Elizabeth C. Forbes

cannot understand
this book

KANT
Selections

KANT
SELECTIONS

1724-1804

EDITED BY
THEODORE MEYER GREENE

CHARLES SCRIBNER'S SONS
NEW YORK

A–10.71 [C]

Printed in the United States of America
SBN 684-12548-X

The following passages from Kant's writings have been selected from "The Critique of Pure Reason," translated by Max Müller, and published by the Macmillan Company, "The Fundamental Principles of the Metaphysic of Morals" and "The Critique of Practical Reason," translated by T. K. Abbott under the title of Kant's "Theory of Ethics" published by Longmans, Green and Co. and the "Kritik of Judgment," translated by J. H. Bernard and published by the Macmillan Co. The Editor wishes hereby to thank the owners and publishers of these volumes for their kind permission to use the passages selected. So far as possible, omissions have been indicated in the text, together with a reference, for each omission, to the page in the Translations of Max Müller, (second edition, revised, 1927), T. K. Abbott (Sixth Edition 1909) and J. H. Bernard (second edition, revised, 1914) on which the omitted passages may be found. Where more has been omitted than retained, on the other hand, the reference given has been to the page or pages on which the selected passage appears. These page references have been included in order to enable the student to relate any of the passages appearing in this volume to the complete translated text from which they were taken.

In all the page references, the letters M., A., and B. refer respectively to the translations by Müller, Abbott, and Bernard mentioned above. Omissions of the translator's footnotes have not been indicated.

CONTENTS

INTRODUCTION

I

The poet Heine once remarked that no life history of Kant was possible for he had neither life nor history. A superficial examination of a biography of Kant and even of his works offers some support for this uncharitable saying. Kant never travelled, but spent his entire life in or near the bleak city of Königsberg in northeastern Prussia. His life-long poverty deprived him of the cultural environment and opportunities which were the heritage of Plato and Aristotle. His physical frailty and the temperamental seriousness of his outlook on life made the youthful adventures of a Goethe uncongenial to him. As time went on he became more and more studious and his habits of life assumed an ever greater regularity and inflexibility. His chief works reflect the austerity and rigor of his character; indeed, their style is so lacking in imaginative warmth, lucidity and literary charm that the student is often tempted to abandon them in despair.

There is another Kant, however, whom even the nonprofessional student of philosophy can discover if he will—the intellectual adventurer who, in his chosen field of study, instituted a 'Copernican revolution'; the courageous thinker so critical of his own beliefs that he was willing, as an old man of over seventy, to abandon arguments and doctrines which he had cherished for years and to set out, even then, in search of new and better ones; the eloquent and devoted teacher who held large classes spell-bound and offered to generations of students his kindly and inspiring counsel; the witty table-companion and gracious host; and the life-long friend of simple men like the English merchants, Green and Motherby. Kant's scholarly pursuits, moreover, were by no means as narrow as is supposed by those who think of him solely as the author of the *Critique of Pure Reason.* In breadth of interest he rivalled the Athenian philosophers, writing with erudition and imaginative insight about science and mathematics, ethics and politics, theology and art. Kant was of course preëminently a philosopher, and his treatment even of these subjects was, for the most part, rigorously philosophical in character. His thinking, however, was saved from the barrenness of abstract intellectualism by having its roots in concrete human experience in one or other of its aspects, and his scholarship was rendered fruitful by his ability to grasp, with imaginative fidelity, those phases of reality which lie nearest to the human heart.

To become acquainted with the real Kant is to see his life and writings in a new light. He disciplined his body and adopted a regular mode of life not from Puritanical motives but because he believed that only thus could he achieve the gigantic task which he had set himself. He refrained from travel and from social life and shrank from active participation in political movements, not because he was unaware of their value but because he felt obliged to sacrifice whatever threatened to tax his time and energy to the detriment of what he conceived to be his life work. Even his philosophical style of writing, whose architectonic and technical abstractness make his books so difficult to read, was chosen deliberately (albeit reluctantly, for Kant knew and loved fine language and apt illustration) as the vehicle best adapted accurately to express his views on questions of supreme importance. The student of the 'Critical Philosophy' must, accordingly, delve beneath the surface and seek to capture for himself the scope and profundity of the philosopher's insight. For to master the works of Immanuel Kant is to have the illuminating experience of coming face to face with the main problems of human life and thought under the guidance of one of the most broad-minded, incisive and honest thinkers of Western Europe.

II

"In the year 1724, on Saturday the 22nd of April, at five in the morning, my son Immanuel was born into the world and on the 23rd received holy baptism . . . May God preserve him in His Covenant of Grace until his blessed end, for Jesus Christ's sake, Amen." This entry in the family Bible symbolizes Kant's early environment and training. His mother was a woman of little education but considerable natural intelligence and a very genuine piety. His deep respect and admiration for her is shown by the way in which he spoke of her, years later, to his friend Jachmann. "My mother was a sweet-tempered, affectionate, pious and upright woman and a tender mother, who led her children in the fear of God by pious teaching and virtuous example. She often took me outside the city, directed my attention to the works of God, expressed herself with pious rapture over His omnipotence, wisdom and goodness, and impressed on my heart a deep reverence for the Creator of all things."

Kant ultimately attained, however, more nearly to his father's ideal than to hers. The father, a Scotchman by descent and a saddler by trade, was morally rather than religiously minded. His chief parental interest lay in making his children industrious and truthful. The moral atmosphere of the Kant household seems to have influenced the philosopher profoundly in his formative years and to have evoked in him a great reverence for moral value. This moral earnestness increased with the passage of years until the objective reality of moral goodness became finally the central motif of his whole philosophical system, and his life grew to be a living embodiment of his own ethical doctrine.

Kant's attitude to evangelical religion, on the contrary, early became one of suspicion and dislike. This was due in large measure, we may be sure, to his unhappy school experience. In 1732 he was sent to the Collegium Fredericianum, a Pietist academy in the city, which he attended as a day-scholar for the next eight years. The Pietist movement had started in Königsberg in the last quarter of the 17th century as a protest against the clerical despotism and creed-bound theology of the Lutheran church. Within fifty years, however, success had crystallized its earlier plea for a more genuine and personal religious devoutness into a dogmatic fanaticism and an intolerance of all expressions of the religious life other than its own. These characteristics of the new orthodoxy seem to have manifested themselves in heightened form in the Collegium. The published aim of the school was to "rescue its charges from their state of spiritual corruption and to implant true Christianity in their hearts from their youth up." Each day opened and closed with devotional exercises and each class hour ended with a "rousing" prayer. The endeavor was made at frequent intervals to warn the pupils concerning the evil state of their souls and to encourage them to confess their sins. Sunday, a weary succession of sermons and catechizings, ended with an hour of soul-searching in which the truths expounded that day were "lovingly pressed home." Not unnaturally, most of the students soon became expert in facile professions of piety; Kant's reaction, on the contrary, was one of loathing and disgust. The remark attributed to him in later life that fear and trembling overcame him whenever he recalled those days of youthful slavery may well be authentic. His lasting abhorrence of all religious emotionalism and his hatred of prayer and hymn-singing certainly dated back to this unhappy period. And though he was able to evaluate the Pietistic movement quite dispassionately in later years and to praise much in the religious consciousness of the time, he never overcame his deep distrust of evangelical religion and never really understood what is regarded by many as the distinctive religious experience.

At the age of sixteen Kant enrolled in the University of Königsberg where he soon came under the influence of Knützen, an able professor of philosophy and an ardent Wolffian. Wolff, the great popularizer of the Leibnizian philosophy, was probably the most influential thinker in Germany in the first half of the 18th century and dominated the philosophical thinking of the land to an amazing degree. It was natural, then, that Kant should have become, under Knützen's influence, a faithful Wolffian. He so enjoyed Knützen's lectures and companionship that he soon gave up his earlier plan of devoting himself to philology and the classics and applied himself to science and to the study of philosophy. Here he found such abundant scope for his intellectual energy and originality that he soon decided to make these two disciplines his chosen fields of endeavor.

On completing his university course, Kant was obliged

for financial reasons to serve as family tutor for several years, an uncongenial task which he performed painstakingly and in such a way as to endear himself to the families whom he served. In 1755 he began his teaching in the University of Königsberg as *privat docent.* Here he lectured for the next fifteen years not only in logic and metaphysics, mathematics and natural science, but also in subjects as varied as physical geography, anthropology and the science of fortification. Twice during this period he applied in vain for a vacant chair in his own university, and it was not till he was forty-six years of age that he was appointed professor of logic and metaphysics. Meanwhile he had been applying himself with tremendous diligence to his writing, with the result that by 1785 he had become the most important figure in the university. By the last decade of the century his fame had extended throughout Germany and his philosophy was being taught in all the universities.

So far we have made no adequate mention of the influence of 18th century science upon Kant's thinking. Newton had died the year of Kant's birth, and by the time Kant entered the university the Newtonian physics had obtained a firm hold upon the German universities. Like other thinkers of the time, Kant was greatly impressed by the simplicity, adequacy, and self-evident truth of the Newtonian system. His belief in the finality and perfection of the new physics remained unshaken to the end of his life. This belief is apparent in the form which he gave, in the *Prolegomena,* to his famous contrasting questions regarding science and metaphysics: *Is* a science of metaphysics possible? he asked, assuming that the answer was by no means self-evident; but, *How* is certain and universal scientific truth possible? assuming that sure scientific truth actually did exist.

His active interest in science is evident from the fact that his earliest writings were purely scientific in character: e. g. his *General History of the Nature and Theory of the Heavens* (1755) in which he gave an original and correct explanation, in terms of the Newtonian principles, of the origin of the tangential movements of the planets, and his lectures on *The Theory of Winds* (1756) in which, working quite independently, he laid the foundation for the explanation of numerous meteorological phenomena. Kant never lost his enthusiasm for scientific research and continued to the end to publish occasional articles on biological, anthropological and astronomical subjects. His main attention, however, gradually shifted, as regards science, to the nature of science as such and to the essential characteristics of scientific thought and method. So greatly did this latter problem occupy his mind in middle life that in the *Critique of Pure Reason,* published when he was fifty-seven, one of his chief aims was to vindicate the work and outlook of the scientist.

His philosophical writing started about 1755, and for the next fifteen years both the titles of his papers and his handling of their subject-matter reveal the profound influence upon him of Leibnizian-Wolffian rationalism. It was only gradually that he became able to appraise critically the basic presuppositions of the traditional rationalistic philosophy and to develop his own distinctive point of view.

The Latin *Dissertation* of 1770, delivered on the assumption of his professorial chair, marks the beginning of Kant's maturer period. For the next eleven years he published only minor articles of a non-technical nature, for he was pouring all his energy into the *Critique of Pure Reason* which appeared in 1781. During these years he seems to have labored successively on the various yet inter-related problems dealt with in that volume, preoccupied now with this argument, now with that, and devoting only the last six months prior to publication to a hurried rearrangement of his notes into book form. This accounts to a considerable extent for the many discrepancies and repetitions which have so endlessly perplexed and annoyed its readers. This, however, is not the whole story. The *Critique* as it stands makes no pretence of being the finished exposition of a rounded metaphysical system; it is rather a record of Kant's prolonged struggle to formulate and reconcile more or less divergent points of view none of which seemed to him to be either wholly adequate or wholly lacking in truth. Like Plato, he was dealing with philosophical problems for which he was unable to discover a single completely satisfactory solution, and he refused to make easy sacrifices in the interests of simplicity and consistency, preferring rather to follow the more fruitful method of doing as full justice as he was able to each point of view as it arose in his mind. The richness of post-Kantian thought testifies to the philosophical value of such procedure. Finally, we can understand his unwillingness to devote still more time to the preparation of this volume when we remember that in the year of its publication he was approaching sixty, with the major portion of his larger philosophical system still to be developed.

After the appearance of the first *Critique,* one important philosophical work followed another in rapid succession. He was so disappointed at the luke-warm reception which the *Critique* received, and found that so few, even among trained philosophers such as Mendelssohn, gave evidence of understanding or appreciating the book, that in 1783 he published *A Prolegomena to Every Future Metaphysic* in which he expounded "for the benefit of teachers of philosophy" the central thesis of the *Critique.* The next five years were devoted to the development of his ethical theory. *The Fundamental Principles of the Metaphysic of Morality,* in which the chief characteristics and immediate implications of the moral life are lucidly and simply portrayed, appeared in 1785, and the *Critique of Practical Reason,* in which morality is more exhaustively and more metaphysically analyzed, three years later. In 1790 came the third volume of the great trilogy, the *Critique of Judgement,* dealing with two apparently unrelated subjects, the nature of beauty and aesthetic taste, and the significance and inter-relation of the principles of mechanism and teleology. Religion remained to be considered, and in 1793-4 there accordingly appeared the *Religion within the Limits of Bare Reason,* in many respects the least illuminating of his main works, yet by far the most profound exposition of 18th century deism produced in Germany.

Through this period of literary productivity Kant continued to publish minor articles and essays on subjects whose wide variety indicates once again the breadth of his interests. Even in the last years of his life he continued to struggle with problems for whose solution his waning strength became increasingly inadequate. The masses of manuscript found in his study at his death, and recently edited by Adickes under the title *Opus Postumum,* give evidence, at once pathetic and inspiring, of the repeated attempts of the aged philosopher to round out his system still further and to reconstruct such portions of it as had been weakened under his own critical scrutiny. "I have undertaken," he writes in 1802, "to complete my account of questions which concern the whole of philosophy, but I am never able to get it done although I am conscious that it is quite possible of accomplishment." Towards the end he suffered from loss of memory and then of eyesight. He died in 1804 at the age of eighty and was buried in Königsberg, the university and city uniting in doing him final honor.

III

Before turning to Kant's philosophical position let us see how he goes about the business of philosophical inquiry. His starting-point invariably is concrete human experience in one or other of its characteristic forms. This experience he regards as a datum, the material for philosophical investigation. Thus, in the *Critique of Pure Reason* his starting-point is man's ordinary knowledge of so-called physical objects; in his ethical writings it is man's moral sense of duty; and in his doctrine of aesthetics it is the appreciation and creation of beauty. If the factual reality of any one of these experiences be denied, Kant's analysis of it loses at once all point and meaning; if, on the other hand, it be admitted as an existential fact, the importance of his subsequent investigation is apparent.

His first step is psychologically to describe and logically to analyze this concrete experience as fully as possible in order to make clear its complex nature and to point out its more immediate implications. At this stage he depicts adequately and precisely the observable nature of the experience which he is trying to understand. Such a *quid facti* analysis at once reveals problems not previously apparent, for as soon as the experience in question is examined with care it is found to be not only far more complex than at first appeared;

it is also seen to be by no means self-explanatory, but logically to presuppose and imply what is not itself revealed to direct observation and to embody within itself logical contradictions calling for solution.

His next step is to ask, regarding the experience which he has been analyzing: Must this experience be thought of merely as a complex psychological activity possessing a logical structure, or does consciousness here transcend itself, revealing to us a reality other than itself? And, if reality be thus knowable, may it be said to embody or sustain objective value so as to satisfy our spiritual needs? In short, though Kant was an eminent psychologist and logician, his fundamental interest was metaphysical, and the ultimate goal of his philosophical thinking was the discovery of the meaning of human experience and the value of human life. Accordingly, his earlier psychological and logical analyses of each type of experience may be said to prepare the way for, and to culminate in, a metaphysical inquiry regarding the normative significance of the experience in question. From these successive explorations of ultimate truth, reality and value there emerges a unified and consistent *Weltanschauung* which takes into account man's nature in its entirety, the whole range of his experience, and the various aspects of that reality which directly or indirectly reveals itself to him. Hence, though the three *Critiques* start out with radically different data they all converge in the end, each making its distinctive contribution to a synoptic account of the nature of reality and man's relation to it.

Such is the general plan of Kant's investigations—exposition and analysis (*Analytic*) being followed by a larger metaphysical inquiry (*Dialectic*). The argument of each *Critique* has, indeed, a certain dramatic quality. The curtain rises on a familiar scene. One by one the actors make their appearance, and their relation to one another and to their environment is explained. Presently the plot thickens as problems and dilemmas reveal themselves. The atmosphere grows tense as one solution after another is rejected. Then at last the tragedy is averted with an account of how the problems may be solved, and when the curtain falls the audience is left assured that somehow, ultimately, the universe is able to sustain man's intellectual and spiritual aspirations.

IV

The *Critique of Pure Reason* [1] opens with a lament. Philosophy, once hailed the queen of the sciences, is in dire straits, for she has failed to substantiate her centuries-old claim of being able to discover and portray the truth regarding the nature of reality. The story of her endeavors is a sad chronicle of disputes and disagreements among her disciples, of ever-renewed beginnings and of conclusions soon abandoned, of vain and unjustified assurance alternating with premature and unprofitable despair. As a result she has now fallen into disrepute and her proud name has become a term of reproach,

[1] The reader is reminded that the following survey of Kant's philosophical position, as expounded in the three *Critiques,* is necessarily based upon the Editor's own interpretation of the Kantian doctrines, and that frequently this interpretation is not the only one which can be given of writings so full of partially developed, and at times irreconcilable, suggestions. Cf. Norman Kemp Smith's *A Commentary to Kant's Critique of Pure Reason* (revised edition, Macmillan 1923), and Edward Caird's *The Critical Philosophy of Kant* (Maclehose, 1909). It should be needless to add that the following account of Kant's philosophy is, as it were, no more than a charcoal sketch of his central theses, of the characteristic tendencies of his thinking, and of the general nature of his conclusions—a sketch which the reader will have to modify and supplement as he proceeds in his study of the text.

for honest men have lost faith in her empty promises and look upon her with indifference or contempt.

Yet the problems which philosophy has thus far failed to solve are too vital to be ignored with impunity. She must renew the battle, for hers is an essential task which she alone is fitted to perform. Before attempting to philosophize anew, however, her disciples must first of all ask themselves in all seriousness whether the so-called science of metaphysics is possible at all, and, if so, how and within what limits? Kant is called the founder and exponent of the 'Critical Philosophy' because, in each of the three *Critiques,* he attaches such importance to this critical examination of the power and scope of our cognitive faculties. He insists that the question as to whether, and how, the possibility of valid judgments about reality can be established must be fully considered and satisfactorily answered *before* the task of developing a new philosophical system is undertaken. This 'critical' approach to all philosophical thinking is well expressed in his later work whose significant title is *A Prolegomena to Every Future Metaphysic,* where he challenges all subsequent metaphysicians to justify their belief in the ability of the human mind to know reality through metaphysical speculation *before* embarking on new speculative ventures. In the *Critique of Pure Reason* Kant applies himself to the statement and solution of this 'critical' problem; true to its title, the book is not primarily an exposition of a new philosophical system but an attempt to take fresh stock of man's metaphysical capacity through a critical examination of the nature and scope of human reason.

Such a critique, however, is bound to lead to conclusions regarding the cognitive capacity of the human mind which carry with them certain metaphysical implications. Indeed, as Kant himself points out, the fruitfulness of his critical inquiry will be shown by the extent to which it enables him to solve the metaphysical problems, and reconcile the doctrinal divergences, of his predecessors. Kant was acutely aware of his philosophical heritage; in writing the *Critique* he had ever in mind the rationalistic and empirical traditions which had emerged out of the Cartesian system. To appreciate the pertinence and originality of his own 'critical' contentions, therefore, we must recall briefly the salient characteristics of these 'pre-critical' traditions and note the main problems to which he had fallen heir and which he tries to solve in 'critical' fashion.

Descartes is called the father of modern philosophy chiefly because he set the stage for subsequent philosophical discussion. His central problem may be formulated thus: What guarantee can be offered that any of our ideas do justice to objective reality? Our ideas are in the mind; reality, presumably, is independent of the mind and external to it. What reason then have we to believe that our thought represents reality to us with any degree of accuracy? Descartes approaches this problem cautiously in a spirit of radical scepticism. The testimony of the senses, he shows, is too conflicting to warrant faith in its validity, and reason's claim to be a guide to truth is challenged by the disturbing thought that we may be at the mercy of a malignant demon who has so warped our minds that a rational knowledge of reality is wholly unattainable. This orgy of distrust is checked by a single certainty; in the very act of doubting everything, the doubt, the thought or *cogito* itself, remains unquestionably real. But thought implies a thinker, *cogito ergo sum.* Thus, thinking substance, conceived of as an enduring psychic entity, becomes the cornerstone of the Cartesian system. Descartes then proceeds to exorcise his malignant demon by proving naïvely (that is, by means of that very faculty of reason whose validity has been radically questioned) the existence of a Deity whose power and beneficence shall reestablish reason's trustworthiness. His "proofs" of God's existence, in short, all rest directly or indirectly on the assumption that necessity of thought implies existence and that it is possible to argue from the content of certain of our ideas to a reality other than these ideas themselves, yet corresponding to them. In this way Descartes assures himself of the existence of an omnipotent Being incapable of guile, an eternal Substance who is the beneficent Creator of all finite substance. He then proceeds to satisfy himself of the existence of a second finite substance, matter, whose essence is space or extension and whose primary attribute is motion. Though we perceive material objects through the distorting medium of color, heat, sound, etc. (later called the "secondary" qualities), he now argues, we can learn their true or primary nature through reasoned contemplation upon the combined testimony of the several senses. Thus in the end Descartes' reality consists of two finite substances, thinking and extended, with God or Infinite Substance as their common ground; and knowledge arises through the coöperation of reason and sense-perception, with reason the responsible and authoritative partner in the alliance.

Out of Descartes there sprang two schools of thought, since labelled rationalism and empiricism; each seized upon an element of truth in the Cartesian philosophy and developed it, in increasing isolation from the other, to its logical and barren conclusion. The weaknesses of Descartes' system were thus to a large extent revealed by his successors, in part deliberately, through critical analysis, at times unwittingly, in an unconscious *reductio ad absurdum*.

The rationalist tradition culminated in one direction in Spinozistic monism, in the other, in the monadology of Leibniz. Kant knew it best in the form expressed by the disciple of Leibniz, Wolff. Descartes' suspicion of the senses as mediators of reality became in Wolff open hostility and contempt. Reason alone, he taught, is qualified to lead man to a knowledge of reality; and to succeed, reason must resolutely shun the allurements of the imagination and wholly ignore the insistent and plausible illusions of the senses. Accordingly, as Malebranche had retreated to his darkened study there to unfold, out of the recesses of his inner thought, the eternal and immutable ways of God, so Wolff, trusting to reason pure and undefiled, expounded in his Rational Psychology, Rational Cosmology and Rational Theology, the true nature of the soul, the world and their Creator.

English empiricism, meanwhile, was exposing this complacent dogmatism of the rationalists by challenging their assumptions and developing a philosophical position of its own. Descartes had, in the end, been unable wholly to ignore the testimony of the senses. Locke, following this clue, sought to make sensation the prime source of all human knowledge. In protest against the doctrine that man is possessed of innate ideas which, when unfolded, yield accurate knowledge of independent reality, he set up the new hypothesis that, at birth, the mind is a blank tablet endowed with a passive, wax-like capacity of receiving sensory impressions from the outer world. Once these have been received, the mind, no longer passive, is able to revive them in the form of images, combine them in new ways, abstract their common character, and so equip itself with new ideas. But all of these ideas must originally, by hypothesis, have been derived from earlier sense-impressions. By the development of this thesis, that all knowledge rests finally on sense experience, Locke started empiricism on its way. Yet he himself continued to believe, in Cartesian fashion, in matter, soul and God as three independent substances which sense cannot reveal to us—matter and soul being relatively, and God absolutely, self-subsistent.

His followers, Berkeley and Hume, adhered to pure empiricism more consistently than did their master and promptly challenged this belief. Berkeley directed his polemic against the idea of an extended substance or material stuff in which an object's qualities were alleged somehow to inhere, and argued with persuasive eloquence that since it is impossible to have a direct sense experience of such a substance, no clear idea of it can be formed and belief in its existence becomes impossible. A physical object, accordingly, is to him nothing but a "cluster of sensations" impressed by God upon the human soul, and spatiality, admittedly a quality of visual sensation, becomes no more than a prophetic intimation of future tactile sensations.

Hume followed suit by submitting Berkeley's "notions" of the soul and God, or finite and infinite thinking substance, to the same empirical criterion with the same negative results. The Scotch philosopher, however, went further and challenged the assumption made quite uncritically by most of his predecessors and contemporaries, rationalist and empiricist alike, that our idea of cause possesses objective validity. After a given series of events has sensuously presented itself to us a number of times in a certain order we form the habit, no doubt, of expecting these events to follow one another in the same sequence, and we believe that the earlier event caused or necessitated its successor. Similarly we believe that on occasion a volition can cause a bodily movement. But try as we may we can never experience, through sensation or introspection, that dynamic 'force' or causal 'energy' whose existence we assume, nor can we rationally prove that such a bond of causal unity must necessarily exist. What philosophical right, then, have we to believe in the objective reality of causation or assume that everything must have a cause? Now this empirical criticism of the objective validity of our ideas both of substance and of causality undermines, it is clear, the very possibility of our knowing objective reality at all. Pure empiricism, in a word, ends with Hume in philosophical scepticism, a result dramatically symbolized by Hume's abandonment, while still a young man, of strictly philosophical inquiry.

Such is the quandary to which Kant, in the prefaces to his *Critique,* directs our gaze. We see reason, 'dogmatically' rejoicing in an illusory power to grasp reality single-handed and unaware that, in the very act of cutting herself loose from sensuous experience, she has deprived herself of all contact with reality; and sense, proud of its escape from rationalistic assumptions but ensnared in 'scepticism' through its inability to attain true philosophical knowledge on a purely empirical basis.

Yet Kant's own reaction to the work of his predecessors was by no means wholly negative. There was, he felt, an important element of truth in each of these philosophical traditions; each school was correct in some of its assertions and erred chiefly in ignoring the insight of its antagonist.

The rationalists were right not only in their contention that philosophical knowledge, to be worthy of the name, must take the form of necessary and universal, or *a priori,* judgments, but also in their insistence that such judgments can never be arrived at by means of mere empirical generalizations from sensuous experience, since such experience is ever incomplete and generalizations based thereon are liable at any moment to be upset by new empirical evidence. The employment of empirical or *a posteriori* judgments[1] is of course indispensable to ordinary life and thought, but philosophy craves greater certainty than such judgments can afford.

Empiricism, on the other hand, was correct both in its assertion that objective reality presents itself to man through the medium of sensuous experience, and in its belief that the rationalists' attempt to know reality merely by analyzing their own innate ideas, and rendering explicit the hidden implications of their own rational concepts according to the criterion of the principle of contradiction, is doomed to failure. These analytical judgments, Kant admits, are valuable in clarifying thought, and the principle of contradiction is too fundamental ever to be disobeyed. Such judgments, however, in and by themselves, can never reveal to us the nature of objective reality, nor can obedience to the law of contradiction produce more than mere internal consistency within the circle of our own ideas. Significant philosophical judgments, in contrast, must be not only self-consistent but instructive and illuminating,

[1] A judgment is 'necessary' and 'universal' if its applicability to all possible cases is certain. For example, the proposition that the sum of the angles of a triangle is equal to two right angles holds true of all possible triangles in plane geometry. It is judged to be necessarily correct because it has been arrived at not by actual measurement of a certain number of triangles but by the logical process of rational analysis and inference. Kant calls such a judgment '*a priori*' because it can be made prior to, and independently of, empirical measurement of actual triangles. That Laplanders have blue eyes, in contrast, is merely a generalization from the experience of seeing a certain number of Laplanders. Such an '*a posteriori*' judgment, based upon and following a limited number of experiences, need not necessarily be true of all Laplanders.

i.e. they must be synthetical,[1] and this synthetic quality must not arise merely through generalization from concrete past experiences, for philosophy is in search of universal truth.

Kant's problem, accordingly, is to establish the possibility of judgments about reality which are both universal and instructive. How, he asks, can we avoid the unfruitful tautology of *a priori* analytical judgments on the one hand, the incompleteness and unavoidable dependence on sense of synthetic *a posteriori* judgments on the other? In a word, how are synthetic *a priori* judgments possible?

The failure of his predecessors, Kant proceeds, was due mainly to their inability to formulate their basic problem in a manner capable of solution. Both schools had defined the problem of knowledge in Cartesian fashion by assuming that our ideas, if true, must correspond to an external reality which, in itself, is wholly independent of the knowing mind. This radical dualism of mind and matter creates at once an insurmountable difficulty. For on this view how *can* we have any possi-

[1] "In all judgments in which there is a relation between subject and predicate . . . that relation can be of two kinds. Either the predicate B belongs to the subject A as something contained (though covertly) in the concept A; or B lies outside the sphere of the concept A, though somehow connected with it. In the former case I call the judgment analytical, in the latter synthetical. Analytical judgments . . . are therefore those in which the connection of the predicate with the subject is conceived through identity, while others in which that connection is conceived without identity, may be called synthetical. The former might be called illustrating, the latter expending judgments, . . ." (Cf. below p. 33) Professor Kemp Smith points out in his *Commentary* (p. 37, ff.) that these hard and fast distinctions between analytical and synthetical judgments, and between *a priori* and *a posteriori* judgments, are not sustained by the subsequent development of Kant's thought in the *Critique*. The student will therefore eventually have to reinterpret these distinctions in the light of Kant's entire argument.

ble guarantee that our ideas do correspond to a reality wholly other than ourselves? To escape this quandary Kant now proposes a complete redefinition of the epistemological problem. Copernicus, finding himself unable to account for certain astronomical data on the assumption that the sun revolves about the earth, reversed his formulation of the problem by risking the heliocentric hypothesis. Following his example, Kant asks us to assume in revolutionary fashion that objective reality, to be known at all, must conform to the essential structure of the human mind. If this be true, the insight which the science of logic gives us into the basic structure of human thought will furnish us with a reliable clue to the discovery of the unvarying structure of knowable reality, and synthetic *a priori* knowledge of reality will be within our grasp. Yet, be it noted, not of reality in its entirety; for an all-important corollary of this 'Copernican hypothesis' is that the only reality of which we can acquire true philosophical knowledge is that which is *capable* of being revealed to *us* in and through our *sensuous* experience. In short, the new hypothesis asserts both the *a priori* knowability of the essential character of 'all possible objects of experience' and, simultaneously, the total inability of the human mind ever to 'know' such reaches of reality as cannot, by their very nature, be sensuously apprehended by beings constituted like ourselves. This need not preclude, however, the possibility that other phases of reality, perhaps more ultimate and significant than what can sensuously be perceived, may reveal themselves to man in non-sensuous fashion, e.g. in the moral experience of goodness or the aesthetic experience of beauty. The nature and importance of these experiences form the subject-matter of the subsequent *Critiques,* and Kant, as we shall find, attaches very great importance to such moral and aesthetic insight. In this first *Critique,* however, he rigorously limits his investigation to what the intellect can know with *a priori* certainty regarding that world of nature which is the object of our sensuous experience.

The concrete problem of the *Critique* may accordingly be restated thus: Assume that the reality which we seek to know with philosophical certainty is the world of nature which we are continually experiencing through our senses; assume further that this reality, in order to enter into our field of consciousness, must, in certain fundamental ways, conform to our cognitive faculties; our task then is to analyze the knowing process, discover its essential character and all that that character implies, and indicate in the form of synthetic *a priori* judgments the pattern to which this world of nature *must* conform if it is to be an object of human knowledge. These judgments will take the form: All natural objects, i.e. 'all possible objects of sensuous experience', must possess such and such a characteristic because our minds are so constituted that they can apprehend sensuously only what has this character. In other words, perception of what we call physical objects and physical events is a fact; if, then, analysis of such perception makes it clear that an object of perception must be substantival in character, or that a natural event must be causally related to other events, it will be true *a priori* that the concepts of substance and causality are necessarily and universally applicable to 'all possible objects of experience', i.e. to the whole world of nature.

Hence the backbone of the *Critique* is Kant's elaborate and highly original analysis of our sensuous experience and his discovery of its implications. As he himself points out, the correctness of his 'Copernican hypothesis', the validity of his *a priori* conclusions regarding the world of nature, and the truth of his subsequent metaphysical doctrines, will all depend upon the cogency of this examination of ordinary perception. Unfortunately, we cannot in this brief Introduction follow through the various stages of his argument, although the reader is warned that he must master this portion of the *Critique* in order to understand the purport and validity of Kant's conclusions. We must content ourselves with a brief summary of these conclusions viewed in their relation to the conclusions of his predecessors. In this summary we shall, for convenience, consider successively the three aspects of ordinary consciousness which Kant clearly differentiates. Like an electric spark leaping from pole to pole, consciousness of objects involves the act of knowing and the two end terms, the knower and the known. Following the order of his own inquiry let us examine first his account of the activity of knowing.

Ordinary sense-perception is by no means, according to Kant, a merely passive reception of sensations; it involves a highly complex mental activity. First, temporally successive sense-impressions must enter consciousness through sensuous intuition. Secondly, they must be preserved in memory and must be revived by means of the reproductive imagination, in order that the given series of impressions may be viewed in its entirety, as a series. Thirdly, the understanding, or mental faculty of grasping relationships, must apprehend the spatial and temporal order in which this series of sense-impressions arrives upon the scene. This act of apprehension is accomplished by means of twelve abstract concepts, or tools of thought, with which the understanding is equipped. These are the categories, or, more correctly, the schemata, of which the most important are the concepts of substance and causality.

Further, in order to deal effectively with the large variety of sensuous objects which the mind is called upon to distinguish, classify and organize, the understanding must also make use of a second and far larger class of tools, namely the empirical concepts. These are, in effect, the abstract schemata particularized through the addition of concrete empirical meaning (e.g. the concept of substance, when empirically limited, becomes the empirical concept of chair, or table, etc.). They differ from the schemata in being not innate but acquired in the course of experience through the process of empirical generalization.

Knowing, in short, involves the coöperation of the faculties of sensuous intuition, imagination and understanding. It is none the less an essentially unified process. To the unity of consciousness Kant attaches great importance, arguing at length that all consciousness involves self-consciousness. A sense of personal identity must pervade all conscious activity if it is to be coherent; the implicit judgment, "I think," must accompany my thought at every instant, else my mental life will disintegrate into wholly unrelated pulses of mere sensuous awareness, and all intelligent apprehension of an orderly sensuous environment will cease.

Kant's doctrine of the knower is but a logical corollary of this conception of the unity of consciousness. As Descartes had argued that the *cogito* implies a *sum,* so Kant maintains that the felt (or empirical) unity of consciousness is unintelligible save by reference to an unchanging subjective center of reference, a self identical throughout the knowing process. This self, no doubt, as Hume correctly pointed out, is empirically discoverable neither through sensation nor introspection. Its reality, however, (and here Kant breaks with Hume) must necessarily be admitted as an explanation of the experienced unity or personal quality of all consciousness. Yet we must be most careful not to admit too much, or more than the actual facts warrant. That is, we are not entitled to infer, as did Descartes, the existence of a self more enduring than the span of conscious memory, nor should we hypostatize this self, as did most of Kant's predecessors, into a self-subsistent psychic entity destined for immortality. Kant's knower, in a word, is strictly correlative to the knowing process and is invoked merely to render this process intelligible.

The known is also defined wholly in terms of its relation to the activity of knowing. It is, in any given instance, that 'object' of which we are sensuously aware; taken universally, it may be described as the sum-total of 'all possible objects of experience'. As such, the known always possesses the following characteristics.

(1) All 'objects of experience' invariably enter consciousness in the forms of space and time. This does not mean, however, that Kant regards space, any more than the self, as a self-subsistent entity, existing, as it were, in its own right and independently of the knowing process. He was well aware that the perplexities of Cartesian dualism could be avoided only by a refusal thus to hypostatize the spatial quality of our sensuous experience into 'extended substance.' Space and time are but the universal and necessary *forms* of all sensuous objects; whatever we apprehend through sense is sure to possess for us a spatial and temporal character.

(2) What is known is in a genuine sense objective to consciousness. The chairs and tables which we perceive in our ordinary sensuous experience are not merely ideas in our own mind or the subjective creations of our own imagination. Kant vehemently repudiates the charge that he is a purely subjective idealist and insists that objectivity has for him a real meaning and

significance. Yet the essence of objectivity is not a total independence of, or spatial externality to, consciousness, as it was for Descartes, but rather the *regular and inescapable spatio-temporal order, or pattern, in which our sense impressions come to us.* In apprehending a chair, for instance, as an 'object', we are aware of a series of sense-impressions which come to us in a *given order* which is not created by us but presented to us; we have to accept it and cannot alter it by any act of will; it has a spatial and temporal character of its own which we cannot destroy or change. An 'object' of sensuous experience, accordingly, is a series of sense impressions which come to us, we know not why nor whence, in a spatio-temporal pattern over which we find ourselves to have no ultimate control; and the world of nature is the sum-total of all such actual and possible 'objects of experience.'

So far we have summarized Kant's conception of 'objectivity' only in general terms. In the second part of the *Analytic* he makes his meaning more precise by showing that, in our experience of 'objects', we invariably grasp the given order of our impressions in terms of the twelve schemata, of which substance and causality are the most fundamental. Let us briefly consider his treatment of these two concepts.

It will at once be admitted that we are continually experiencing the natural phenomenon of change. 'Objects' of our experience grow and decay, intensify and fade in color and sound, heat and odor, and vary in spatial relation to one another. Now this fact of temporal change is seen, when analyzed, to be complex in character. The paradox of change is this, that only the changeless can change; that is, all change necessarily implies a core or a back-ground of permanence against which the change is observed and in terms of which it is interpreted. To say "*It* has changed," is to say that "it", a complex entity, has in certain respects remained the same whereas in others it is now different from what it was. How then do we actually, and necessarily, conceive of this abiding "it", this element of permanence in our changing sensuous manifold? [1] In terms, says Kant, of the concept of substance and changing attributes. Yet, be it noted again, Kant does not mean by substance an invisible, self-subsistent entity or an hypostatized spatial stuff in which certain qualities inhere more fixedly than others. We must not forget that he is wholly in sympathy with Berkeley's criticism of 'matter' thus conceived. Substance for Kant is merely a fundamental interpretive *concept* in terms of which we must apprehend the element of permanence in the given spatio-temporal order of our impressions. This observed element of fixity in the pattern of these impressions we conceive substantively and call 'the object itself'; the simultaneously observed variations we think of as the object's 'qualities' or attributes. But the concept of substance and quality is, from first to last, nothing but a tool of thought.

Take next our sensuous experience of what is commonly, and properly, called a causal series of events. We see a ship gliding down a stream and are quite sure that what we see is not the product of our own imagination, but real. What then makes this series of sense-impressions so real to us? Merely the inescapable spatio-temporal order of their occurrence. We test the objectivity of such an experience by seeking, by an act of will, to reverse this order. Were we to succeed, we should refuse to ascribe objectivity to the succession

[1] By the 'sensuous manifold' Kant means the aggregate of sense-impressions which come to us at successive instants and are therefore temporally distinct from one another.

of our mental states and call them merely subjective. When, on the other hand, we fail in this attempt, we judge ourselves to be in the presence of an objective series of events and entitle the earlier event the cause, its successor, the effect. Observe, however, that Kant does not hypostatize the experienced necessity of a causal order into a self-subsistent force or dynamic energy.[1] Causal necessity is not a 'something' which a spatial object mysteriously conveys to another spatial object. For the world of nature is a world of actual and possible sense-impressions, and a causal series of impressions is merely one whose order we cannot alter or reverse but must accept as given. This order is for *us* a 'necessary' or 'causal' order simply because it eludes our voluntary control. The concept of causality then, like that of substance, is but a mental tool which we must employ in apprehending the innumerable series of impressions which constitute our world of natural events.

It is obvious that Kant is defining the terms 'object' and 'objective' in a new way. Descartes had conceived of reality in radically dualistic fashion. Thought and the spatial world of objects were for him wholly independent of one another. Objects somehow impressed themselves upon the mind, and our ideas of objects were true and adequate to the extent to which they corresponded to, or represented, them with fidelity. This is the 'doctrine of representative perception' in terms of which we tend, even today, to conceive of the epistemological problem. To avoid the insoluble perplexities incident to this doctrine Kant approached the problem of knowledge from another angle. His starting-point was our actual experience of sense-perception,

[1] Kant's handling of the concept of force is somewhat ambiguous, but the interpretation here given is, in the Editor's opinion, in line with his general teaching.

which differs so radically from our 'inner', subjective experiences such as day-dreaming, controlled imagination and reasoning. Now what, he asks, is the precise difference between these two types of experience? Time as such is not the distinguishing feature, for both types of experience occur in time, sense-impressions following one another in temporal sequence and images or rational concepts succeeding one another from moment to moment.[1] The crucial difference between our 'subjective' and 'objective' experiences can be defined only in terms of our ability to control or determine the temporal and spatial pattern of what sensuously presents itself to us. When I *imagine* a moving ship, I can picture it to myself as sailing up-stream or down-stream, rapidly or slowly; when I *imagine* a chair I can alter its shape at will and freely determine its position in an imagined room. But when I *perceive* a moving ship or a chair, the spatial and temporal pattern of the object of my awareness is determined for me and I must accept it for what it is. What I perceive, accordingly, is objective to me, for in the act of perception I am in the presence of that which has a character of its own. This spatio-temporal character, in turn, I can apprehend *only* in terms of the *concepts* of substance, causality, and the other schemata. An 'object of experience', then, is that which is (1) sensuously perceived, and (2) endowed with a spatial and temporal order which cannot be altered by an act of will, and the 'world of nature' is the sum-total of all such actual and possible 'objects of experience.'

Kant's conception of 'objectivity' may also be explained in terms of the distinction between public and

[1] Vividness is not the primary basis of distinction, neither is spatiality, for mental images are sometimes extraordinarily vivid, and such images frequently, perhaps always, possess a spatial quality.

private. In a sense, each individual's 'world of nature' is private to himself, since each can know *at first hand* only those 'objects' which reveal themselves to him in and through his own conscious states. Yet in all its significant aspects it is also the public property of all conscious beings like ourselves, for in essential structure and, to a large extent, in sensuous quality, it is the same for each of us; sensuous 'objects' display the same spatio-temporal pattern to all conscious beings alike and arouse similar or identical sensations of color, sound, touch, etc. In short, the world we know through sense is private to each of us to the precise extent to which our experience of it differs from individual to individual; it is public in so far as our fields of consciousness over-lap so as to include the self-same 'objects' of perception. What the scientist seeks to do is to abstract this common quality of all the 'objects' of human experience, ignore what is unique to this or that individual, and formulate with mathematical precision the intricate spatio-temporal pattern of events of which all men are, or can be, conscious. These spatio-temporal sequences of which he is in search are what he calls the laws of nature; they are those regularities in our common sensuous experience which we cannot change but which we can apprehend in terms of the interpretative concepts with which we are equipped. In a word, the phrases, 'subject to natural law', 'independent of human volition' and 'actually or potentially public', may all be taken as synonymous descriptions of that in our sensuous experience which is objectively real.

The general nature of Kant's own answer to the question: "How are synthetic *a priori* judgments possible?" should now be clear. 'Reality' for him is the sum of all possible 'objects' of human experience. As such, it must necessarily conform in essential structure to the structure of the knowing mind. It must possess a spatio-temporal pattern such that the mind can apprehend this pattern through the employment of the mental tools of cognition in its possession. Were nature's structure fundamentally different from what it is, our sense-impressions would be a chaotic, meaningless jumble and all knowledge would be impossible. Accordingly we can be *a priori* certain that every possible 'object of experience' will be in space and time and will be knowable in terms of substance, causality and the remaining schematic concepts. This being so, the possibility of true philosophical knowledge about that reality which we can sensuously experience has been established. Furthermore the scientist can now rest assured that every natural event which he may care to study must have a natural cause and must be knowable in terms of substance and the other basic forms of thought. The scientific assumption of the regularity and uniformity of natural events has thus been justified by philosophical analysis.

We have already pointed out that Kant succeeds in rescuing philosophy from Humean scepticism only at the cost of *limiting* man's field of knowledge to the world of natural occurrences. We must now ask how this concept of a limit arises. The mind, says Kant, is endowed with the faculties not only of sensuous intuition and understanding but also of 'speculative' reason. This faculty of reason is the source of the unique and highly important idea of the Infinite, which in various contexts may also be called the idea of the Unlimited, Totality, Completeness or Wholeness. When the nature and scope of our experience of sensuous objects is examined according to this criterion of absolute completeness, its limitation is at once apparent. For why should we assume that the whole of reality is of such a nature as to be capable of being sensuously experienced by beings like ourselves? Reason accordingly suggests to us the wisdom of recognizing the possibility that our world of nature may be no more than the partial and inadequate appearance to us, through our senses, of a reality whose farther reaches can never be thus sensuously apprehended, by entitling our world of objects the world of phenomenal appearance, and what remains, the realm of ultimate or noumenal reality. The second and third *Critiques* are devoted to an exploration of this noumenal realm with reference to its existence, its nature and its relation to the world of phenomenal appearances. In the *Dialectic* of the first *Critique,* however, Kant limits himself to showing first, that the attempt of the rationalists like Wolff to discover the positive content of noumenal reality solely by means of abstract ratiocination is doomed to failure, and secondly, that the concept of nature as merely phenomenal and hence not the whole of reality provides the key to the solution of certain philosophical problems which otherwise would be insoluble.

Kant's rationalistic predecessors, it will be recalled, had claimed that human reason was able to establish the noumenal existence and to portray the noumenal nature of the soul and God with absolute certainty and finality. In his chapters on the *Paralogisms* and the *Ideal of Reason* Kant shows this claim to be unfounded by testing the "proofs" of an immortal, substantival soul, and of a Deity infinitely perfect in every respect, according to the criterion of objective reality which he has already developed in the *Analytic.* Reason, no doubt, can conceive of a soul as an immaterial, incorruptible, spiritual substance, animating the body in life and surviving it at death; but no such psychic entity can be sensuously experienced, nor need it be invoked to explain the activity of consciousness. All that we can be sure of on a purely intellectual basis is that whenever consciousness exists for me, 'I' am the simple and identical subject of my own cognitive experience. Similarly, reason can form the idea of an omniscient and omnipotent Deity. This abstract thought, however, receives no guarantee of objective truth from our sensuous experience, for we cannot know God as we know sensuous objects. Nor can His existence be established by means of the logical principle of contradiction, as the ontological argument claims, because necessity of thought can never prove necessity of existence; nor need He be regarded as the necessary Cause of the phenomenal world as a whole, since the concept of causation is, as we have seen, applicable only *within* the confines of phenomenal existence and cannot be extended validly beyond these limits into the noumenal realm; nor, finally, is it legitimate to argue with dogmatic certainty that a good Deity is responsible for such evidence of purposive design as our phenomenal world exhibits, because this evidence is ambiguous and lends itself to alternative explanations. All such attempts of reason to penetrate to the heart of ultimate reality are bound to fail.

The chapter on the *Antinomies* deals with four problems which, according to Kant, are insoluble save in terms of the distinction which he has made between the phenomenal and the noumenal. These problems arise through the application of reason's idea of wholeness or totality to the spatial and temporal series of phenomenal events. In the first two antinomies Kant asks whether the world of natural events is infinite or finite in space, and time, and inner constitution. Both alternatives, he insists, can be supported with perfectly valid arguments—hence the 'antinomy,' or fundamental philosophical contradiction—provided nature is judged to be the whole of reality and not merely its phenomenal appearance. When nature is defined, however, in accordance with the teaching of the *Analytic,* as merely the sum of all possible 'objects of experience,' it is seen to be finite in the sense that our experience of it up to any given moment is finite, infinite in the sense that our investigation of it can be, so far as we can see, indefinitely continued. This 'solution' of these age-long philosophical dilemmas is hailed by Kant as further proof of the correctness of his earlier contentions.

The second pair of antinomies deals with the question of the relation of natural causal law to human freedom and to God. All natural events, it has already been shown, are subject to the law of causal necessity. Now man, by virtue of his physical nature, is part and parcel of this phenomenal world; as such, accordingly, he must be wholly subject to its laws. The problem therefore arises as to whether he can in any sense be judged to be free. Again, since every phenomenal event must have an antecedent cause, God cannot be thought of as the first member of this causal series, for, so defined, He too would have to have a cause. Can God then be in any sense related to the world of phenomenal events, taken in its entirety? To solve these problems Kant once again falls back on his distinction between phenomenal and noumenal reality. If the world of nature is the only world there is, no place can be found for God and human freedom. If, on the other hand, a noumenal world exists, man may (provided his nature, though partly phenomenal, is also partly noumenal) be able to identify himself with a noumenal law of freedom; and God (conceived of as a purely noumenal Being) may be the ultimate or noumenal ground of all phenomenal appearance. Pure 'speculative' reason can conceive of such a possibility; further than this, however, it cannot go because, once and for all, man's merely sensuous experience of phenomenal fact can never provide the data for positive belief in a noumenal realm of value. 'Speculative' reason, however, in its insistence upon the possibility of such a noumenal realm, has provided a place in its metaphysical scheme of things for whatever aspects of noumenal reality may be revealed to man in his moral, religious or aesthetic experiences. The *Critique of Pure Reason,* in short, has prepared the way for the ethical, theological and aesthetic doctrines developed in the second and third *Critiques.*

V

The central fact of Kant's own spiritual life was his deep and unshakable conviction that the distinction between right and wrong, good and bad, had its roots in the nature of ultimate reality. His theory of ethics is but an exposition and philosophical defense of the objective validity of this belief.

Where, first of all, does moral worth reside? Not primarily in conduct, as the casuists have maintained, for acts as such are neither good nor bad. The locus of moral value is man's own mind, and moral goodness is, in essence, the tone and quality of his inner life. The measure of a man's moral worth is not the degree of his conformity to any social standard nor mere passive submission to the pronouncements of religious authority.

This does not mean however that a moral judgment is merely an expression of a subjective preference. The hedonistic identification of the good with pleasure or happiness robs goodness of its distinctive quality and makes moral endeavor meaningless. Pleasure results whenever the demands of our sensuous nature are satisfied, and the desire for happiness is our natural motive of action. It is therefore absurd to say that we *ought* to seek happiness or that we *ought* to prefer one variety of happiness to another. At the naturalistic level our only rule is prudence based on a pleasure-pain calculus; we are prudentially wise to the extent to which we direct our lives so as to secure the greatest amount of happiness for ourselves, foolish in so far as we choose present pleasures blindly and fail to take the future into account.

But happiness is not the only goal for which we consciously can strive, and our sense of moral obligation is both genuine and significant. For we are able deliberately to attach supreme value to an objective moral standard, or, as Kant puts it, to respect the moral law for its own sake. The truly moral motive, accordingly, is conscious and whole-hearted allegiance to the moral law; to the extent to which we voluntarily revere this law our will is good; and "nothing can possibly . . . be called good without qualification except a good will."

This sense of loyalty to a moral standard is, in essence, a sense of universal justice. Our natural impulse is to think only of ourselves and our immediate circle of friends and relatives, our natural attitude being one of self-love and a spontaneous affection for those about us whose lives are more or less identified with our own. Morality, in contrast, demands of us strict impartiality in our ultimate evaluation of all human beings and condemns our natural tendency to regard ourselves and our own interests as possessing exceptional importance. The moral law, then, takes this concrete form: That act is good which expresses a spirit of fair-mindedness towards humanity at large and is in accord with pure dispassionate justice to all men.

Now man is able to envisage and cherish this ideal

of justice because of his rational nature. Apart from reason he is hopelessly self-centered; each instinct demands its own immediate satisfaction, and prudence, aiming at the happiness of the "dear self" alone, is indifferent to the welfare of society. In so far as men are dominated by their desire for pleasure they tend either to pull in opposite directions towards satisfaction of divergent tastes, or else to fight with one another in order to secure what all cannot possess. On this basis social concord is impossible. Moral or 'practical' reason, on the other hand, leads to social harmony. Kant holds that man's moral faculty is reason because social justice is a rational ideal, and because conduct motivated by the thought of a universal moral standard is possible through the activity of reason alone. And reason is called 'practical' because of its ability to determine conduct; when once conformity to its dictates becomes the dominant motive of action, man is able to 'practice' what it teaches. Kant adds that it is this faculty of practical reason alone, present in all men at least potentially, which distinguishes men from animals and awakens our respect for humanity at large.

Kant's two complementary formulations of the moral law bring out clearly what is most distinctive in his conception of morality. Here, as elsewhere, Kant is an objective idealist. In the moral experience man has an immediate and poignant realization that goodness is objectively real. It has a character of its own which expresses itself in the form of the moral *law,* and it is *universally* valid for all men endowed with moral sensitivity. The first formulation of the moral law emphasizes the universal character of the moral motive: "Act as if the maxim of thy action were to become by thy will a universal law of nature"—that is, appraise each contemplated act according to the criterion of a universal standard and refrain from action which seems to constitute a violation of, or exception to, that standard. The second formulation of the moral law defines its social setting: "So act as to treat humanity, whether in thine own person or that of another, in every case as an end withal, never as a means"—that is, show your respect for every human being by honoring his right to make his own moral decisions and by recognizing his ability to determine his conduct according to the dictates of his own conscience. The essence of the moral attitude is an allegiance to the ideal of freedom of conscience, a championing of each man's inalienable right to distinguish for himself between right and wrong. Yet just because this is an ideal which all men can hold in common, loyalty to it is the ultimate basis of social harmony. This two-fold aspect of the moral law is expressed by Kant in the form of a paradox, that on the one hand the moral law is the law of my own nature, yet at the same time the law of all rational beings. It is my law since my own reason or sense of justice has prescribed it to me; it is the law of all rational creatures because reason, which is its source, is the same in all men. In so far as men are rational they will of necessity be motivated by the self-same ideal of justice and fair play which makes it appeal to me. The universal law of reason is therefore at once the safeguard of human individuality and the basis of social coöperation.

Kant has been criticized for defining the moral law in such abstract and universal terms as to rob it of all concrete value. Surely this criticism is unsound. For individuals differ endlessly in temperament and in social background; each of us is in many respects unique, and each envisages the good life concretely according to his own distinctive nature. Even within the life of a single individual new concrete values are continually making their appearance, and new concrete problems are forever presenting themselves for solution. Amid this endless variety of interests and values the casuistic attempt to lay down minute rules of conduct cannot succeed without impoverishing and finally destroying individuality. The wiser course is to define the moral *attitude* in terms of a universal formula which each individual can apply for himself to his own concrete situation. We must have faith, says Kant, in the ability of man to solve his own specific moral problems and to allow others to do likewise.

Curiously enough, Kant has also been criticised for robbing men of their individuality by seeking to make all conform to the same concrete pattern of conduct. This charge seems to be based upon a misinterpretation of his first formulation of the moral law, in which he suggests that the morality of an act be tested by being universalized in thought.[1] Here he is advocating common allegiance to the same *motive* of conduct, namely, love of justice and respect for human personality, and not a machine-like uniformity of conduct. The question we should ask ourselves is not: Would we want all men, irrespective of their nature and temporal circumstances, always to act in this particular way? but rather: Would we be willing to have all men, in exactly similar circumstances, act thus? According to this criterion a desire to deceive by lying might well be morally condemned, whereas devotion to a particular task for which perhaps only a single individual is fitted might be approved. It is in order to make clear this distinction between motive and action that Kant lays such stress upon the good will behind the act rather than upon the

[1] Kant's own illustrations of how the formula is to be applied to concrete cases are not free from a certain ambiguity which is in part responsible for this misconception.

act itself. Men's fundamental motive can be identical without impairing individuality, for the same motive is bound to express itself in conduct differently with different men.

A far more difficult question arises with reference to the freedom of the moral will. The problem may be expressed briefly in the form of three separate dilemmas which are related to one another in all being concerned with human freedom and in yielding ultimately to solution through the development of the same metaphysical doctrine. (1) The moral law is not a law of nature, nor can it in the least disturb the regular sequence of natural events; yet man is morally required to translate his mental allegiance to it into the concrete terms of actual conduct, and such obligation indicates his freedom so to act. (2) The moral law is, on the one hand, the law of freedom and moral liberty; yet it is a law which commands complete and absolute obedience and expresses itself in the form of the 'categorical' (or inescapable) imperative. (3) The moral law is in no sense imposed upon man by an omnipotent Deity, nor does it derive its force from a divine sanction; yet the essence of the truly religious attitude consists in regarding it as the law of God.

The key to the solution of these dilemmas is the distinction, suggested in the first *Critique,* between phenomenal and noumenal reality in general and between the phenomenal and noumenal aspects of man's own nature. In the earlier work this distinction was advanced merely as an hypothesis, for 'speculative' reason could offer no coercive proof of the reality of the noumenal world and could obtain no knowledge of its nature; the thought of it was but a negative or limiting concept of a possible something else, it knew not what. 'Practical' reason, however, possesses in the moral experience of obligation to be good a new and positive insight into this noumenal realm. The latter is now seen to be the realm of value in contrast to the phenomenal realm of fact, and man's noumenal nature is now defined as his capacity to think and act not merely mechanically but in terms of moral value.

Let us consider the three dilemmas in turn in the light of this doctrine. (1) How are phenomenal necessity and moral freedom to be reconciled? Man is, both physically and psychically, part of the phenomenal world. His body is subject to all the physical laws which express the regularity of structure and occurrence of physical events, and his mental life conforms perfectly to the psychological laws of association and the like. His every thought and act is embedded in a causal series, being preceded by its invariable and necessary antecedents and followed by its unavoidable effects. In modern terms, man is, from the phenomenal (or scientific) point of view, the product of his heredity and his environment taken in conjunction. Now rational freedom and moral value are quite meaningless at this naturalistic level. Phenomenal events, as such, simply are; it is absurd to say that they ought to have been otherwise, or that man, regarded merely as a phenomenal being, is free, or that any of his thoughts or actions possess value. From the scientific point of view man's physical behavior is exhaustively describable and explicable in naturalistic terms, and, to the psychologist, his mental life is a mere succession of psychical events whose sequence conforms to the laws of thought and whose contents, though susceptible to classification, possess no value or significance. In the moral experience, on the other hand, man thinks in terms of value. He judges this motive to be good, that bad, this action right, that wrong. In so doing, he contemplates his own mental and physical life from within in terms of a normative standard of which the scientist as such can know nothing. This raises his whole inner life, as it were, to a new level; and the new meaning which now pervades his conscious thought transfigures his every act so that what was previously mere physical behavior is now the phenomenal expression of his moral attitude.

A difficulty, however, still remains. For to define freedom of thought and conduct merely as approval or disapproval of ideas and acts which, none the less, are wholly necessitated by their phenomenal antecedents, is but a "miserable subterfuge." Man can be really free and morally responsible only if he is able to *initiate* action and to *control* his mental activity. How is this possible without upsetting the causal series of phenomenal events? To answer this question we must recall the precise way in which Kant has defined causal necessity in the first *Critique*. A series of events is objective and causally related whenever it presents itself to us in a *given order*. Phenomenal events, however, are mere appearances related to one another by no discoverable dynamic link of 'force' or 'energy'; the necessity of their sequence is purely relative to our own inability to alter this spatio-temporal order by an act of will. The ultimate explanation of this order remains an enigma to 'speculative' reason, and the scientist must just accept it as the pattern of appearances. Let us assume now that the final explanation of all phenomena is to be found in ultimate or noumenal reality, regarded as their 'ground'. The noumenal world then, taken as a whole, would be the ultimate basis of all appearances, and man, by virtue of his noumenal capacity to apprehend value, would be able to act so as to express the moral ideal revealed to him by reason. His physical behavior and the succession of his mental states would still present themselves to an external observer as an objective or causal series of events. The man himself, however, seeing his own thought and action from within, would know them to be the *expressions of his own noumenal nature,* and his experience of being able by an act of will freely to select his motive of action and to translate this motive into appropriate behavior would lead him to hold himself responsible for his own character and conduct. The scientist would explain each act and thought of his in terms of its given antecedents; the man himself would recognize these phenomenal antecedents and still look upon himself as a free moral agent, a responsible noumenal being.

Now clearly such a noumenal interpretation of the freedom of the human will is valid only if man's moral experience of obligation be taken seriously. Kant himself never for an instant doubted the significance of this experience; his belief in the reality of the moral order began, as we saw, in childhood, continued in maturity, as each of the *Critiques* testify, and persisted to old age. Duty and freedom are accordingly the pillars of his moral 'faith', his sense of duty convincing him of his freedom and the thought of freedom enabling him to render the thought of duty intelligible and significant.

(2) This brings us to the second dilemma. How can the moral law be at once the law of absolute compulsion and of perfect freedom? The intensity of Kant's belief in duty provides the explanation for his insistence that the moral imperative is 'categorical' in its commands. All hedonistic imperatives, which take the form: 'If happiness is desired, this course of action must be pursued,' are 'hypothetical' in character, since we are always at liberty to renounce the goal of happiness. But moral goodness, whose source is ultimate reality itself, commands us with a voice of absolute authority;

we cannot escape the obligation to be good. Yet the requirement is, in the truest sense, one which we impose upon ourselves for it is but the expression of our own inmost nature. The noumenal spark in us, or conscience, requires that our sensuous inclinations submit to its behest and that our thoughts and actions conform with the ideal which it sets up.

(3) Kant's solution of the third dilemma, concerning the relation of the moral law to God, brings out his deistic conception of the Deity and of man's relation to Him. We have already suggested that his attitude to religion is in large measure the result of his early contact with Pietistic mysticism in the Collegium, while the rationalistic temper of the age in which he lived and his own intellectualism were doubtless contributing factors. But whatever the cause, his most characteristic [1] conception of God and His relation to man shows all the signs of 18th century deism. God is not known directly through the religious experience nor does He reveal himself to man in history. Therefore His existence must be proved. Pure 'speculative' reason is unequal to this task, as was shown in the first *Critique*. Hence 'practical' reason must develop a new argument to justify belief in God and immortality. The moral individual, surveying life and reality dispassionately and rationally, is forced to believe that the cosmos is prepared to sustain moral endeavor through the ultimate equating of perfect happiness with perfect virtue. Since we cannot achieve in this life the perfect virtue which duty requires of us, we must believe in immortality; and since virtue and happiness do not in essence imply one another, either being attainable in this life disproportionately to the other, we must believe in the existence of a moral and omnipotent Deity who, in the life

[1] Yet cf. below pp. 370 ff.

to come, will measure out happiness as it is deserved. Kant was aware of the inadequacy of this conception of God's relation to the moral order, and he struggled manfully to avoid the hedonistic implication that the final incentive to virtue is eternal bliss. His dissatisfaction with the entire argument is shown by the fact that he abandoned it in his last years and attempted, shortly before his death, to give a more convincing account of our knowledge of God and of His relation to the moral law. Even then, however, his approach to the problem was moral rather than religious. Kant never seems to have doubted a personal God's existence. Yet the idea of God was to him less significant and vital than the idea of an impersonal moral order. In the *Religion within the Limits of Bare Reason* God, or the personification of the moral law, is referred to as the anthropomorphic form in which objective value is described in religious literature for the benefit of the uneducated and the simple-minded, and the essence of religion is said to be obedience to the moral law "regarded as" the law of God. In the *Critique of Practical Reason* He is described not as the source of moral value but as a noumenal Being worthy of our respect because of His perfect conformity to its objective standard, not as a Despot who imposes His will upon us in the form of the moral law but as an independent Being who makes the moral law His own. We must conclude that Kant's chief concern was to preserve man's spiritual autonomy at all costs, proclaiming that neither the world of nature nor the Deity can rob him of his moral freedom.

VI

There remain to be considered two other aspects of human experience to which men have always attached great importance, the appreciation and creation of beauty and the discovery of scientific truth. Kant seeks in the *Critique of Judgement* to relate these experiences to one another on the ground that each is clearly distinguishable both from our ordinary consciousness of objects and from morality, each involves pleasure as an essential ingredient, and each throws new light upon the interrelation of the phenomenal and noumenal worlds. This attempt to discover what the two experiences have in common is less illuminating, however, than are his highly suggestive interpretations of each experience in turn.

His study of the aesthetic experience starts off as usual with an analysis of its unique characteristics. The judgment of taste is, first, disinterested. This does not mean that a beautiful[1] object is uninteresting—on the contrary, it interests us profoundly—but merely that it awakens in us no desire, moral or sensuous, to do anything with reference to it other than contemplate it and enjoy it. It does not arouse our appetites nor call forth our moral approval or condemnation but merely delights us in being what it is. Secondly, the judgment of taste is at once universal and non-conceptual. It is universal in being not merely an expression of private preference but in laying claim to universal acceptance. To say that an object is beautiful is to suggest that others possessed of taste will agree with this judgment, always provided that the judgment has been correctly made. In short, we look upon beauty as though it were objective and possessed of a character of its own,

[1] The use of the word 'beauty' should not lead the reader to suppose that Kant is conceiving of the object of the aesthetic experience more narrowly than does the modern student of aesthetics. Such a term as 'the aesthetically satisfying' might be employed as a synonym for 'the beautiful,' as he uses it.

and as though our aesthetic judgments might be true or false. Yet beauty, unlike truth and goodness, is not objective in the sense of being susceptible to analysis and proof. No intellectual criterion of beauty can be found and judgments of taste cannot be tested according to objective standards. We cannot approach a work of art with a clear idea in mind of what constitutes beauty and measure it in terms of this idea, for beauty does not lend itself to such conceptual treatment.

By this characterization of taste, Kant disassociated himself from the explanations of the beautiful, current in his day—the sensationalist, which identified it with the sensuously pleasant, and the rationalist, which regarded it as the object of confused thought. The aesthetic experience is, he insists, unique, however hard it may be accurately to describe it. It is "the feeling of purposiveness without the idea of purpose", the sense of meaning without conceptual definition of what is meant, the awareness of finality or completeness without an intellectual realization of what was aimed at or achieved.

Now this paradoxical nature of taste calls for an explanation. How are we to account for the fact that beauty, though not a quality of the sensuously apprehended object, and though not apprehended conceptually but merely 'felt,' occasions, none the less, judgments of taste which carry with them the implication that beauty is the same for all, an object of necessary satisfaction to all who are aesthetically sensitive? Kant explains this paradox first in terms of man's faculties of cognition and then, more illuminatingly, in terms of his noumenal nature.

The first solution rests on his earlier analysis of our cognitive activity. In our ordinary awareness of physical objects the faculty of imagination (whereby the temporally successive impressions are presented to consciousness all at once) and the faculty of understanding (whereby the relation of these impressions to one another is apprehended) coöperate to produce intelligent perception. In the aesthetic experience these same faculties are aroused by the object called beautiful to a more harmonious and complete activity than is occasioned by ordinary objects. The feeling of this greater and unexpected harmony is aesthetic pleasure. And, since all men's cognitive faculties are essentially alike, what gives me aesthetic enjoyment may be expected to do the same for others. The communicability of our delight in beauty is thus explained and the paradox of taste is psychologically resolved.

The metaphysical solution is developed by Kant in answer to the question: How are we to interpret the beauty of nature and the creations of artistic genius? Genius, says Kant, baffles mere scientific explanation. For though the genius employs a definite technique, the value of his work lies not primarily in its technical excellence but in its 'spirit'; though nature is his model, he does not copy nature slavishly; and though each work of art which he produces is an expression of his artistic insight, he is himself more often than not unaware of what he meant to say until, in the finished product, it has said itself. Such unique activity can be accounted for only in terms of inspiration. Genius is the vehicle of a supra-individual force whose comings and goings the artist himself can only partially control. Works of art are phenomenal expressions of the noumenal realm of value. Beauty, like goodness, is born in mysterious fashion, and its discovery by genius is not to be explained solely in terms of psychological and physical antecedents. It is created; yet not, like goodness, by an act of will and through the agency of reason, but rather through the spontaneous activity of our noumenal nature. And since all genuine works of art are perfect and complete, they may well be regarded as the most adequate expressions of noumenal value which the phenomenal world affords.

This account of genius at once suggests a more illuminating explanation of the universality and communicability of taste. May it not be the super-sensible or noumenal in each of us which, though in most cases too feeble to produce great art, yet makes possible our apprehension and enjoyment of the beauty which genius has created? Genius, moreover, provides us with the key for natural beauty. For nature is not beautiful to the aesthetically untutored mind; the artist teaches us to find beauty in it and in so doing opens up to us a new and deeply satisfying approach to nature. In the aesthetic experience natural objects are apprehended not as embodiments of universal law, but, on the analogy of art, concretely, each object being regarded as complete and perfect in itself. The understanding still clings, in science, to the mechanical interpretation of nature; our aesthetic sense meanwhile releases us from this conceptual yoke and, calling upon us to view nature from within rather than from without, opens our eyes to a beauty which the scientist cannot see. This new experience does not of itself justify the definite assertion that natural beauty has been created by nature for our special benefit, but it does enable us to envisage nature as the phenomenal embodiment of the selfsame noumenal reality, or 'super-sensible substrate,' as Kant now calls it, which, in creative genius and aesthetic insight, stirs the human soul.

This brings us, finally, to the consideration of a problem to which Kant devotes the second part of the *Critique of Judgement*. In the appreciation of natural beauty we feel nature's response to our aesthetic needs. Is she as ready to meet our intellectual needs? Can we be sure that she is willing to reveal all her secrets to man's inquiring mind and place no insurmountable obstacle in the way of scientific knowledge?

Kant's analysis, in the first *Critique,* of ordinary consciousness made it clear that, in essential structure, nature must conform to our faculties of cognition and always be knowable in general mechanistic terms. The scientist is thus assured that his search for the causal antecedents of any natural occurrence, or his attempt to measure nature quantitatively, is always legitimate and possible of accomplishment. A fundamental difficulty, however, seems to arise in the explanation of living organisms, such as trees, which are, no doubt, quantitatively measurable and causally dependent upon their physical environment, but which are also possessed of certain *distinctive* characteristics which seem to elude a mechanistic explanation. Trees, for example, are self-multiplying, each tree being at once the generic product and parent of other trees. How is this reproductive capacity to be explained mechanistically? Again, each tree grows, and growth is not mere addition of new parts through mechanical or quantitative increase but involves the qualitative transformation of the inorganic into the organic. Finally, the various parts of a tree such as the leaves and roots depend upon the life of the whole tree, flourishing and dying with it; the tree itself, in turn, depends upon the active functioning of its parts, as is shown by the effect of repeatedly defoliating it or severing its roots. A tree, in short, like every other living organism, is not a mere aggregate of unrelated inorganic constituents but a functionally related system of parts bound each to each in organic unity. The failure of mechanism to explain this phenomenon of organic life is due not to the admitted incompleteness of our present mechanistic knowledge but to its inherent disqualification to deal with such phenomena. Even an omniscient mechanist, Kant believes, would be unable to explain what is distinctive in a living organism, namely its life and inner organic unity.

Now were we to discover a regular hexagon traced upon the sand of a supposedly uninhabited island we should have to abandon the attempt to explain it solely as the effect of wind and waves and, regarding it as necessarily the product of a conscious mind, decide that the island must be inhabited after all. Similarly our natural impulse is to account for living organisms in terms of the explanatory principle of design. Nature, we feel, must be the product of a purposive Intellect who has left the impress of His wisdom upon His handiwork. Such a theistic explanation, says Kant, is preferable to materialistic mechanism which fails completely to illuminate the salient facts, or pantheistic fatalism which, in regarding the whole of nature as a part of God, gives no account of its specific organic structure, or hylozoism which falls back on the unintelligible notion of 'living matter' while offering no satisfactory explanation of life itself. Even theism, however, cannot be accepted as either an adequate or a certain explanation of natural organization. Its inadequacy is most apparent if God be conceived deistically as the artificer of nature who, like the maker of a watch, constructed the world and then turned it loose to run itself. For an inanimate machine, constructed according to a design, is external to its designing cause and can neither repair its outworn parts nor reproduce itself, whereas a living organism gives every indication of being a 'self-caused cause' and is able to supply its own needs and propagate its kind. But even though we think of God as immanent in nature and as directing its behavior at every turn, what coercive reason have we for believing that such a God exists or that, if He exists, His activity is purposive like our own, action following deliberate design in temporal sequence. In short, teleology like mechanism gives every indication of being a faulty explanation of organic life.

What then is the solution of our dilemma? How is the scientist to proceed towards an understanding of natural phenomena? Both mechanism and design, says Kant, must be employed as explanatory principles, and, of the two, the latter must finally be given preference as the more adequate and inclusive. The scientist must, on the one hand, continue to explore the universe along mechanistic lines and never wholly abandon this approach; yet he should bear in mind that organic life can best be understood by minds like ours in terms of the principle of natural teleology. The biologist is wise in refraining from theistic speculation and the employment of an anthropocentric teleology, for he can never discover scientifically for what human or divine purpose nature is organized as it is. Yet even he must conceive of every living organism as possessing a 'natural' purpose, its structure and activity having a teleological value for the preservation of its own life and that of its own species. The modern evolutionary point of view would seem to sustain Kant in this conclusion.

Reason, meanwhile, suggests to us the possibility that ultimate reality, or the 'super-sensible substrate' of nature, may contain within itself an explanation of organic life other than mechanism or design, yet possibly similar to either or both. This thought should lead us to refrain from uncritical faith in the adequacy of either mechanism or teleology, as we understand them, as final explanatory principles. There seems to be in nature an element of mystery which our minds are unable to fathom and which science may never be able fully to resolve. Despite the marvelous success of science in learning nature's secrets, therefore, the thoughtful scientist will never forget the limitations of his own insight and will refrain from a complacent faith in his own powers to solve all the riddles of the universe. An honest theologian, on the other hand, will realize that the existence of a moral Deity can never be inferred with certainty from nature's structure and behavior and that morality, not science, must be counted on to justify his faith in God and a cosmic moral order.

VII

A careful study of Kant's writings leaves us with the conviction that the outstanding characteristic of his personality was hatred of all intellectual and spiritual superficiality and a passion for honest and profound scrutiny of man's fundamental problems. The goal of his philosophical endeavor was always the discovery of the final meaning and significance of human experience; his method was endless analysis and exploration. The tone of dogmatic finality which often characterizes his literary style is but the accidental result of his desire for precise utterance. At heart he is a highly undogmatic thinker, possessed to an unusual degree of the Socratic spirit—questioning every conclusion, testing every argument, and tireless in the endeavor to lay bare all hidden presuppositions and avoid all blinding prejudice. "I cling to nothing," he wrote Herder in

1767, "and, whether they be my own opinions or those of another, I frequently, and with complete impartiality, rotate the entire structure and study it from various points of view in the hope of discovering finally an angle of approach which will delineate the truth."

Hegel, it has been said, was chiefly interested in his solutions, Kant in his problems. The latter statement at least is unquestionably true. Kant was too suspicious of easy thinking ever to rest content with what other thinkers might regard either as satisfactory or as inevitable. The rationalistic belief in the power of reason to discover the deepest secrets of ultimate reality seemed to him to betray a blindness to the limits of human knowledge. The naturalism fostered by some of the empiricists was, he thought, lacking in philosophical insight and spiritual profundity. He revealed the failure of students of aesthetics like Baumgarten and Burke rightly to comprehend the true nature of taste and genius, and challenged the presumptuous claim of science to be able eventually to solve all human problems. The faith of 18th century humanitarianism in man's pristine goodness and its explanation of moral evil as the artificial product of civilization he regarded as superficial and childish; there is in human nature, he felt sure, a mysterious root of evil which can be eradicated only through painful moral struggle. Thus there seems to have been awakened in Kant in the presence of each of the major human problems—of knowledge, reality, goodness and beauty—a sense of human finitude and of ultimate mystery. Let us by all means, he says, study as exhaustively as possible the nature of our cognitive, moral and aesthetic experiences; there will always remain a something which the intellect cannot grasp and which must yet be accepted as supremely significant. In this larger and perhaps truer sense Kant was a deeply religious thinker who, at the conclusion of each of his major philosophical inquiries seems to exclaim: "The wind bloweth where it listeth and thou hearest the sound thereof, but canst not tell whence it cometh and whither it goeth; so is every one born of the Spirit."

THEODORE MEYER GREENE

KANT
Selections

CRITIQUE OF PURE REASON[1]

PREFACE TO THE FIRST EDITION[2]

OUR reason (Vernunft) has this peculiar fate that with reference to one class of its knowledge, it is always troubled with questions which cannot be ignored, because they spring from the very nature of reason, and which cannot be answered, because they transcend the powers of human reason.

Nor is human reason to be blamed for this. It begins with principles which, in the course of experience, it *must* follow, and which are sufficiently confirmed by experience. With these again, according to the necessities of its nature, it rises higher and higher to more remote conditions. But when it perceives that in this way its work remains for ever incomplete, because the questions never cease, it finds itself constrained to take refuge in principles which exceed every possible experimental application, and nevertheless seem so unobjectionable that even ordinary common sense agrees with them. Thus, however, reason becomes involved in darkness and contradictions, from which, no doubt, it may conclude that errors must be lurking somewhere, but without being able to discover them, because the principles which it follows transcend all the limits of

[1] [The following selections have been taken from the revised second edition of Max Müller's translation, published by Macmillan & Co. All page references are to this edition.]

[2] [M. xvii ff.]

experience and therefore withdraw themselves from all experimental tests. It is the battle-field of these endless controversies which is called *Metaphysic.*

There was a time when Metaphysic held a royal place among all the sciences, and, if the will were taken for the deed, the exceeding importance of her subject might well have secured to her that place of honour. At present it is the fashion to despise Metaphysic, and the poor matron, forlorn and forsaken, complains like Hecuba, *Modo maxima rerum, tot generis natisque potens—nunc trahor exul, inops* (Ovid, Metam. xiii. 508).

At first the rule of Metaphysic, under the dominion of the dogmatists, was despotic. But as the laws still bore the traces of an old barbarism, intestine wars and complete anarchy broke out, and the sceptics, a kind of nomads, despising all settled culture of the land, broke up from time to time all civil society. Fortunately their number was small, and they could not prevent the old settlers from returning to cultivate the ground afresh, though without any fixed plan or agreement. Not long ago one might have thought, indeed, that all these quarrels were to have been settled and the legitimacy of her claims decided once for all through a certain physiology of the human understanding, the work of the celebrated *Locke.* But, though the descent of that royal pretender, traced back as it had been to the lowest mob of common experience, ought to have rendered her claims very suspicious, yet, as that genealogy turned out to be in reality a false invention, the old queen (Metaphysic) continued to maintain her claims, everything fell back into the old rotten dogmatism, and the contempt from which metaphysical science was to have been rescued, remained the same as ever. At present, after everything has been tried, so they say, and tried in vain, there reign in philosophy weariness and complete indifferentism, the mother of chaos and night in all sciences but, at the same time, the spring or, at least, the prelude of their near reform and of a new light, after an ill-applied study has rendered them dark, confused, and useless.

It is in vain to assume a kind of artificial indifferentism in respect to enquiries the object of which cannot be indifferent to human nature. Nay, those pretended indifferentists (however they may try to disguise themselves by changing scholastic terminology into popular language), if they think at all, fall back inevitably into those very metaphysical dogmas which they profess to despise. Nevertheless this indifferentism, showing itself in the very midst of the most flourishing state of all sciences, and affecting those very sciences the teachings of which, if they could be had, would be the last to be surrendered, is a phenomenon well worthy of our attention and consideration. It is clearly the result, not of the carelessness, but of the matured judgment [1] of our age, which will no longer rest satisfied with the mere appearance of knowledge. It is, at the same time, a powerful appeal to reason to undertake anew the most diffi-

[1] We often hear complaints against the shallowness of thought in our own time, and the decay of sound knowledge. But I do not see that sciences which rest on a solid foundation, such as mathematics, physics, etc., deserve this reproach in the least. On the contrary, they maintain their old reputation of solidity, and with regard to physics, even surpass it. The same spirit would manifest itself in other branches of knowledge, if only their principles had first been properly determined. Till that is done, indifferentism and doubt, and ultimately severe criticism, are rather signs of honest thought. Our age is, in every sense of the word, the age of criticism, and everything must submit to it. Religion, on the strength of its sanctity, and law, on the strength of its majesty, try to withdraw themselves from it; but by so doing they arouse just suspicions, and cannot claim that sincere respect which reason pays to those only who have been able to stand its free and open examination.

cult of its duties, namely, self-knowledge, and to institute a court of appeal which should protect the just rights of reason, but dismiss all groundless claims, and should do this not by means of irresponsible decrees, but according to the eternal and unalterable laws of reason. This court of appeal is no other than the *Critique of Pure Reason.*

I do not mean by this a criticism of books and systems, but of the faculty of reason in general, touching that whole class of knowledge which it may strive after, unassisted by experience. This must decide the question of the possibility or impossibility of metaphysic in general, and the determination of its sources, its extent, and its limits—and all this according to fixed principles.

This, the only way that was left, I have followed, and I flatter myself that I have thus removed all those errors which have hitherto brought reason, whenever it was unassisted by experience, into conflict with itself. I have not evaded its questions by pleading the insufficiency of human reason, but I have classified them according to principles, and, after showing the point where reason begins to misunderstand itself, solved them satisfactorily. It is true that the answer of those questions is not such as a dogma-enamoured curiosity might wish for, for such curiosity could not have been satisfied except by juggling tricks in which I am no adept. But this was not the intention of the natural destiny of our reason, and it became the duty of philosophy to remove the deception which arose from a false interpretation, even though many a vaunted and cherished dream should vanish at the same time. In this work I have chiefly aimed at completeness, and I venture to maintain that there ought not to be one single metaphysical problem that has not been solved here, or to the solution of which the key at least has not been supplied. In fact Pure

Reason is so perfect a unity that, if its principle should prove insufficient to answer any one of the many questions started by its very nature, one might throw it away altogether, as insufficient to answer the other questions with perfect certainty.

While I am saying this I fancy I observe in the face of my readers an expression of indignation, mixed with contempt, at pretensions apparently so self-glorious and extravagant; and yet they are in reality far more moderate than those made by the writer of the commonest essay professing to prove the simple nature of the soul or the necessity of a first beginning of the world. For, while he pretends to extend human knowledge beyond the limits of all possible experience, I confess most humbly that this is entirely beyond my power. I mean only to treat of reason and its pure thinking, a knowledge of which is not very far to seek, considering that it is to be found within myself. Common logic gives an instance how all the simple acts of reason can be enumerated completely and systematically. Only between the common logic and my work there is this difference, that my question is,—what can we hope to achieve with reason, when all the material and assistance of experience is taken away?

So much with regard to the completeness in our laying hold of every single object, and the thoroughness in our laying hold of all objects, as the material of our critical enquiries—a completeness and thoroughness determined, not by a casual idea, but by the nature of knowledge itself.

Besides this, certainty and clearness with regard to form are two essential demands that may very properly be addressed to an author who ventures on so slippery an undertaking.

First, with regard to certainty, I have pronounced

judgment against myself by saying that in this kind of enquiries it is in no way permissible to propound mere opinions, and that everything looking like a hypothesis is counterband, that must not be offered for sale at however low a price, but must, as soon as it has been discovered, be confiscated. For every kind of knowledge which professes to be certain *a priori,* proclaims itself that it means to be taken for absolutely necessary. And this applies, therefore, still more to a definition of all pure knowledge *a priori,* which is to be the measure, and therefore also an example, of all apodictic philosophical certainty. Whether I have fulfilled what I have here undertaken to do, must be left to the judgment of the reader; for it only behooves the author to propound his arguments, and not to determine beforehand the effect which they ought to produce on his judges. . . . [M. xxii-xxiii]

Secondly, as to clearness, the reader has a right to demand not only what may be called logical or discursive clearness, which is based on concepts, but also what may be called æsthetic or intuitive clearness produced by intuitions, i.e. by examples and concrete illustrations. With regard to the former I have made ample provision. That arose from the very nature of my purpose, but it became at the same time the reason why I could not fully satisfy the latter, if not absolute, yet very just claim. Nearly through the whole of my work I have felt doubtful what to do. Examples and illustrations seemed always to be necessary, and therefore found their way into the first sketch of my work. But I soon perceived the magnitude of my task and the number of objects I should have to treat; and, when I saw that even in their driest scholastic form they would considerably swell my book, I did not consider it expedient to extend it still further through examples and illustrations required for popular purposes only. This work can never satisfy the popular taste, and the few who know, do not require that help which, though it is always welcome, yet might here have defeated its very purpose. The Abbé Terrasson writes indeed that, if we measured the greatness of a book, not by the number of its pages, but by the time we require for mastering it, many a book might be said to be much shorter, if it were not so short. But, on the other hand, if we ask how a complicated, yet in principle coherent whole of speculative thought can best be rendered intelligible, we might be equally justified in saying that many a book would have been more intelligible, if it had not tried to be so very intelligible. For the helps to clearness, though they may be missed with regard to details, often distract with regard to the whole. The reader does not arrive quickly enough at a survey of the whole, because the bright colours of illustrations hide and distort the articulation and concatenation of the whole system, which, after all, if we want to judge of its unity and sufficiency, are more important than anything else.

Surely it should be an attraction to the reader if he is asked to join his own efforts with those of the author in order to carry out a great and important work, according to the plan here proposed, in a complete and lasting manner. Metaphysic, according to the definitions here given, is the only one of all sciences which, through a small but united effort, may count on such completeness in a short time, so that nothing will remain for posterity but to arrange everything according to its own views for didactic purposes, without being able to add anything to the subject itself. For it is in reality nothing but an inventory of all our possessions acquired through Pure Reason, systematically arranged. Nothing can escape us, because whatever reason produces entirely out of itself, cannot hide itself, but is brought to light by reason itself, so soon as the common principle has been discovered. This absolute completeness is rendered not only possible, but necessary, through the perfect unity of this kind of knowledge, all derived from pure concepts, without any influence from experience, or from special intuitions leading to a definite kind of experience, that might serve to enlarge and increase it. *Tecum habita et noris quam sit tibi curta supellex* (Persius, Sat. iv. 52).

Such a system of pure (speculative) reason I hope myself to produce under the title of "Metaphysic of Nature." It will not be half so large, yet infinitely richer than this Critique of Pure Reason, which has, first of all, to discover its source, nay, the conditions of its possibility, in fact, to clear and level a soil quite overgrown with weeds. Here I expect from my readers the patience and impartiality of a judge, there the goodwill and aid of a fellow-worker. For however completely all the principles of the system have been propounded in my Critique, the completeness of the whole system requires also that no derivative concepts should be omitted, such as cannot be found out by an estimate *a priori,* but have to be discovered step by step. There the synthesis of concepts has been exhausted, here it will be requisite to do the same for their analysis, a task which is easy and an amusement rather than a labour. . . . [M. xxvi]

PREFACE TO THE SECOND EDITION.[1]

Whether the treatment of that class of knowledge with which reason is occupied follows the secure method of a science or not, can easily be determined by the result.

[1] [Cf. M. 688 ff.]

If, after repeated preparations, it comes to a standstill, as soon as its real goal is approached, or is obliged, in order to reach it, to retrace its steps again and again, and strike into fresh paths; again, if it is impossible to produce unanimity among those who are engaged in the same work, as to the manner in which their common object should be obtained, we may be convinced that such a study is far from having attained to the secure method of a science, but is groping only in the dark. In that case we are conferring a great benefit on reason, if we only find out the right method, though many things should have to be surrendered as useless, which were comprehended in the original aim that had been chosen without sufficient reflection.

That *Logic,* from the earliest times, has followed that secure method, may be seen from the fact that since *Aristotle* it has not had to retrace a single step, unless we choose to consider as improvements the removal of some unnecessary subtleties, or the clearer definition of its matter, both of which refer to the elegance rather than to the solidity of the science. It is remarkable also, that to the present day, it has not been able to make one step in advance, so that, to all appearance, it may be considered as completed and perfect. If some modern philosophers thought to enlarge it, by introducing *psychological* chapters on the different faculties of knowledge (faculty of imagination, wit, etc.), or *metaphysical* chapters on the origin of knowledge, or the different degrees of certainty according to the difference of objects (idealism, scepticism, etc.), or lastly, *anthropological* chapters on prejudices, their causes and remedies, this could only arise from their ignorance of the peculiar nature of logical science. We do not enlarge, but we only disfigure the sciences, if we allow their respective limits to be confounded: and the limits of logic are definitely fixed by the fact, that it is a science which has nothing to do but fully to exhibit and strictly to prove all formal rules of thought (whether it be *a priori* or empirical, whatever be its origin or its object, and whatever be the impediments, accidental or natural, which it has to encounter in the human mind).

That logic should in this respect have been so successful, is due entirely to its limitation, whereby it has not only the right, but the duty, to make abstraction of all the objects of knowledge and their differences, so that the understanding has to deal with nothing beyond itself and its own forms. It was, of course, far more difficult for reason to enter on the secure method of science, when it has to deal not with itself only, but also with objects. Logic, therefore, as a kind of preparation *(propaedeutic)* forms, as it were, the vestibule of the sciences only, and where real knowledge is concerned, is presupposed for critical purposes only, while the acquisition of knowledge must be sought for in the sciences themselves, properly and objectively so called. . . . [M. 689]

Mathematics and *physics* are the two theoretical sciences of reason, which have to determine their *objects a priori;* the former quite purely, the latter partially so, and partially from other sources of knowledge besides reason.

Mathematics, from the earliest times to which the history of human reason can reach, has followed, among that wonderful people of the Greeks, the safe way of a science. But it must not be supposed that it was as easy for mathematics as for logic, in which reason is concerned with itself alone, to find, or rather to make for itself that royal road. I believe, on the contrary, that there was a long period of tentative work (chiefly still among the Egyptians), and that the change is to be ascribed to a *revolution,* produced by the happy thought of a single man, whose experiment pointed unmistakably to the path that had to be followed, and opened and traced out for the most distant times the safe way of a science. The history of that intellectual revolution, which was far more important than the discovery of the passage round the celebrated Cape of Good Hope, and the name of its fortunate author, have not been preserved to us. But the story preserved by Diogenes Laertius, who names the reputed author of the smallest elements of ordinary geometrical demonstrations, even of such as, according to general opinion, do not require to be proved, shows, at all events, that the memory of the revolution, produced by the very first traces of the discovery of a new method, appeared extremely important to the mathematicians, and thus remained unforgotten. A new light flashed on the first man who demonstrated the properties of the isosceles triangle (whether his name was *Thales* or any other name), for he found that he had not to investigate what he saw in the figure, or the mere concept of that figure, and thus to learn its properties; but that he had to produce (by construction) what he had himself, according to concepts *a priori,* placed into that figure and represented in it, so that, in order to know anything with certainty *a priori,* he must not attribute to that figure anything beyond what necessarily follows from what he has himself placed into it, in accordance with the concept.

It took a much longer time before physics entered on the high way of science: for no more than a century and a half has elapsed, since Bacon's ingenious proposal partly initiated that discovery, partly, as others were already on the right track, gave a new impetus to it,—a discovery which, like the former, can only be explained by a rapid intellectual revolution. In what

I have to say, I shall confine myself to natural science, so far as it is founded on *empirical* principles.

When Galilei let balls of a particular weight, which he had determined himself, roll down an inclined plane, or Torricelli made the air carry a weight, which he had previously determined to be equal to that of a definite volume of water; or when, in later times, Stahl [1] changed metal into lime, and lime again into metal, by withdrawing and restoring something, a new light flashed on all students of nature. They comprehended that reason has insight into that only, which she herself produces on her own plan, and that she must move forward with the principles of her judgments, according to fixed law, and compel nature to answer her questions, but not let herself be led by nature, as it were in leading strings, because otherwise accidental observations, made on no previously fixed plan, will never converge towards a necessary law, which is the only thing that reason seeks and requires. Reason, holding in one hand its principles, according to which concordant phenomena alone can be admitted as laws of nature, and in the other hand the experiment, which it has devised according to those principles, must approach nature, in order to be taught by it: but not in the character of a pupil, who agrees to everything the master likes, but as an appointed judge, who compels the witnesses to answer the questions which he himself proposes. Therefore even the science of physics entirely owes the beneficial revolution in its character to the happy thought, that we ought to seek in nature (and not import into it by means of fiction) whatever reason must learn from nature, and could not know by itself, and that we must do this in accordance with what reason itself has originally placed

[1] I am not closely following here the course of the history of the experimental method, nor are the first beginnings of it very well known.

into nature. Thus only has the study of nature entered on the secure method of a science, after having for many centuries done nothing but grope in the dark.

Metaphysic, a completely isolated and speculative science of reason, which declines all teaching of experience, and rests on concepts only (not on their application to intuition, as mathematics), in which reason therefore is meant to be her own pupil, has hitherto not been so fortunate as to enter on the secure path of a science, although it is older than all other sciences, and would remain, even if all the rest were swallowed up in the abyss of an all-destroying barbarism. In metaphysic, reason, even if it tries only to understand *a priori* (as it pretends to do) those laws which are confirmed by the commonest experience, is constantly brought to a standstill, and we are obliged again and again to retrace our steps, because they do not lead us where we want to go; while as to any unanimity among those who are engaged in the same work, there is so little of it in metaphysic, that it has rather become an arena, specially destined, it would seem, for those who wish to exercise themselves in mock fights, and where no combatant has, as yet, succeeded in gaining an inch of ground that he could call permanently his own. It cannot be denied, therefore, that the method of metaphysic has hitherto consisted in groping only, and, what is the worst, in groping among mere concepts.

What then can be the cause that hitherto no secure method of science has been discovered? Shall we say that it is impossible? Then why should nature have visited our reason with restless aspiration to look for it, as if it were its most important concern? Nay more, how little should we be justified in trusting our reason if, with regard to one of the most important objects we wish to know, it not only abandons us, but lures us on by vain hopes, and in the end betrays us! Or, if hitherto we have only failed to meet with the right path, what indications are there to make us hope that, if we renew our researches, we shall be more successful than others before us?

The examples of mathematics and natural science, which by one revolution have become what they now are, seem to me sufficiently remarkable to induce us to consider, what may have been the essential element in that intellectual revolution which has proved so beneficial to them, and to make the experiment, at least, so far as the analogy between them, as sciences of reason, with metaphysic allows it, of imitating them. Hitherto it has been supposed that all our knowledge must conform to the objects: but, under that supposition, all attempts to establish anything about them *a priori,* by means of concepts, and thus to enlarge our knowledge, have come to nothing. The experiment therefore ought to be made, whether we should not succeed better with the problems of metaphysic, by assuming that the objects must conform to our mode of cognition, for this would better agree with the demanded possibility of an *a priori* knowledge of them, which is to settle something about objects, before they are given us. We have here the same case as with the first thought of Copernicus, who, not being able to get on in the explanation of the movements of the heavenly bodies, as long as he assumed that all the stars turned round the spectator, tried, whether he could not succeed better, by assuming the spectator to be turning round, and the stars to be at rest. A similar experiment may be tried in metaphysic, so far as the *intuition* of objects is concerned. If the intuition had to conform to the constitution of objects, I do not see how we could know anything of it *a priori;* but if the object (as an object of the senses) conforms to the constitution of our faculty of intuition, I can very well conceive such a possibility. As, however, I cannot rest in these intuitions, if they are to become knowledge, but have to refer them, as representations, to something as their object, and must determine that object by them, I have the choice of admitting, either that the *concepts,* by which I carry out that determination, conform to the object, being then again in the same perplexity on account of the manner how I can know anything about it *a priori;* or that the objects, or what is the same, the experience in which alone they are known (as given objects), must conform to those concepts. In the latter case, the solution becomes more easy, because experience, as a kind of knowledge, requires understanding, and I must therefore, even before objects are given to me, presuppose the rules of the understanding as existing within me *a priori,* these rules being expressed in concepts *a priori,* to which all objects of experience must necessarily conform, and with which they must agree. . . . [M. 694]

This experiment succeeds as well as we could desire, and promises to metaphysic, in its first part, which deals with concepts *a priori,* of which the corresponding objects may be given in experience, the secure method of a science. For by thus changing our point of view, the possibility of knowledge *a priori* can well be explained, and, what is still more, the laws which *a priori* lie at the foundation of nature, as the sum total of the objects of experience, may be supplied with satisfactory proofs, neither of which was possible with the procedure hitherto adopted. But there arises from this deduction of our faculty of knowing *a priori,* as given in the first part of metaphysic, a somewhat startling result, apparently most detrimental to the objects of metaphysic that have to be treated in the second part, namely, the impossibility of going with it beyond the frontier of possible experience, which is precisely the most essential purpose of metaphysical science. But here we have exactly the experiment which, by disproving the opposite, establishes the truth of our first estimate of the knowledge of reason *a priori,* namely, that it can refer to phenomena only, but must leave the thing by itself as unknown to us, though as existing by itself. For that which impels us by necessity to go beyond the limits of experience and of all phenomena, is the *unconditioned,* which reason postulates in all things by themselves, by necessity and by right, for everything conditioned, so that the series of conditions should thus become complete. If then we find that, under the supposition of our experience conforming to the objects as things by themselves, it is *impossible to conceive* the unconditioned *without contradiction,* while, under the supposition of our representation of things, as they are given to us, not conforming to them as things by themselves, but, on the contrary, of the objects conforming to our mode of representation, that *contradiction vanishes,* and that therefore the unconditioned must not be looked for in things, so far as we know them (so far as they are given to us), but only so far as we do not know them (as things by themselves), we clearly perceive that, what we at first assumed tentatively only, is fully confirmed.[1] But, after all progress in the field of the supersensuous has thus been denied to speculative reason, it is still open to us to see, whether in the practical knowledge of reason *data* may not be found which enable us to determine that transcendent concept of the unconditioned which is demanded by reason, in order thus, according to the wish of metaphysic, to get beyond the limits of all possible experience, by means of our

[1] [Note, M. 695]

knowledge *a priori,* which is possible to us for practical purposes only. In this case, speculative reason has at least gained for us room for such an extension of knowledge, though it had to leave it empty, so that we are not only at liberty, but are really called upon to fill it up, if we are able, by *practical data* of reason.[1]

The very object of the critique of pure speculative reason consists in this attempt at changing the old procedure of metaphysic, and imparting to it the secure method of a science, after having completely revolutionised it, following the example of geometry and physical science. That critique is a treatise on the method *(Traité de la méthode),* not a system of the science itself; but it marks out nevertheless the whole plan of that science, both with regard to its limits, and to its internal organisation. For pure speculative reason has this peculiar advantage that it is able, nay, bound to measure its own powers, according to the different ways in which it chooses its own objects, and to completely enumerate the different ways of choosing problems; thus tracing a complete outline of a system of metaphysic. This is due to the fact that, with regard to the first point, nothing can be attributed to objects in knowledge *a priori,* except what the thinking subject takes from within itself; while, with regard to the second point, reason, so far as its principles of cognition are concerned, forms a separate and independent unity, in which, as in an organic body, every member exists for the sake of all others, and all others exist for the sake of the one, so that no principle can be safely applied in *one* relation, unless it has been carefully examined in *all* its relations, to the whole employment of pure reason. Hence, too, metaphysic has this singular advantage, an advantage which cannot be shared by any other sci-

[1] [Note, M. 696]

ence, in which reason has to deal with objects (for *Logic* deals only with the form of thought in general) that, if it has once attained, by means of this critique, to the secure method of a science, it can completely comprehend the whole field of knowledge pertaining to it, and thus finish its work and leave it to posterity, as a capital that can never be added to, because it has only to deal with principles and the limits of their employment, which are fixed by those principles themselves. And this completeness becomes indeed an obligation, if it is to be a fundamental science, of which we must be able to say, '*nil actum reputans, si quid superesset agendum.*'

But it will be asked, what kind of treasure is it which we mean to bequeath to posterity in this metaphysic of ours, after it has been purified by criticism, and thereby brought to a permanent condition? After a superficial view of this work, it may seem that its advantage is *negative* only, warning us against venturing with speculative reason beyond the limits of experience. Such is no doubt its primary use: but it becomes *positive,* when we perceive that the principles with which speculative reason ventures beyond its limits, lead inevitably, not to an *extension,* but, if carefully considered, to a *narrowing* of the employment of reason, because, by indefinitely extending the limits of sensibility, to which they properly belong, they threaten entirely to supplant the pure (practical) employment of reason. Hence our *critique,* by limiting sensibility to its proper sphere, is no doubt *negative;* but by thus removing an impediment, which threatened to narrow, or even entirely to destroy its practical employment, it is in reality of *positive,* and of very important use, if only we are convinced that there is an absolutely necessary practical use of pure reason (the moral use), in which reason must inevitably go beyond the limits of sensibility, and though not requiring for this purpose the assistance of speculative reason, must at all events be assured against its opposition, lest it be brought in conflict with itself. To deny that this service, which is rendered by criticism, is a *positive* advantage, would be the same as to deny that the police confers upon us any positive advantage, its principal occupation being to prevent violence, which citizens have to apprehend from citizens, so that each may pursue his vocation in peace and security. We had established in the analytical part of our critique the following point:—First, that space and time are only forms of sensuous intuition, therefore conditions of the existence of things, as phenomena only; Secondly, that we have no concepts of the understanding, and therefore nothing whereby we can arrive at the knowledge of things, except in so far as an intuition corresponding to these concepts can be given, and consequently that we cannot have knowledge of any object, as a thing by itself, but only in so far as it is an object of sensuous intuition, that is, a phenomenon. This proves no doubt that all speculative knowledge of reason is limited to objects of *experience;* but it should be carefully borne in mind, that this leaves it perfectly open to us, to *think* the same objects as things by themselves, though we cannot *know* them.[1] For otherwise we should arrive at the absurd conclusion, that there is phenomenal ap-

[1] In order to *know* an object, I must be able to prove its possibility, either from its reality, as attested by experience, or *a priori* by means of reason. But I can *think* whatever I please, provided only I do not contradict myself, that is, provided my conception is a possible thought, though I may be unable to answer for the existence of a corresponding object in the sum total of all possibilities. Before I can attribute to such a concept objective reality (real possibility, as distinguished from the former, which is purely logical), something more is required. This something more, however, need not be sought for in the sources of theoretical knowledge, for it may be found in those of practical knowledge also.

pearance without something that appears. Let us suppose that the necessary distinction, established in our critique, between things as objects of experience and the same things by themselves, had not been made. In that case, the principle of causality, and with it the mechanism of nature, as determined by it, would apply to all things in general, as efficient causes. I should then not be able to say of one and the same being, for instance the human soul, that its will is free, and, at the same time, subject to the necessity of nature, that is, not free, without involving myself in a palpable contradiction: and this because I had taken the soul, in both propositions, in *one and the same sense,* namely, as a thing in general (as something by itself), as, without previous criticism, I could not but take it. If, however, our criticism was true, in teaching us to take an object in two senses, namely, either as a phenomenon, or as a thing by itself, and if the deduction of our concepts of the understanding was correct, and the principle of causality applies to things only, if taken in the first sense, namely, so far as they are objects of experience, but not to things, if taken in their second sense, we can, without any contradiction, think the same will when phenomenal (in visible actions) as necessarily conforming to the law of nature, and so far, *not free,* and yet, on the other hand, when belonging to a thing by itself, as not subject to that law of nature, and therefore *free.* Now it is quite true that I may not *know* my soul, as a thing by itself, by means of speculative reason (still less through empirical observation), and consequently may not know freedom either, as the quality of a being to which I attribute effects in the world of sense, because, in order to do this, I should have to know such a being as determined in its existence, and yet as not determined in time (which, as I cannot provide my concept with any intuition, is impossible). This, however, does not prevent me from *thinking* freedom; that is, my representation of it contains at least no contradiction within itself, if only our critical distinction of the two modes of representation (the sensible and the intelligible), and the consequent limitation of the concepts of the pure understanding, and of the principles based on them, has been properly carried out. If, then, morality necessarily presupposed freedom (in the strictest sense) as a property of our will, producing, as *a priori data* of it, practical principles, belonging originally to our reason, which, without freedom, would be absolutely impossible, while speculative reason had proved that such a freedom cannot even be thought, the former supposition, namely, the moral one, would necessarily have to yield to another, the opposite of which involves a palpable contradiction, so that *freedom,* and with it morality (for its opposite contains no contradiction, unless freedom is presupposed), would have to make room for the *mechanism* of nature. Now, however, as morality requires nothing but that freedom should not only contradict itself, and that, though unable to understand, we should at least be able to think it, there being no reason why freedom should interfere with the natural mechanism of the same act (if only taken in a different sense), the doctrine of morality may well hold its place, and the doctrine of nature may hold its place too, which would have been impossible, if our critique had not previously taught us our inevitable ignorance with regard to things by themselves, and limited everything, which we are able to *know* theoretically, to mere phenomena. The same discussion as to the positive advantage to be derived from the critical principles of pure reason might be repeated with regard to the concept of *God,* and of the *simple nature* of our *soul;* but, for the sake of brevity, I shall pass this by. I am not allowed therefore even to *assume,* for the sake of the necessary practical employment of my reason, *God, freedom,* and *immortality,* if I cannot *deprive* speculative reason of its pretensions to transcendent insights, because reason, in order to arrive at these, must use principles which are intended originally for objects of possible experience only, and which, if in spite of this, they are applied to what cannot be an object of experience, really changes this into a phenomenon, thus rendering all *practical extension* of pure reason impossible. I had therefore to remove *knowledge,* in order to make room for *belief.* For the dogmatism of metaphysic, that is, the presumption that it is possible to achieve anything in metaphysic without a previous criticism of pure reason, is the source of all that unbelief, which is always very dogmatical, and wars against all morality.

If, then, it may not be too difficult to leave a bequest to posterity, in the shape of a systematical metaphysic, carried out according to the critique of pure reason, such a bequest is not to be considered therefore as of little value, whether we regard the improvement which reason receives through the secure method of a science, in place of its groundless groping and uncritical vagaries, or whether we look to the better employment of the time of our enquiring youth, who, if brought up in the ordinary dogmatism, are early encouraged to indulge in easy speculations on things of which they know nothing, and of which they, as little as anybody else, will ever understand anything; neglecting the acquirement of sound knowledge, while bent on the discovery of new metaphysical thoughts and opinions. The greatest benefit however will be, that such work will enable us to put an end for ever to all objections to morality and religion, according to the Socratic method, namely, by the clearest proof of the ignorance of our opponents. Some kind of metaphysic has always existed, and will always exist, and with it a dialectic of pure reason, as being natural to it. It is therefore the first and most important task of philosophy to deprive metaphysic, once for all, of its pernicious influence, by closing up the sources of its errors.

In spite of these important changes in the whole field of science, and of the *losses* which speculative reason must suffer in its fancied possessions, all general human interests, and all the advantages which the world hitherto derived from the teachings of pure reason, remain just the same as before. The loss, if any, affects only the *monopoly of the schools,* and by no means the *interests* of *humanity.* I appeal to the staunchest dogmatist, whether the proof of the continued existence of our soul after death, derived from the simplicity of the substance, or that of the freedom of the will, as opposed to the general mechanism of nature, derived from the subtle, but inefficient, distinction between subjective and objective practical necessity, or that of the existence of God, derived from the concept of an *Ens realissimum* (the contingency of the changeable, and the necessity of a prime mover), have ever, after they had been started by the schools, penetrated the public mind, or exercised the slightest influence on its convictions? If this has not been, and in fact could not be so, on account of the unfitness of the ordinary understanding for such subtle speculations; and if, on the contrary, with regard to the first point, the hope of a *future life* has chiefly rested on that peculiar character of human nature, never to be satisfied by what is merely temporal (and insufficient, therefore, for the character of its whole destination); if with regard to the second, the clear consciousness of *freedom* was produced only by the clear exhibition of duties in opposition to all the claims of sensuous desires; and if, lastly, with regard to the third, the belief in a great and wise *Author of the world* has been supported entirely by the wonderful beauty, order, and providence, everywhere displayed in nature, then this possession remains not only undisturbed, but acquires even greater authority, because the schools have now been taught, not to claim for themselves any higher or fuller insight on a point which concerns general human interests, than what is equally within the reach of the great mass of men, and to confine themselves to the elaboration of these universally comprehensible, and, for moral purposes, quite sufficient proofs. The change therefore affects the arrogant pretensions of the schools only, which would fain be considered as the only judges and depositaries of such truth (as they are, no doubt, with regard to many other subjects), allowing to the public its use only, and trying to keep the key to themselves, *quod mecum nescit, solus vult scire videri*. At the same time full satisfaction is given to the more moderate claims of speculative philosophers. They still remain the exclusive depositaries [1] of a science which benefits the masses without their knowing it, namely, the critique of reason. That critique can never become popular, nor does it need to be so, because, if on the one side the public has no understanding for the fine-drawn arguments in support of useful truths, it is not troubled on the other by the equally subtle objections. It is different with the schools which, in the same way as every man who has once risen to the height of speculation, must know both the pro's and the con's and are bound, by means of a careful investigation of the rights of speculative reason, to prevent, once for all, the scandal which, sooner or later, is sure to be caused even to

[1] [M. reads "depositors."]

the masses, by the quarrels in which metaphysicians (and as such, theologians also) become involved, if ignorant of our critique, and by which their doctrine becomes in the end entirely perverted. Thus, and thus alone, can the very root be cut off of *materialism, fatalism, atheism, free-thinking, unbelief, fanaticism,* and *superstition,* which may become universally injurious, and finally of *idealism* and *sceptism* also, which are dangerous rather to the schools, and can scarcely ever penetrate into the public. If governments think proper ever to interfere with the affairs of the learned, it would be far more consistent with their wise regard for science as well as for *society,* to favour the freedom of such a criticism by which alone the labours of reason can be established on a firm footing, than to support the ridiculous despotism of the schools, which raise a loud clamour of public danger, whenever the cobwebs are swept away of which the public has never taken the slightest notice, and the loss of which it can therefore never perceive.

Our critique is not opposed to the *dogmatical procedure* of reason, as a science of pure knowledge (for this must always be dogmatical, that is, derive its proof from sure principles *a priori*), but to *dogmatism* only, that is, to the presumption that it is possible to make any progress with pure (philosophical) knowledge, consisting of concepts, and guided by principles, such as reason has long been in the habit of employing, without first enquiring in what way, and what right, it has come possessed of them. Dogmatism is therefore the dogmatical procedure of pure reason, *without a previous criticism of its own powers;* and our opposition to this is not intended to defend either that loquacious shallowness which arrogates to itself the good name of popularity, much less that scepticism which makes short work with the whole of metaphysic. On the contrary, our critique is meant to form a necessary preparation in support of a thoroughly scientific system of metaphysic, which must necessarily be carried out dogmatically and strictly systematically, so as to satisfy all the demands, not so much of the public at large, as of the schools, this being an indispensable condition, as it has undertaken to carry out its work entirely *a priori,* and thus to the complete satisfaction of speculative reason. . . . [M. 704-8] [1]

INTRODUCTION

I. Of the Difference between Pure and Empirical Knowledge [2]

That all our knowledge begins with experience there can be no doubt. For how should the faculty of knowledge be called into activity, if not by objects which affect our senses, and which either produce representations by themselves, or rouse the activity of our understanding to compare, to connect, or to separate them; and thus to convert the raw material of our sensuous impressions into a knowledge of objects, which we call experience? In respect of time, therefore, no knowledge within us is antecedent to experience, but all knowledge begins with it.

But although all our knowledge begins with experience, it does not follow that it arises from experience. For it is quite possible that even our empirical experience is a compound of that which we receive through

[1] [The Note on M. 705-6 appears below pp. 142-3.]

[2] [Cf. M. 715 ff. Selections from the *Introduction* have been made from both the 1st and 2nd Editions, as indicated.]

impressions, and of that which our own faculty of knowledge (incited only by sensuous impressions), supplies from itself, a supplement which we do not distinguish from that raw material, until long practice has roused our attention and rendered us capable of separating one from the other.

It is therefore a question which deserves at least closer investigation, and cannot be disposed of at first sight, whether there exists a knowledge independent of experience, and even of all impressions of the senses? Such *knowledge* is called *a priori,* and distinguished from *empirical* knowledge, which has its sources *a posteriori,* that is, in experience.

This term *a priori,* however, is not yet definite enough to indicate the full meaning of our question. For people are wont to say, even with regard to knowledge derived from experience, that we have it, or might have it, *a priori,* because we derive it from experience, not *immediately,* but from a general rule, which, however, has itself been derived from experience. Thus one would say of a person who undermines the foundations of his house, that he might have known *a priori* that it would tumble down, that is, that he need not wait for the experience of its really tumbling down. But still he could not know this entirely *a priori,* because he had first to learn from experience that bodies are heavy, and will fall when their supports are taken away.

We shall therefore, in what follows, understand by knowledge *a priori* knowledge which is *absolutely* independent of all experience, and not of this or that experience only. Opposed to this is empirical knowledge, or such as is possible *a posteriori* only, that is, by experience. Knowledge *a priori,* if mixed up with nothing empirical, is called *pure.* Thus the proposition, for example, that every change has its cause, is a proposition *a priori,* but not pure: because change is a concept which can only be derived from experience.

II. We are in Possession of Certain Cognitions a priori, *and even the Ordinary Understanding is never without them* [1]

All depends here on a criterion, by which we may safely distinguish between pure and empirical knowledge. Now experience teaches us, no doubt, that something is so or so, but not that it cannot be different. *First,* then, if we have a proposition, which is thought, together with its necessity, we have a judgment *a priori;* and if, besides, it is not derived from any proposition, except such as is itself again considered as necessary, we have an absolutely *a priori* judgment. *Secondly,* experience never imparts to its judgments true or strict, but only assumed or relative universality (by means of induction), so that we ought always to say, so far as we have observed hitherto, there is no exception to this or that rule. If, therefore, a judgment is thought with strict universality, so that no exception is admitted as possible, it is not derived from experience, but valid absolutely *a priori.* Empirical universality, therefore, is only an arbitrary extension of a validity which applies to most cases, to one that applies to all: as, for instance, in the proposition, all bodies are heavy. If, on the contrary, strict universality is essential to a judgment, this always points to a special source of knowledge, namely, a faculty of knowledge *a priori.* Necessity, therefore, and strict universality are safe criteria of knowledge *a priori,* and are inseparable one from the

[1] [Cf. M. 716 ff.]

other. As, however, in the use of these criteria, it is sometimes easier to show the contingency than the empirical limitation of judgments, and as it is sometimes more convincing to prove the unlimited universality which we attribute to a judgment than its necessity, it is advisable to use both criteria separately, each being by itself infallible.

That there really exist in our knowledge such necessary, and in the strictest sense universal, and therefore pure judgments *a priori*, is easy to show. If we want a scientific example, we have only to look to any of the propositions of mathematics; if we want one from the sphere of the ordinary understanding, such a proposition as that each change must have a cause, will answer the purpose; nay, in the latter case, even the concept of cause contains so clearly the concept of the necessity of its connection with an effect, and of the strict universality of the rule, that it would be destroyed altogether if we attempted to derive it, as Hume does, from the frequent concomitancy of that which happens with that which precedes, and from a habit arising thence (therefore from a purely subjective necessity), of connecting representations. It is possible even, without having recourse to such examples in proof of the reality of pure propositions *a priori* within our knowledge, to prove their indispensability for the possibility of experience itself, thus proving it *a priori*. For whence should experience take its certainty, if all the rules which it follows were always again and again empirical, and therefore contingent and hardly fit to serve as first principles? For the present, however, we may be satisfied for having shown the pure employment of the faculty of our knowledge as a matter of fact, with the criteria of it. . . .[M. 718]

III. Philosophy requires a Science to determine the Possibility, the Principles, and the Extent of all Cognitions a priori [1]

. . . [M. 1-2] Certain kinds of knowledge leave the field of all possible experience, and seem to enlarge the sphere of our judgments beyond the limits of experience by means of concepts to which experience can never supply any corresponding objects.

And it is in this very kind of knowledge which transcends the world of the senses, and where experience can neither guide nor correct us, that reason prosecutes its investigations, which by their importance we consider far more excellent and by their tendency far more elevated than anything the understanding can find in the sphere of phenomena. Nay, we risk rather anything, even at the peril of error, than that we should surrender such investigations, either on the ground of their uncertainty, or from any feeling of indifference or contempt. These inevitable problems of pure reason itself are, *God, Freedom,* and *Immortality.* The science which with all its apparatus is really intended for the solution of these problems, is called *Metaphysic.* Its procedure is at first *dogmatic,* i.e. unchecked by a previous examination of what reason can and cannot do, before it engages confidently in so arduous an undertaking.

Now it might seem natural that, after we have left the solid ground of experience, we should not at once proceed to erect an edifice with knowledge which we possess without knowing whence it came, and trust to

[1] [M. 2 ff.]

principles the origin of which is unknown, without having made sure of the safety of the foundations by means of careful examination. It would seem natural, I say, that philosophers should first of all have asked the question how the mere understanding could arrive at all this knowledge *a priori,* and what extent, what truth, and what value it could possess. If we take natural to mean what is just and reasonable, then indeed nothing could be more natural. But if we understand by natural what takes place ordinarily, then, on the contrary, nothing is more natural and more intelligible than that this examination should have been neglected for so long a time. For one part of this knowledge, namely, the mathematical, has always been in possession of perfect trustworthiness; and thus produces a favourable presumption with regard to other parts also, although these may be of a totally different nature. Besides, once beyond the precincts of experience, and we are certain that experience can never contradict us, while the charm of enlarging our knowledge is so great that nothing will stop our progress until we encounter a clear contradiction. This can be avoided if only we are cautious in our imaginations, which nevertheless remain what they are, imaginations only. How far we can advance independent of all experience in *a priori* knowledge is shown by the brilliant example of mathematics. It is true they deal with objects and knowledge so far only as they can be represented in intuition. But this is easily overlooked, because that intuition itself may be given *a priori,* and be difficult to distinguish from a pure concept. Thus inspirited by a splendid proof of the power of reason, the desire of enlarging our knowledge sees no limits. The light dove, piercing in her easy flight the air and perceiving its resistance, imagines that flight would be easier still in empty space. It was thus that Plato left the world of sense, as opposing so many hindrances to our understanding, and ventured beyond on the wings of his ideas into the empty space of pure understanding. He did not perceive that he was making no progress by these endeavours, because he had no resistance as a fulcrum on which to rest or to apply his powers, in order to cause the understanding to advance. It is indeed a very common fate of human reason first of all to finish its speculative edifice as soon as possible, and then only to enquire whether the foundation be sure. Then all sorts of excuses are made in order to assure us as to its solidity, or to decline altogether such a late and dangerous enquiry. The reason why during the time of building we feel free from all anxiety and suspicion and believe in the apparent solidity of our foundation, is this:—A great, perhaps the greatest portion of what our reason finds to do consists in the analysis of our concepts of objects. This gives us a great deal of knowledge which, though it consists in no more than in simplifications and explanation of what is comprehended in our concepts (though in a confused manner), is yet considered as equal, at least in form, to new knowledge. It only separates and arranges our concepts, it does not enlarge them in matter or contents. As by this process we gain a kind of real knowledge *a priori,* which progresses safely and usefully, it happens that our reason, without being aware of it, appropriates under that pretence propositions of a totally different character, adding to given concepts new and strange ones *a priori,* without knowing whence they come, nay without even thinking of such a question. I shall therefore at the very outset treat of the distinction between these two kinds of knowledge.

IV. Of the Distinction between Analytical and Synthetical Judgments [1]

In all judgments in which there is a relation between subject and predicate (I speak of affirmative judgments only, the application to negative ones being easy), that relation can be of two kinds. Either the predicate B belongs to the subject A as something contained (though covertly) in the concept A; or B lies outside the sphere of the concept A, though somehow connected with it. In the former case I call the judgment analytical, in the latter synthetical. Analytical judgments (affirmative) are therefore those in which the connection of the predicate with the subject is conceived through identity, while others in which that connection is conceived without identity, may be called synthetical. The former might be called illustrating, the latter expanding judgments, because in the former nothing is added by the predicate to the concept of the subject, but the concept is only divided into its constituent concepts which were always conceived as existing within it, though confusedly; while the latter add to the concept of the subject a predicate not conceived as existing within it, and not to be extracted from it by any process of mere analysis. If I say, for instance, All bodies are extended, this is an analytical judgment. I need not go beyond the concept connected with the name of body, in order to find that extension is connected with it. I have only to analyse that concept and become conscious of the manifold elements always contained in it, in order to find that predicate. This is therefore an analytical judgment. But if I say, All

[1] [Cf. M. 5 ff.]

bodies are heavy, the predicate is something quite different from what I think as the mere concept of body. The addition of such a predicate gives us a synthetical judgment.

It becomes clear from this,

1. That our knowledge is in no way extended by analytical judgments, but that all they effect is to put the concepts which we possess into better order and render them more intelligible.

2. That in synthetical judgments I must have besides the concept of the subject something else (x) on which the understanding relies in order to know that a predicate, not contained in the concept, nevertheless belongs to it.

In empirical judgments this causes no difficulty, because this x is here simply the complete experience of an object which I conceive by the concept A, that concept forming one part of my experience. For though I do not include the predicate of gravity in the general concept of body, that concept nevertheless indicates the complete experience through one of its parts, so that I may add other parts also of the same experience, all belonging to that concept. I may first, by an analytical process, realise the concept of body through the predicates of extension, impermeability, form, etc., all of which are contained in it. Afterwards I expand my knowledge, and looking back to the experience from which my concept of body was abstracted, I find gravity always connected with the before-mentioned predicates. Experience therefore is the x which lies beyond the concept A, and on which rests the possibility of a synthesis of the predicate of gravity B with the concept A.

In synthetical judgments *a priori*, however, that help

is entirely wanting. If I want to go beyond the concept A in order to find another concept B connected with it, where is there anything on which I may rest and through which a synthesis might become possible, considering that I cannot have the advantage of looking about in the field of experience? Take the proposition that all which happens has its cause. In the concept of something that happens I no doubt conceive of something existing preceded by time, and from this certain analytical judgments may be deduced. But the concept of cause is entirely outside that concept, and indicates something different from that which happens, and is by no means contained in that representation. How can I venture then to predicate of that which happens something totally different from it, and to represent the concept of cause, though not contained in it, as belonging to it, and belonging to it by necessity? What is here the unknown *x,* on which the understanding may rest in order to find beyond the concept A a foreign predicate B, which nevertheless is believed to be connected with it? It cannot be experience, because the proposition that all which happens has its cause represents this second predicate as added to the subject not only with greater generality than experience can ever supply, but also with a character of necessity, and therefore purely *a priori,* and based on concepts. All our speculative knowledge *a priori* aims at and rests on such synthetical, i.e. expanding propositions, for the analytical are no doubt very important and necessary, yet only in order to arrive at that clearness of concepts which is requisite for a safe and wide synthesis, serving as a really new addition to what we possess already. . . . [M. 8-12, 727]

V. In all Theoretical Sciences of Reason Synthetical Judgments a priori *are contained as Principles*[1]

1. *All mathematical judgments are synthetical.* This proposition, though incontestably certain, and very important to us for the future, seems to have hitherto escaped the observation of those who are engaged in the anatomy of human reason: nay, to be directly opposed to all their conjectures. For as it was found that all mathematical conclusions proceed according to the principle of contradiction (which is required by the nature of all apodictic certainty), it was supposed that the fundamental principles of mathematics also rested on the authority of the same principle of contradiction. This, however, was a mistake: for though a synthetical proposition may be understood according to the principle of contradiction, this can only be if another synthetical proposition is presupposed, from which the latter is deduced, but never by itself. First of all, we ought to observe, that mathematical propositions, properly so called, are always judgments *a priori,* and not empirical, because they carry along with them necessity, which can never be deduced from experience. If people should object to this, I am quite willing to confine my statement to pure mathematics, the very concept of which implies that it does not contain empirical, but only pure knowledge *a priori.*

At first sight one might suppose indeed that the proposition $7+5=12$ is merely analytical, following, according to the principle of contradiction, from the concept of a sum of 7 and 5. But, if we look more closely, we shall find that the concept of the sum of 7 and 5 contains nothing beyond the union of both sums

[1] [Cf. M. 720 ff.]

into one, whereby nothing is told us as to what this single number may be which combines both. We by no means arrive at a concept of Twelve, by thinking that union of Seven and Five; and we may analyse our concept of such a possible sum as long as we will, still we shall never discover in it the concept of Twelve. We must go beyond these concepts, and call in the assistance of the intuition corresponding to one of the two, for instance, our five fingers, or, as Segner does in his arithmetic, five points, and so by degrees add the units of the Five, given in intuition, to the concept of the Seven. For I first take the number 7, and taking the intuition of the fingers of my hand, in order to form with it the concept of the 5, I gradually add the units, which I before took together, to make up the number 5, by means of the image of my hand, to the number 7, and I thus see the number 12 arising before me. That 5 should be added to 7 was no doubt implied in my concept of a sum 7+5, but not that that sum should be equal to 12. An arithmetical proposition is, therefore, always synthetical, which is seen more easily still by taking larger numbers, where we clearly perceive that, turn and twist our conceptions as we may, we could never, by means of the mere analysis of our concepts and without the help of intuition, arrive at the sum that is wanted.

Nor is any proposition of pure geometry analytical. That the straight line between two points is the shortest, is a synthetical proposition. For my concept of *straight* contains nothing of magnitude (quantity), but a quality only. The concept of the *shortest* is, therefore, purely adventitious, and cannot be deduced from the concept of the straight line by any analysis whatsoever. The aid of intuition, therefore, must be called in, by which alone the synthesis is possible.

It is true that some few propositions, presupposed by

the geometrician, are really analytical, and depend on the principle of contradiction: but then they serve only, like identical propositions, to form the chain of the method, and not as principles. Such are the propositions, $a=a$, the whole is equal to itself, or $(a+b) > a$, that the whole is greater than its part. And even these, though they are valid according to mere concepts, are only admitted in mathematics, because they can be represented in intuition. What often makes us believe that the predicate of such apodictic judgments is contained in our concept, and the judgment therefore analytical, is merely the ambiguous character of the expression. We are told that we *ought* to join in thought a certain predicate to a given concept, and this necessity is inherent in the concepts themselves. But the question is not what we *ought* to join to the given concept, but what we *really think* in it, though confusedly only, and then it becomes clear that the predicate is no doubt inherent in those concepts by necessity, not, however, as thought in the concept itself, but by means of an intuition, which must be added to the concept.

2. *Natural science (physica) contains synthetical judgments* a priori *as principles.* I shall adduce, as examples, a few propositions only, such as, that in all changes of the material world the quantity of matter always remains unchanged: or that in all communication of motion, action and reaction must always equal each other. It is clear not only that both convey necessity, and that, therefore, their origin is *a priori,* but also that they are synthetical propositions. For in the concept of matter I do not conceive its permanency, but only its presence in the space which it fills. I therefore go beyond the concept of matter in order to join something to it *a priori,* which I did not before conceive *in it.* The proposition is, therefore, not analytical, but

synthetical, and yet *a priori,* and the same applies to the other propositions of the pure part of natural science.

3. *Metaphysic,* even if we look upon it as hitherto a tentative science only, which, however, is indispensable to us, owing to the very nature of human reason, is meant to *contain synthetical knowledge a priori.* Its object is not at all merely to analyse such concepts as we make to ourselves of things *a priori,* and thus to explain them analytically, but to expand our knowledge *a priori.* This we can only do by means of concepts which add something to a given concept that was not contained in it; nay, we even attempt, by means of synthetical judgments *a priori,* to go so far beyond a given concept that experience itself cannot follow us: as, for instance, in the proposition that the world must have a first beginning. Thus, according at least to its intentions, metaphysic consists merely of synthetical propositions *a priori.*

VI. The General Problem of Pure Reason

Much is gained if we are able to bring a number of investigations under the formula of one single problem. For we thus not only facilitate our own work by defining it accurately, but enable also everybody else who likes to examine it to form a judgment, whether we have really done justice to our purpose or not. Now the real problem of pure reason is contained in the question, *How are synthetical judgments* a priori *possible?*

That metaphysic has hitherto remained in so vacillating a state of ignorance and contradiction is entirely due to people not having thought sooner of this problem, or perhaps even of a distinction between *analytical* and *synthetical* judgments. The solution of this problem, or a sufficient proof that a possibility which is to be explained does in reality not exist at all, is the question of life or death to metaphysic. *David Hume,* who among all philosophers approached nearest to that problem, though he was far from conceiving it with sufficient definiteness and universality, confining his attention only to the synthetical proposition of the connection of an effect with its causes (*principium causalitatis*), arrived at the conclusion that such a proposition *a priori* is entirely impossible. According to his conclusions, everything which we call metaphysic would turn out to be a mere delusion of reason, fancying that it knows by itself what in reality is only borrowed from experience, and has assumed by mere habit the appearance of necessity. If he had grasped our problem in all its universality, he would never have thought of an assertion which destroys all pure philosophy, because he would have perceived that, according to his argument, no pure mathematical science was possible either, on account of its certainty containing synthetical propositions *a priori;* and from such an assertion his good sense would probably have saved him.

On the solution of our problem depends, at the same time, the possibility of the pure employment of reason, in establishing and carrying out all sciences which contain a theoretical knowledge *a priori* of objects, i.e. the answer to the questions

How is pure mathematical science possible?

How is pure natural science possible?

As these sciences really exist, it is quite proper to ask, *How* they are possible? for *that* they must be possible, is proved by their reality.[1]

But as to *metaphysic,* the bad progress which it has

[1] [Note M. 724]

hitherto made, and the impossibility of asserting of any of the metaphysical systems yet brought forward that it really exists, so far as its essential aim is concerned, must fill every one with doubts as to its possibility.

Yet, in a certain sense, this *kind of knowledge* also must be looked upon as given, and though not as a science, yet as a natural disposition (*metaphysica naturalis*) metaphysic is real. For human reason, without being moved merely by the conceit of omniscience, advances irresistibly, and urged on by its own need, to questions such as cannot be answered by any empirical employment of reason, or by principles thence derived, so that we may really say, that all men, as soon as their reason became ripe for speculation, have at all times possessed some kind of metaphysic, and will always continue to possess it. And now it will also have to answer the question,

How is metaphysic possible, as a natural disposition? that is, how does the nature of universal human reason give rise to questions which pure reason proposes to itself, and which it is urged on by its own need to answer as well as it can?

As, however, all attempts which have hitherto been made at answering these natural questions (for instance, whether the world has a beginning, or exists from all eternity) have always led to inevitable contradictions, we cannot rest satisfied with the mere natural disposition to metaphysic, that is, with the pure faculty of reason itself, from which some kind of metaphysic (whatever it may be) always arises; but it must be possible to arrive with it at some certainty as to our either knowing or not knowing its objects; that is, we must either decide that we can judge of the objects of these questions, or of the power or want of power of reason, in deciding anything upon them,—therefore that we can either enlarge our pure reason with certainty, or that we have to impose on it fixed and firm limits. This last question, which arises out of the former more general problem, would properly assume this form,

How is metaphysic possible, as a science?

The critique of reason leads, therefore, necessarily, to true science, while its dogmatical use, without criticism, lands us in groundless assertions, to which others, equally specious, can always be opposed, that is, in *scepticism.*

Nor need this science be very formidable by its great prolixity, for it has not to deal with the objects of reason, the variety of which is infinite, but with reason only, and with problems, suggested by reason and placed before it, not by the nature of things, which are different from it, but by its own nature; so that, if reason has only first completely understood its own power, with reference to objects given to it in experience, it will have no difficulty in determining completely and safely the extent and limits of its attempted application beyond the limits of all experience.

We may and must therefore regard all attempts which have hitherto been made at building up a metaphysic dogmatically, as *non-avenu.* For the mere analysis of the concepts that dwell in our reason *a priori,* which has been attempted in one or other of those metaphysical systems, is by no means the aim, but only a preparation for true metaphysic, namely, the answer to the question, how we can enlarge our knowledge *a priori* synthetically; nay, it is utterly useless for that purpose, because it only shows what is contained in those concepts, but not by what process *a priori* we arrive at them, in order thus to determine the validity of their employment with reference to all objects of knowledge in general. Nor does it require much self denial to give up these pretensions, considering that the undeniable and, in the dogmatic procedure, inevitable contradictions of reason with itself, have long deprived every system of metaphysic of all authority. More firmness will be required in order not to be deterred by difficulties from within and resistance from without, from trying to advance a science, indispensable to human reason (a science of which we may lop off every branch, but will never be able to destroy the root), by a treatment entirely opposed to all former treatments, which promises, at last, to ensure the successful and fruitful growth of metaphysical science.

TRANSCENDENTAL ÆSTHETIC [1]

[INTRODUCTION]

WHATEVER [2] the process and the means may be by which knowledge reaches its objects, there is one that reaches them directly, and forms the ultimate material of all thought, viz. intuition (Anschauung). This is possible only when the object is given, and the object can be given only (to human beings at least) through a certain affection of the mind (Gemüth).

This faculty (receptivity) of receiving representations (Vorstellungen), according to the manner in which we are affected by objects, is called sensibility (Sinnlichkeit).

Objects therefore are given to us through our sensibility. Sensibility alone supplies us with intuitions (Anschauungen). These intuitions become thought through the understanding (Verstand), and hence arise concep-

[1] [Selections have been made from both Editions. Cf. M. 15-39, 728-736. The order and numbering of the paragraphs have been changed in some cases, as indicated.]

[2] [Cf. M. 15 ff.]

tions (Begriffe). All thought therefore must, directly or indirectly, go back to intuitions (Anschauungen), i.e. to our sensibility, because in no other way can objects be given to us.

The effect produced by an object upon the faculty of representation (Vorstellungsfähigkeit), so far as we are affected by it, is called sensation (Empfindung). An intuition (Anschauung) of an object, by means of sensation, is called empirical. The undefined object of such an empirical intuition is called phenomenon (Erscheinung).

In a phenomenon I call that which corresponds to the sensation its *matter;* but that which causes the manifold matter of the phenomenon to be perceived as arranged in a certain order, I call its *form.*

Now it is clear that it cannot be sensation again through which sensations are arranged and placed in certain forms. The matter only of all phenomena is given us *a posteriori;* but their form must be ready for them in the mind (Gemüth) *a priori,* and must therefore be capable of being considered as separate from all sensations.

I call all representations in which there is nothing that belongs to sensation, *pure* (in a transcendental sense). The pure form therefore of all sensuous intuitions, that form in which the manifold elements of the phenomena are seen in a certain order, must be found in the mind *a priori.* And this pure form of sensibility may be called the pure intuition (Anschauung).

Thus, if we deduct from the representation (Vorstellung) of a body what belongs to the thinking of the understanding, viz. substance, force, divisibility, etc., and likewise what belongs to sensation, viz. impermeability, hardness, colour, etc., there still remains something of that empirical intuition (Anschauung), viz. extension and form. These belong to pure intuition, which *a priori,* and even without a real object of the senses or of sensation, exists in the mind as a mere form of sensibility.

The science of all the principles of sensibility *a priori* I call *Transcendental Æsthetic.*[1] There must be such a science, forming the first part of the Elements of Transcendentalism, as opposed to that which treats of the principles of pure thought, and which should be called *Transcendental Logic.*

In Transcendental Æsthetic therefore we shall first isolate sensibility, by separating everything which the understanding adds by means of its concepts, so that nothing remains but empirical intuition (Anschauung).

Secondly, we shall separate from this all that belongs to sensation (Empfindung), so that nothing remains but pure intuition (reine Anschauung) or the mere form of the phenomena, which is the only thing which sensibility *a priori* can supply. In the course of this investigation it will appear that there are, as principles of *a priori* knowledge, two pure forms of sensuous intuition (Anschauung), namely, *Space* and *Time.* We now proceed to consider these more in detail.

First Section. *Of Space* [2]

Metaphysical Exposition of the Concept of Space

By means of our external sense, a property of our mind (Gemüth), we represent to ourselves objects as external or outside ourselves, and all of these in space. It is within space that their form, size, and relative

[1] [Note M. 17]
[2] [Cf. M. 18 ff.]

position are fixed or can be fixed. The internal sense by means of which the mind perceives itself or its internal state, does not give an intuition (Anschauung) of the soul (Seele) itself, as an object, but it is nevertheless a fixed form under which alone an intuition of its internal state is possible, so that whatever belongs to its internal determinations (Bestimmungen) must be represented in relations of time. Time cannot be perceived (angeschaut) externally, as little as space can be perceived as something within us.

What then are space and time? Are they real beings? Or, if not that, are they determinations or relations of things, but such as would belong to them even if they were not perceived? Or lastly, are they determinations and relations which are inherent in the form of intuition only, and therefore in the subjective nature of our mind, without which such predicates as space and time would never be ascribed to anything?

In order to understand this more clearly, let us first consider space.

1. Space is not an empirical concept which has been derived from external experience. For in order that certain sensations should be referred to something outside myself, i.e. to something in a different part of space from that where I am; again, in order that I may be able to represent them (vorstellen) as side by side, that is, not only as different, but as in different places, the representation (Vorstellung) of space must already be there. Therefore the representation of space cannot be borrowed through experience from relations of external phenomena, but, on the contrary, this external experience becomes possible only by means of the representation of space.

2. Space is a necessary representation *a priori*, forming the very foundation of all external intuitions.

It is impossible to imagine that there should be no space, though one might very well imagine that there should be space without objects to fill it. Space is therefore regarded as a condition of the possibility of phenomena, not as a determination produced by them; it is a representation *a priori* which necessarily precedes all external phenomena. . . . [M. 19]

3.[1] Space is not a discursive or so-called general concept of the relations of things in general, but a pure intuition. For, first of all, we can imagine one space only and if we speak of many spaces, we mean parts only of one and the same space. Nor can these parts be considered as antecedent to the one and all-embracing space and, as it were, its component parts out of which an aggregate is formed, but they can be thought of as existing within it only. Space is essentially one; its multiplicity, and therefore the general concept of spaces in general, arises entirely from limitations. . . . [M. 20]

4.[1] Space is represented as an infinite quantity. Now a general concept of space, which is found in a foot as well as in an ell, could tell us nothing in respect to the quantity of the space. If there were not infinity in the progression of intuition, no concept of relations of space could ever contain a principle of infinity.

Transcendental Exposition of the Concept of Space [2]

. . . [M. 728] Geometry is a science which determines the properties of space synthetically, and yet *a priori*. What then must be the representation of space, to render such a knowledge of it possible? It must be originally intuitive; for it is impossible from a mere con-

[1] [Second Edition numbering of these paragraphs.]
[2] [Cf. M. 728 ff.]

cept to deduce propositions which go beyond that concept, as we do in geometry. That intuition, however, must be *a priori,* that is, it must exist within us before any perception of the object, and must therefore be pure, not empirical intuition. For all geometrical propositions are apodictic, that is, connected with the consciousness of their necessity, as for instance the proposition, that space has only three dimensions; and such propositions cannot be empirical judgments, nor conclusions from them.

How then can an external intuition dwell in the mind anterior to the objects themselves, and in which the concept of objects can be determined *a priori?* Evidently not otherwise than so far as it has its seat in the subject only, as the formal condition under which the subject is affected by the objects and thereby is receiving an *immediate representation,* that is, *intuition* of them; therefore as a form of the external *sense* in general.

It is therefore by our explanation only that the *possibility* of *geometry* as a synthetical science *a priori* becomes intelligible. Every other explanation, which fails to account for this possibility, can best be distinguished from our own by that criterion, although it may seem to have some similarity with it.

Conclusions from the Foregoing Concepts [1]

a. Space does not represent any quality of objects by themselves, or objects in their relation to one another; i.e. space does not represent any determination which is inherent in the objects themselves, and would remain, even if all subjective conditions of intuition were removed. For no determinations of objects, whether be-

[1] [Cf. M. 20 ff.]

longing to them absolutely or in relation to others, can enter into our intuition before the actual existence of the objects themselves, that is to say, they can never be intuitions *a priori*.

b. Space is nothing but the form of all phenomena of the external senses; it is the subjective condition of our sensibility, without which no external intuition is possible for us. If then we consider that the receptivity of the subject, its capacity of being affected by objects, must necessarily precede all intuition of objects, we shall understand how the form of all phenomena may be given before all real perceptions, may be, in fact, *a priori* in the soul, and may, as the pure intuition, by which all objects must be determined, contain, prior to all experience, principles regulating their relations.

It is therefore from the human standpoint only that we can speak of space, extended objects, etc. If we drop the subjective condition under which alone we can gain external intuition, that is, so far as we ourselves may be affected by objects, the representation of space means nothing. For this predicate is applied to objects only in so far as they appear to us, and are objects of our senses. The constant form of this receptivity, which we call sensibility, is a necessary condition of all relations in which objects, as without us, can be perceived; and, when abstraction is made of these objects, what remains is that pure intuition which we call space. As the peculiar conditions of our sensibility cannot be looked upon as conditions of the possibility of the objects themselves, but only of their appearance as phenomena to us, we may say indeed that space comprehends all things which may appear to us externally, but not all things by themselves, whether perceived by us or not, or by any subject whatsoever. We cannot judge whether the intuitions of other thinking beings are subject to the same conditions which determine our intuition, and which for us are generally binding. If we add the limitation of a judgment to a subjective concept, the judgment gains absolute validity. The proposition 'all things are beside each other in space,' is valid only under the limitation that things are taken as objects of our sensuous intuition (Anschauung). If I add that limitation to the concept and say 'all things, as external phenomena, are beside each other in space,' the rule obtains universal and unlimited validity. Our discussions teach therefore the reality, i.e. the objective validity, of space with regard to all that can come to us externally as an object, but likewise the *ideality* of space with regard to things, when they are considered in themselves by our reason, and independent of the nature of our senses. We maintain the empirical reality of space, so far as every possible external experience is concerned, but at the same time its transcendental ideality; that is to say, we maintain that space is nothing, if we leave out of consideration the condition of a possible experience, and accept it as something on which things by themselves are in any way dependent. . . . [M. 22-4, 730]

SECOND SECTION. *Of Time* [1]

Metaphysical Exposition of the Concept of Time

1. Time is not an empirical concept deduced from any experience, for neither coexistence nor succession would enter into our perception, if the representation of time were not given *a priori*. Only when this representation *a priori* is given, can we imagine that certain things happen at the same time (simultaneously) or at different times (successively).

[1] [Cf. M. 24 ff.]

2. Time is a necessary representation on which all intuitions depend. We cannot take away time from phenomena in general, though we can well take away phenomena out of time. Time therefore is given *a priori*. In time alone is reality of phenomena possible. All phenomena may vanish, but time itself (as the general condition of their possibility) cannot be done away with.

[3].[1] Time is not a discursive, or what is called a general concept, but a pure form of sensuous intuition. Different times are parts only of one and the same time. Representation, which can be produced by a single object only, is called an intuition. The proposition that different times cannot exist at the same time cannot be deduced from any general concept. Such a proposition is synthetical, and cannot be deduced from concepts only. It is contained immediately in the intuition and representation of time.

[4]. To say that time is infinite means no more than that every definite quantity of time is possible only by limitations of one time which forms the foundation of all times. The original representation of time must therefore be given as unlimited. But when the parts themselves and every quantity of an object can be represented as determined by limitation only, the whole representation cannot be given by concepts (for in that case the partial representations come first), but it must be founded on immediate intuition.

Transcendental Exposition of the Concept of Time

On[2] this *a priori* necessity depends also the possibility of apodictic principles of the relations of time, or

[1] [Paragraph 3 appears below as the first paragraph of the *Transcendental Exposition.*]
[2] [Cf. M. 25]

of axioms of time in general. Time has one dimension only; different times are not simultaneous, but successive, while different spaces are never successive, but simultaneous. Such principles cannot be derived from experience, because experience could not impart to them absolute universality nor apodictic certainty. We should only be able to say that common experience teaches us that it is so, but not that it must be so. These principles are valid as rules under which alone experience is possible; they teach us before experience, not by means of experience.

. . . [M. 731] The [1] concept of change, and with it the concept of motion (as change of place), is possible only through and in the representation of time; if this representation were not intuitive (internal) *a priori,* no concept, whatever it be, could make us understand the possibility of a change, that is, of a connection of contradictorily opposed predicates (for instance, the being and not-being of one and the same thing in one and the same place) in one and the same object. It is only in time that both contradictorily opposed determinations can be met with in the same object, that is, one after the other. Our concept of time, therefore, exhibits the possibility of as many synthetical cognitions *a priori* as are found in the general doctrine of motion, which is very rich in them.

Conclusions from the Foregoing Concepts [2]

a. Time is not something existing by itself, or inherent in things as an objective determination of them, something therefore that might remain when abstraction is made of all subjective conditions of intuition. For

[1] [Cf. M. 731]
[2] [Cf. M. 26 ff.]

in the former case it would be something real, without being a real object. In the latter it could not, as a determination or order inherent in things themselves, be antecedent to things as their condition, and be known and perceived by means of synthetical propositions *a priori*. All this is perfectly possible if time is nothing but a subjective condition under which alone intuitions take place within us. For in that case this form of internal intuition can be represented prior to the objects themselves, that is, *a priori*.

b. Time is nothing but the form of the internal sense, that is, of our intuition of ourselves, and of our internal state. Time cannot be a determination peculiar to external phenomena. It refers neither to their shape, nor their position, etc., it only determines the relation of representations in our internal state. And exactly because this internal intuition supplies no shape, we try to make good this deficiency by means of analogies, and represent to ourselves the succession of time by a line progressing to infinity, in which the manifold constitutes a series of one dimension only; and we conclude from the properties of this line as to all the properties of time, with one exception, i.e. that the parts of the former are simultaneous, those of the latter successive. From this it becomes clear also, that the representation of time is itself an intuition, because all its relations can be expressed by means of an external intuition.

c. Time is the formal condition, *a priori*, of all phenomena whatsoever. Space, as the pure form of all external intuition, is a condition, *a priori*, of external phenomena only. But, as all representations, whether they have for their objects external things or not, belong by themselves, as determinations of the mind, to our inner state, and as this inner state falls under the formal conditions of internal intuition, and therefore of time,

time is a condition, *a priori,* of all phenomena whatsoever, and is so directly as a condition of internal phenomena (of our mind) and thereby indirectly of external phenomena also. If I am able to say, *a priori,* that all external phenomena are in space, and are determined, *a priori,* according to the relations of space, I can, according to the principle of the internal sense, make the general assertion that all phenomena, that is, all objects of the senses, are in time, and stand necessarily in relations of time.

If we drop our manner of looking at ourselves internally, and of comprehending by means of that intuition all external intuitions also within our power of representation, and thus take objects as they may be by themselves, then time is nothing. Time has objective validity with reference to phenomena only, because these are themselves things which we accept as objects of our senses; but time is no longer objective, if we remove the sensuous character of our intuitions, that is to say, that mode of representation which is peculiar to ourselves, and speak of things in general. Time is therefore simply a subjective condition of our (human) intuition (which is always sensuous, that is so far as we are affected by objects), but by itself, apart from the subject, nothing. Nevertheless, with respect to all phenomena, that is, all things which can come within our experience, time is necessarily objective. We cannot say that all things are in time, because, if we speak of things in general, nothing is said about the manner of intuition, which is the real condition under which time enters into our representation of things. If therefore this condition is added to the concept, and if we say that all things as phenomena (as objects of sensuous intuition) are in time, then such a proposition has its full objective validity and *a priori* universality.

What we insist on therefore is the empirical reality of time, that is, its objective validity, with reference to all objects which can ever come before our senses. And as our intuition must at all times be sensuous, no object can ever fall under our experience that does not come under the conditions of time. What we deny is, that time has any claim on absolute reality, so that, without taking into account the form of our sensuous condition, it should by itself be a condition or quality inherent in things; for such qualities which belong to things by themselves can never be given to us through the senses. This is what constitutes the transcendental ideality of time, so that, if we take no account of the subjective conditions of our sensuous intuitions, time is nothing, and cannot be added to the objects by themselves (without their relation to our intuition) whether as subsisting or inherent. . . . [M. 29-39]

[General Conclusion]

. . . [M. 732-4]. In[1] natural theology, where we think of an object which not only can never be an object of intuition to us, but which even to itself can never be an object of *sensuous* intuition, great care is taken to remove all conditions of space and time from its intuition (for all its knowledge must be intuitive, and not *thought,* which always involves limitation). But how are we justified in doing this, when we have first made space and time forms of things by themselves, such as would remain as conditions of the existence of things *a priori,* even if the things themselves had been removed? If conditions of all existence, they would also be conditions of the existence of God. If we do not wish to change space and time into objective forms of all things,

[1] [Cf. M. 734 ff.]

nothing remains but to accept them as subjective forms of our external as well as internal intuition, which is called sensuous, for the very reason that it is not originally spontaneous, that is such, that it could itself give us the existence of the objects of intuition (such an intuition, so far as we can understand, can belong to the First Being only), but dependent on the existence of objects, and therefore possible only, if the faculty of representation in the subject is affected by them.

It is not necessary, moreover, that we should limit this intuition in space and time to the sensibility of man; it is quite possible that all finite thinking beings must necessarily agree with us on this point (though we cannot decide this). On account of this universal character, however, it does not cease to be sensibility, for it always is, and remains derivative (*intuitus derivativus*), not original (*intuitus originarius*), and therefore not intellectual intuition. For the reason mentioned before, the latter intuition seems only to belong to the First Being, and never to one which is dependent, both in its existence and its intuition (which intuition determines its existence with reference to given objects). This latter remark, however, must only be taken as an illustration of our æsthetic theory, and not as a proof. . . . [M. 735-6]

TRANSCENDENTAL LOGIC

INTRODUCTION [1]

I. Of Logic in General

Our knowledge springs from two fundamental sources of our soul; the first receives representations (recep-

[1] [Cf. M. 40 ff.]

tivity of impressions), the second is the power of knowing an object by these representations (spontaneity of concepts). By the first an object is *given* us, by the second the object is *thought,* in relation to that representation which is a mere determination of the soul. Intuition therefore and concepts constitute the elements of all our knowledge, so that neither concepts without an intuition corresponding to them, nor intuition without concepts can yield any real knowledge.

Both are either pure or empirical. They are empirical when sensation, presupposing the actual presence of the object, is contained in it. They are pure when no sensation is mixed up with the representation. The latter may be called the material of sensuous knowledge. Pure intuition therefore contains the form only by which something is seen, and pure conception the form only by which an object is thought. Pure intuitions and pure concepts only are possible *a priori,* empirical intuitions and empirical concepts *a posteriori.*

We call *sensibility* the *receptivity* of our soul, or its power of receiving representations whenever it is in any wise affected, while the *understanding,* on the contrary, is with us the power of producing representations, or the *spontaneity* of knowledge. We are so constituted that our intuition must always be sensuous, and consist of the mode in which we are affected by objects. What enables us to think the objects of our sensuous intuition is the understanding. Neither of these qualities or faculties is preferable to the other. Without sensibility objects would not be given to us, without understanding they would not be thought by us. *Thoughts without contents are empty, intuitions without concepts are blind.* Therefore it is equally necessary to make our concepts sensuous, i.e. to add to them their object in intuition, as to make our intuitions intelligible, i.e. to bring them under concepts. These two powers or faculties cannot exchange their functions. The understanding cannot see, the senses cannot think. By their union only can knowledge be produced. But this is no reason for confounding the share which belongs to each in the production of knowledge. On the contrary, they should always be carefully separated and distinguished, and we have therefore divided the science of the rules of sensibility in general, i.e. æsthetic, from the science of the rules of the understanding in general, i.e. logic. . . . [M. 42]

General logic is either pure or applied. In the former no account is taken of any empirical conditions under which our understanding acts, i.e. of the influence of the senses, the play of imagination, the laws of memory, the force of habit, the inclinations, and therefore the sources of prejudice also, nor of anything which supplies or seems to supply particular kinds of knowledge; for all this applies to the understanding under certain circumstances of its application only, and requires experience as a condition of knowledge. General but pure logic has to deal with principles *a priori* only, and is a *canon of the understanding and of reason,* though with reference to its formal application only, irrespective of any contents, whether empirical or transcendental. . . . [M. 43-4]

II. Of Transcendental Logic

General logic, as we saw, takes no account of the contents of knowledge, i.e. of any relation between it and its objects, and considers the logical form only in the relation of cognitions to each other, that is, it treats of the form of thought in general. But as we found, when treating of Transcendental Æsthetic, that there are pure as well as empirical intuitions, it is possible that a similar distinction might appear between pure and empirical thinking. In this case we should have a logic in which the contents of knowledge are not entirely ignored, for such a logic which should contain the rules of pure thought only, would exclude only all knowledge of a merely empirical character. It would also treat of the origin of our knowledge of objects, so far as that origin cannot be attributed to the objects, while general logic is not at all concerned with the origin of our knowledge, but only considers representations (whether existing originally *a priori* in ourselves or empirically given to us), according to the laws followed by the understanding, when thinking and treating them in their relation to each other. It is confined therefore to the form imparted by the understanding to the representations, whatever may be their origin. . . . [M. 45]

On the supposition therefore that there may be concepts, having an *a priori* reference to objects, not as pure or sensuous intuitions, but as acts of pure thought, being concepts in fact, but neither of empirical nor æsthetic origin, we form by anticipation an idea of a science of that knowledge which belongs to the pure understanding and reason, and by which we may think objects entirely *a priori*. Such a science, which has to determine the origin, the extent, and the objective validity of such knowledge, might be called *Transcendental Logic,* having to deal with the laws of the understanding and reason in so far only as they refer *a priori* to objects, and not, as general logic, in so far as they refer promiscuously to the empirical as well as to the pure knowledge of reason.

IV.[1] *Of the Division of Transcendental Logic into Transcendental Analytic and Dialectic*

In transcendental logic we isolate the understanding, as before in transcendental æsthetic the sensibility, and fix our attention on that part of thought only which has its origin entirely in the understanding. The application of this pure knowledge has for its condition that objects are given in intuition, to which it can be applied, for without intuition all our knowledge would be without objects, and it would therefore remain entirely empty. That part of transcendental logic therefore which teaches the elements of the pure knowledge of the understanding, and the principles without which no object can be thought, is transcendental Analytic, and at the same time a logic of truth. No knowledge can contradict it without losing at the same time all contents, that is, all relation to any object, and therefore all truth. But as it is very tempting to use this pure knowledge of the understanding and its principles by themselves, and even beyond the limits of all experience, which alone can supply the material or the objects to which those pure concepts of the understanding can be applied, the understanding runs the risk of making, through mere sophisms, a material use of the purely formal principles of the pure understanding, and thus of judging indiscriminately of objects which are not given to us, nay, perhaps can never be given. As it is properly meant to be a mere canon for criticising the empirical use of the understanding, it is a real abuse if it is allowed as an organum of its general and unlimited application, by our venturing, with the pure understanding

[1] [For Section III, see M. 46-9]

alone, to judge synthetically of objects in general, or to affirm and decide anything about them. In this case the employment of the pure understanding would become dialectical.

The second part of transcendental logic must therefore form a critique of that dialectical semblance, and is called transcendental Dialectic, not as an art of producing dogmatically such semblance (an art but too popular with many metaphysical jugglers), but as a critique of the understanding and reason with regard to their hyper-physical employment, in order thus to lay bare the false semblance of its groundless pretensions, and to reduce its claims to discovery and expansion, which was to be achieved by means of transcendental principles only, to a mere critique, serving as a protection of the pure understanding against all sophistical illusions.

TRANSCENDENTAL ANALYTIC

. . . [M. 52-3]

Book I. ANALYTIC OF CONCEPTS [1]

BY ANALYTIC of concepts I do not understand their analysis, or the ordinary process in philosophical disquisitions of dissecting any given concepts according to their contents, and thus rendering them more distinct; but a hitherto seldom attempted dissection of the faculty of the understanding itself, with the sole object of discovering the possibility of concepts *a priori,* by looking for them nowhere but in the understanding itself as their birthplace, and analysing the pure use of the understanding. This is the proper task of a transcendental philosophy, all the rest is mere logical treat-

[1] [Cf. M. 54 ff.]

ment of concepts. We shall therefore follow up the pure concepts to their first germs and beginnings in the human understanding, in which they lie prepared, till at last, on the occasion of experience, they become developed, and are represented by the same understanding in their full purity, freed from all inherent empirical conditions.

CHAPTER I

METHOD OF DISCOVERING ALL PURE CONCEPTS OF THE UNDERSTANDING [1]

. . . [M. 55-6]

I. Of the Logical Use of the Understanding in General

. . . [M. 56-7] As all acts of the understanding can be reduced to judgments, the understanding may be defined as *the faculty of judging.* For we saw before that the understanding is the faculty of thinking, and thinking is knowledge by means of concepts, while concepts, as predicates of possible judgments, refer to some representation of an object yet undetermined. Thus the concept of body means, for instance, metal, which can be known by that concept. It is only a concept, because it comprehends other representations, by means of which it can be referred to objects. It is therefore the predicate of a possible judgment, such as, that every metal is a body. Thus the functions of the understanding can be discovered in their completeness, if it is possible to represent the functions of unity in *judgments.* That this is possible will be seen in the following section.

[1] [Cf. M. 55 ff.]

II. Of the Logical Function of the Understanding in Judgments

If we leave out of consideration the contents of any judgment and fix our attention on the mere form of the understanding, we find that the function of thought in a judgment can be brought under four heads, each of them with three subdivisions. They may be represented in the following table:—

TABLE OF JUDGMENTS

I

Quantity of Judgments

Universal.
Particular.
Singular.

II

Quality

Affirmative.
Negative.
Infinite.

III

Relation

Categorical.
Hypothetical.
Disjunctive.

IV

Modality

Problematical.
Assertory.
Apodictic.

. . . [M. 58-63]

III. Of the Pure Concepts of the Understanding, or of the Categories

General logic, as we have often said, takes no account of the contents of our knowledge, but expects that representations will come from elsewhere in order to be turned into concepts by an analytical process. Transcendental logic, on the contrary, has before it the manifold contents of sensibility *a priori,* supplied by transcendental æsthetic as the material for the concepts of the pure understanding, without which those concepts would be without any contents, therefore entirely empty. It is true that space and time contain what is manifold in the pure intuition *a priori,* but they belong also to the conditions of the receptivity of our mind under which alone it can receive representations of objects, and which therefore must affect the concepts of them also. The spontaneity of our thought requires that what is manifold in the pure intuition should first be in a certain way examined, received, and connected, in order to produce a knowledge of it. This act I call *synthesis.*

In its most general sense, I understand by synthesis the act of arranging different representations together, and of comprehending what is manifold in them under one form of knowledge. Such a synthesis is pure, if the manifold is not given empirically, but *a priori* (as in time and space). Before we can proceed to an analysis of our representations, these must first be given, and, as far as their contents are concerned, no concepts can arise analytically. Knowledge is first produced by the synthesis of what is manifold (whether given empirically or *a priori*). That knowledge may at first be crude and confused and in need of analysis, but it is synthesis which really collects the elements of knowledge, and unites them to a certain extent. It is therefore the first thing which we have to consider, if we want to form an opinion on the first origin of our knowledge.

We shall see hereafter that synthesis in general is the

mere result of what I call the faculty of imagination, a blind but indispensable function of the soul, without which we should have no knowledge whatsoever, but of the existence of which we are scarcely conscious. But to reduce this synthesis to concepts is a function that belongs to the understanding, and by which the understanding supplies us for the first time with knowledge properly so called. . . . [M. 65]

By means of analysis different representations are brought under one concept, a task treated of in general logic; but how to bring, not the representations, but the pure synthesis of representations, under concepts, that is what transcendental logic means to teach. The first that must be given us *a priori* for the sake of knowledge of all objects, is the manifold in pure intuition. The second is, the synthesis of the manifold by means of imagination. But this does not yet produce true knowledge. The concepts which impart unity to this pure synthesis and consist entirely in the representation of this necessary synthethical unity, add the third contribution towards the knowledge of an object, and rest on the understanding.

The same function which imparts unity to various representations in one judgment imparts unity likewise to the mere synthesis of various representations in one intuition, which in a general way may be called the pure concept of the understanding. The same understanding, and by the same operations by which in concepts it achieves through analytical unity the logical form of a judgment, introduces also, through the synthetical unity of the manifold in intuition, a transcendental element into its representations. They are therefore called pure concepts of the understanding, and they refer *a priori* to objects, which would be quite impossible in general logic.

In this manner there arise exactly so many pure concepts of the understanding which refer *a priori* to objects of intuition in general, as there were in our table logical functions in all possible judgments, because those functions completely exhaust the understanding, and comprehend every one of its faculties. Borrowing a term of Aristotle, we shall call these concepts *categories,* our intention being originally the same as his, though widely diverging from it in its practical application.

TABLE OF CATEGORIES

I

Of Quantity

Unity.
Plurality.
Totality.

II

Of Quality

Reality.
Negation.
Limitation.

III

Of Relation

Of Inherence and Subsistence (*substantia et accidens*).
Of Causality and Dependence (cause and effect).
Of Community (reciprocity between the active and the passive).

IV

Of Modality

Possibility. Impossibility.
Existence. Non-existence.
Necessity. Contingency.

This then is a list of all original pure concepts of synthesis, which belong to the understanding *a priori,* and for which alone it is called pure understanding; for it is by them alone that it can understand something in the manifold of intuition, that is, think an object in it. The classification is systematical, and founded on a common principle, namely, the faculty of judging (which is the same as the faculty of thinking). . . . [M. 67-9, 737-41]

CHAPTER II

OF THE DEDUCTION OF THE PURE CONCEPTS OF THE UNDERSTANDING [1]

SECTION I. *Of the Principles of a Transcendental Deduction in General* [2]

JURISTS, when speaking of rights and claims, distinguish in every lawsuit the question of right *(quid juris)* from the question of fact *(quid facti)*, and in demanding proof of both they call the former, which is to show the right or, it may be, the claim, the *deduction*. We, not being jurists, make use of a number of empirical concepts, without opposition from anybody, and consider ourselves justified, without any deduction, in attaching to them a sense or imaginary meaning, because we can always appeal to experience to prove their objective reality. There exist however illegitimate concepts also,

[1] [The argument of this chapter, as it appears in the First and Second Editions, is so involved, repetitious, and, in places, at least seemingly contradictory, that each student of the chapter must, of necessity, resort to a certain amount of interpretation. The following passages, taken from both Editions, have been selected and arranged so as to bring out what the Editor of this volume conceives to be the main stages of the argument.]

[2] [Cf. M. 70 ff.]

such as, for instance, chance, or fate, which through an almost general indulgence are allowed to be current, but are yet from time to time challenged by the question *quid juris.* In that case we are greatly embarrassed in looking for their deduction, there being no clear legal title, whether from experience or from reason, on which their claim to employment could be clearly established.

Among the many concepts, however, which enter into the complicated code of human knowledge, there are some which are destined for pure use *a priori,* independent of all experience, and such a claim requires at all times a deduction,[1] because proofs from experience would not be sufficient to establish the legitimacy of such a use, though it is necessary to know how such concepts can refer to objects which they do not find in experience. I call the explanation of the manner how such concepts can *a priori* refer to objects their transcendental deduction, and distinguish it from the empirical deduction which shows the manner how a concept may be gained by experience and by reflection on experience; this does not touch the legitimacy, but only the fact whence the possession of the concept arose.

We have already become acquainted with two totally distinct classes of concepts, which nevertheless agree in this, that they both refer *a priori* to objects, namely, the concepts of space and time as forms of sensibility, and the categories as concepts of the understanding. It would be labour lost to attempt an empirical deduction of them, because their distinguishing characteristic is that they refer to objects without having borrowed anything from experience for their representation. If

[1] That is, a transcendental deduction.

therefore a deduction of them is necessary, it can only be transcendental.

It is possible, however, with regard to these concepts, as with regard to all knowledge, to try to discover in experience, if not the principle of their possibility, yet the contingent causes of their production. And here we see that the impressions of the senses give the first impulse to the whole faculty of knowledge with respect to them, and thus produce experience which consists of two very heterogeneous elements, namely, matter for knowledge, derived from the senses, and a certain form according to which it is arranged, derived from the internal source of pure intuition and pure thought, first brought into action by the former, and then producing concepts. Such an investigation of the first efforts of our faculty of knowledge, beginning with single perceptions and rising to general concepts, is no doubt very useful, and we have to thank the famous Locke for having been the first to open the way to it. A deduction of the pure concepts *a priori,* however, is quite impossible in that way. It lies in a different direction, because, with reference to their future use, which is to be entirely independent of experience, a very different certificate of birth will be required from that of mere descent from experience. We may call this attempted physiological [1] derivation (which cannot properly be called deduction, because it refers to a *quaestio facti*), the explanation of the possession of pure knowledge. It is clear therefore that of these pure concepts *a priori* a transcendental deduction only is possible, and that to attempt an empirical deduction of them is mere waste of time, which no one would think of except those who have never understood the very peculiar nature of that kind of knowledge. . . . [M. 72-6]

[1] [In modern terms, psychological.]

Transition to a Transcendental Deduction of the Categories[1]

. . . [M. 76-7] To know a thing as an object is possible only under two conditions. First, there must be intuition by which the object is given us, though as a phenomenon only; secondly, there must be a concept by which an object is thought as corresponding to that intuition. From what we have said before it is clear that the first condition, namely, that under which alone objects can be seen, exists, so far as the form of intuition is concerned, in the soul *a priori*. All phenomena therefore must conform to that formal condition of sensibility, because it is through it alone that they appear, that is, that they are given and empirically seen.

Now the question arises whether there are not also antecedent concepts *a priori,* forming conditions under which alone something can be, if not seen, yet thought as an object in general; for in that case all empirical knowledge of objects would necessarily conform to such concepts, it being impossible that anything should become an object of experience without them. All experience contains, besides the intuition of the senses by which something is given, a concept also of the object, which is given in intuition as a phenomenon. Such concepts of objects in general therefore must form conditions *a priori* of all knowledge produced by experience, and the objective validity of the categories, as being such concepts *a priori,* rests on this very fact that by them alone, so far as the form of thought is concerned, experience becomes possible. If by them only it is possible to think any object of experience, it follows

[1] [Cf. M. 76 ff.]

that they refer by necessity and *a priori* to all objects of experience.

There is therefore a principle for the transcendental deduction of all concepts *a priori* which must guide the whole of our investigation, namely, that all must be recognized as conditions *a priori* of the possibility of experience, whether of intuition, which is found in it, or of thought. Concepts which supply the objective ground of the possibility of experience are for that very reason necessary. An analysis of the experience in which they are found would not be a deduction, but a mere illustration, because they would there have an accidental character only. Nay, without their original relation to all possible experience in which objects of knowledge occur, their relation to any single object would be quite incomprehensible. . . . [M. 78-9]

If therefore we wish to know how pure concepts of the understanding are possible, we must try to find out what are the conditions *a priori* on which the possibility of experience depends, nay, on which it is founded, apart from all that is empirical in phenomena. A concept expressing this formal and objective condition of experience with sufficient generality might properly be called a pure concept of the understanding. . . . [M. 80] Such concepts, then, which comprehend the pure thinking *a priori* involved in every experience, are discovered in the categories, and it is really a sufficient deduction of them and a justification of their objective validity, if we succeed in proving that by them alone an object can be thought. . . . [M. 80-1]

Locke,[1] for want of this reflection, and because he met with pure concepts of the understanding in experience, derived them also from experience, and yet acted so

[1] [Cf. M. 742-3]

inconsistently that he attempted to use them for knowledge which far exceeds all limits of experience. David Hume saw that, in order to be able to do this, these concepts ought to have their origin *a priori;* but as he could not explain how it was possible that the understanding should be constrained to think concepts, which by themselves are not united in the understanding, as necessarily united in the object, and never thought that possibly the understanding might itself, through these concepts, be the author of that experience in which its objects are found, he was driven by necessity to derive them from experience (namely, from a subjective necessity, produced by frequent association in experience, which at last is wrongly supposed to be *objective,* that is, from habit). He acted, however, very consistently, by declaring it to be impossible to go with these concepts, and with the principles arising from them, beyond the limits of experience. This empirical deduction, which was adopted by both philosophers, cannot be reconciled with the reality of our scientific knowledge *a priori,* namely, pure *mathematics* and *general natural science,* and is therefore refuted by facts. The former of these two celebrated men opened a wide door to *fantastic extravagance,* because reason, if it has once established such pretensions, can no longer be checked by vague praises of moderation; the other, thinking that he had once discovered so general an illusion of our faculty of knowledge, which had formerly been accepted as reason, gave himself over entirely to *scepticism.* We now intend to make the experiment whether it is not possible to conduct reason safely between these two rocks, to assign to her definite limits, and yet to keep open for her the proper field for all her activities? . . . [M. 743]

SECTION II. *Transcendental Deduction of the Pure Concepts of the Understanding*

[I.] *Of the Possibility of Connecting* (conjunctio) *in General*[1]

The manifold of representations may be given in an intuition which is purely sensuous, that is, nothing but receptivity, and the form of that intuition may lie *a priori* in our faculty of representation, without being anything but the manner in which a subject is affected. But the connection (*conjunctio*) of anything manifold can never enter into us through the senses, and cannot be contained, therefore, already in the pure form of sensuous intuition, for it is a spontaneous act of the power of representation; and as, in order to distinguish this from sensibility, we must call it understanding, we see that all connecting, whether we are conscious of it or not, and whether we connect the manifold of intuition or several concepts together, and again, whether that intuition be sensuous or not sensuous, is an act of the understanding. This act we shall call by the general name of *synthesis,* in order to show that we cannot represent to ourselves anything as connected in the object, without having previously connected it ourselves, and that of all representations *connection* is the only one which cannot be given through the objects, but must be carried out by the subject itself, because it is an act of its spontaneity. It can be easily perceived that this act must be originally one and the same for every kind of connection, and that its dissolution, that is, the *analysis,* which seems to be its opposite, does always presuppose it. For where the understanding has not previously

[1] [Cf. M. 744-5]

connected, there is nothing for it to disconnect, because, as connected, it could only be given by the understanding to the faculty of representation. . . . [M. 745]

If [1] every single representation stood by itself, as if isolated and separated from the others, nothing like what we call knowledge could ever arise, because knowledge forms a whole of representations connected and compared with each other. If therefore I ascribe to the senses a synopsis, because in their intuition they contain something manifold, there corresponds to it always a synthesis, and receptivity can make knowledge possible only when joined with spontaneity. This spontaneity, now, appears as a threefold synthesis which must necessarily take place in every kind of knowledge, namely, first, that of the *apprehension* of representations as modifications of the soul in intuition, secondly, of the *reproduction* of them in the imagination, and, thirdly, that of their *recognition* in concepts. This leads us to three subjective sources of knowledge which render possible the understanding, and through it all experience as an empirical product of the understanding. It is [therefore] necessary for us to consider the subjective sources which form the foundation *a priori* for the possibility of experience, not according to their empirical, but according to their transcendental character. . . . [M. 81-2]

[II. *Connection involves, subjectively, a Threefold Synthesis.*]

1. *Of the Synthesis of Apprehension in Intuition* [2]

Whatever the origin of our representations may be, whether they be due to the influence of external things

[1] [Cf. M. 81. The position of one sentence has been changed.]
[2] [Cf. M. 82-3]

or to internal causes, whether they have arisen *a priori* or empirically as phenomena, as modifications of the mind they must always belong to the internal sense, and all our knowledge must therefore finally be subject to the formal condition of that internal sense, namely, time, in which they are all arranged, joined, and brought into certain relations to each other. This is a general remark which must never be forgotten in all that follows.

Every representation contains something manifold, which could not be represented as such, unless the mind distinguished the time in the succession of one impression after another; for as contained in one moment, each representation can never be anything but absolute unity. In order to change this manifold into a unity of intuition (as, for instance, in the representation of space), it is necessary first to run through the manifold and then to hold it together. It is this act which I call the synthesis of apprehension, because it refers directly to intuition which no doubt offers something manifold, but which, without a synthesis, can never make it such, as it is contained in *one* representation.

This synthesis of apprehension must itself be carried out *a priori* also, that is, with reference to representations which are not empirical. For without it we should never be able to have the representations either of space or time *a priori,* because these cannot be produced except by a synthesis of the manifold which the senses offer in their original receptivity. It follows therefore that we have a pure synthesis of apprehension.

2. *Of the Synthesis of Reproduction in Imagination* [1]

. . . [M. 83-4] Now, when I draw a line in thought, or if I think the time from one noon to another, or if I

[1] [Cf. M. 83-5]

only represent to myself a certain number, it is clear that I must first necessarily apprehend one of these manifold representations after another. If I were to lose from my thoughts what precedes, whether the first parts of a line or the antecedent portions of time, or the numerical unities representing one after the other, and if, while I proceed to what follows, I were unable to reproduce what came before, there would never be a complete representation, and none of the before-mentioned thoughts, not even the first and purest representations of space and time, could ever arise within [me.] [1]

The synthesis of apprehension is therefore inseparably connected with the synthesis of reproduction, and as the former constitutes the transcendental ground of the possibility of all knowledge in general (not only of empirical, but also of pure *a priori* knowledge), it follows that a reproductive synthesis of imagination belongs to the transcendental acts of the soul. We may therefore call this faculty the transcendental faculty of imagination.

3. *Of the Synthesis of Recognition in Concepts* [2]

Without our being conscious that what we are thinking now is the same as what we thought a moment before, all reproduction in the series of representations would be vain. Each representation would, in its present state, be a new one, and in no wise belonging to the act by which it was to be produced by degrees, and the manifold in it would never form a whole, because deprived of that unity which consciousness alone can impart to it. If in counting I forget that the unities which now present themselves to my mind have been

[1] [M. read "us"]
[2] [Cf. M. 85-6]

added gradually one to the other, I should not know the production of the quantity by the successive addition of one to one, nor should I know consequently the number, produced by the counting, this number being a concept consisting entirely in the consciousness of that unity of synthesis.

[*III and IV. The Synthesis of Recognition depends upon Empirical Self-Consciousness, which, in turn, presupposes the Transcendental Unity of Apperception.*]

[III.] The [1] very word of concept (Begriff) could have suggested this remark, for it is the *one* consciousness which unites the manifold that has been perceived successively, and afterwards reproduced into one representation. This consciousness may often be very faint, and we may connect it with the effect only, and not with the act itself, i.e. with the production of a representation. But in spite of this, that consciousness, though deficient in pointed clearness, must always be there, and without it, concepts, and with them, knowledge of objects are perfectly impossible. . . . [M. 86-8]

[IV. But] the [2] consciousness of oneself, according to the determinations of our state, is, with all our internal perceptions, empirical only, and always transient. There can be no fixed or permanent self in that stream of internal phenomena. It is generally called the *internal sense,* or the empirical apperception. What is necessarily to be represented as numerically identical with itself, cannot be thought as such by means of empirical data only. It must be a condition which precedes all experience, and in fact renders it possible, for thus only could such a transcendental supposition acquire validity.

[1] [Cf. M. 86]
[2] [Cf. M. 88]

No knowledge can take place in us, no conjunction or unity of one kind of knowledge with another, without that unity of consciousness which precedes all data of intuition, and without reference to which no representation of objects is possible. This pure, original, and unchangeable consciousness I shall call *transcendental apperception*. . . . [M. 89-90]

It [1] must be *possible* that the *I think* should accompany all my representations: for otherwise something would be represented within me that could not be thought, in other words, the representation would either be impossible or nothing, at least so far as I am concerned. That representation which can be given before all thought, is called *intuition,* and all the manifold of intuition has therefore a necessary relation to the *I think* in the same subject in which that manifold of intuition is found. That representation, however (that *I think*), is an act of *spontaneity,* that is, it cannot be considered as belonging to sensibility. I call it *pure apperception,* in order to distinguish it from empirical apperception, or *original apperception* also, because it is that self-consciousness which by producing the representation, *I think* (which must accompany all others, and is one and the same in every act of consciousness), cannot itself be accompanied by any other. I also call the unity of it the transcendental unity of self-consciousness, in order to indicate that it contains the possibility of knowledge *a priori.*

For the manifold representations given in any intuition would not all be *my* representations, if they did not all belong to one self-consciousness. What I mean is that, as my representations (even though I am not conscious of them as such), they must be in accordance with that condition, under which alone they can stand to-

[1] [Cf. M. 745-6]

gether in one common self-consciousness, because otherwise they would not all belong to me.[1] . . . [M. 746].

[V. Empirical Self-consciousness is Possible, and the Transcendental Unity of Apperception is Thinkable, only in and through Consciousness of Other-than-Self.]

The [2] unbroken identity of apperception of the manifold that is given in intuition contains a synthesis of representations, and is possible only through the consciousness of that synthesis. The empirical consciousness, which accompanies various representations, is itself various and disunited, and without reference to the

[1] [The following note, from the 1st Edition (M. 96), summarizes the relation of the transcendental unity of apperception to empirical self-consciousness.] . . . All representations have a necessary relation to some possible empirical consciousness, for if they did not possess that relation, and if it were entirely impossible to become conscious of them, this would be the same as if they did not exist. All empirical consciousness has a necessary relation to a transcendental consciousness, which precedes all single experiences, namely, the consciousness of my own self as the original apperception. It is absolutely necessary therefore that in my knowledge all consciousness should belong to one consciousness of my own self. Here we have a synthetical unity of the manifold (consciousness) which can be known *a priori,* and which may thus supply a foundation for synthetical propositions *a priori* concerning pure thinking in the same way as space and time supply a foundation for synthetical propositions which concern the form of mere intuition.

The synthetical proposition that the different kinds of empirical consciousness must be connected in one self-consciousness, is the very first and synthetical foundation of all our thinking. It should be remembered that the mere representation of the Ego in reference to all other representations (the collective unity of which would be impossible without it) constitutes our transcendental consciousness. It does not matter whether that representation is clear (empirical consciousness) or confused, not even whether it is real; but the possibility of the logical form of all knowledge rests necessarily on the relation to this apperception *as a faculty.*

[2] [Cf. M. 746-8]

identity of the subject. Such a relation takes place, not by my simply accompanying every relation with consciousness, but by my *adding* one to the other and being conscious of that act of adding, that is, of that synthesis. Only because I am able to connect the manifold of given representations in *one consciousness,* is it possible for me to represent to myself the *identity* of the *consciousness* in these *representations,* that is, only under the supposition of some synthetical unity of apperception does the analytical unity of apperception become possible.[1]

The thought that the representations given in intuition belong all of them to me, is therefore the same as that I connect them in one self-consciousness, or am able at least to do so; and though this is not yet the *consciousness* of the *synthesis* of representations, it nevertheless presupposes the possibility of this synthesis. In other words, it is only because I am able to comprehend the manifold of representations in one consciousness, that I call them altogether my representations, for otherwise, I should have as manifold and various a self as I have representations of which I am conscious. The synthetical unity of the manifold of intuitions as given *a priori* is therefore the ground also of the identity of that apperception itself which precedes *a priori* all definite thought. Connection, however, does never lie in the objects, and cannot be borrowed from them by perception, and thus be taken into the understanding, but it is always an act of the understanding, which itself is nothing but a faculty of connecting *a priori,* and of bringing the manifold of given representations under the unity of apperception, which is, in fact, the highest principle of all human knowledge.

It is true, no doubt, that this principle of the neces-

[1] [Note M. 747]

sary unity of apperception is itself identical, and therefore an analytical proposition; but it shows, nevertheless, the necessity of a synthesis of the manifold which is given in intuition, without which synthesis it would be impossible to think the unbroken identity of self-consciousness. For through the *Ego,* as a simple representation, nothing manifold is given; in the intuition, which is different from that, it can be given only, and then, by *connection,* be thought in one consciousness. An understanding in which, by its self-consciousness, all the manifold would be given at the same time, would possess *intuition;* our understanding can do nothing but think, and must seek for its intuition in the senses. I am conscious, therefore, of the identical self with respect to the manifold of the representations, which are given to me in an intuition, because I call them, altogether, my representations, as constituting *one.* This means, that I am conscious of a necessary synthesis of them *a priori,* which is called the original synthetical unity of apperception under which all representations given to me must stand, but have to be brought there, first, by means of a synthesis.

[VI. *Consciousness of Other-than-Self is a Consciousness of a Connected Manifold, i.e. of Objects.*]

[1.] *The Principle of the Synthetical Unity of Apperception is the Highest Principle of all Employment of the Understanding*[1]

The highest principle of the possibility of all intuition, in relation to sensibility, was, according to the transcendental Æsthetic, that all the manifold in it

[1] [Cf. M. 748-50]

should be subject to the formal conditions of space and time. The highest principle of the same possibility in relation to the understanding is, that all the manifold in intuition must be subject to the conditions of the original synthetical unity of apperception.[1]

All the manifold representations of intuition, so far as they are *given* us, are subject to the former, so far as they must admit of being connected in one consciousness, to the latter; and without that nothing can be thought or known by them, because the given representations would not share the act of apperception (I think) in common, and could not be comprehended in one self-consciousness.

The *understanding* in its most general sense is the faculty of *cognitions.* These consist in a definite relation of given representations to an object; and an *object* is that in the concept of which the manifold of a given intuition is *connected.* All such connection of representations requires of course the unity of the consciousness in their synthesis: consequently, the unity of consciousness is that which alone constitutes the relation of representations to an object, that is, their objective validity, and consequently their becoming cognitions, so that the very possibility of the understanding depends on it.

The first pure cognition of the understanding, therefore, on which all the rest of its employment is founded, and which at the same time is entirely independent of all conditions of sensuous intuition, is this very principle of the original synthetical unity of apperception. Space, the mere form of external sensuous intuition, is not yet cognition: it only supplies the manifold of intuition *a priori* for a possible cognition. In order to

[1] [Note M. 748]

know anything in space, for instance, a line, I must *draw* it, and produce synthetically a certain connection of the manifold that is given, so that the unity of that act is at the same time the unity of the consciousness (in the concept of a line), and (so that) an object (a determinate space) is then only known for the first time. The synthetical unity of consciousness is, therefore, an objective condition of all knowledge; a condition, not necessary for myself only, in order to know an object, but one to which each intuition must be subject, in order to become an *object* for me, because the manifold could not become connected in one consciousness in any other way, and without such a synthesis.

No doubt, that proposition, as I said before, is itself analytical, though it makes synthetical unity a condition of all thought, for it really says no more than that all my representations in any given intuition must be subject to the condition under which alone I can ascribe them, as my representations, to the identical self, and therefore comprehend them, as synthetically connected, in one apperception through the general expression, *I think*.

And yet this need not be a principle for every possible understanding, but only for that which gives nothing manifold through its pure apperception in the representation, *I am*. An understanding which through its self-consciousness could give the manifold of intuition, and by whose representation the objects of that representation should at the same time exist, would not require a special act of the synthesis of the manifold for the unity of its consciousness, while the human understanding, which possesses the power of thought only, but not of intuition, requires such an act. To the human understanding that first principle is so indispensable that it really cannot form the least concept of any other possible understanding, whether it be intuitive by itself, or possessed of a sensuous intuition, different from that in space and time.

[2.] *What is the Objective Unity of Self-consciousness?*[1]

The transcendental *unity* of apperception connects all the manifold given in an intuition into a concept of an object. It is therefore called *objective,* and must be distinguished from the *subjective unity* of consciousness, which is a form of the *internal sense,* by which the manifold of intuition is empirically given, to be thus connected. Whether I can become *empirically* conscious of the manifold, as either simultaneous or successive, depends on circumstances, or empirical conditions. The empirical unity of consciousness, therefore, through the association of representations, is itself phenomenal and wholly contingent, while the pure form of intuition in time, merely as general intuition containing the manifold that is given, is subject to the original unity of the consciousness, through the necessary relation only of the manifold of intuition to the one, *I think,*—that is, through the pure synthesis of the understanding, which forms the *a priori* ground of the empirical synthesis. That unity alone is, therefore, valid objectively; the empirical unity of apperception, which we do not consider here, and which is only derived from the former, under given conditions *in concreto,* has subjective validity only. One man connects the representation of a word with one thing, another with another, and the unity of consciousness, with regard to what is empirical, is not necessary nor universally valid with reference to that which is given.

[1] [Cf. M. 750-1]

[3.] *The Logical Form of all Judgments consists in the Objective Unity of Apperception of the Concepts contained therein* [1]

I could never feel satisfied with the definition of a judgment in general, given by our logicians, who say that it is the representation of a relation between two concepts. Without disputing with them in this place as to the defect of that explanation, that it may possibly apply to categorical, but not to hypothetical and disjunctive judgments (the latter containing, not a relation of concepts, but of judgments themselves),—though many tedious consequences have arisen from this mistake of logicians,—I must at least make this observation, that we are not told in what that *relation* consists.[2]

But, if I examine more closely the relation of given cognitions in every judgment, and distinguish it, as belonging to the understanding, from the relation according to the rules of reproductive imagination (which has subjective validity only), I find that a judgment is nothing but the mode of bringing given cognitions into the *objective* unity of apperception. This is what is intended by the copula *is,* which is meant to distinguish the objective unity of given representations from the subjective. It (the copula *is*) indicates their relation to the original apperception, and their necessary *unity,* even though the judgment itself be empirical, and therefore contingent; as, for instance, bodies are heavy. By this I do not mean to say that these representations belong *necessarily* to each other, in the empirical intuition, but that they belong to each other by means of the *necessary unity* of apperception in the synthesis of in-

[1] [Cf. M. 751-2]
[2] [Note M. 751]

tuitions, that is, according to the principles of the objective determination of all representations, so far as any cognition is to arise from them, these principles being all derived from the principle of the transcendental unity of apperception. Thus, and thus alone, does the relation become a *judgment,* that is, a relation that is valid objectively, and can thus be kept sufficiently distinct from the relation of the same representations, if it has subjective validity only, for instance, according to the laws of association. In the latter case, I could only say, that if I carry a body I feel the pressure of its weight, but not, that it, the body, is heavy, which is meant to say that these two representations are connected together in the object, whatever the state of the subject may be, and not only associated or conjoined in the perception, however often it may be repeated.

[VII. *Consciousness of Objects involves the Use of the Categories.*]

All Sensuous Intuitions are subject to the Categories as to Conditions under which alone their Manifold Contents can come together in one Consciousness [1]

The manifold which is given us in a sensuous intuition is necessarily subject to the original synthetical unity of apperception, because by it alone the unity of intuition becomes possible. That act of the understanding, further, by which the manifold of given representations (whether intuitions or concepts) is brought under one apperception in general, is the logical function of a judgment. The manifold, therefore, so far as it is given in an empirical intuition, is *determined* with regard to one of the logical functions of judgment, by which, indeed, it is brought to consciousness in general.

[1] [Cf. M. 752-3]

The *categories,* however, are nothing but these functions of judgment, so far as the manifold of a given intuition is determined with respect to them. Therefore the manifold in any given intuition is naturally subject to the categories.

Note [1]

The manifold, contained in an intuition which I call my own, is represented through the synthesis of the understanding, as belonging to the necessary unity of self-consciousness, and this takes place through the category.[2]

This category indicates, therefore, that the empirical consciousness of the manifold, given in any intuition, is subject to a pure self-consciousness *a priori,* in the same manner as the empirical intuition is subject to a pure sensuous intuition which likewise takes place *a priori.*

In the above proposition a beginning is made of a *deduction* of the pure concepts of the understanding. In this deduction, as the categories arise in the understanding only, *independent of all sensibility,* I ought not yet to take any account of the manner in which the manifold is given for an empirical intuition, but attend exclusively to the unity which, by means of the category, enters into the intuition through the understanding. In what follows we shall show, from the manner in which the empirical intuition is given in sensibility, that its unity is no other than that which is prescribed by the category to the manifold of any given intuition. Thus only, that is, by showing their validity *a priori* with respect to all

[1] [Cf. M. 753-4]
[2] [Note M. 753]

objects of our senses, the purpose of our deduction will be fully attained.

There is one thing, however, of which, in the above demonstration, I could not make abstraction: namely, that the manifold for an intuition must be given antecedently to the synthesis of the understanding, and independently of it;—how, remains uncertain. For if I were to imagine an understanding, itself intuitive (for instance, a divine understanding, which should not represent to itself given objects, but produce them at once by his representation), the categories would have no meaning with respect to such cognition. They are merely rules for an understanding whose whole power consists in thinking, that is, in the act of bringing the synthesis of the manifold, which is given to it in intuition from elsewhere, to the unity of apperception; an understanding which therefore knows nothing by itself, but connects only and arranges the material for cognition, that is, the intuition which must be given to it by the object. This peculiarity of our understanding of producing unity of apperception *a priori* by means of the categories only, and again by such and so many, cannot be further explained, any more than why we have these and no other functions of judgment, and why time and space are the only forms of a possible intuition for us.

There[1] is but one experience in which all perceptions are represented as in permanent and regular connection, as there is but one space and one time in which all forms of phenomena and all relations of being or not being take place. If we speak of different experiences, we only mean different perceptions so far as they belong to one and the same general experience. It is the per-

[1] [Cf. M. 91 ff.]

manent and synthetical unity of perceptions that constitutes the form of experience, and experience is nothing but the synthetical unity of phenomena according to concepts.

Unity of synthesis, according to empirical concepts, would be purely accidental, nay, unless these were founded on a transcendental ground of unity, a whole crowd of phenomena might rush into our soul, without ever forming real experience. All relation between our knowledge and its objects would be lost at the same time, because that knowledge would no longer be held together by general and necessary laws; it would therefore become thoughtless intuition, never knowledge, and would be to us the same as nothing.

The conditions *a priori* of any possible experience in general are at the same time conditions of the possibility of any objects of our experience. Now I maintain that the categories of which we are speaking are nothing but the conditions of thought which make experience possible, as much as space and time contain the conditions of that intuition which forms experience. These categories therefore are also fundamental concepts by which we think objects in general for the phenomena, and have therefore *a priori* objective validity. This is exactly what we wish to prove.

The possibility, nay the necessity of these categories rests on the relation between our whole sensibility, and therefore all possible phenomena, and that original apperception in which everything must be necessarily subject to the conditions of the permanent unity of self-consciousness, that is, must submit to the general functions of that synthesis which we call synthesis according to concepts, by which alone our apperception can prove its permanent and necessary identity *a priori.* Thus the concept of cause is nothing but a synthesis of that which follows in temporal succession, with other phenomena, but a synthesis according to concepts: and without such a unity which rests on a rule *a priori,* and subjects all phenomena to itself, no permanent and general, and therefore necessary unity of consciousness would be formed in the manifold of our perceptions. Such perceptions would then belong to no experience at all, they would be without an object, a blind play of representations,—less even than a dream. . . .[1]

. . . [M. 94-103] We[2] have before given various definitions of the understanding, by calling it the spontaneity of knowledge (as opposed to the receptivity of the senses), or the faculty of thinking, or the faculty of concepts or of judgments; all of these explanations, if more closely examined, coming to the same. We may now characterise it as *the faculty of rules.* This characteristic is more significant, and approaches nearer to the essence of the understanding. The senses give us forms (of intuition), the understanding rules, being always busy to examine phenomena, in order to discover in them some kind of rule. Rules, so far as they are objective (therefore necessarily inherent in our knowledge of an object), are called laws. Although experience teaches us many laws, yet these are only particular determinations of higher laws, the highest of them, to which all others are subject, springing *a priori* from the understanding; not being derived from experience, but, on the contrary, imparting to the phenomena their regularity, and thus making experience possible. The understanding therefore is not only a power of making rules by a comparison of phenomena, it is itself the law-

[1] [The next two pages of the 1st Edition appear below pp. 94-5]

[2] [Cf. M. 103 ff.]

giver of nature, and without the understanding nature, that is, a synthetical unity of the manifold of phenomena, according to rules, would be nowhere to be found, because phenomena, as such, cannot exist without us, but exist in our sensibility only. This sensibility, as an object of our knowledge in any experience, with everything it may contain, is possible only in the unity of apperception, which unity of apperception is transcendental ground of the necessary order of all phenomena in an experience. The same unity of apperception with reference to the manifold of representations (so as to determine it out of one) [1] forms what we call the rule, and the faculty of these rules I call the understanding. As possible experience therefore, all phenomena depend in the same way *a priori* on the understanding, and receive their formal possibility from it as, when looked upon as mere intuitions, they depend on sensibility, and become possible through it, so far as their form is concerned.

However exaggerated therefore and absurd it may sound, that the understanding is itself the source of the laws of nature, and of its formal unity, such a statement is nevertheless correct and in accordance with experience. It is quite true, no doubt, that empirical laws, as such, cannot derive their origin from the pure understanding, as little as the infinite manifoldness of phenomena could be sufficiently comprehended through the pure form of sensuous intuition. But all empirical laws are only particular determinations of the pure laws of the understanding, under which and according to which the former become possible, and phenomena assume a regular form, quite as much as all phenomena, in spite of the variety of their empirical form, must

[1] That is, out of one, or out of the unity of apperception.

always submit to the conditions of the pure form of sensibility.

The pure understanding is therefore in the categories the law of the synthetical unity of all phenomena, and thus makes experience, so far as its form is concerned, for the first time possible. This, and no more than this, we were called upon to prove in the transcendental deduction of the categories, namely, to make the relation of the understanding to our sensibility, and through it to all objects of experience, that is the objective validity of the pure concepts *a priori* of the understanding, conceivable, and thus to establish their origin and their truth. . . . [M. 105-6]

[VIII. *General Nature of the Deduction*]

. . . [M. 756-64] Categories [1] are concepts which *a priori* prescribe laws to all phenomena, and therefore to nature as the sum total of all phenomena *(natura materialiter spectata)*. The question therefore arises, as these laws are not derived from nature, nor conform to it as their model (in which case they would be empirical only), how we can understand that nature should conform to them, that is, how they can determine *a priori* the connection of the manifold in nature, without taking that connection from nature. The solution of that riddle is this.

It is no more surprising that the laws of phenomena in nature must agree with the understanding and its form *a priori*, that is, with its power of *connecting* the manifold in general, than that the phenomena themselves must agree with the form of sensuous intuition *a priori*. For laws exist as little in phenomena themselves, but relatively only, with respect to the subject to which, so

[1] [Cf. M. 764 ff.]

far as it has understanding, the phenomena belong, as phenomena exist by themselves, but relatively only, with respect to the same being so far as it has senses. Things by themselves would necessarily possess their conformity to the law, independent also of any understanding by which they are known. But phenomena are only representations of things, unknown as to what they may be by themselves. As mere representations they are subject to no law of connection, except that which is prescribed by the connecting faculty. Now that which connects the manifold of sensuous intuition is the faculty of imagination, which receives from the understanding the unity of its intellectual synthesis, and from sensibility the manifoldness of apprehension. Thus, as all possible perceptions depend on the synthesis of apprehension, and that synthesis itself, that empirical synthesis, depends on the transcendental, and, therefore, on the categories, it follows that all possible perceptions, everything in fact that can come to the empirical consciousness, that is, all phenomena of nature, must, so far as their connection is concerned, be subject to the categories. On these categories, therefore, nature (considered as nature in general) depends, as on the original ground of its necessary conformity to law (as *natura formaliter spectata*). Beyond the laws, on which *nature is general,* as a lawful order of phenomena in space and time depends, the pure faculty of the understanding is incapable of prescribing *a priori,* by means of mere categories, laws to phenomena. Special laws, therefore, as they refer to phenomena which are empirically determined, cannot be completely derived from the categories, although they are all subject to them. Experience must be superadded in order to know such special laws: while those other *a priori* laws inform us only with regard to experience in general, and what can be known as an object of it. . . . [M. 766-8]

All[1] attempts therefore at deriving those pure concepts of the understanding from experience, and ascribing to them a purely empirical origin, are perfectly vain and useless. I shall not dwell here on the fact that a concept of cause, for instance, contains an element of necessity, which no experience can ever supply, because experience, though it teaches us that after one phenomenon something else follows habitually, can never teach us that it follows necessarily, nor that we could *a priori*, and without any limitation, derive from it, as a condition, any conclusion as to what must follow. And thus I ask with reference to that empirical rule of association, which must always be admitted if we say that everything in the succession of events is so entirely subject to rules that nothing ever happens without something preceding it on which it always follows,— What does it rest on, if it is a law of nature, nay, how is that very association possible? You call the ground for the possibility of the association of the manifold, so far as it is contained in the objects themselves, the *affinity* of the manifold. I ask, therefore, how do you make that permanent affinity by which phenomena stand, nay, must stand, under permanent laws, conceivable to yourselves?

According to my principles it is easily conceivable. All possible phenomena belong, as representations, to the whole of our possible self-consciousness. From this, as a transcendental representation, numerical identity is inseparable and *a priori* certain, because nothing can become knowledge except by means of that original apperception. As this identity must necessarily enter

[1] [Cf. M. 92-4]

into the synthesis of the whole of the manifold of phenomena, if that synthesis is to become empirical knowledge, it follows that the phenomena are subject to conditions *a priori* to which their synthesis (in apprehension) must always conform. The representation of a general condition according to which something manifold *can* be arranged (with uniformity) is called *a rule,* if it *must* be so arranged, *a law*. All phenomena therefore stand in a permanent connection according to necessary laws, and thus possess that transcendental affinity of which the empirical is a mere consequence.

It sounds no doubt very strange and absurd that nature should have to conform to our subjective ground of apperception, nay, be dependent on it, with respect to her laws. But if we consider that what we call nature is nothing but a whole of phenomena, not a thing by itself, but a number of representations in our soul, we shall no longer be surprised that we only see her through the fundamental faculty of all our knowledge, namely, the transcendental apperception, and in that unity without which it could not be called the object (or the whole) of all possible experience, that is, nature. We shall thus also understand why we can recognise this unity *a priori,* and therefore as necessary, which would be perfectly impossible if it were given by itself and independent of the first sources of our own thinking. In that case I could not tell whence we should take the synthetical propositions of such general unity of nature. They would have to be taken from the objects of nature themselves, and as this could be done empirically only, we could derive from it none but an accidental unity, which is very different from that necessary connection which we mean when speaking of nature.

[IX. *The Only Valid Employment of the Categories.*]

The Category admits of no other Employment for the Cognition of Things, but its Application to Objects of Experience [1]

We have seen that to think an object is not the same as to know an object. In order to know an object, we must have the concept by which any object is thought (the category), and likewise the intuition by which it is given. If no corresponding intuition could be given to a concept, it would still be a thought, so far as its form is concerned: but it would be without an object, and no knowledge of anything would be possible by it, because, so far as I know, there would be nothing, and there could be nothing, to which my thought could be referred. Now the only possible intuition for us is sensuous (see Æsthetic); the thought of any object, therefore, by means of a pure concept of the understanding, can with us become knowledge only, if it is referred to objects of the senses. Sensuous intuition is either pure (space and time), or empirical, i.e. if it is an intuition of that which is represented in space and time, through sensation as immediately real. By means of pure intuition we can gain knowledge *a priori* of things as phenomena (in mathematics), but only so far as their form in concerned; but whether there are things which must be perceived, according to that form, remains unsettled. Mathematical concepts, by themselves, therefore, are not yet knowledge, except under the supposition that there are things which admit of being represented by us, according to the form of that pure sensuous intuition only. Consequently, as things in *space* and *time*

[1] [Cf. M. 754-6]

are only given as perceptions (as representations accompanied by sensations), that is, through empirical representations, the pure concepts of the understanding, even if applied to intuitions *a priori*, as in mathematics, give us knowledge in so far only as these pure intuitions, and therefore through them the concepts of the understanding also, can be applied to empirical intuitions. Consequently the categories, by means of intuition, do not give us any knowledge of things, except under the supposition of their possible application to empirical *intuition;* they serve, in short, for the possibility of empirical *knowledge* only, which is called *experience.* From this it follows that the categories admit of no other employment for the cognition of things, except so far only as these are taken as objects of possible experience.[1]

The foregoing proposition is of the greatest importance, for it determines the limits of the employment of the pure concepts of the understanding with reference to objects, in the same manner as the transcendental Æsthetic determined the limits of the employment of the pure form of our sensuous intuition. Space and time are conditions of the possibility of how objects can be given to us, so far only as objects of

[1] [The following note, appearing on M. 766, is inserted here as throwing light on the preceding paragraph.] Lest anybody should be unnecessarily frightened by the dangerous consequences of this proposition, I shall only remark that the categories are not limited for the purpose of *thought* by the conditions of our sensuous intuition, but have really an unlimited field. It is only the *knowledge* of that which we think, the determining of an object, that requires intuition, and even in the absence of intuition, the thought of the object may still have its true and useful consequences, so far as the subjective *use of reason* is concerned. That use of reason, however, as it is not always directed to the determination of the object, that is, to knowledge, but also to the determination of the subject, and its volition, cannot be treated of in this place.

the senses, therefore of experience, are concerned. Beyond these limits they represent nothing, for they belong only to the senses, and have no reality beyond them. Pure concepts of the understanding are free from this limitation, and extend to objects of intuition in general, whether that intuition be like our own or not, if only it is sensuous and not intellectual. This further extension, however, of concepts beyond our sensuous intuition, is of no avail to us; for they are in that case empty concepts of objects, and the concepts do not even enable us to say, whether such objects be possible or not. They are mere forms of thought, without objective reality: because we have no intuition at hand to which the synthetical unity of apperception, which is contained in the concepts alone, could be applied, so that they might determine an object. Nothing can give them sense and meaning, except our sensuous and empirical intuition.

If, therefore, we assume an object of a non-sensuous intuition as given, we may, no doubt, determine it through all the predicates, which follow from the supposition that *nothing belonging to sensuous intuition belongs to it,* that, therefore, it is not extended, or not in space, that its duration is not time, that no change (succession of determinations in time) is to be met in it, etc. But we can hardly call this knowledge, if we only indicate how the intuition of an object *is not,* without being able to say what is contained in it, for, in that case, I have not represented the possibility of an object, corresponding to my pure concept of the understanding, because I could give no intuition corresponding to it, but could only say that our intuition did not apply to it. But what is the most important is this, that not even a single category could be applied to such a thing; as, for instance, the concept of substance, that is, of something that can exist as a subject only, but never as a mere predicate. For I do not know whether there can be anything corresponding to such a determination of thought, unless empirical intuition supplies the case for its application. Of this more hereafter.

Book II. ANALYTIC OF PRINCIPLES

. . . [M. 107-8]

INTRODUCTION

OF THE TRANSCENDENTAL FACULTY OF JUDGMENT IN GENERAL

. . . [M. 108-10]

WHAT [1] distinguishes transcendental philosophy is, that besides giving the rules (or rather the general condition of rules) which are contained in the pure concept of the understanding, it can at the same time indicate *a priori* the case to which each rule may be applied. The superiority which it enjoys in this respect over all other sciences, except mathematics, is due to this, that it treats of concepts which are meant to refer to their objects *a priori,* so that their objective validity cannot be proved *a posteriori,* because this would not affect their own peculiar dignity. It must show, on the contrary, by means of general but sufficient marks, the conditions under which objects can be given corresponding to those concepts; otherwise these would be without any contents, mere logical forms, and not pure concepts of the understanding.

Our transcendental doctrine of the faculty of judgment will consist of two chapters. The first will treat of the sensuous condition under which alone pure concepts of the understanding can be used. This is what I

[1] [M. 111]

call the *schematism* of the pure understanding. The second will treat of the synthetical judgments, which can be derived *a priori* under these conditions from pure concepts of the understanding, and on which all knowledge *a priori* depends. It will treat, therefore, of the principles of the pure understanding.

CHAPTER I

OF THE SCHEMATISM OF THE PURE CONCEPTS OF THE UNDERSTANDING [1]

In comprehending any object under a concept, the representation of the former must be homogeneous with the latter, that is, the concept must contain that which is represented in the object to be comprehended under it, for this is the only meaning of the expression that an object is comprehended under a concept. Thus, for instance, the empirical concept of a plate is homogeneous with the pure geometrical concept of a circle, the roundness which is conceived in the first forming an object of intuition in the latter.

Now it is clear that pure concepts of the understanding, as compared with empirical or sensuous impressions in general, are entirely heterogeneous, and can never be met with in any intuition. How then can the latter be comprehended under the former, or how can the categories be applied to phenomena, as no one is likely to say that causality, for instance, could be seen through the senses, and was contained in the phenomenon? It is really this very natural and important question which renders a transcendental doctrine of the faculty of judgment necessary, in order to show how it is possible that any of the pure concepts of the understanding can be

[1] [M. 112 ff.]

applied to phenomena. In all other sciences in which the concepts by which the object is thought in general are not so heterogeneous or different from those which represent it *in concreto*, and as it is given, there is no necessity to enter into any discussions as to the applicability of the former to the latter.

In our case there must be some third thing homogeneous on the one side with the category, and on the other with the phenomenon, to render the application of the former to the latter possible. This intermediate representation must be pure (free from all that is empirical) and yet intelligible on the one side, and sensuous on the other. Such a representation is the *transcendental schema*.

The concept of the understanding contains pure synthetical unity of the manifold in general. Time, as the formal condition of the manifold in the internal sense, consequently of the conjunction of all representations, contains a manifold *a priori* in pure intuition. A transcendental determination of time is so far homogeneous with the category (which constitutes its unity) that it is general and founded on a rule *a priori;* and it is on the other hand so far homogeneous with the phenomenon, that time must be contained in every empirical representation of the manifold. The application of the category to phenomena becomes possible therefore by means of the transcendental determination of time, which, as a *schema* of the concepts of the understanding, allows the phenomena to be comprehended under the category.

After what has been said in the deduction of the categories, we hope that nobody will hesitate in answering the question whether these pure concepts of the understanding allow only of an empirical or also of a transcendental application, that is, whether, as conditions of a possible experience, they refer *a priori* to phenomena only, or whether, as conditions of the possibility of things in general, they may be extended to objects by themselves (without restriction to our sensibility). For there we saw that concepts are quite impossible, and cannot have any meaning unless there be an object given either to them or, at least, to some of the elements of which they consist, and that they can never refer to things by themselves (without regard as to whether and how things may be given to us). We likewise saw that the only way in which objects can be given to us, consists in a modification of our sensibility, and lastly, that pure concepts *a priori* must contain, besides the function of the understanding in the category itself, formal conditions *a priori* of sensibility (particularly of the internal sense) which form the general condition under which alone the category may be applied to any object. We shall call this formal and pure condition of sensibility, to which the concept of the understanding is restricted in its application, its *schema;* and the function of the understanding in these schemata, the *schematism of the pure understanding.*

The schema by itself is no doubt a product of the imagination only, but as the synthesis of the imagination does not aim at a single intuition, but at some kind of unity alone in the determination of sensibility, the schema ought to be distinguished from the image. Thus, if I place five points, one after the other . . . . ., this is an image of the number five. If, on the contrary, I think of a number in general, whether it be five or a hundred, this thinking is rather the representation of a method of representing in one image a certain quantity (for instance a thousand) according to a certain concept, than the image itself, which, in the case of a thousand, I could hardly take in and compare with the concept. This representation of a general procedure of the imagination by which a concept receives its image, I call the schema of such concept. . . . [M. 115-6]

This schematism of our understanding applied to phenomena and their mere form is an art hidden in the depth of the human soul, the true secrets of which we shall hardly ever be able to guess and reveal. So much only we can say, that the *image* is a product of the empirical faculty of the productive imagination, while the *schema* of sensuous concepts (such as of figures in space) is a product and so to say a monogram of the pure imagination *a priori,* through which and according to which images themselves become possible, though they are never fully adequate to the concept, and can be connected with it by means of their schema only. The schema of a pure concept of the understanding, on the contrary, is something which can never be made into an image; for it is nothing but the pure synthesis determined by a rule of unity, according to concepts, a synthesis as expressed by the category, and represents a transcendental product of the imagination, a product which concerns the determination of the internal sense in general, under the conditions of its form (time), with reference to all representations, so far as these are meant to be joined *a priori* in one concept, according to the unity of apperception.

Without dwelling any longer on a dry and tedious determination of all that is required for the transcendental schemata of the pure concepts of the understanding in general, we shall proceed at once to represent them according to the order of the categories, and in connection with them.

The pure image of all quantities (*quanta*) before the external sense, is space; that of all objects of the senses in general, time. The pure schema of quantity (*quan-*

titas), however, as a concept of the understanding, is *number,* a representation which comprehends the successive addition of one to one (homogeneous). Number therefore is nothing but the unity of the synthesis of the manifold (repetition) of a homogenous intuition in general, I myself producing the time in the apprehension of the intuition.

Reality is, in the pure concept of the understanding, that which corresponds to a sensation in general: that, therefore, the concept of which indicates by itself being (in time), while negation is that the concept of which represents not-being (in time). The opposition of the two takes place therefore by a distinction of one and the same time, as either filled or empty. As time is only the form of intuition, that is, of objects as phenomena, that which in the phenomena corresponds to sensation, constitutes the transcendental matter of all objects, as things by themselves (reality, Sachheit). Every sensation, however, has a degree of quantity by which it can fill the same time (that is, the internal sense, with reference to the same representation of an object), more or less, till it vanishes into nothing (equal to nought or negation). There exists, therefore, a relation and connection, or rather a transition from reality to negation, which makes every reality representable as a quantum; and the schema of a reality, as the quantity of something which fills time, is this very continuous and uniform production of reality in time; while we either descend from the sensation which has a certain degree, to its vanishing in time, or ascend from the negation of sensation to some quantity of it.

The schema of substance is the permanence of the real in time, that is, the representation of it as a substratum for the empirical determination of time in general, which therefore remains while everything else changes. (It is not time that passes, but the existence of the changeable passes in time. What corresponds therefore in the phenomena to time, which in itself is unchangeable and permanent, is the unchangeable in existence, that is, substance; and it is only in it that the succession and the coexistence of phenomena can be determined according to time.)

The schema of cause and of the causality of a thing in general is the real which, when once supposed to exist, is always followed by something else. It consists therefore in the succession of the manifold, in so far as that succession is subject to a rule.

The schema of community (reciprocal action) or of the reciprocal causality of substances, in respect to their accidents, is the coexistence, according to a general rule, of the determinations of the one with those of the other.

The schema of possibility is the agreement of the synthesis of different representations with the conditions of time in general, as, for instance, when opposites cannot exist at the same time in the same thing, but only one after the other. It is therefore the determination of the representation of a thing at any time whatsoever.

The schema of reality is existence at a given time.

The schema of necessity is the existence of an object at all times.

It is clear, therefore, if we examine all the categories, that the schema of quantity contains and represents the production (synthesis) of time itself in the successive apprehension of an object; the schema of quality, the synthesis of sensation (perception) with the representation of time or the filling-up of time; the schema of relation, the relation of perceptions to each other at all times (that is, according to a rule which determines time); lastly, the schema of modality and its categories, time itself as the correlative of the determination of an object as to whether and how it belongs to time. The schemata therefore are nothing but determinations of time *a priori* according to rules, and these, as applied to all possible objects, refer in the order of the categories to the *series of time,* the *contents of time,* the *order of time,* and lastly, the *comprehension of time.*

We have thus seen that the schematism of the understanding, by means of a transcendental synthesis of imagination, amounts to nothing else but to the unity of the manifold in the intuition of the internal sense, and therefore indirectly to the unity of apperception, as an active function corresponding to the internal sense (as receptive). These schemata therefore of the pure concepts of the understanding are the true and only conditions by which these concepts can gain a relation to objects, that is, a *significance,* and the categories are thus in the end of no other but a possible empirical use, serving only, on account of an *a priori* necessary unity (the necessary connection of all consciousness in one original apperception) to subject all phenomena to general rules of synthesis, and thus to render them capable of a general connection in experience. . . . [M. 119-20]

CHAPTER II

SYSTEM OF ALL PRINCIPLES OF THE PURE UNDERSTANDING [1]

We have in the preceding chapter considered the transcendental faculty of judgment with reference to those general conditions only under which it is justified in using the pure concepts of the understanding for synthetical judgments. It now becomes our duty to repre-

[1] [Cf. M. 121 ff.]

sent systematically those judgments which, under that critical provision, the understanding can really produce *a priori*. For this purpose our table of categories will be without doubt our natural and best guide. For it is the relation of the categories to all possible experience which must constitute all pure *a priori* knowledge of the understanding; and their relation to sensibility in general will therefore exhibit completely and systematically all the transcendental principles of the use of the understanding.

Principles *a priori* are so called, not only because they contain the grounds for other judgments, but also because they themselves are not founded on higher and more general kinds of knowledge. This peculiarity, however, does not enable them to dispense with every kind of proof; for although this could not be given objectively, as all knowledge of any object really rests on it, this does not prevent us from attempting to produce a proof drawn from the subjective sources of the possibility of a knowledge of the object in general; nay, it may be necessary to do so, because, without it, our assertion might be suspected of being purely gratuitous. . . . [M. 122-3]

SECTION I. *Of the Highest Principle of all Analytical Judgments*

Whatever the object of our knowledge may be, and whatever the relation between our knowledge and its object, it must always submit to that general, though only negative condition of all our judgments, that they do not contradict themselves; otherwise these judgments, without any reference to their object, are in themselves nothing. But although there may be no contradiction in our judgment, it may nevertheless connect concepts in a manner not warranted by the object, or without there being any ground, whether *a priori* or *a posteriori,* to confirm such a judgment. A judgment may therefore be false or groundless, though in itself it is free from all contradiction.

The proposition that no subject can have a predicate which contradicts it, is called *the principle of contradiction.* It is a general though only negative criterion of all truth, and belongs to logic only, because it applies to knowledge as knowledge only, without reference to its object, and simply declares that such contradiction would entirely destroy and annihilate it. . . . [M. 123-4]

It must therefore be admitted that the principle of contradiction is the general and altogether sufficient principle of all analytical knowledge, though beyond this its authority and utility, as a sufficient criterion of truth, must not be allowed to extend. For the fact that no knowledge can run counter to that principle, without destroying itself, makes it no doubt a *conditio sine qua non,* but never the determining reason of the truth of our knowledge. Now, as in our present enquiry we are chiefly concerned with the synthetical part of our knowledge, we must no doubt take great care never to offend against that inviolable principle, but we ought never to expect from it any help with regard to the truth of this kind of knowledge. . . . [M. 124-5]

Section II. *Of the Highest Principle of all Synthetical Judgments*

The explanation of the possibility of synthetical judgments is a subject of which general logic knows nothing, not even its name, while in a transcendental logic it is the most important task of all, nay, even the only one, when we have to consider the possibility of synthetical judgments *a priori,* their conditions, and the extent of their validity. For when that task is accomplished, the object of transcendental logic, namely, to determine the extent and limits of the pure understanding, will have been fully attained. . . . [M. 126-7]

If knowledge is to have any objective reality, that is to say, if it is to refer to an object, and receive by means of it any sense and meaning, the object must necessarily be given in some way or other. Without that all concepts are empty. We have thought in them, but we have not, by thus thinking, arrived at any knowledge. We have only played with representations. To give an object, if this is not meant again as mediate only, but if it means to represent something immediately in intuition, is nothing else but to refer the representation of the object to experience (real or possible). Even space and time, however pure these concepts may be of all that is empirical, and however certain it is that they are represented in the mind entirely *a priori,* would lack nevertheless all objective validity, all sense and meaning, if we could not show the necessity of their use with reference to all objects of experience. Nay, their representation is a pure schema, always referring to that reproductive imagination which calls up the objects of experience, without which objects would be meaningless. The same applies to all concepts without any distinction.

It is therefore the *possibility of experience* which alone gives objective reality to all our knowledge *a priori.* Experience, however, depends on the synthetical unity of phenomena, that is, on a synthesis according to concepts of the object of phenomena in general. Without it, it would not even be knowledge, but only a rhapsody of perceptions, which would never grow into a connected text according to the rules of an altogether coherent (possible) consciousness, nor into a transcendental and necessary unity of apperception. Experience depends therefore on *a priori* principles of its form, that is, on general rules of unity in the synthesis of phenomena, and the objective reality of these (rules) can always be shown by their being the necessary conditions in all experience; nay, even in the possibility of all experience. Without such a relation synthetical propositions *a priori* would be quite impossible, because they have no third medium, that is, no object in which the synthetical unity of their concepts could prove their objective reality. . . . [M. 128-9]

The highest principle of all synthetical judgments is therefore this, that every object is subject to the necessary conditions of a synthetical unity of the manifold of intuition in a possible experience.

Thus synthetical judgments *a priori* are possible, if we refer the formal conditions of intuition *a priori*, the synthesis of imagination, and the necessary unity of it in a transcendental apperception, to a possible knowledge in general, given in experience, and if we say that the conditions of the possibility of experience in general are at the same time conditions of the possibility of the objects of experience themselves, and thus possess objective validity in a synthetical judgment *a priori*.

Section III. *Systematical Representation of all Synthetical Principles of the Understanding*

That there should be principles at all is entirely due to the pure understanding, which is not only the faculty of rules in regard to all that happens, but itself the source of principles, according to which everything (that can become an object to us) is necessarily subject to rules, because, without such, phenomena would never become objects corresponding to knowledge. Even laws of nature, if they are considered as principles of the empirical use of the understanding, carry with them a character of necessity, and thus lead to the supposition that they rest on grounds which are valid *a priori* and before all experience. Nay, all laws of nature without distinction are subject to higher principles of the understanding, which they apply to particular cases of experience. They alone therefore supply the concept which contains the condition, and, as it were, the exponent of a rule in general, while experience furnishes each case to which the general rule applies.

There can hardly be any danger of our mistaking purely empirical principles for principles of the pure understanding or *vice versa,* for the character of necessity which distinguishes the concepts of the pure understanding, and the absence of which can easily be perceived in every empirical proposition, however general it may seem, will always prevent their confusion. . . . [M. 130-1]

Our table of categories gives us naturally the best instructions for drawing up a table of principles, because these are nothing but rules for the objective use of the former.

All principles of the pure understanding are therefore,

I
Axioms of Intuition.

II
Anticipations of
Perception.

III
Analogies of
Experience.

IV
Postulates of Empirical
Thought in General.

. . . [M. 132-5, 769]

I. Axioms of Intuition

Their [1] principle is: All intuitions are extensive quantities.

Proof

All phenomena contain, so far as their form is concerned, an intuition in space and time, which forms the *a priori* foundation of all of them. They cannot, therefore, be apprehended, that is, received into empirical consciousness, except through the synthesis of the manifold, by which the representations of a definite space or time are produced, i.e. through the synthesis of the homogeneous, and the consciousness of the synthetical unity of that manifold (homogeneous). Now the consciousness of the manifold and homogeneous in intuition, so far as by it the representation of an object is first rendered possible, is the concept of quantity (quantum). Therefore even the perception of an object as a phenomenon is possible only through the same synthetical unity of the manifold of the given sensuous intuition, by which the unity of the composition of the manifold and homogeneous is conceived in the concept of a *quantity;* that is, phenomena are always quantities, and *extensive quantities;* because as intuitions in space and time, they must be represented through the same synthesis through which space and time in general are determined.

Phenomena [2] are not things in themselves. Empirical intuition is possible only through pure intuition (of space and time), and whatever geometry says of the latter is valid without contradiction of the former. All evasions, as if objects of the senses should not conform to the rules of construction in space (for instance, to

[1] [Cf. M. 770]
[2] [Cf. M. 135-6]

the rule of the infinite divisibility of lines or angles) must cease, for one would thus deny all objective validity to space and with it to all mathematics, and would no longer know why and how far mathematics can be applied to phenomena. The synthesis of spaces and times, as the synthesis of the essential form of all intuition, is that which renders possible at the same time the apprehension of phenomena, that is, every external experience, and therefore also all knowledge of its objects, and whatever mathematics, in their pure use prove of that synthesis is valid necessarily also of this knowledge. All objections to this are only the chicaneries of a falsely guided reason, which wrongly imagines that it can separate the objects of the senses from the formal conditions of our sensibility, and represents them, though they are phenomena only, as objects by themselves, given to the understanding. In this case, however, nothing could be known of them *a priori*, nothing could be known synthetically through pure concepts of space, and the science which determines those concepts, namely, geometry, would itself become impossible.

II. Anticipations of Perception

Their [1] principle is: In all *phenomena* the *Real,* which is the *object of a sensation, has intensive quantity,* that is, a degree.

Proof

. . . [M. 136-7] If [2] . . . there should be something in every sensation that could be known *a priori* as sensation in general, even if no particular sensation be given, this would, in a very special sense, deserve to be called

[1] [Cf. M. 771]
[2] [Cf. M. 137]

anticipation, because it seems extraordinary that we should anticipate experience in that which concerns the matter of experience and can be derived from experience only. Yet such is really the case. . . . [M. 137-8]

Perception[1] is empirical consciousness, that is, a consciousness in which there is at the same time sensation. Phenomena, as objects of perception, are not pure (merely formal) intuitions, like space and time (for space and time can never be perceived by themselves). They contain, therefore, over and above the intuition, the material for some one object in general (through which something existing in space and time is represented); that is, they contain the real of sensation, as a merely subjective representation, which gives us only the consciousness that the subject is affected, and which is referred to some object in general. Now there is a gradual transition possible from empirical to pure consciousness, till the real of it vanishes completely and there remains a merely formal consciousness (*a priori*) of the manifold in space and time; and, therefore, a synthesis also is possible in the production of the quantity of a sensation, from its beginning, that is, from the pure intuition=0, onwards to any quantity of it, As sensation by itself is no objective representation, and as in it the intuition of neither space nor time can be found, it follows that though not an extensive, yet some kind of quantity must belong to it (and this through the apprehension of it, in which the empirical consciousness may grow in a certain time from nothing=0 to any amount). That *quantity* must be *intensive*, and corresponding to it, an intensive quantity, i.e. a degree of influence upon the senses, must be attributed to all objects of perception, so far as it contains sensation.

[1] [Cf. M. 771]

Every[1] sensation, therefore, and every reality in phenomena, however small it may be, has a degree, that is, an intensive quantity which can always be diminished, and there is between reality and negation a continuous connection of possible realities, and of possible smaller perceptions. Every colour, red, for instance, has a degree, which, however small, is never the smallest; and the same applies to heat, the momentum of gravity, etc. . . . [M. 138-40]

If therefore all reality in perception has a certain degree, between which and negation there is an infinite sucession of ever smaller degrees, and if every sense must have a definite degree of receptivity of sensations, it follows that no perception, and therefore no experience, is possible, that could prove, directly or indirectly, by any roundabout syllogisms, a complete absence of all reality in a phenomenon. We see therefore that experience can never supply a proof of empty space or empty time, because the total absence of reality in a sensuous intuition can itself never be perceived, neither can it be deduced from any phenomenon whatsoever and from the difference of degree in its reality; nor ought it ever to be admitted in explanation of it. For although the total intuition of a certain space or time is real all through, no part of it being empty, yet as every reality has its degree which, while the extensive quality of the phenomenon remains unchanged, may diminish by infinite degrees down to the nothing or void, there must be infinitely differing degrees in which space and time are filled, and the intensive quantity in phenomena may be smaller or greater, although the extensive quantity as given in intuition remains the same. . . . [M. 141-4]

[1] [Cf. M. 138]

III. Analogies of Experience

Their[1] principle is: Experience is possible only through the representation of a necessary connection of perceptions.

Proof

Experience is empirical knowledge, that is, knowledge which determines an object by means of perceptions. It is, therefore, a synthesis of perceptions, which synthesis itself is not contained in the perception, but contains the synthetical unity of the manifold of the perceptions in a consciousness, that unity constituting the essential of our knowledge of the objects of the senses, i.e. of experience (not only of intuition or of sensation of the senses). In experience perceptions come together contingently only, so that no necessity of their connection could be discovered in the perceptions themselves, apprehension being only a composition of the manifold of empirical intuition, but containing no representation of the necessity of the connected existence, in space and time, of the phenomena which it places together. Experience, on the contrary, is a knowledge of objects by perceptions, in which therefore the relation in the existence of the manifold is to be represented, not as it is put together in time, but as it is in time, objectively. Now, as time itself cannot be perceived, the determination of the existence of objects in time can take place only by their connection in time in general, that is, through concepts connecting them *a priori*. As these concepts always imply necessity, we are justified in saying that experience is possible only through a repre-

[1] [Cf. M. 772]

sentation of the necessary connection of perceptions. . . . [M. 773-7]

The [1] three modi of time are *permanence, succession,* and *coexistence.* There will therefore be three rules of all relations of phenomena in time, by which the existence of every phenomenon with regard to the unity of time is determined, and these rules will precede all experience, nay, render experience possible.

The general principle of the three analogies depends on the necessary unity of apperception with reference to every possible empirical consciousness (perception) *at every time,* and, consequently, as that unity forms an *a priori* ground, on the synthetical unity of all phenomena, according to their relation in time. For the original apperception refers to the internal sense (comprehending all representations), and it does so *a priori* to its form, that is, to the relation of the manifold of the empirical consciousness in time. The original apperception is intended to combine all this manifold according to its relations in time, for this is what is meant by its transcendental unity *a priori,* to which all is subject which is to belong to my own and my uniform knowledge, and thus to become an object for me. This synthetical unity in the time relations of all perceptions, which is determined *a priori,* is expressed therefore in the law, that all empirical determinations of time must be subject to rules of the general determination of time; and the analogies of experience, of which we are now going to treat, are exactly rules of this kind. . . . [M. 145-7]

What has been remarked of all synthetical principles and must be enjoined here more particularly is this, that these analogies have their meaning and validity, not as principles of the transcendent, but only as principles

[1] [Cf. M. 144]

of the empirical use of the understanding. They can be established in this character only, nor can phenomena ever be comprehended under the categories directly, but only under their schemata. If the objects to which these principles refer were things by themselves, it would be perfectly impossible to know anything of them *a priori* and synthetically. But they are nothing but phenomena, and our whole knowledge of them, to which, after all, all principles *a priori* must relate, is only our possible experience of them. Those principles therefore can aim at nothing but the conditions of the unity of empirical knowledge in the synthesis of phenomena, which synthesis is represented only in the schema of the pure concepts of the understanding, while the category contains the function, restricted by no sensuous condition, of the unity of that synthesis as synthesis in general. Those principles will therefore authorise us only to connect phenomena, according to analogy, with the logical and universal unity of concepts, so that, though in using the principle we use the category, yet in practice (in the application to phenomena) we put the schema of the category, as a practical key, in its place, or rather put it by the side of the category as a restrictive condition, or, as what may be called, a formula of the category.

FIRST ANALOGY

Principle of Permanence

All [1] phenomena contain the permanent (substance) as the object itself, and the changeable as its determination only, that is, as a mode in which the object exists.

[1] [Cf. M. 149 ff.]

Proof of the First Analogy

All phenomena take place in time. Time can determine in two ways the relation in the existence of phenomena, so far as they are either successive or coexistent. In the first case time is considered as a series, in the second as a whole.

Our apprehension of the manifold of phenomena is always successive, and therefore always changing. By it alone therefore we can never determine whether the manifold, as an object of experience, is coexistent or successive, unless there is something in it which exists always, that is, something constant and permanent, while change and succession are nothing but so many kinds (*modi*) of time in which the permanent exists. Relations of time are therefore possible in the permanent only (coexistence and succession being the only relations of time) so that the permanent is the substratum of the empirical representation of time itself, and in it alone all determination of time is possible. Permanence expresses time as the constant correlative of all existence of phenomena, of all change and concomitancy. For change does not affect time itself, but only phenomena in time (nor is coexistence a mode of time itself, because in it no parts can be coexistent, but successive only). If we were to ascribe a succession to time itself, it would be necessary to admit another time in which such succession should be possible. Only through the permanent does *existence* in different parts of a series of time assume a *quantity* which we call *duration*. For in mere succession existence always comes and goes, and never assumes the slightest quantity. Without something permanent therefore no relation of time is possible. Time by itself, however, cannot be perceived, and it is therefore the permanent in phenomena that forms the substratum for all determination of time, and at the same time the condition of the possibility of all synthetical unity of perceptions, that is, of experience; while with regard to that permanent all existence and all change in time can only be taken as a mode of existence of what is permanent. In all phenomena therefore the permanent is the object itself, that is, the substance (phenomenon), while all that changes or can change belongs only to the mode in which substance or substances exist, therefore to their determinations. . . . [M. 150-2]

The different determinations of a substance, which are nothing but particular modes in which it exists, are called accidents. They are always real, because they concern the existence of a substance (negations are nothing but determinations which express the non-existence of something in the substance). If we want to ascribe a particular kind of existence to these real determinations of the substance, as, for instance, to motion, as an accident of matter, we call it *inherence,* in order to distinguish it from the existence of substance, which we call *subsistence.* This, however, has given rise to many misunderstandings, and we shall express ourselves better and more correctly, if we define the accident through the manner only in which the existence of a substance is positively determined. It is inevitable, however, according to the conditions of the logical use of our understanding, to separate, as it were, whatever can change in the existence of a substance, while the substance itself remains unchanged, and to consider it in its relation to that which is radical and truly permanent. Hence a place has been assigned to this category under the title of relations, not so much because it contains itself a relation, as because it contains their condition.

On this permanence depends also the right understanding of the concept of *change*. To arise and to perish are not changes of that which arises or perishes. Change is a mode of existence, which follows another mode of existence of the same object. Hence whatever changes is permanent, and its condition only changes. As this alteration refers only to determinations which may have an end or a beginning, we may use an expression that seems somewhat paradoxical and say: the permanent only (substance) is changed, the changing itself suffers no change, but only an alteration, certain determinations ceasing to exist, while others begin.

It is therefore in substances only that change can be perceived. Arising or perishing absolutely, and not referring merely to a determination of the permanent can never become a possible perception, because it is the permanent only which renders the representations of a transition from one state to another, from not being to being, possible, which (changes) consequently can only be known empirically, as alternating determinations of what is permanent. . . . [M. 153-4]

Substances therefore (as phenomena) are the true substrata of all determinations of time. If some substances could arise and others perish, the only condition of the empirical unity of time would be removed, and phenomena would then be referred to two different times, in which existence would pass side by side, which is absurd. For there is but one time in which all different times must be placed, not as simultaneous, but as successive.

Permanence, therefore, is a necessary condition under which alone phenomena, as things or objects, can be determined in a possible experience. What the empirical criterion of this necessary permanence, or of the substantiality of phenomena may be, we shall have to explain in the sequel.

SECOND ANALOGY

Principle of Production

Everything that happens (begins to be), presupposes something on which it follows according to a rule.

Proof [1]

[1.] The [2] apprehension of the manifold of phenomena is always successive. The representations of the parts follow one upon another. Whether they also follow one upon the other in the object is a second point for reflection, not contained in the former. We may indeed call everything, even every representation, so far as we are conscious of it, an object; but it requires a more profound investigation to discover what this word may mean with regard to phenomena, not in so far as they (as representations) are objects, but in so far as they only signify an object. So far as they, as representations only, are at the same time objects of consciousness, they cannot be distinguished from our apprehension, that is from their being received in the synthesis of our imagination, and we must therefore say, that the manifold of phenomena is always produced in the mind successively. If phenomena were things by themselves, the succession of the representations of their manifold would never enable us to judge how that manifold is

[1] [The following section contains not one but three separate proofs, as indicated by the inserted numerals.]
[2] [Cf. M. 155 ff.]

connected in the object. We have always to deal with our representations only; how things may be by themselves (without reference to the representations by which they affect us) is completely beyond the sphere of our knowledge. Since, therefore, phenomena are not things by themselves, and are yet the only thing that can be given to us to know, I am asked to say what kind of connection in time belongs to the manifold of the phenomena itself, when the representation of it in our apprehension is always successive. Thus, for instance, the apprehension of the manifold in the phenomenal appearance of a house that stands before me, is successive. The question then arises, whether the manifold of the house itself be successive by itself, which of course no one would admit. Whenever I ask for the transcendental meaning of my concepts of an object, I find that a house is not a thing by itself, but a phenomenon only, that is, a representation the transcendental object of which is unknown. What then can be the meaning of the question, how the manifold in the phenomenon itself (which is not a thing by itself) may be connected? Here that which is contained in our successive apprehension is considered as representation, and the given phenomenon, though it is nothing but the whole of those representations, as their object, with which my concept, drawn from the representations of my apprehension, is to accord. As the accord between knowledge and its object is truth, it is easily seen, that we can ask here only for the formal conditions of empirical truth, and that the phenomenon, in contradistinction to the representations of our apprehension, can only be represented as the object different from them, if it is subject to a rule distinguishing it from every other apprehension, and necessitating a certain kind of conjunction of the manifold. That which in the phenomenon contains the condition of this necessary rule of apprehension is *the object.*

Let us now proceed to our task. That something takes place, that is, that something, or some state, which did not exist before, begins to exist, cannot be perceived empirically, unless there exists antecedently a phenomenon which does not contain that state; for a reality, following on empty time, that is a beginning of existence, preceded by no state of things, can be apprehended as little as empty time itself. Every apprehension of an event is therefore a perception following on another perception. But as this applies to all synthesis of apprehension, as I showed before in the phenomenal appearance of a house, that apprehension would not thereby be different from any other. But I observe at the same time, that if in a phenomenon which contains an event I call the antecedent state of perception A, and the subsequent B, B can only follow A in my apprehension, while the perception A can never follow B, but can only precede it. I see, for instance, a ship gliding down a stream. My perception of its place below follows my perception of its place higher up in the course of the stream, and it is impossible in the apprehension of this phenomenon that the ship should be perceived first below and then higher up. We see therefore that the order in the succession of perceptions in our apprehension is here determined, and our apprehension regulated by that order. In the former example of a house my perceptions could begin in the apprehension at the roof and end in the basement, or begin below and end above: they could apprehend the manifold of the empirical intuition from right to left or from left to right. There was therefore no determined order in the succession of these perceptions, determining the point where I had to begin in apprehension, in order to connect the manifold empirically; while in the apprehension of an event there is always a rule, which makes the order of the successive perceptions (in the apprehension of this phenomenon) necessary.

In our case, therefore, we shall have to derive the subjective succession in our apprehension from the objective succession of the phenomena, because otherwise the former would be entirely undetermined, and unable to distinguish one phenomenon from another. The former alone proves nothing as to the connection of the manifold in the object, because it is quite arbitrary. The latter must therefore consist in the order of the manifold in a phenomenon, according to which the apprehension of what is happening follows upon the apprehension of what has happened, in conformity with a rule. Thus only can I be justified in saying, not only of my apprehension, but of the phenomenon itself, that there exists in it a succession, which is the same as to say that I cannot arrange the apprehension otherwise than in that very succession.

In conformity with this, there must exist in that which always precedes an event the condition of a rule, by which this event follows at all times, and necessarily; but I cannot go back from the event and determine by apprehension that which precedes. For no phenomenon goes back from the succeeding to the preceding point of time, though it is related to some preceding point of time, while the progress from a given time to a determined following time is necessary. Therefore, as there certainly is something that follows, I must necessarily refer it to something else which precedes, and upon which it follows by rule, that is, by necessity. So that the event, as being conditional, affords a safe indication of some kind of condition, while that condition itself determines the event. . . . [M. 159-60]

[2.] It [1] is necessary therefore to show by examples that we never, even in experience, ascribe the sequence or consequence (of an event or something happening that did not exist before) to the object, and distinguish it from the subjective sequence of our apprehension, except when there is a rule which forces us to observe a certain order of perceptions, and no other; nay, that it is this force which from the first renders the representation of a succession in the object possible.

We have representations within us, and can become conscious of them; but however far that consciousness may extend, and however accurate and minute it may be, yet the representations are always representations only, that is, internal determinations of our mind in this or that relation of time. What right have we then to add to these representations an object, or to ascribe to these modifications, beyond their subjective reality, another objective one? Their objective character cannot consist in their relation to another representation (of that which one wished to predicate of the object), for thus the question would only arise again, how that representation could again go beyond itself, and receive an objective character in addition to the subjective one, which belongs to it, as a determination of our mind. If we try to find out what new quality or dignity is imparted to our representations by their relation to an *object*, we find that it consists in nothing but the rendering necessary the connection of representations in a certain way, and subjecting them to a rule; and that on the other hand they receive their objective character only because a certain order is necessary in the time relations of our representations.

In th synthesis of phenomena the manifold of our representations is always successive. No object can

[1] [Cf. M. 160 ff.]

thus be represented, because through the succession which is common to all apprehensions, nothing can be distinguished from anything else. But as soon as I perceive or anticipate that there is in this succession a relation to an antecedent state from which the representation follows by rule, then something is represented as an event, or as something that happens: that is to say, I know an object to which I must assign a certain position in time, which, after the preceding state, cannot be different from what it is. If therefore I perceive that something happens, this representation involves that something preceded, because the phenomenon receives its position in time with reference to what preceded, that is, it exists after a time in which it did not exist. Its definite position in time can only be assigned to it, if in the antecedent state something is presupposed on which it always follows by rule. It thus follows that, first of all, I cannot invert the order, and place that which happens before that on which it follows; secondly, that whenever the antecedent state is there, the other event must follow inevitably and necessarily. Thus it happens that there arises an order among our representations, in which the present state (as having come to be), points to an antecedent state, as a correlative of the event that is given; a correlative which, though as yet indefinite, refers as determining to the event, as its result, and connects that event with itself by necessity, in the succession of time. . . . [M. 162-3]

[3.] What[1] is required for all experience and renders it possible is the understanding, and the first that is added by it is not that it renders the representation of objects clear, but that it really renders the representation of any object for the first time possible. This takes place by the understanding transferring the order

[1] [Cf. M. 163 ff.]

of time to the phenomena and their existence, and by assigning to each of them as to a consequence a certain *a priori* determined place in time, with reference to antecedent phenomena, without which place phenomena would not be in accord with time, which determines *a priori* their places to all its parts. This determination of place cannot be derived from the relation in which phenomena stand to absolute time (for that can never be an object of perception); but, on the contrary, phenomena must themselves determine to each other their places in time, and render them necessary in the series of time. In other words, what happens or follows must follow according to a general rule on that which was contained in a previous state. We thus get a series of phenomena which, by means of the understanding, produces and makes necessary in the series of possible perceptions the same order and continuous coherence which exists *a priori* in the form of internal intuition (time), in which all perceptions must have their place.

That something happens is therefore a perception which belongs to a possible experience, and this experience becomes real when I consider the phenomenon as determined with regard to its place in time, that is to say, as an object which can always be found, according to a rule, in the connection of perceptions. This rule, by which we determine everything according to the succession of time, is this: the condition under which an event follows at all times (necessarily) is to be found in what precedes. All possible experience therefore, that is, all objective knowledge of phenomena with regard to their relation in the succession of time, depends on 'the principle of sufficient reason.'

The proof of this principle rests entirely on the following considerations. All empirical knowledge requires synthesis of the manifold by imagination, which is always successive, one representation following upon the other. That succession, however, in the imagination is not at all determined with regard to the order in which something precedes and something follows, and the series of successive representations may be taken as retrogressive as well as progressive. If that synthesis, however, is a synthesis of apperception (of the manifold in a given phenomenon), then the order is determined in the object, or, to speak more accurately, there is then in it an order of successive synthesis which determines the object, and according to which something must necessarily precede, and, when it is once there, something else must necessarily follow. If therefore my perception is to contain the knowledge of an event, or something that really happens, it must consist of an empirical judgment, by which the succession is supposed to be determined, so that the event presupposes another phenomenon in time on which it follows necessarily and according to a rule. If it were different, if the antecedent phenomenon were there, and the event did not follow on it necessarily, it would become to me a mere play of my subjective imaginations, or if I thought it to be objective, I should call it a dream. It is therefore the relation of phenomena (as possible perceptions) according to which the existence of the subsequent (what happens) is determined in time by something antecedent necessarily and by rule, or, in other words, the relation of cause and effect, which forms the condition of the objective validity of our empirical judgments with regard to the series of perceptions, and therefore also the condition of the empirical truth of them, and of experience. The principle of the causal relation in the succession of phenomena is valid therefore for all objects of experience, also (under the conditions of succession), because that principle is itself the ground of the possibility of such experience. . . . [M. 165-72]

THIRD ANALOGY

Principle of Community

All substances, in so far as they are coexistent, stand in complete community, that is, reciprocity one to another.

Proof

Things [1] are coexistent in so far as they exist at one and the same time. But how can we know that they exist at one and the same time? Only if the order in the synthesis of apprehension of the manifold is indifferent, that is, if I may advance from A through B, C, D, to E, or contrariwise from E to A. For, if the synthesis were successive in time (in the order beginning with A and ending with E), it would be impossible to begin the apprehension with the perception of E and to go backwards to A, because A belongs to past time, and can no longer be an object of apprehension.

If we supposed it possible that in a number of substances, as phenomena, each were perfectly isolated, so that none influenced another or received influences from another, then the coexistence of them could never become an object of possible perception, nor could the existence of the one through any process of empirical synthesis lead us on to the existence of another. For if we imagined that they were separated by a perfectly empty space, a perception, proceeding from the one in time to the other might no doubt determine the existence of it by means of a subsequent perception, but would never be able to determine whether that phe-

[1] [Cf. M. 172 ff.]

nomenon followed objectively on the other or was coexistent with it.

There must therefore be something besides their mere existence by which *A* determines its place in time for *B*, and *B* for *A*, because thus only can these two substances be represented empirically as coexistent. Nothing, however, can determine the place of anything else in time, except that which is its cause or the cause of its determinations. Therefore every substance (since it can be effect with regard to its determinations only) must contain in itself the causality of certain determinations in another substance, and, at the same time, the effects of the causality of that other substance, that is, substances must stand in dynamical communion, immediately or mediately, with each other, if their coexistence is to be known in any possible experience. Now, everything without which the experience of any objects would be impossible, may be said to be necessary with reference to such objects of experience; from which it follows that it is necessary for all substances, so far as they are coexistent as phenomena, to stand in a complete communion of reciprocity with each other.

The word *communion* (Gemeinschaft) may be used in two senses, meaning either *communio* or *commercium*. We use it here in the latter sense: as a dynamical communion without which even the local *communio spatii* could never be known empirically. We can easily perceive in our experience, that continuous influences only can lead our senses in all parts of space from one object to another; that the light which plays between our eyes and celestial bodies produces a mediate communion between us and them, and proves the coexistence of the latter; that we cannot change any place empirically (perceive such a change) unless matter itself renders the perception of our own place possible to us, and that by means of its reciprocal influence only matter can evince its simultaneous existence, and thus (though mediately only) its coexistence, even to the most distant objects. Without this communion every perception (of any phenomenon in space) is separated from the others, and the chain of empirical representations, that is, experience itself, would have to begin *de novo* with every new object, without the former experience being in the least connected with it, or standing to it in any temporal relation. I do not want to say anything here against empty space. Empty space may exist where perception cannot reach, and where therefore no empirical knowledge of coexistence takes place, but, in that case, it is no object for any possible experience.

The following remarks may elucidate this. It is necessary that in our mind all phenomena, as being contained in a possible experience, must share a communion of apperception, and if the objects are to be represented as connected in coexistence, they must reciprocally determine their place in time, and thus constitute a whole. If this subjective communion is to rest on an objective ground, or is to refer to phenomena as substances, then the perception of the one as cause must render possible the perception of the other, and *vice versa*: so that the succession which always exists in perceptions, as apprehensions, may not be attributed to the objects, but that the objects should be represented as existing simultaneously. This is a reciprocal influence, that is a real *commercium* of substances, without which the empirical relation of co-existence would be impossible in our experience. . . . [M. 175]

. . . Hence [1] the coexistence of substances in space cannot be known in experience otherwise but under the supposition of reciprocal action: and this is therefore the

[1] [Cf. M. 777]

condition also of the possibility of things themselves as objects of experience.

* * * * * * * * *

These[1] are the three analogies of experience. They are nothing but principles for determining the existence of phenomena in time, according to its three modes. First, the relation of time itself, as to a quantity (quantity of existence, that is duration). Secondly, the relation in time, as in a series (successively). And thirdly, likewise in time, as the whole of all existence (simultaneously). This unity in the determination of time is dynamical only, that is, time is not looked upon as that in which experience assigns immediately its place to every existence, for this would be impossible; because absolute time is no object of perception by which phenomena could be held together; but the rule of the understanding through which alone the existence of phenomena can receive synthetical unity in time determines the place of each of them in time, therefore *a priori* and as valid for all time.

By nature (in the empirical sense of the word) we mean the coherence of phenomena in their existence, according to necessary rules, that is, laws. There are therefore certain laws, and they exist *a priori,* which themselves make nature possible, while the empirical laws exist and are discovered through experience, but in accordance with those original laws which first render experience possible. Our analogies therefore represent the unity of nature in the coherence of all phenomena, under certain exponents, which express the relation of time (as comprehending all existence) to the unity of apperception, which apperception can only take place in the synthesis according to rules. The three analogies,

[1] [Cf. M. 175 ff.]

therefore, simply say, that all phenomena exist in one nature, and must so exist because, without such unity *a priori* no unity of experience, and therefore no determination of objects in experience, would be possible.

With regard to the mode of proof, by which we have arrived at these transcendental laws of nature and its peculiar character, a remark must be made which will become important as a rule for any other attempt to prove intelligible, and at the same time synthetical propositions *a priori.* If we had attempted to prove these analogies dogmatically, that is from concepts, showing that all which exists is found only in that which is permanent, that every event presupposes something in a previous state on which it follows by rule, and lastly, that in the manifold which is coexistent, states coexist in relation to each other by rule, all our labour would have been in vain. For we may analyse as much as we like, we shall never arrive from one object and its existence at the existence of another, or at its mode of existence by means of the concepts of these things only. What else then remained? There remained the possibility of experience, as that knowledge in which all objects must in the end be capable of being given to us, if their representation is to have any objective reality for us. In this, namely in the synthetical unity of apperception of all phenomena, we discovered the conditions *a priori* of an absolute and necessary determination in time of all phenomenal existence. Without this even the empirical determinations in time would be impossible, and we thus established the rules of the synthetical unity *a priori,* by which we might anticipate experience. It was because people were ignorant of this method, and imagined that they could prove dogmatically synthetical propositions which the empirical use of the understanding follows as its principles, that so many and always unsuccessful attempts have been made to prove the proposition of the 'sufficient reason.' The other two analogies have not even been thought of, though everybody followed them unconsciously,[1] because the method of the categories was wanting, by which alone every gap in the understanding, both with regard to concepts and principles, can be discovered and pointed out.

IV. The Postulates of Empirical Thought in General

1. What agrees with the formal conditions of experience (in intuition and in concepts) is possible.
2. What is connected with the material conditions of experience (sensation) is real.
3. That which, in its connection with the real, is determined by universal conditions of experience, is (exists as) necessary.

Explanation

The[1] categories of modality have this peculiar character that, as determining an object, they do not enlarge in the least the concept to which they are attached as predicates, but express only a relation to our faculty of knowledge. Even when the concept of a thing is quite complete, I can still ask with reference to that object, whether it is possible only, or real also, and, if the latter, whether it is necessary? No new determinations of the object are thereby conceived, but it is only asked in what relation it (with all its determinations) stands to the understanding and its empirical employ-

[1] [Note M. 177]
[1] [Cf. M. 178 ff.]

ment, to the empirical faculty of judgment, and to reason, in its application to experience?

The principles of modality are therefore nothing but explanations of the concepts of possibility, reality, and necessity, in their empirical employment, confining all categories to an empirical employment only, and prohibiting their transcendental use. For if these categories are not to have a purely logical character, expressing the forms of thought analytically, but are to refer to things, their possibility, reality, or necessity, they must have reference to possible experience and its synthetical unity, in which alone objects of knowledge can be given.

[1.] The postulate of the possibility of things demands that the concept of these should agree with the formal conditions of experience in general. This, the objective form of experience in general, contains all synthesis which is required for a knowledge of objects. A concept is to be considered as empty, and as referring to no object, if the synthesis which it contains does not belong to experience, whether as borrowed from it (in which case it is called an empirical concept), or as a synthesis on which, as a condition *a priori,* all experience (in its form) depends, in which case it is a pure concept, but yet belonging to experience, because its object can only be found in it. For whence could the character of the possibility of an object, which can be conceived by a synthetical concept *a priori,* be derived, except from the synthesis which constitutes the form of all empirical knowledge of objects? It is no doubt a necessary logical condition, that such a concept must contain nothing contradictory, but this is by no means sufficient to establish the objective reality of a concept, that is, the possibility of such an object, as is conceived by a concept. . . . [M. 179-80] The objective reality of these concepts is only known when we see that they express *a priori* the relations of perceptions in every kind of experience; and this objective reality, that is, their transcendental truth, though independent of all experience, is nevertheless not independent of all relation to the form of experience in general, and to that synthetical unity in which alone objects can be known empirically. . . . [M. 180-1]

I here pass by everything the possibility of which can only be learned from its reality in experience, and I only mean to consider the possibility of things through concepts *a priori*. Of these (concepts) I persist in maintaining that they can never exist as such concepts by themselves alone, but only as formal and objective conditions of experience in general. . . . [M. 182] If we are able to know and determine the possibility of things without any previous experience, this is only with reference to those formal conditions under which anything may become an object in experience. This takes place entirely *a priori*, but nevertheless in constant reference to experience, and within its limits.

[2.] The postulate concerning our knowledge of the *reality* of things, requires *perception*, therefore sensation and consciousness of it, not indeed immediately of the object itself, the existence of which is to be known, but yet of a connection between it and some real perception, according to the analogies of experience which determine in general all real combinations in experience.[1]

In the *mere concept* of a thing no sign of its existence can be discovered. For though the concept be ever so perfect, so that nothing should be wanting in it to enable

[1] [The following note appears on M. 191] . . . While possibility is only the positing of a thing in reference to the understanding (in its empirical use), reality is, at the same time, a connection of it with perception.

us to conceive the thing with all its own determinations, existence has nothing to do with all this. It depends only on the question whether such a thing be given us, so that its perception may even precede its concept. A concept preceding experience implies its possibility only, while perception, which supplies the material of a concept, is the only characteristic of reality. It is possible, however, even before the perception of a thing, and therefore, in a certain sense, *a priori,* to know its existence, provided it hang together with some other perceptions, according to the principles of their empirical connection (analogies). For in that case the existence of a thing hangs together at least with our perceptions in a possible experience, and guided by our analogies we can, starting from our real experience, arrive at some other thing in the series of possible perceptions. Thus we know the existence of some magnetic matter pervading all bodies from the perception of the attracted iron filings, though our organs are so constituted as to render an immediate perception of that matter impossible. According to the laws of sensibility and the texture of our perceptions, we ought in our experience to arrive at an immediate empirical intuition of that magnetic matter, if only our senses were more acute, for their actual obtuseness does not concern the form of possible experience. Wherever, therefore, perception and its train can reach, according to empirical laws, there our knowledge also of the existence of things can reach. But if we do not begin with experience, or do not proceed according to the laws of the empirical connection of phenomena, we are only making a vain display, as if we could guess and discover the existence of anything.

An [1] important protest, however, against these rules

[1] [Cf. M. 778-81]

for proving existence mediately is brought forward by *Idealism,* and this is therefore the proper place for its refutation.

Refutation of Idealism

Idealism (I mean *material* idealism) is the theory which declares the existence of objects in space, without us, as either doubtful only and not demonstrable, or as false and impossible. The *former* is the *problematical* idealism of Descartes, who declares one empirical assertion only to be undoubted, namely, that of *I am;* the *latter* is the *dogmatical* idealism of Berkeley, who declares space and all things to which it belongs as an inseparable condition, as something impossible in itself, and, therefore, the things in space as mere imaginations. Dogmatic idealism is inevitable, if we look upon space as a property belonging to things by themselves, for in that case space and all of which it is a condition, would be a non-entity. The ground on which that idealism rests has been removed by us in the transcendental Æsthetic. Problematical idealism, which asserts nothing, but only pleads our inability of proving any existence except our own by means of immediate experience, is reasonable and in accordance with a sound philosophical mode of thought, which allows of no decisive judgment, before a sufficient proof has been found. The required proof will have to demonstrate that we may have not only an *imagination,* but also an *experience* of external things, and this it seems can hardly be effected in any other way except by proving that even our internal experience, which Descartes considers as undoubted, is possible only under the supposition of external experience.

Theorem

The simple, but empirically determined consciousness of my own existence, proves the existence of objects in space outside myself.

Proof

I am conscious of my own existence as determined in time, and all determination in time presupposes something *permanent* in the perception. That *permanent*, however, cannot be an intuition within me, because all the causes which determine my existence, so far as they can be found within me, are representations, and as such require themselves something permanent, different from them, in reference to which their change, and therefore my existence in time in which they change, may be determined. The perception of this permanent, therefore, is possible only through a thing *outside* me, and not through the mere *representation* of a thing outside me, and the determination of my existence in time is, consequently, possible only by the existence of real things, which I perceive outside me. Now, as the consciousness in time is necessarily connected with the consciousness of the possibility of that determination of time, it is also necessarily connected with the existence of things outside me, as the condition of the determination of time. In other words, the consciousness of my own existence is, at the same time, an immediate consciousness of the existence of other things.

NOTE 1.—It will have been perceived that in the foregoing proof the trick played by idealism has been turned against it, and with greater justice. Idealism assumed that the only immediate experience is the internal, and that from it we can no more than *infer* external things, though in an untrustworthy manner only, as always happens if from given effects we infer *definite* causes: it being quite possible that the cause of the representations, which are ascribed by us, it may be wrongly, to external things, may lie within ourselves. We, however, have proved that external experience is really immediate,[1] and that only by means of it, though not the consciousness of our own existence, yet its determination in time, that is, internal experience, becomes possible. No doubt this representation of *I am,* which expresses the consciousness that can accompany all thought, is that which immediately includes the existence of a subject: but it does not yet include a *knowledge* of it, and therefore no empirical knowledge, that is, experience. For that we require, besides the thought of something existing, intuition, also, and in this case internal intuition in respect to which, that is, to time, the subject must be determined. For that purpose external objects are absolutely necessary, so that internal experience itself is possible, mediately only, and through external experience.

Note 3.[2]—Because the existence of external objects is required for the possibility of a definite consciousness

[1] The *immediate* consciousness of the existence of external things is not simply assumed in the preceding thereorem, but proved, whether we can understand the possibility of this consciousness or not. The question with regard to that possibility would come to this, whether we have an internal sense only, and no external sense, but merely an external imagination. It is clear, however, that, even in order to imagine only something as external, that is, to represent it to the senses in intuition, we must have an external sense, and thus distinguish immediately the mere receptivity of an external intuition from that spontaneity which characterizes every act of imagination. For merely to imagine an external *sense* would really be to destroy the faculty of intuition, which is to be determined by the faculty of imagination.

[2] [For Note 2, see M. 780-1]

of ourselves, it does not follow that every intuitional representation of external things involves, at the same time, their existence; for such a representation may well be the mere effect of the faculty of imagination (in dreams as well as in madness); but it can be such an effect only through the reproduction of former external perceptions, which, as we have shown, is impossible without the reality of *external* objects. What we wanted to prove here was only that internal experience in general is possible only through external experience in general. Whether this or that supposed experience be purely imaginary, must be settled according to its own particular determinations, and through a comparison with the criteria of all real experience.[1]

[1] [The following note appears in the Preface to the Second Edition, M. 705-6]: The only thing which might be called an addition [to the Second Edition], though in the method of proof only, is the new refutation of *psychological idealism,* and the strict (and as I believe the only possible) proof of the objective reality of external phenomena. That idealism may be considered entirely innocent with respect to the essential aims of metaphysic (though it is not so in reality), yet it remains a scandal to philosophy, and to human reason in general, that we should have to accept the existence of things without us (from which we derive the whole material of knowledge for our own internal sense) on faith only, unable to meet with any satisfactory proof an opponent, who is pleased to doubt it. It will probably be urged against this proof that, after all, I am immediately conscious of that only which is within me, that is, of my *representation* of external things, and that consequently it must still remain uncertain whether there be outside me anything corresponding to it or not. But by internal *experience* I am conscious of *my existence in time* (consequently also, of its determinability in time); and this is more than to be conscious of my representation only, and yet identical with the *empirical consciousness of my existence,* which can be itself determined only by something connected with my existence, yet outside me. This consciousness of my existence in time is therefore connected as identical with the consciousness of relation to something *outside* me; so that it is experience, and not fiction, sense, and not imagination, which indissolubly connects the external with my internal sense. The external sense is by itself a relation

[3.] With[1] reference to the third postulate we find that it refers to the material necessity in existence, and not to the merely formal and logical necessity in the

of intuition to something real outside me; and its real, in contradistinction to a purely imaginary character, rests entirely on its being indissolubly connected with internal experience, as being the condition of its possibility. This is what happens here. If with the *intellectual consciousness* of my existence in the representation, *I am,* which accompanies all my judgments and all acts of my understanding, I could at the same time connect a determination of that existence of mine by means of *intellectual intuition,* then that determination would not require the consciousness of relation to something outside me. But although that intellectual consciousness comes first, the inner intuition, in which alone any existence can be determined, is sensuous and dependent on the condition of time; and that determination again, and therefore internal experience itself, depends on something permanent which is not within me, consequently on something outside me only, to which I must consider myself as standing in a certain relation. Hence the reality of the external sense is necessarily connected, in order to make experience possible at all, with the reality of the internal sense; that is, I am conscious, with the same certainty, that there are things outside me which have a reference to my sense, as that I exist myself in time. In order to ascertain to what given intuitions objects outside me really correspond (these intuitions belonging to the *external sense,* and not to the faculty of imagination), we must in each single case apply the rules according to which experience in general (even internal) is distinguished from imaginations, the proposition that there really is an external experience being always taken for granted. It may be well to add here the remark that the *representation of something permanent* in existence is not the same as a *permanent representation;* for this (the representation of something permanent in existence) can change and alternate, as all our representations, even those of matter, and may yet refer to something permanent, which must therefore be something external, and different from all my representations, the *existence* of which is necessarily involved in the *determination* of my own existence, and constitutes with it but one experience, which could never take place internally, unless (in part) it were external also. The *how* admits here of as little explanation as the permanent in time in general, the coexistence of which with the variable produces the concept of change.

[1] [Cf. M. 184]

connection of concepts. As it is impossible that the existence of the objects of the senses would ever be known entirely *a priori,* though it may be known to a certain extent *a priori,* namely, with reference to another already given existence, and as even in that case we can only arrive at such an existence as must somewhere be contained in the whole of the experience of which the given perception forms a part, it follows that the necessity of existence can never be known from concepts, but always from the connection only with what is actually perceived, according to general rules of experience. Now, there is no existence that can be known as necessary under the condition of other given phenomena, except the existence of effects from given causes, according to the laws of causality. It is not therefore the existence of things (substances), but the existence of their state, of which alone we can know the necessity, and this from other states only, which are given in perception, and according to the empirical laws of causality. Hence it follows that the criterion of necessity can only be found in the law of possible experience, viz. that everything that happens is determined *a priori* by its cause in phenomena. We therefore know in nature the necessity of those effects only of which the causes are given, and the character of necessity in existence never goes beyond the field of possible experience, and even there it does not apply to the existence of things, as substances, because such substances can never be looked upon as empirical effects or as something that happens and arises. Necessity, therefore, affects only the relations of phenomena according to the dynamical law of causality, and the possibility, dependent upon it, of concluding *a priori* from a given existence (of a cause) to another existence (that of an effect). Thus the principle that everything which happens is hypothetically necessary, subjects all the changes in the world to a law, that is, to a rule of necessary existence, without which there would not even be such a thing as nature. Hence the proposition that nothing happens by blind chance (*in mundo non datur casus*) is an *a priori* law of nature, and so is likewise the other, that no necessity in nature is a blind, but always a conditional and therefore an intelligible, necessity (*non datur fatum*). Both these are laws by which the mere play of changes is rendered subject to a *nature of things* (as phenomena), or what is the same, to that unity of the understanding in which alone they can belong to experience, as the synthetical unity of phenomena. . . . [M. 186-9]

Absolute possibility (which has no regard for the formal conditions of experience) is really no concept of the understanding, and can never be used empirically, but belongs to reason alone, which goes beyond all possible empirical use of the understanding. . . . [M. 189-91, 782-6]

CHAPTER III

ON THE GROUND OF DISTINCTION OF ALL SUBJECTS INTO PHENOMENA AND NOUMENA

WE [1] HAVE now not only traversed the whole domain of the pure understanding, and carefully examined each part of it, but we have also measured its extent, and assigned to everything in it its proper place. This domain, however, is an island and enclosed by nature itself within limits that can never be changed. It is the country of truth (a very attractive name), but surrounded by a wide and stormy ocean, the true home of

[1] [Cf. M. 192 ff.]

illusion, where many a fog bank and ice that soon melts away tempt us to believe in new lands, while constantly deceiving the adventurous mariner with vain hopes, and involving him in adventures which he can never leave, and yet can never bring to an end. Before we venture ourselves on this sea, in order to explore it on every side, and to find out whether anything is to be hoped for there, it will be useful to glance once more at the map of that country which we are about to leave, and to ask ourselves, first, whether we might not be content with what it contains, nay, whether we must not be content with it, supposing that there is no solid ground anywhere else on which we could settle; secondly, by what title we possess even that domain, and may consider ourselves safe against all hostile claims. Although we have sufficiently answered these questions in the course of the analytic, a summary recapitulation of their solutions may help to strengthen our conviction, by uniting all arguments in one point.

We have seen that the understanding possesses everything which it draws from itself, without borrowing from experience, for no other purpose but for experience. The principles of the pure understanding, whether constitutive *a priori* (as the mathematical) or simply relative (as the dynamical), contain nothing but, as it were, the pure schema of possible experience; for that experience derives its unity from that synthetical unity alone which the understanding originally and spontaneously imparts to the synthesis of imagination, with reference to apperception, and to which all phenomena, as data of a possible knowledge, must conform *a priori*. But although these rules of the understanding are not only true *a priori*, but the very source of all truth, that is, of the agreement of our knowledge with objects, because containing the conditions of the possibility of experience, as the complete sphere of all knowledge in which objects can be given to us, nevertheless we do not seem to be content with hearing only what is true, but want to know a great deal more. If therefore this critical investigation does not teach us any more than what, even without such subtle researches, we should have practised ourselves in the purely empirical use of the understanding, it would seem as if the advantages derived from it were hardly worth the labour. One might reply that nothing would be more prejudicial to the enlargement of our knowledge than that curiosity which, before entering upon any researches, wishes to know beforehand the advantages likely to accrue from them, though quite unable as yet to form the least conception of such advantages, even though they were placed before our eyes. There is, however, one advantage in this transcendental investigation which can be rendered intelligible, nay, even attractive to the most troublesome and reluctant apprentice, namely this, that the understanding confined to its empirical use only and unconcerned with regard to the sources of its own knowledge, may no doubt fare very well in other respects, but can never determine for itself the limits of its own use and know what is inside or outside its own sphere. It is for that purpose that such profound investigations are required as we have just instituted. If the understanding cannot decide whether certain questions lie within its own horizon or not, it can never feel certain with regard to its claims and possessions, but must be prepared for many humiliating corrections, when constantly transgressing, as it certainly will, the limits of its own domain, and losing itself in follies and fancies.

That the understanding cannot make any but an empirical, and never a transcendental, use of all its principles *a priori*, nay, of all its concepts, is a proposition which, if thoroughly understood, leads indeed to most important consequences. What we call the transcendental use of a concept in any proposition is its being referred to things in general and to things by themselves, while its empirical use refers to phenomena only, that is, to objects of a possible experience. That the latter use alone is admissible will be clear from the following considerations. What is required for every concept is, first, the logical form of a concept (of thought) in general; and, secondly, the possibility of an object to which it refers. Without the latter, it has no sense, and is entirely empty, though it may still contain the logical function by which a concept can be formed out of any data. The only way in which an object can be given to a concept is in intuition, and though a pure intuition is possible *a priori* and before the object, yet even that pure intuition can receive its object, and with it its objective validity, by an empirical intuition only, of which it is itself nothing but the form. All concepts, therefore, and with them all principles, though they may be possible *a priori,* refer nevertheless to empirical intuitions, that is, to data of a possible experience. Without this, they can claim no objective validity, but are a mere play, whether of the imagination or of the understanding with their respective representations. Let us take the concepts of mathematics as an example, and, first, with regard to pure intuitions. Although such principles as 'space has three dimensions,' 'between two points there can be only one straight line,' as well as the representation of the object with which that science is occupied, may be produced in the mind *a priori,* they would have no meaning, if we were not able at all times to show their meaning as applied to phenomena (empirical objects). It is for this reason that an abstract concept is required to be made *sensuous,* that is, that its corresponding object is required to be shown in intuition, because, without this, the concept (as people say) is without *sense*, that is, without meaning. Mathematics fulfil this requirement by the construction of the figure, which is a phenomenon present to the senses (although constructed *a priori*). In the same science the concept of quantity finds its support and sense in number; and this in turn in the fingers, the beads of the abacus, or in strokes and points which can be presented to the eyes. The concept itself was produced *a priori*, together with all the synthetical principles or formulas which can be derived from such concepts; but their use and their relation to objects can nowhere be found except in experience, of which those concepts contain *a priori* the (formal) possibility only.

That this is the case with all categories and with all the principles drawn from them, becomes evident from the fact that we could not define any one of them (really, that is, make conceivable the possibility of their object), without at once having recourse to the conditions of sensibility or the form of phenomena, to which, as their only possible objects, these categories must necessarily be restricted, it being impossible, if we take away these conditions, to assign to them any meaning, that is, any relation to an object, or to make it intelligible to ourselves by an example what kind of thing could be intended by such concepts. . . . [M. 196-201]

In [1] one word, none of these concepts admit of being *authenticated*, nor can their real possibility be proved, if all sensuous intuition (the only one which we possess) is removed, and there remains in that case a *logical* possibility only, that is, that a concept (a thought) is possible. This, however, does not concern us here, but

[1] [Cf. M. 787]

only whether the concept refers to an object and does therefore signify anything.

From [1] this it follows incontestably, that the pure concepts of the understanding never admit of a transcendental, but only of an empirical use, and that the principles of the pure understanding can only be referred, as general conditions of a possible experience, to objects of the senses, never to things by themselves (without regard to the manner in which we have to look at them).

Transcendental Analytic has therefore yielded us this important result, that the understanding *a priori* can never do more than anticipate the form of a possible experience; and as nothing can be an object of experience except the phenomenon, it follows that the understanding can never go beyond the limits of sensibility, within which alore objects are given to us. Its principles are principles for the exhibition of phenomena only; and the proud name of Ontology, which presumes to supply in a systematic form different kinds of synthetical knowledge *a priori* of things by themselves (for instance the principle of causality), must be replaced by the more modest name of a mere Analytic of the pure understanding. . . . [M. 202]

It might therefore be advisable to express ourselves in the following way: the pure categories, without the formal conditions of sensibility, have a transcendental character only, but do not admit of any transcendental use, because such use in itself is impossible, as the categories are deprived of all the conditions of being used in judgments, that is, of the formal conditions of the subsumption of any possible object under these concepts. As therefore (as pure categories) they are not meant to be used empirically, and cannot be used tran-

[1] [Cf. M. 201 ff.]

scendentally, they admit, if separated from sensibility, of no use at all; that is, they cannot be applied to any possible object, and are nothing but the pure form of the use of the understanding with reference to objects in general, and of thought, without ever enabling us to think or determine any object by their means alone. . . . [M. 203-7]

We [1] are met here by an illusion which is difficult to avoid. The categories do not depend in their origin on sensibility, like the forms of *intuition,* space, and time, and seem, therefore, to admit of an application extending beyond the objects of the senses. But, on the other side, they are nothing but *forms of thought,* containing the logical faculty only of comprehending *a priori* in one consciousness the manifold that is given in intuition, and they would therefore, if we take away the only intuition which is possible to us, have still less significance than those pure sensuous forms by which at least an object is given, while a peculiar mode of our understanding of connecting the manifold (unless that intuition, in which the manifold alone can be given, is added), signifies nothing at all. . . . [M. 788]

At the very outset, however, we meet with an ambiguity which may cause great misapprehension. The understanding, by calling an object in one aspect a phenomenon only, makes to itself, apart from that aspect, another representation of *an object by itself,* and imagines itself able to form *concepts* of such an object. As, then, the understanding yields no other concepts but the categories, it supposes that the object in the latter aspect can be thought at least by those pure concepts of the understanding, and is thus induced to take the entirely indefinite concept of a being of the understanding, as of a something in general outside our sensibility, as

[1] [Cf. M. 788 ff.]

a *definite* concept of a being which we might know to a certain extent through the understanding.

If by noumenon we mean a thing so far as it is *not an object of our sensuous intuition,* and make abstraction of our mode of intuition, it may be called a noumenon in a *negative* sense. If, however, we mean by it an *object* of a *non-sensuous intuition,* we admit thereby a peculiar mode of intuition, namely, the intellectual, which, however, is not our own, nor one of which we can understand even the possibility. This would be the noumenon in a *positive* sense.

The doctrine of sensibility is at the same time the doctrine of noumena in their negative sense; that is, of things which the understanding must think without reference to our mode of intuition, and therefore, not as phenomena only, but as things by themselves, but to which, after it has thus separated them, the understanding knows that it must not, in this new aspect, apply its categories; because these categories have significance only with reference to the unity of intuitions in space and time, and can therefore *a priori* determine that unity, on account of the mere ideality of space and time only, by means of general connecting concepts. Where that unity in time cannot be found, i.e. in the noumenon, the whole use, nay, the whole significance of categories comes to an end: because even the possibility of things that should correspond to the categories, would be unintelligible. On this point I may refer the reader to what I have said at the very beginning of the general note to the previous chapter. The possibility of a thing can never be proved from the fact that its concept is not self-contradictory, but only by being authenticated by an intuition corresponding to it. If, therefore, we at tempted to apply the categories to objects which are not considered as phenomena, we should have to admit an intuition other than the sensuous, and thus the object would become a noumenon in a *positive sense*. As, however, such an intuition, namely, an intellectual one, is entirely beyond our faculty of knowledge, the use of the categories also can never reach beyond the limits of the objects of experience. Beings of the understanding correspond no doubt to beings of the senses, and there may be beings of the understanding to which our faculty of sensuous intuition has no relation at all; but our concepts of the understanding, being forms of thought for our sensuous intuition only, do not reach so far, and what is called by us a noumenon must be understood as such in a *negative sense* only.

If [1] all thought (by means of categories) is taken away from empirical knowledge, no knowledge of any object remains, because nothing can be thought by mere intuition, and the mere fact that there is within me an affection of my sensibility, establishes in no way any relation of such a representation to any object. If, on the contrary, all intuition is taken away, there always remains the form of thought, that is, the mode of determining an object for the manifold of a possible intuition. In this sense the categories may be said to extend further than sensuous intuition, because they can think objects in general without any regard to the special mode of sensibility in which they may be given; but they do not thus prove a larger sphere of objects, because we cannot admit that such objects can be given, without admitting the possibility of some other but sensuous intuition, for which we have no right whatever.

I call a concept problematic, if it is not self-contradictory, and if, as limiting other concepts, it is connected with other kinds of knowledge, while its objective reality cannot be known in any way. Now the con-

[1] [Cf. M. 207]

cept of a noumenon, that is of a thing which can never be thought as an object of the senses, but only as a thing by itself (by the pure understanding), is not self-contradictory, because we cannot maintain that sensibility is the only form of intuition. That concept is also necessary, to prevent sensuous intuition from extending to things by themselves; that is, in order to limit the objective validity of sensuous knowledge (for all the rest to which sensuous intuition does not extend is called noumenon, for the very purpose of showing that sensuous knowledge cannot extend its domain over everything that can be thought by the understanding). But, after all, we cannot understand the possibility of such noumena, and whatever lies beyond the sphere of phenomena is (to us) empty; that is, we have an understanding which *problematically* extends beyond that sphere, but no intuition, nay not even the conception of a possible intuition, by which, outside the field of sensibility, objects could be given to us, and our understanding could extend beyond that sensibility in its assertory use. The concept of a noumenon is therefore merely *limitative,* and intended to keep the claims of sensibility within proper bounds, therefore of negative use only. But it is not a mere arbitrary fiction, but closely connected with the limitation of sensibility, though incapable of adding anything positive to the sphere of the senses.

A real division of objects into phenomena and noumena, and of the world into a sensible and intelligible world (in a positive sense), is therefore quite inadmissible, although concepts may very well be divided into sensuous and intellectual. For no objects can be assigned to these intellectual concepts, nor can they be represented as objectively valid. If we drop the senses, how are we to make it conceivable that our categories (which would be the only remaining concepts for noumena) have any meaning at all, considering that, in order to refer them to any object, something more must be given than the mere unity of thought, namely, a possible intuition, to which the categories could be applied? With all this the concept of a noumenon, if taken as problematical only, remains not only admissible, but as a concept to limit the sphere of sensibility, indispensable. In this case, however, it is not a particular *intelligible object* for *our* understanding, but an understanding to which it could belong is itself a problem, if we ask how it could know an object, not discursively by means of categories, but intuitively, and yet in a non-sensuous intuition,—a process of which we could not understand even the bare possibility. Our understanding thus acquires a kind of negative extension, that is, it does not become itself limited by sensibility, but, on the contrary, limits it, by calling things by themselves (not considered as phenomena) noumena. In doing this, it immediately proceeds to prescribe limits to itself, by admitting that it cannot know these noumena by means of the categories, but can only think of them under the name of something unknown. . . . [M. 209-37, 791.]

TRANSCENDENTAL DIALECTIC

INTRODUCTION

1. Of Transcendental Appearance (Illusion) . . . [M. 238-40.]

It[1] is not at present our business to treat of empirical, for instance, optical appearance or illusion, which occurs in the empirical use of the otherwise correct rules

[1] [Cf. M. 240 ff.]

of the understanding, and by which, owing to the influence of imagination, the faculty of judgment is misled. We have to deal here with nothing but the *transcendental illusion,* which touches principles never even intended to be applied to experience, which might give us a test of their correctness,—an illusion which, in spite of all the warnings of criticism, tempts us far beyond the empirical use of the categories, and deludes us with the mere dream of an extension of the pure understanding. All principles the application of which is entirely confined within the limits of possible experience, we shall call *immanent;* those, on the contrary, which tend to transgress those limits, *transcendent.* I do not mean by this the transcendental use or abuse of the categories, which is a mere fault of the faculty of the judgment, not being as yet sufficiently subdued by criticism nor sufficiently attentive to the limits of the sphere within which alone the pure understanding has full play, but real principles which call upon us to break down all those barriers, and to claim a perfectly new territory, which nowhere recognises any demarcation at all. Here *transcendental* and *transcendent* do not mean the same thing. The principles of the pure understanding, which we explained before, are meant to be only of empirical, and not of transcendental application, that is, they cannot transcend the limits of experience. A principle, on the contrary, which removes these landmarks, nay, insists on our transcending them, is called *transcendent.* If our critique succeeds in laying bare the illusion of those pretended principles, the other principles of a purely empirical use may, in opposition to the former, be called *immanent.*

Logical illusion, which consists in a mere imitation of the forms of reason (the illusion of sophistic syllogisms), arises entirely from want of attention to logical rules. It disappears at once, when our attention is roused. Transcendental illusion, on the contrary, does not disappear, although it has been shown up, and its worthlessness rendered clear by means of transcendental criticism, as, for instance, the illusion inherent in the proposition that the world must have a beginning in time. The cause of this is that there exists in our reason (considered subjectively as a faculty of human knowledge) principles and maxims of its use, which have the appearance of objective principles, and lead us to mistake the subjective necessity of a certain connection of our concepts in favour of the understanding for an objective necessity in the determination of things by themselves. This illusion is as impossible to avoid as it is to prevent the sea from appearing to us higher at a distance than on the shore, because we see it by higher rays of light; or to prevent the moon from appearing, even to an astronomer, larger at its rising, although he is not deceived by that illusion.

Transcendental Dialectic must, therefore, be content to lay bare the illusion of transcendental judgments and guard against its deceptions—but it will never succeed in removing the transcendental illusion (like the logical), and putting an end to it altogether. For we have here to deal with a natural and inevitable illusion, which itself rests on subjective principles, representing them to us as objective, while logical Dialectic, in removing sophisms, has to deal merely with a mistake in applying the principles, or with an artificial illusion produced by an imitation of them. There exists, therefore, a natural and inevitable Dialectic of pure reason, not one in which a mere bungler might get entangled from want of knowledge, or which a sophist might artificially devise to confuse rational people, but one that is inherent in, and inseparable from human reason, and which, even after its illusion has been exposed, will never cease to fascinate our reason, and to precipitate it into momentary errors, such as require to be removed again and again.

2. Of Pure Reason, as the Seat of Transcendental Illusion

A. *Of Reason in General*

. . . [M. 242-5]

If [1] the understanding is a faculty for producing unity among phenomena, according to rules, reason is the faculty for producing unity among the rules of the understanding, according to principles. Reason therefore never looks directly to experience, or to any object, but to the understanding, in order to impart *a priori* through concepts to its manifold kinds of knowledge a unity that may be called the unity of reason, and is very different from the unity which can be produced by the understanding.

This is a general definition of the faculty of reason, so far as it was possible to make it intelligible without the help of illustrations, which are to be given hereafter.

C.[2] *Of the Pure Use of Reason*

The question to which we have at present to give an answer, though a preliminary one only, is this, whether reason can be isolated and thus constitute by itself an independent source of concepts and judgments, which spring from it alone, and through which it has reference to objects, or whether it is only a subordinate faculty

[1] [Cf. M. 245]
[2] [Cf. M. 247. For Sec. B, see M. 246-7]

for imparting a certain form to any given knowledge, namely, a logical form, a faculty whereby the cognitions of the understanding are arranged among themselves only, and lower rules placed under higher ones (the condition of the latter comprehending in its sphere the condition of the former) so far as all this can be done by their comparison. Variety of rules with unity of principles is a requirement of reason for the purpose of bringing the understanding into perfect agreement with itself, just as the understanding brings the variety of intuition under concepts, and thus imparts to intuition a connected form. Such a principle however prescribes no law to the objects themselves, nor does it contain the ground on which the possibility of knowing and determining objects depends. It is merely a subjective law of economy, applied to the stores of our understanding; having for its purpose, by means of a comparison of concepts, to reduce the general use of them to the smallest possible number, but without giving us a right to demand of the objects themselves such a uniformity as might conduce to the comfort and the extension of our understanding, or to ascribe to that maxim any objective validity. In one word, the question is, whether reason in itself, that is pure reason, contains synthetical principles and rules *a priori,* and what those principles are? . . . [M. 248-9]

Reason, in its logical employment, looks for the general condition of its judgment (the conclusion), and the syllogism produced by reason is itself nothing but a judgment by means of bringing its condition under a general rule (the major). But as this rule is again liable to the same experiment, reason having to seek, as long as possible, the condition of a condition (by means of a pro-syllogism), it is easy to see that it is the peculiar principle of reason (in its logical use) to find for every conditioned knowledge of the understanding the unconditioned, whereby the unity of that knowledge may be completed.

This logical maxim, however, cannot become a principle of *pure reason,* unless we admit that, whenever the condition is given, the whole series of conditions, subordinated to one another, a series, which consequently is itself unconditioned, is likewise given (that is, is contained in the object and its connection). . . . [M. 250]

The principles resulting from this highest principle of pure reason will however be *transcendent,* with regard to all phenomena; that is to say, it will be impossible ever to make any adequate empirical use of such a principle. It will thus be completely different from all principles of the understanding, the use of which is entirely *immanent* and directed to the possibility of experience only. The task that is now before us in the transcendental Dialectic which has to be developed from sources deeply hidden in the human reason, is this: to discover the correctness or otherwise the falsehood of the principle that the series of conditions (in the synthesis of phenomena, or of objective thought in general) extends to the unconditioned, and what consequences result therefrom with regard to the empirical use of the understanding:—to find out whether there is really such an objectively valid principle of reason, and not only, in place of it, a logical rule which requires us, by ascending to ever higher conditions, to approach their completeness, and thus to bring the highest unity of reason, which is possible to us, into our knowledge: to find out, I say, whether, by some misconception, a mere tendency of reason has not been mistaken for a transcendental principle of pure reason, postulating, without sufficient reflection, absolute completeness in the series of conditions in the objects themselves. . . . [M. 251]

Book I. OF THE CONCEPTS OF PURE REASON . . . [M. 252]

THE [1] very name, however, of a *concept of reason* gives a kind of intimation that it is not intended to be limited to experience, because it refers to a kind of knowledge of which every empirical knowledge is a part only (it may be, the whole of possible experience or of its empirical synthesis): and to which all real experience belongs, though it can never fully attain to it. Concepts of reason serve for conceiving or comprehending; concepts of the understanding for understanding (perceptions). If they contain the unconditioned, they refer to something to which all experience may belong, but which itself can never become an object of experience;—something to which reason in its conclusions from experience leads up, and by which it estimates and measures the degree of its own empirical use, but which never forms part of empirical synthesis. If such concepts possess, notwithstanding, objective validity, they may be called *conceptus ratiocinati* (concepts legitimately formed); if they have only been surreptitiously obtained, by a kind of illusory conclusion, they may be called *conceptus ratiocinantes* (sophistical concepts). But as this subject can only be fully treated in the chapter on the dialectical conclusions of pure reason, we shall say no more of it now, but shall only, as we gave the name of categories to the pure concepts of the understanding, give a new name to the concepts of pure reason, and call them *transcendental ideas,* a name that has now to be explained and justified.

[1] [Cf. M. 252 ff.]

Section II.[1] *Of Transcendental Ideas* . . . [M. 261-5]

It[2] is . . . the absolute totality in the synthesis of conditions at which the transcendental concept of reason aims, nor does it rest satisfied till it has reached that which is unconditioned absolutely and in every respect. Pure reason leaves everything to the understanding, which has primarily to do with the objects of intuition, or rather their synthesis in imagination. It is only the absolute totality in the use of the concepts of the understanding, which reason reserves for itself, while trying to carry the synthetical unity, which is realised in the category, to the absolutely unconditioned. We might therefore call the latter the unity of the phenomena in reason, the former, which is expressed by the category, the unity in the understanding. Hence reason is only concerned with the use of the understanding, not so far as it contains the basis of possible experience (for the absolute totality of conditions is not a concept that can be used in experience, because no experience is unconditioned), but in order to impart to it a direction towards a certain unity of which the understanding knows nothing, and which is meant to comprehend all acts of the understanding, with regard to any object, into an absolute whole. On this account the objective use of the pure concepts of reason must always be *transcendent*: while that of the pure concepts of the understanding must always be *immanent,* being by its very nature restricted to possible experience.

By idea I understand the necessary concept of reason, to which the senses can supply no corresponding

[1] [For Section I, Cf. M. 254-61]
[2] [Cf. M. 265]

object. The concepts of reason, therefore, of which we have been speaking, are *transcendental ideas.* They are concepts of pure reason, so far as they regard all empirical knowledge as determined by an absolute totality of conditions. They are not mere fancies, but supplied to us by the very nature of reason, and referring by necessity to the whole use of the understanding. They are, lastly, transcendent, as overstepping the limits of all experience which can never supply an object adequate to the transcendental idea. If we speak of an idea, we say a great deal with respect to the object (as the object of the pure understanding) but very little with respect to the subject, that is, with respect to its reality under empirical conditions, because an idea, being the concept of a maximum, can never be adequately given *in concreto*. As the latter is really the whole aim in the merely speculative use of reason, and as the mere approaching a concept, which in reality can never be reached, is the same as if the concept were missed altogether, people, when speaking of such a concept, are wont to say, it is an idea only. Thus one might say, that the absolute whole of all phenomena is an idea only, for as we can never form a representation of such a whole, it remains a problem without a solution. . . . [M. 266-7]

Although we must say that all transcendental concepts of reason are ideas only, they are not therefore to be considered as superfluous and useless. For although we cannot by them determine any object, they may nevertheless, even unobserved, supply the understanding with a canon or rule of its extended and consistent use, by which, though no object can be better known than it is according to its concepts, yet the understanding may be better guided onwards in its knowledge. . . . [M. 267-70]

SECTION III. *System of Transcendental Ideas* . . . [M. 270-1]

All [1] pure concepts in general aim at a synthetical unity of representations, while concepts of pure reason (transcendental ideas) aim at unconditioned synthetical unity of all conditions. All transcendental ideas therefore can be arranged in three classes: the *first* containing the absolute (unconditioned) *unity of the thinking subject;* the *second* the absolute *unity of the series of conditions of phenomena;* the *third* the absolute *unity of the condition of all objects of thought in general.*

The thinking subject is the object-matter of *psychology,* the system of all phenomena (the world) the object-matter of *cosmology,* and the being which contains the highest condition of the possibility of all that can be thought (the Being of all beings), the object-matter of *theology.* Thus it is pure reason which supplies the idea of a transcendental science of the soul (*psychologia rationalis*), of a transcendental science of the world (*cosmologia rationalis*), and, lastly, of a transcendental science of God (*theologia transcendentalis*). Even the mere plan of any one of these three sciences does not come from the understanding, even if connected with the highest logical use of reason, that is, with all possible conclusions, leading from one of its objects (phenomenon) to all others, and on to the most remote parts of any possible empirical synthesis,—but is altogether a pure and genuine product or rather problem of pure reason. . . . [M. 272-4]

Metaphysic [2] has for the real object of its investigation three ideas only, *God, Freedom,* and *Immortality;*

[1] [Cf. M. 271]
[2] [Cf. M. 792]

the second concept connected with the first leading by necessity to the third as conclusion. Everything else treated by that science is a means only in order to establish those ideas and their reality. Metaphysic does not require these ideas for the sake of natural science; but in order to go beyond nature. A right insight into them would make *theology, morality,* and, by the union of both, *religion* also, therefore the highest objects of our existence, dependent on the speculative faculty of reason only, and on nothing else. In a systematical arrangement of those ideas the above order, being *synthetical,* would be the most appropriate; but in their elaboration, which must necessarily come first, the *analytical* or inverse order is more practical, enabling us, by starting from what is given us by experience, namely, the *study of the soul* (psychology), and proceeding thence to the *study of the world* (cosmology), and lastly, to a *knowledge of God* (theology), to carry out the whole of our great plan in its entirety.

Book II. OF THE DIALECTICAL CONCLUSIONS OF PURE REASON

. . . [M. 275-7]

CHAPTER I

OF THE PARALOGISMS OF PURE REASON [1]

THE [2] logical paralogism consists in the formal faultiness of a conclusion, without any reference to its contents. But a transcendental paralogism arises from a transcendental cause, which drives us to a formally false conclusion. Such a paralogism, therefore, depends

[1] [Selections for this Chapter have been made from both 1ST and 2ND Editions, as indicated.]

[2] [Cf. M. 278 ff.]

most likely on the very nature of human reason, and produces an illusion which is inevitable, though not insoluble.

We now come to a concept which was not inserted in our general list of transcendental concepts, and yet must be reckoned with them, without however changing that table in the least, or proving it to be deficient. This is the concept, or, if the term is preferred, the judgment, *I think.* It is easily seen, however, that this concept is the vehicle of all concepts in general, therefore of transcendental concepts also, being always comprehended among them, and being itself transcendental also, though without any claim to a special title, inasmuch as it serves only to introduce all thought, as belonging to consciousness. However free that concept may be from all that is empirical (impressions of the senses), it serves nevertheless to distinguish two objects within the nature of our faculty of representation. *I,* as thinking, am an object of the internal sense, and am called soul. That which is an object of the external senses is called body. The term *I,* as a thinking being, signifies the object of psychology, which may be called the rational science of the soul, supposing that we want to know nothing about the soul except what, independent of all experience (which determines the *I* more especially and *in concreto*), can be deduced from the concept of *I,* so far as it is present in every act of thought.

Now the rational science of the soul is really such an undertaking; for if the smallest empirical element of my thought or any particular perception of my internal state were mixed up with the sources from which that science derives its materials, it would be an empirical, and no longer a purely rational science of the soul. There is therefore a pretended science, founded on the single proposition of *I think,* and the soundness or unsoundness of which may well be examined in this place, according to the principles of transcendental philosophy. It should not be objected that even in that proposition, which expresses the perception of oneself, I have an internal experience, and that therefore the rational science of the soul, which is founded on it, can never be quite pure, but rests, to a certain extent, on an empirical principle. For this inner perception is nothing more than the mere apperception, *I think,* without which even all transcendental concepts would be impossible, in which we really say, I think the substance, I think the cause, etc. This internal experience in general and its possibility, or perception in general and its relation to other perceptions, there being no special distinction or empirical determination of it, cannot be regarded as empirical knowledge, but must be regarded as knowledge of the empirical in general, and falls therefore under the investigation of the possibility of all experience, which investigation is certainly transcendental. The smallest object of perception (even pleasure and pain), if added to the general representation of self-consciousness, would at once change rational into empirical psychology.

I think is, therefore, the only text of rational psychology, out of which it must evolve all its wisdom. It is easily seen that this thought, if it is to be applied to any object (my self), cannot contain any but transcendental predicates, because the smallest empirical predicate would spoil the rational purity of the science, and its independence of all experience.

We shall therefore follow the thread of the categories, with this difference, however, that as here the first thing which is given is a thing, the I, a thinking being, we must begin with the category of substance, by which a thing in itself is represented, and then proceed backwards, though without changing the respective order of the categories, as given before in our table. The topic of the rational science of the soul, from which has to be derived whatever else that science may contain, is therefore the following.

I

The Soul is *substance.*

II

As regards its quality, *simple.*

III

As regards the different times in which it exists, numerically identical, that is *unity* (not plurality).

IV

It is in relation to *possible* objects in space.[1]

All concepts of pure psychology arise from these elements, simply by way of combination, and without the admixture of any other principle. This substance, taken simply as the object of the internal sense, gives us the concept of *immateriality;* and as simple substance, that of *incorruptibility;* its identity, as that of an intellectual substance, gives us *personality;* and all these three together, *spirituality;* its relation to objects in space gives us the concept of *commercium* (intercourse) with *bodies;* the pure psychology thus representing the thinking substance as the principle of life in matter, that is, as soul (*anima*), and as the ground of *animality;* which again, as restricted by spirituality, gives us the concept of *immortality.*

To these concepts refer four paralogisms of a transcendental psychology, which is falsely supposed to be

[1] [Note on M. 281]

a science of pure reason, concerning the nature of our thinking being. We can, however, use as the foundation of such a science nothing but the single, and itself perfectly empty, representation of the *I*, of which we cannot even say that it is a concept, but merely a consciousness that accompanies all concepts. By this *I*, or *he*, or *it* (the thing), which thinks, nothing is represented beyond a transcendental subject of thoughts=x, which is known only through the thoughts that are its predicates, and of which, apart from them, we can never have the slightest concept, so that we are really turning round it in a perpetual circle, having already to use its representation, before we can form any judgment about it. And this inconvenience is really inevitable, because consciousness in itself is not so much a representation, distinguishing a particular object, but really a form of representation in general, in so far as it is to be called knowledge, of which alone I can say that I think something by it. . . . [M. 282-3]

The proposition *I think* is used in this case, however, as problematical only; not so far as it may contain the perception of an existence (the Cartesian, *cogito, ergo sum*), but with regard to its mere possibility, in order to see what properties may be deduced from such a simple proposition with regard to its subject, whether such subject exists or not . . . [M. 283-4]

. . . [M. 793] I[1] do not know any object by merely thinking, but only by determining a given intuition with respect to that unity of consciousness in which all thought consists; therefore, I do not know myself by being conscious of myself, as thinking, but only if I am conscious of the intuition of myself as determined with respect to the function of thought. All modes of self-

[1] [Cf. M. 793]

consciousness in thought are therefore by themselves not yet concepts of understanding of objects (categories), but mere logical functions, which present no object to our thought to be known, and therefore do not present myself either as an object. It is not a consciousness of the *determining,* but only that of the *determinable* self, that is, of my internal intuition (so far as the manifold in it can be connected in accordance with the general condition of the unity of apperception in thought) which forms the object.

The First Paralogism of Substantiality

That [1] the representation of which is the absolute subject of our judgments, and cannot be used therefore as the determination of any other thing, is the *substance.*

I, as a thinking being, am the absolute subject of all my possible judgments, and this representation of myself can never be used as the predicate of any other thing.

Therefore I, as a thinking being (Soul), am *Substance.*

Criticism of the First Paralogism of Transcendental Psychology

In [2] all judgments I am always the *determining subject* only of the relation which constitutes the judgment. That I, who think, can be considered in thinking as *subject* only, and as something not simply inherent in the thinking, as predicate, is an apodictical and even *identical* proposition; but it does not mean that, as an

[1] [Cf. M. 284]
[2] [Cf. M. 793-4]

object, I am a *self-dependent being* or a *substance.* The latter would be saying a great deal, and requires for its support *data* which are not found in the thinking, perhaps (so far as I consider only the thinking subject as such) more than I shall ever find in it.

. . . [M. 284-5] Hence [1] it follows that in the first syllogism of transcendental psychology reason imposes upon us an apparent knowledge only, by representing the constant logical subject of thought as the knowledge of the real subject in which that knowledge inheres. Of that subject, however, we have not and cannot have the slightest knowledge, because consciousness is that which alone changes representations into thoughts, and in which therefore, as the transcendental subject, all our perceptions must be found. Beside this logical meaning of the I, we have no knowledge of the subject in itself, which forms the substratum and foundation of it and of all our thoughts. In spite of this, the proposition that the soul is a substance may well be allowed to stand, if only we see that this concept cannot help us on in the least or teach us any of the ordinary conclusions of rationalising psychology, as, for instance, the everlasting continuance of the soul amid all changes and even in death, and that it therefore signifies a substance in idea only, and not in reality.

The Second Paralogism of Simplicity

Everything, the action of which can never be considered as the concurrence of several acting things, is simple.

Now the Soul, or the thinking I, is such a thing:—

Therefore, etc.

[1] [Cf. M. 285-6]

Criticism of the Second Paralogism of Transcendental Psychology

That [1] the *Ego* of apperception, and therefore the *Ego* in every act of thought, is a *singular* which cannot be dissolved into a plurality of subjects, and that it therefore signifies a logically simple subject, follows the very concept of thinking, and is consequently an analytical proposition. But this does not mean that a thinking *Ego* is a simple *substance,* which would indeed be a synthetical proposition. The concept of substance always relates to intuitions which, with me, cannot be other but sensuous, and which therefore lie completely outside the field of the understanding and its thinking, which alone is intended here, when we say that the *Ego,* in thinking, is simple. It would indeed be strange, if what elsewhere requires so great an effort, namely, to distinguish in what is given by intuition what is substance, and still more, whether that substance can be simple (as in the case of the component parts of matter), should in our case be given to us so readily in what is really the poorest of all representations, and, as it were, by an act of revelation.

. . . [M. 286-9.] Thus [2] we see that the famous psychological argument is founded merely on the indivisible unity of a representation, which only determines the verb with reference to a person; and it is clear that the subject of inherence is designated transcendentally only by the I, which accompanies the thought, without our perceiving the smallest quality of it, in fact, without our knowing anything about it. It signifies a something in general (a transcendental subject) the repre-

1 [Cf. M. 794]
2 [Cf. M. 289]

sentation of which must no doubt be simple, because nothing is determined in it, and nothing can be represented more simple than by the concept of a mere something. The simplicity however of the representation of a subject is not therefore a knowledge of the simplicity of the subject, because no account whatever is taken of its qualities when it is designated by the entirely empty expression I, an expression that can be applied to every thinking subject.

So much is certain therefore that though I always represent by the I an absolute, but only logical, unity of the subject (simplicity), I never know thereby the real simplicity of my subject. We saw that the proposition, I am a substance, signified nothing but the mere category of which I must not make any use (empirically) *in concreto*. In the same manner, I may well say, I am a simple substance, that is, a substance the representation of which contains no synthesis of the manifold; but that concept, or that proposition also, teaches us nothing at all with reference to myself, as an object of experience, because the concept of substance itself is used as a function of synthesis only, without any intuition to rest on, and therefore without any object, valid with reference to the condition of our knowledge only, but not with reference to any object of it. . . . [M. 290-3]

Thus collapses the whole of rational psychology, with its fundamental support, and neither here nor elsewhere can we hope by means of mere concepts (still less through the mere subjective form of all our concepts, that is, through our consciousness) and without referring these concepts to a possible experience, to extend our knowledge, particularly as even the fundamental concept of a *simple nature* is such that it can never be met with in experience, so that no chance remains of arriving at it as a concept of objective validity.

The Third Paralogism of Personality

Whatever is conscious of the numerical identity of its own self at different times, is in so far a person.
Now the Soul, etc.
Therefore the Soul is a person.

Criticism of the Third Paralogism of Transcendental Psychology

The [1] proposition of the identity of myself amidst the manifold of which I am conscious, likewise follows from the concepts themselves, and is therefore analytical; but the identity of the subject of which, in all its representations, I may become conscious, does not refer to the intuition by which it is given as an object, and cannot therefore signify the identity of the person, by which is understood the consciousness of the identity of one's own substance, as a thinking being, in all the changes of circumstances. In order to prove this, the mere analysis of the proposition, I think, would avail nothing: but different synthetical judgments would be required, which are based on the given intuition.

. . . [M. 294-5] The [2] identity of my consciousness at different times is therefore a formal condition only of my thoughts and their coherence, and proves in no way the numerical identity of my subject, in which, in spite of the logical identity of the I, such a change may have passed as to make it impossible to retain its identity, though we may still attribute to it the same name of I,

[1] [Cf. M. 794]
[2] [Cf. M. 295-6]

which in every other state, and even in the change of the subject, might yet retain the thought of the preceding and hand it over to the subsequent subject.[1]

Although the teaching of some old schools that everything is in a flux, and nothing in the world permanent, cannot be admitted, if we admit substances, yet it must not be supposed that it can be refuted by the unity of self-consciousness. For we ourselves cannot judge from our own consciousness whether, as souls, we are permanent or not, because we reckon as belonging to our own identical self that only of which we are conscious, and therefore are constrained to admit that, during the whole time of which we are conscious, we are one and the same. From the point of view of a stranger, however, such a judgment would not be valid, because, perceiving in the soul no permanent phenomena, except the representation of the I, which accompanies and connects them all, we cannot determine whether that I (being a mere thought) be not in the same state of flux as the other thoughts which are chained together by the I. . . . [M. 296-7]

Like the concept of substance and of the simple, however, the concept of personality also may remain, so long as it is used as transcendental only, that is, as a

[1] An elastic ball, which impinges on another in a straight line, communicates to it its whole motion, and therefore (if we only consider the places in space) its whole state. If then, in analogy with such bodies, we admit substances of which the one communicates to the other representations with consciousness, we could imagine a whole series of them, in which the first communicates its state and its consciousness to the second, the second its own state with that of the first substance to a third, and this again all the states of the former, together with its own, and a consciousness of them, to another. That last substance would be conscious of all the states of the previously changed substances, as of its own, because all of them had been transferred to it with the consciousness of them; but for all that it would not have been the same person in all those states.

concept of the unity of the subject which is otherwise unknown to us, but in the determinations of which there is an uninterrupted connection by apperception. In this sense such a concept is necessary for practical purposes and sufficient, but we can never pride ourselves on it as helping to expand our knowledge of our self by means of pure reason, which only deceives us if we imagine that we can conclude an uninterrupted continuance of the subject from the mere concept of the identical self. . . . [M. 297-8]

The Fourth Paralogism of Ideality (with Regard to External Relations)

That, the existence of which can only be inferred as a cause of given perceptions, has a doubtful existence only:—

All external phenomena are such that their existence cannot be perceived immediately, but that we can only infer them as the cause of given perceptions:—

Therefore the existence of all objects of the external senses is doubtful. This uncertainty I call the ideality of external phenomena, and the doctrine of that ideality is called *idealism;* in comparison with which the other doctrine, which maintains a possible certainty of the objects of the external senses, is called *dualism.*

Criticism of the Fourth Paralogism of Transcendental Psychology

. . . [M. 298-327]

To [1] say that I distinguish my own existence, as that of a thinking being, from other things outside me (one of them being my body) is likewise an analytical propo-

[1] [Cf. M. 794-5]

sition; for *other* things are things which I conceive as *different* from myself. But, whether such a consciousness of myself is even possible without things outside me, whereby representations are given to me, and whether I could exist merely as a thinking being (without being a man), I do not know at all by that proposition.

[*Conclusion*]

Nothing[1] therefore is gained by the analysis of the consciousness of myself, in thought in general, towards the knowledge of myself as an object. The logical analysis of thinking in general is simply mistaken for a metaphysical determination of the object.

It would be a great, nay, even the only objection to the whole of our critique, if there were a possibility of proving *a priori* that all thinking beings are by themselves simple substances, that as such (as a consequence of the same argument) personality is inseparable from them, and that they are conscious of their existence as distinct from all matter. For we should thus have made a step beyond the world of sense and entered into the field of noumena, and after that no one could dare to question our right of advancing further, of settling in it, and, as each of us is favoured by luck, taking possession of it. The proposition that every thinking being is, as such, a simple substance, is synthetical *a priori,* because, first, it goes beyond the concept on which it rests, and adds to act of thinking in general the *mode of existence*; and secondly, because it adds to that concept a predicate (simplicity) which cannot be given in any experience. Hence synthetical propositions *a priori* would be not only admissible, as we maintained, in reference to objects of possible experience, and then

[1] [Cf. M. 795 ff.]

only as principles of the possibility of that experience, but could be extended to things in general and to things by themselves, a result which would put an end to the whole of our critique, and bid us to leave everything as we found it. However, the danger is not so great, if only we look more closely into the matter. . . . [M. 795-9]

If, on the contrary, we proceed *analytically*, taking the proposition, I think, which involves existence (according to the category of *modality*) as given, and analyse it, in order to find out whether, and how, the *Ego* determines its existence in space and time by it alone, the propositions of rational psychology would not start from the concept of a thinking being, in general, but from a reality, and the inference would consist in determining from the manner in which that reality is thought, after everything that is empirical in it has been removed, what belongs to a thinking being in general. This may be shown by the following Table.

1.
I think,

2.	3.
as Subject,	as simple Subject,

4.
as identical Subject,
in every state of my thought.

As it has not been determined in the second proposition, whether I can exist and be conceived to exist as a subject only, and not also as a predicate of something else, the concept of subject is here taken as logical only, and it remains undetermined whether we are to understand by it a substance or not. In the third proposition, however, the absolute unity of apperception, the simple I, being the representation to which all connection or separation (which constitute thought) relate, assumes its own importance, although nothing is determined as yet with regard to the nature of the subject, or its subsistence. The apperception is something real, and it is only possible, if it is simple. In space, however, there is nothing real that is simple, for points (the only simple in space) are limits only, and not themselves something which, as a part, serves to constitute space. From this follows the impossibility of explaining the nature of myself, as merely a thinking subject, from the *materialistic* point of view. As, however, in the first proposition, my existence is taken for granted, for it is not said in it that every thinking being exists (this would predicate too much, namely, absolute necessity of them), but only, *I exist,* as thinking, the proposition itself is empirical, and contains only the determinability of my existence, in reference to my representations in time. But as for that purpose again I require, first of all, something permanent, such as is not given to me at all in internal intuition, so far as I think myself, it is really impossible by that simple self-consciousness to determine the manner in which I exist, whether as a substance or as an accident. Thus, if *materialism* was inadequate to explain my existence, *spiritualism* is equally insufficient for that purpose, and the conclusion is, that, in no way whatsoever can we know anything of the nature of our soul, so far as the possibility of its separate existence is concerned.

And how indeed should it be possible by means of that unity of consciousness which we only know because it is indispensable to us for the very possibility of experience, to get beyond experience (our existence in life), and even to extend our knowledge to the nature of all thinking beings in general, by the empirical, but, with reference to every kind of intuition, undetermined proposition, I think.

There is, therefore, no rational psychology, as a *doctrine,* furnishing any addition to our self-knowledge, but only as a *discipline,* fixing unpassable limits to speculative reason in this field, partly to keep us from throwing ourselves into the arms of a soulless materialism, partly to warn us against losing ourselves in a vague, and, with regard to practical life, baseless spiritualism. It reminds us at the same time to look upon this refusal of our reason to give a satisfactory answer to such curious questions, which reach beyond the limits of this life, as a hint to turn our self-knowledge away from fruitless speculations to a fruitful practical use—a use which, though directed always to objects of experience only, derives its principle from a higher source, and so regulates our conduct, as if our destination reached far beyond experience, and therefore far beyond this life.

We see from all this, that rational psychology owes its origin to a mere misunderstanding. The unity of consciousness, on which the categories are founded, is mistaken for an intuition of the subject as object, and the category of substance applied to it. But that unity is only the unity in *thought,* by which alone no object is given, and to which, therefore, the category of substance, which always presupposes a given *intuition,* cannot be applied, and therefore the subject cannot be known. The subject of the categories, therefore, cannot, by thinking them, receive a concept of itself, as an object of the categories; for in order to think the categories, it must presuppose its pure self-consciousness, the very thing that had to be explained. In like manner the subject, in which the representation of time has its original source, cannot determine by it its own existence in time; and if the latter is impossible, the former, as a determination of oneself (as of a thinking being in general) by means of the categories, is equally so. . . . [M. 802-7]

CHAPTER II

THE ANTINOMY OF PURE REASON[1]

. . . [M. 328-9] When we apply reason to the *objective synthesis* of phenomena [we find that it] tries at first, with great plausibility, to establish its principle of unconditioned unity, but becomes soon entangled in so many contradictions, that it must give up its pretensions with regard to cosmology also.

For here we are met by a new phenomenon in human reason, namely, a perfectly natural Antithetic, which is not produced by any artificial efforts, but into which reason falls by itself, and inevitably. Reason is no doubt preserved thereby from the slumber of an imaginary conviction, which is often produced by a purely one-sided illusion; but it is tempted at the same time, either to abandon itself to sceptical despair, or to assume a dogmatical obstinacy, taking its stand on certain assertions, without granting a hearing and doing justice to the arguments of the opponent. In both cases, a death-blow is dealt to sound philosophy, although in the former we might speak of the *Euthanasia* of pure reason.

Before showing the scenes of discord and confusion produced by the conflict of the laws (antinomy) of pure reason, we shall have to make a few remarks in order to explain and justify the method which we mean to follow in the treatment of this subject. I shall call all transcendental ideas, so far as they relate to the abso-

[1] [Cf. M. 328 ff.]

lute totality in the synthesis of phenomena, *cosmical concepts*. . . . [M. 330] As therefore the paralogisms of pure reason formed the foundation for a dialectical psychology, the antinomy of pure reason will place before our eyes the transcendental principles of a pretended pure (rational) cosmology, not in order to show that it is valid and can be accepted, but, as may be guessed from the very name of the antinomy of reason, in order to expose it as an idea surrounded by deceptive and false appearances, and utterly irreconcileable with phenomena.

SECTION I.[1] *System of Cosmological Ideas*

Before we are able to enumerate these ideas according to a principle and with systematic precision, we must bear in mind,

1st, That pure and transcendental concepts arise from the understanding only, and that reason does not in reality produce any concept, but only *frees*, it may be, the *concept of the understanding* of the inevitable limitation of a possible experience, and thus tries to enlarge it, beyond the limits of experience, yet in connection with it. Reason does this by demanding for something that is given as conditioned, absolute totality on the side of the conditions (under which the understanding subjects all phenomena to the synthetical unity). It thus changes the category into a transcendental idea, in order to give absolute completeness to the empirical synthesis, by continuing it up to the unconditioned (which can never be met with in experience, but in the idea only). In doing this, reason follows the principle that, *if the conditioned is given, the whole sum of conditions, and therefore the absolutely unconditioned must be given*

[1] [Cf. M. 330 ff.]

likewise, the former being impossible without the latter. Hence the transcendental ideas are in reality nothing but categories, enlarged till they reach the unconditioned, and those ideas must admit of being arranged in a table, according to the titles of the categories.

2ndly, Not all categories will lend themselves to this, but those only in which the synthesis constitutes a *series*, and a series of subordinated (not of co-ordinated) conditions. Absolute totality is demanded by reason, with regard to an ascending series of conditions only, not therefore when we have to deal with a descending line of consequences, or with an aggregate of co-ordinated conditions. . . . [M. 331-2]

I shall call the synthesis of a series on the side of the conditions, beginning with the one nearest to a given phenomenon, and advancing to the more remote conditions, *regressive;* the other, which on the side of the conditioned advances from the nearest effect to the more remote ones, *progressive*. The former proceeds in *antecedentia*, the second in *consequentia*. Cosmological ideas therefore, being occupied with the totality of regressive synthesis, proceed in *antecedentia*, not in *consequentia*. If the latter should take place, it would be a gratuitous, not a necessary problem of pure reason, because for a complete comprehension of what is given us in experience we want to know the causes, but not the effects.

In order to arrange a table of ideas in accordance with the table of the categories, we must take, *first* the two original *quanta* of all our intuition, time and space. Time is in itself a series (and the formal condition of all series), and in it, therefore, with reference to any given present, we have to distinguish *a priori* the *antecedentia* as conditions (the past) from the *consequentia* (the future). Hence the transcendental idea of the absolute totality of the series of conditions of anything conditioned refers to time past only. The whole of time past is looked upon, according to the idea of reason, as a necessary condition of the given moment. With regard to space there is in it no difference between *progressus* and *regressus,* because all its parts exist together and form an aggregate, but *no series.* . . . [M. 333] Nevertheless the synthesis by which we apprehend the many parts of space is successive, takes place in time, and contains a series. And as in that series of aggregated spaces (as, for instance, of feet in a rood) the spaces added to a given space are always the *condition of the limit* of the preceding spaces, we ought to consider the *measuring* of a space also as a synthesis of a series of conditions of something given as conditioned, with this difference only, that the side of the conditions is by itself not different from the other side which comprehends the conditioned, so that *regressus* and *progressus* seem to be the same in space. As however every part of space is limited only, and not given by another, we must look upon every limited space as conditioned also, so far as it presupposes another space as the condition of its limit, and so on. With reference to limitation therefore *progressus* in space is also *regressus,* and the transcendental idea of the absolute totality of the synthesis in the series of conditions applies to space also. I may ask then for the absolute totality of phenomena in space, quite as well as in time past, though we must wait to see whether an answer is ever possible.

Secondly, reality in space, that is, matter, is something conditioned, the parts of which are its internal conditions, and the parts of its parts, its remoter conditions. We have therefore here a regressive synthesis the absolute totality of which is demanded by reason, but which cannot take place except by a complete division, whereby the reality of matter dwindles away into nothing, or into that at least which is no longer matter, namely, the simple; consequently we have here also a series of conditions, and a progress to the unconditioned.

Thirdly, when we come to the categories of the real relation between phenomena, we find that the category of substance with its accidents does not lend itself to a transcendental idea; that is, reason has here no inducement to proceed regressively to conditions. . . . [M. 334-5] The same applies to substances in community, which are aggregates only, without having an exponent of a series, since they are not subordinate to each other, as conditions of their possibility, in the same way as spaces were, the limits of which can never be determined by itself, but always through another space. There remains therefore only the category of *causality,* which offers a series of causes to a given effect, enabling us to ascend from the latter, as the conditioned, to the former as the conditions, and thus to answer the question of reason.

Fourthly, the concepts of the possible, the real, and the necessary do not lead to any series, except so far as the *accidental* in existence must always be considered as conditioned, and point, according to a rule of the understanding, to a condition which makes it necessary to ascend to a higher condition, till reason finds at last, only, in the totality of that series, the unconditioned *necessity* which it requires.

If therefore we select those categories which necessarily imply a series in the synthesis of the manifold, we shall have no more than four cosmological ideas, according to the four titles of the categories.

I

Absolute completeness
of the composition
of the given whole of all phenomena.

II

Absolute completeness
of the division
of a given whole
in phenomenal appearance.

III

Absolute completeness
of the origination
of a phenomenon
in general.

IV

Absolute completeness
of the dependence of the existence
of the changeable in phenomenal appearance.

It should be remarked, *first,* that the idea of absolute totality refers to nothing else but the exhibition of phenomena, and not therefore to the pure concept, formed by the understanding, of a totality of things in general. Phenomena, therefore, are considered here as given, and reason postulates the absolute completeness of the conditions of their possibility, so far as these conditions constitute a series, that is, an absolutely (in every respect) complete synthesis, whereby phenomena could be exhibited according to the laws of the understanding.

Secondly, it is in reality the unconditioned alone which reason is looking for in the synthesis of conditions, continued regressively and serially, as it were a completeness in the series of premisses, which taken together require no further premisses. This *unconditioned* is always contained in *the absolute totality of a series,* as represented in imagination. But this absolutely complete synthesis is again an idea only, for it is impossible to know beforehand, whether such a synthesis be possible in phenomena. . . . [M. 336-7] But the idea of that completeness is no doubt contained in reason, without reference to the possibility or impossibility of connecting with it adequate empirical concepts. As therefore in the absolute totality of the regressive synthesis of the manifold in intuition (according to the categories which represent that totality as a series of conditions of something given as conditioned) the unconditioned is necessarily contained without attempting to determine whether and how such a totality be possible, reason here takes the road to start from the idea of totality, though her final aim is the *unconditioned,* whether of the whole series or of a part thereof. . . . [M. 337-8]

We have two expressions, *world* and *nature,* which frequently run into each other. The first denotes the mathematical total of all phenomena and the totality of their synthesis of large and small in its progress whether by composition or division. That world, however, is called nature [1] if we look upon it as a dynamical whole, and consider not the aggregation in space and time, in order to produce a quantity, but the unity in the *existence* of phenomena. In this case the condition of that which happens is called *cause,* the unconditioned causality of the cause as phenomenal, *liberty,* while the conditioned causality, in its narrower meaning, is called *natural cause.* That of which the existence is conditioned is called *contingent,* that of which it is unconditioned, *necessary.* The unconditioned necessity of phenomena may be called *natural necessity.*

I have called the ideas, which we are at present discussing, cosmological, partly because we understand by *world* the totality of all phenomena, our ideas being directed to that only which is unconditioned among the phenomena; partly, because world, in its transcendental meaning, denotes the totality of all existing things, and

[1] [Note M. 338]

we are concerned only with the completeness of the synthesis (although properly only in the *regressus* to the conditions). Considering, therefore, that all these ideas are transcendent because, though not transcending in kind their object, namely, phenomena, but restricted to the world of sense (and excluded from all noumena) they nevertheless carry synthesis to a *degree* which transcends all possible experience, they may, according to my opinion, very properly be called *cosmical concepts*. With reference to the distinction, however, between the mathematically or the dynamically unconditioned at which the *regressus* aims, I might call the two former, in a narrower sense, *cosmical concepts* (macrocosmically or microcosmically) and the remaining two *transcendent concepts of nature*. This distinction, though for the present of no great consequence, may become important hereafter.

SECTION II.[1] *Antithetic of Pure Reason*

. . . [M. 339-40] If we apply our reason, not only to objects of experience, in order to make use of the principles of the understanding, but venture to extend it beyond the limit of experience, there arise rationalising or sophistical propositions, which can neither hope for confirmation nor need fear refutation from experience. Every one of them is not only in itself free from contradiction, but can point to conditions of its necessity in the nature of reason itself, only that, unfortunately, its opposite can produce equally valid and necessary grounds for its support. . . . [M. 340-1]

This dialectical doctrine will not refer to the unity of the understanding in concepts of experience, but to the unity of reason in mere ideas, the condition of which,

[1] [Cf. M. 339 ff.]

as it is meant to agree, as a synthesis according to rules, with the understanding, and yet at the same time, as the absolute unity of that synthesis, with reason, must either, if it is adequate to the unity of reason, be too great for the understanding, or, if adequate to the understanding, too small for reason. Hence a conflict must arise, which cannot be avoided, do what we will.

These apparently rational, but really sophistical assertions open a dialectical battle-field, where that side always obtains the victory which is allowed to make the attack, and where those must certainly succumb who are obliged to keep on the defensive. . . . [M. 341] As impartial judges we must take no account of whether it be the good or the bad cause which the two champions defend. It is best to let them fight it out between themselves in the hope that, after they have rather tired out than injured each other, they may themselves perceive the uselessness of their quarrel, and part as good friends. . . . [M. 342-3]

FIRST CONFLICT OF THE TRANSCENDENTAL IDEAS [1]

Thesis

The world has a beginning in time, and is limited also with regard to space.

Proof

For if we assumed that the world had no beginning in time, then an eternity must have elapsed up to every given point of time, and therefore an infinite series of

[1] [Cf. M. 344 ff. The *Statements* and *Proofs* of the four theses and antheses are given in full. The *Observations* have been omitted; cf. M. 346-51, 356-61, 364-9, 372-8.]

successive states of things must have passed in the world. The infinity of a series, however, consists in this, that it never can be completed by means of a successive synthesis. Hence an infinite past series of worlds is impossible, and the beginning of the world a necessary condition of its existence. This was what had to be proved first.

With regard to the second, let us assume again the opposite. In that case the world would be given as an infinite whole of co-existing things. Now we cannot conceive in any way the extension of a quantum, which is not given within certain limits to every intuition,[1] except through the synthesis of its parts, nor the totality of such a quantum in any way, except through a completed synthesis, or by the repeated addition of unity to itself.[2] In order therefore to conceive the world, which fills all space, as a whole, the successive synthesis of the parts of an infinite world would have to be looked upon as complete; that is, an infinite time would have to be looked upon as elapsed, during the enumeration of all co-existing things. This is impossible. Hence an infinite aggregate of real things cannot be regarded as a given whole, nor, therefore, as given at the same time. Hence it follows that the world is not infinite, as regards extension in space, but enclosed in limits. This was the second that had to be proved.

[1] We may perceive an indefinite quantum as a whole, if it is included in limits, without having to build up its totality by means of measuring, that is, by the successive synthesis of its parts. The limits themselves determine its completeness, by cutting off everything beyond.

[2] The concept of totality is in this case nothing but the representation of the completed synthesis of its parts, because, as we cannot deduce the concept from the intuition of the whole (this being in this case impossible), we can conceive it only through the synthesis of its parts, up to the completion of the infinite, at least in the idea.

Antithesis

The world has no beginning and no limits in space, but is infinite, in respect both to time and space.

Proof

For let us assume that it has a beginning. Then, as beginning is an existence which is preceded by a time in which the thing is not, it would follow that antecedently there was a time in which the world was not, that is, an empty time. In an empty time, however, it is impossible that anything should take its beginning, because of such a time no part possesses any condition as to existence rather than non-existence, which condition could distinguish that part from any other (whether produced by itself or through another cause). Hence, though many a series of things may take its beginning in the world, the world itself can have no beginning, and in reference to time past is infinite.

With regard to the second, let us assume again the opposite, namely, that the world is finite and limited in space. In that case the world would exist in an empty space without limits. We should therefore have not only a relation of things *in space,* but also of things *to space.* As however the world is an absolute whole, outside of which no object of intuition, and therefore no correlate of the world can be found, the relation of the world to empty space would be a relation to *no object.* Such a relation, and with it the limitation of the world by empty space, is nothing, and therefore the world is not limited with regard to space, that is, it is infinite in extension.[1]

[1] Space is merely the form of external intuition (formal intuition) and not a real object that can be perceived by exter-

SECOND CONFLICT OF THE TRANSCENDENTAL IDEAS

Thesis

Every compound substance in the world consists of simple parts, and nothing exists anywhere but the simple, or what is composed of it.

Proof

For let us assume that compound substances did not consist of simple parts, then, if all composition is removed in thought, there would be no compound part, and (as no simple parts are admitted) no simple part either, that is, there would remain nothing, and there would therefore be no substance at all. Either, therefore, it is impossible to remove all composition in thought, or, after its removal, there must remain something that exists without composition, that is the simple. In the former case the compound could not itself con-

---

nal intuition. Space, as prior to all things which determine it (fill or limit it), or rather which give an empirical intuition determined by its form, is, under the name of absolute space, nothing but a mere possibility of external phenomena, so far as they either exist already, or can be added to given phenomena. Empirical intuition, therefore, is not a compound of phenomena and of space (perception and empty intuition). The one is not a correlate of the other in a synthesis, but the two are only connected as matter and form in one and the same empirical intuition. If we try to separate one from the other, and to place space outside all phenomena, we arrive at a number of empty determinations of external intuition, which, however, can never be possible perceptions; for instance, motion or rest of the world in an infinite empty space, i.e. a determination of the mutual relation of the two, which can never be perceived, and is therefore nothing but the predicate of a mere idea.

sist of substances (because with them composition is only an accidental relation of substances, which substances, as permanent beings, must subsist without it). As this contradicts the supposition, there remains only the second view, namely, that the substantial compounds in the world consist of simple parts.

It follows as an immediate consequence that all the things in the world are simple beings, that their composition is only an external condition, and that, though we are unable to remove these elementary substances from their state of composition and isolate them, reason must conceive them as the first subjects of all composition, and therefore, antecedently to it, as simple beings.

Antithesis

No compound thing in the world consists of simple parts, and there exists nowhere in the world anything simple.

Proof

Assume that a compound thing, a substance, consists of simple parts. Then as all external relation, and therefore all composition of substances also, is possible in space only, it follows that space must consist of as many parts as the parts of the compound that occupies the space. Space, however, does not consist of simple parts, but of spaces. Every part of a compound, therefore, must occupy a space. Now the absolutely primary parts of every compound are simple. It follows therefore that the simple occupies a space. But as everything real, which occupies a space, contains a manifold, the parts of which are by the side of each other, and which therefore is compounded, and, as a real compound, compounded not of accidents (for these could not exist by the side of each other, without a substance), but of substances, it would follow that the simple is a substantial compound, which is self-contradictory.

The second proposition of the antithesis, that there exists nowhere in the world anything simple, is not intended to mean more than that the existence of the absolutely simple cannot be proved from any experience or perception, whether external or internal, and that the absolutely simple is a mere idea, the objective reality of which can never be shown in any possible experience, so that in the explanation of phenomena it is without any application or object. For, if we assumed that an object of this transcendental idea might be found in experience, the empirical intuition of some one object would have to be such as to contain absolutely nothing manifold by the side of each other, and combined to a unity. But as, from our not being conscious of such a manifold, we cannot form any valid conclusion as to the entire impossibility of it in any objective intuition, and as without this no absolute simplicity can be established, it follows that such simplicity cannot be inferred from any perception whatsoever. As, therefore, an absolutely simple object can never be given in any possible experience, while the world of sense must be looked upon as the sum total of all possible experience, it follows that nothing simple exists in it.

This second part of the antithesis goes far beyond the first, which only banished the simple from the intuition of the composite, while the second drives it out of the whole of nature. Hence we could not attempt to prove it out of the concept of any given object of external intuition (of the compound), but from its relation to a possible experience in general.

THIRD CONFLICT OF THE TRANSCENDENTAL IDEAS

Thesis

Causality, according to the laws of nature, is not the only causality from which all the phenomena of the world can be deduced. In order to account for these phenomena it is necessary also to admit another causality, that of freedom.

Proof

Let us assume that there is no other causality but that according to the laws of nature. In that case everything that *takes place;* presupposes an anterior state, on which it follows inevitably according to a rule. But that anterior state must itself be something which has taken place (which has come to be in time, and did not exist before), because, if it had always existed, its effect too would not have only just arisen, but have existed always. The causality, therefore, of a cause, through which something takes place, is itself an *event,* which again, according to the law of nature, presupposes an anterior state and its causality, and this again an anterior state, and so on. If, therefore, everything takes place according to mere laws of nature, there will always be a secondary only, but never a primary beginning, and therefore no completeness of the series, on the side of successive causes. But the law of nature consists in this, that nothing takes place without a cause sufficiently determined *a priori.* Therefore the proposition, that all causality is possible according to the laws of nature only, contradicts itself, if taken in unlimited generality, and it is impossible, therefore, to admit that causality as the only one.

We must therefore admit another causality, through which something takes place, without its cause being further determined according to necessary laws by a preceding cause, that is, an *absolute spontaneity* of causes, by which a series of phenomena, proceeding according to natural laws, begins by itself; we must consequently admit transcendental freedom, without which, even in the course of nature, the series of phenomena on the side of causes, can never be perfect.

Antithesis

There is no freedom, but everything in the world takes place entirely according to the laws of nature.

Proof

If we admit that there is *freedom*, in the transcendental sense, as a particular kind of causality, according to which the events in the world could take place, that is a faculty of absolutely originating a state, and with it a series of consequences, it would follow that not only a series would have its absolute beginning through this spontaneity, but the determination of that spontaneity itself to produce the series, that is, the causality, would have an absolute beginning, nothing preceding it by which this act is determined according to permanent laws. Every beginning of an act, however, presupposes a state in which the cause is not yet active, and a dynamically primary beginning of an act presupposes a state which has no causal connection with the preceding state of that cause, that is, in no wise follows from it. Transcendental freedom is therefore opposed to the law of causality, and represents such a connection of successive states of effective causes, that no unity of experience is possible with it. It is therefore an empty fiction of the mind, and not to be met with in any experience.

We have, therefore, nothing but *nature*, in which we must try to find the connection and order of cosmical events. Freedom (independence) from the laws of nature is no doubt a *deliverance* from restraint, but also from the *guidance* of all rules. For we cannot say that, instead of the laws of nature, laws of freedom may enter into the causality of the course of the world, because, if determined by laws, it would not be freedom, but nothing else but nature. Nature, therefore, and transcendental freedom differ from each other like legality and lawlessness. The former, no doubt, imposes upon the understanding the difficult task of looking higher and higher for the origin of events in the series of causes, because their causality is always conditioned. In return for this, however, it promises a complete and well-ordered unity of experience; while, on the other side, the fiction of freedom promises, no doubt, to the enquiring mind, rest in the chain of causes, leading him up to an unconditioned causality, which begins to act by itself, but which, as it is blind itself, tears the thread of rules by which alone a complete and coherent experience is possible.

FOURTH CONFLICT OF THE TRANSCENDENTAL IDEAS

Thesis

There exists an absolutely necessary Being belonging to the world, either as a part or as a cause of it.

Proof

The world of sense, as the sum total of all phenomena, contains a series of changes without which even the representation of a series of time, which forms the condition of the possibility of the world of sense, would not be given us.[1] But every change has its condition which precedes it in time, and renders it necessary. Now, everything that is given as conditional presupposes, with regard to its existence, a complete series of conditions, leading up to that which is entirely unconditioned, and alone absolutely necessary. Something absolutely necessary therefore must exist, if there exists a change as its consequence. And this absolutely necessary belongs itself to the world of sense. For if we supposed that it existed outside that world, then the series of changes in the world would derive its origin from it, while the necessary cause itself would not belong to the world of sense. But this is impossible. For as the beginning of a temporal series can be determined only by that which precedes it in time, it follows that the highest condition of the beginning of a series of changes must exist in the time when that series was not yet (because the beginning is an existence, preceded by a time in which the thing which begins was not yet). Hence the causality of the necessary cause of changes and that cause itself belong to time and therefore to phenomena (in which alone time, as their form, is possible), and it cannot therefore be conceived as separated from the world of sense, as the sum total of all phe-

[1] As formal condition of the possibility of changes, time is no doubt objectively prior to them; subjectively, however, and in the reality of our consciousness the representation of time, like every other, is occasioned solely by perceptions.

nomena. It follows, therefore, that something absolutely necessary is contained in the world, whether it be the whole cosmical series itself, or only a part of it.

Antithesis

There nowhere exists an absolutely necessary Being, either within or without the world, as the cause of it.

Proof

If we supposed that the world itself is a necessary being, or that a necessary being exists in it, there would then be in the series of changes either a beginning, unconditionally necessary, and therefore without a cause, which contradicts the dynamical law of the determination of all phenomena in time; or the series itself would be without any beginning, and though contingent and conditioned in all its parts, yet entirely necessary and unconditioned as a whole. This would be self-contradictory, because the existence of a multitude cannot be necessary, if no single part of it possesses necessary existence.

If we supposed, on the contrary, that there exists an absolutely necessary cause of the world, outside the world, then that cause, as the highest member in *the series of causes* of cosmical changes, would begin the existence of the latter and their series.[1] In that case, however, that cause would have to begin to act, and its causality would belong to time, and therefore to the sum total of phenomena. It would belong to the world,

[1] The word *to begin* is used in two senses. The first is active when the cause begins, or starts (infit), a series of states as its effect. The second is passive (or neuter) when the causality begins in the cause itself (fit). I reason here from the former to the latter meaning.

and would therefore not be outside the world, which is contrary to our supposition. Therefore, neither in the world, nor outside the world (yet in causal connection with it), does there exist anywhere an absolutely necessary Being.

SECTION III.[1] *Of the Interest of Reason in these Conflicts*

. . . [M. 379-81] For the present we shall . . . consider which side we should like to take, if it should become necessary to take sides at all. As in this case we do not consult the logical test of truth, but only our own interest, such an enquiry, though settling nothing as to the contested rights of both parties, will have this advantage, that it makes us understand why those who take part in this contest embrace one rather than the other side, without being guided by any special insight into the subject. It may also explain some other things, as, for instance, the zelotic heat of the one and the calm assurance of the other party, and why the world greets one party with rapturous applause, and entertains towards the other an irreconcileable prejudice.

There is something which in this preliminary enquiry determines the right point of view, from which alone it can be carried on with proper completeness, and this is the comparison of the principles from which both parties start. If we look at the propositions of the antithesis, we shall find in it a perfect uniformity in the mode of thought and a complete unity of principle, namely, the principle of pure empiricism, not only in the explanation of the phenomena of the world, but also in the solution of the transcendental ideas of the cosmical universe

[1] [Cf. M. 379 ff.]

itself. The propositions of the thesis, on the contrary, rest not only on the empirical explanation within the series of phenomena, but likewise on intelligible beginnings, and its maxim is therefore not simple. With regard to its essential and distinguishing characteristic, I shall call it the *dogmatism* of pure reason.

On the side of *dogmatism* we find in the determination of the cosmological ideas, or in the *Thesis:*—

First, A certain *practical interest,* which every right-thinking man, if he knows his true interests, will heartily share. That the world has a beginning; that my thinking self is of a simple and therefore indestructible nature; that the same self is free in all his voluntary actions, and raised above the compulsion of nature; that, finally, the whole order of things, or the world, derives its origin from an original Being, whence everything receives both unity and purposeful connection—these are so many foundation stones on which morals and religion are built up. The antithesis robs us, or seems to rob us, of all these supports.

Secondly, Reason has a certain *speculative interest* on the same side. For if we take and employ the transcendental ideas as they are in the thesis, one may quite *a priori* grasp the whole chain of conditions and comprehend the derivation of the conditioned by beginning with the unconditioned. This cannot be done by the antithesis, which presents itself in a very unfavorable light, because it cannot return to the question as to the conditions of its synthesis any answer which does not lead to constantly new questions. According to it one has always to ascend from a given beginning to a higher one, every part leads always to a still smaller part, every event has always before it another event as its cause, and the conditions of existence in general always rest on others, without ever receiving unconditioned strength and support from a self-subsisting thing, as the original Being.

Thirdly, This side has also the advantage of *popularity,* which is by no means its smallest recommendation. The common understanding does not see the smallest difficulty in the idea of the unconditioned beginning of all synthesis, being accustomed rather to descend to consequences, than to ascend to causes. It finds comfort in the ideas of the absolutely first (the possibility of which does not trouble it), and at the same time a firm point to which the leading strings of its life may be attached, while there is no pleasure in a restless ascent from condition to condition, and keeping one foot always in the air.

On the side of *empiricism,* so far as it determines the cosmological ideas, or the *antithesis,* there is:—

First, No such practical interest, arising from the pure principles of reason, as morality and religion possess. On the contrary, empiricism seems to deprive both of their power and influence. If there is no original Being, different from the world; if the world is without a beginning, and therefore without a Creator; if our will is not free, and our soul shares the same divisibility and perishableness with matter, *moral ideas* also and principles lose all validity, and fall with the *transcendental* ideas, which formed their theoretic support.

But, on the other side, empiricism offers advantages to the speculative interests of reason, which are very tempting, and far exceed those which the dogmatical teacher can promise. With the empiricist the understanding is always on its own proper ground, namely, the field of all possible experience, the laws of which may be investigated and serve to enlarge certain and intelligible knowledge without end. Here every object can and ought to be represented to intuition, both in itself and in its relations, or at least in concepts, the images of which can be clearly and distinctly represented in given similar intuitions. Not only is there no necessity for leaving the chain of the order of nature in order to lay hold of ideas, the objects of which are not known, because, as mere products of thought, they can never be given, but the understanding is not even allowed to leave its proper business and, under pretence of its being finished, to cross into the domain of idealising reason and transcendental concepts, where it need no longer observe and investigate according to the laws of nature, but only *think* and *dream*, without any risk of being contradicted by the facts of nature, not being bound by their evidence, but justified in passing them by, or in even subordinating them to a higher authority, namely, that of pure reason.

Hence the empiricist will never allow that any epoch of nature should be considered as the absolutely first, or any limit of his vision into the extent of nature should be considered as the last. He will not approve of a transition from the objects of nature, which he can analyse by observation and mathematics and determine synthetically in intuition (the extended), to those which neither sense nor imagination can ever represent *in concreto* (the simple); nor will he concede that a faculty be presupposed, even in nature, to act independent of the laws of nature (freedom), thus narrowing the operations of the understanding in investigating, according to the necessary rules, the origin of phenomena. Lastly, he will never tolerate that the cause of anything should be looked for anywhere outside of nature (in the original Being), because we know nothing but nature, which alone can offer us objects and instruct us as to their laws.

If the empirical philosopher had no other purpose with his antithesis but to put down the rashness and presumption of reason in mistaking her true purpose, while boasting of *insight* and *knowledge,* where insight and knowledge come to an end, nay, while representing, what might have been allowed to pass on account of practical interests, as a real advancement of speculative enquiry, in order, when it is so disposed, either to tear the thread of physical enquiry, or to fasten it, under the pretence of enlarging our knowledge, to those transcendental ideas, which really teach us only *that we know nothing;* if, I say, the empiricist were satisfied with this, then his principle would only serve to teach moderation in claims, modesty in assertions, and encourage the greatest possible enlargement of our understanding through the true teacher given to us, namely, experience. For in such a case we should not be deprived of our own intellectual *presumptions* or of our *faith* in their influence on our practical interests. They would only have lost the pompous titles of science and rational insight, because true speculative *knowledge* can never have any other object but experience; and, if we transcend its limits, our synthesis, which attempts new kinds of knowledge independent of experience, lacks that substratum of intuition to which alone it could be applied.

As it is, empiricism becomes often itself dogmatical with regard to ideas, and boldly denies what goes beyond the sphere of its intuitive knowledge, and thus becomes guilty itself of a want of modesty, which here is all the more reprehensible, because an irreparable injury is thereby inflicted on the practical interests of reason. . . . [M. 386-96]

SECTION V.[1] *Sceptical Representation of the Cosmological Questions in the Four [2] Transcendental Ideas*

We should no doubt gladly desist from wishing to have our questions answered dogmatically, if we understood beforehand that, whatever the answer might be, it would only increase our ignorance, and throw us from one incomprehensibility into another, from one obscurity into a still greater obscurity, or it may be even into contradictions. If our question can only be answered by yes or no, it would seem to be prudent to take no account at first of the probable grounds of the answer, but to consider before, what we should gain, if the answer was yes, and what, if the answer was no. If we should find that in either case nothing comes of it but mere nonsense, we are surely called upon to examine our question critically, and to see whether it does not rest on a groundless supposition, playing only with an idea which betrays its falsity in its application and its consequences better than when represented by itself. This is the great advantage of the sceptical treatment of questions which pure reason puts to pure reason. We get rid by it, with a little effort, of a great amount of dogmatical rubbish, in order to put in its place sober criticism which, as a true cathartic, removes successfully all illusion with its train of omniscience.

If, therefore, I could know beforehand that a cosmological idea, in whatever way it might try to realise the unconditioned of the regressive synthesis of phenomena (whether in the manner of the thesis or in that

[1] [Cf. 396 ff. For Section IV, Cf. M. 389-96.]

[2] [As will appear presently, what Kant says in this section really applies only to the first two antinomies. The portions of the section least consistent with Section IX, below, have therefore been omitted. Cf. below p. 217.]

of the antithesis), that, I say, the cosmological idea would always be either *too large* or *too small* for any *concept of the understanding,* I should understand that, as that cosmological idea refers only to an object of experience which is to correspond to a possible concept of the understanding, it must be empty and without meaning,[1] because the object does not fit into it, whatever I may do to adapt it. And this must really be the case with all [2] cosmical concepts, which on that very account involve reason, so long as it remains attached to them, in inevitable antinomy. For suppose: —

First, That the *world has no beginning,* and you will find that it is too large for your concept, which, as it consists in a successive regressus, can never reach the whole of past eternity. Or, suppose, *that the world has a beginning,* then it is again too small for the concept of your understanding engaged in the necessary empirical regressus. For as a beginning always presupposes a time preceding, it is not yet unconditioned; and the law of the empirical use of the understanding obliges you to look for a higher condition of time, so that, with reference to such a law, the world (as limited in time) is clearly too small.

The same applies to the twofold answer to the question regarding the extent of the world in space. For if *it is infinite* and unlimited, it is *too large* for every possible empirical concept. If *it is finite* and limited, you have a perfect right to ask what determines that limit. Empty space is not an independent correlate of things, and cannot be a final condition, still less an empirical condition forming a part of a possible experience;—for how can there be experience of what is absolutely void? But, in order to produce an absolute totality in an em-

[1] [This extreme statement is modified in later sections.]
[2] [Cf. Ed.'s note above p. 205.]

pirical synthesis, it is always requisite that the unconditioned should be an empirical concept. Thus it follows that a *limited world* would be *too small* for your concept.

Secondly, If every phenomenon in space (matter) consists of an *infinite number of parts,* the regressus of a division will always be too large for your concept, while if the *division* of space is to *stop* at any member (the simple), it would be *too small* for the idea of the unconditioned, because that member always admits of a regressus to more parts contained in it. . . . [M. 398-9]

We have said that in all these cases, the *cosmical idea* is either too large or too small for the empirical regressus, and therefore for every possible concept of the understanding. But why did we not take the opposite view and say that in the former case the empirical concept is always too small for the idea, and in the latter too large, so that blame should attach to the empirical regressus, and not to the cosmological idea, which we accused of deviating from its object, namely, possible experience, either by its too-much or its too-little? The reason was this. It is possible experience alone that can impart reality to our concepts; without this, a concept is only an idea without truth, and without any reference to an object. Hence the possible empirical concept was the standard by which to judge the idea, whether it be an idea and fiction only, or whether it has an object in the world. For we then only say that anything is relatively to something else either too large or too small, if it is required for the sake of the other and ought to be adapted to it. . . . [M. 399-400] You would never say that the man is too large for his coat, but that the coat is too small for the man.

We have thus been led at least to a well-founded suspicion that the cosmological ideas, and with them all the conflicting sophistical assertions, may rest on an empty and merely imaginary conception of the manner in which the object of those ideas can be given, and this suspicion may lead us on the right track to discover the illusion which has so long led us astray.

SECTION VI.[1] *Transcendental Idealism as the Key to the Solution of Cosmological Dialectic*

It has been sufficiently proved in the transcendental Æsthetic that everything which is perceived in space and time, therefore all objects of an experience possible to us, are nothing but phenomena, that is, mere representations which, such as they are represented, namely, as extended beings, or series of changes, have no independent existence outside our thoughts. This system I call *Transcendental Idealism*. . . . [M. 400-1]

I [2] have sometimes called it *formal* idealism also, in order to distinguish it from the *material* or common idealism, which doubts or denies the very existence of external things. In some cases it seems advisable to use these terms rather than those in the text, in order to prevent all misunderstanding.

[This] transcendental [3] idealism . . . allows that the objects of external intuition may be real, as they are perceived in space, and likewise all changes in time, as they are represented by the internal sense. For as space itself is a form of that intuition which we call external, and as there would be no empirical representation at all, unless there were objects in space, we can and must admit the extended beings in it as real; and the same applies to time. Space itself, however, as well as time,

[1] [Cf. M. 400]
[2] [Cf. M. 808]
[3] [Cf. M. 401 ff.]

and with them all phenomena, are not *things* by themselves, but representations, and cannot exist outside our mind; and even the internal sensuous intuition of our mind (as an object of consciousness) which is represented as determined by the succession of different states in time, is not a real self, as it exists by itself, or what is called the transcendental subject, but a phenomenon only, given to the sensibility of this to us unknown being. It cannot be admitted that this internal phenomenon exists as a thing by itself, because it is under the condition of time, which can never be the determination of anything by itself. In space and time, however, the empirical truth of phenomena is sufficiently established, and kept quite distinct from a dream, if both are properly and completely connected together in experience, according to empirical laws.

The objects of experience are therefore *never given by themselves,* but in our experience only, and do not exist outside it. That there may be inhabitants in the moon, though no man has ever seen them, must be admitted; but it means no more than that, in the possible progress of our experience, we may meet with them; for everything is real that hangs together with a perception, according to the laws of empirical progress. They are therefore real, if they are empirically connected with any real consciousness, although they are not therefore real by themselves, that is, apart from that progress of experience. . . . [M. 402]

The faculty of sensuous intuition is really some kind of receptivity only, according to which we are affected in a certain way by representations the mutual relation of which is a pure intuition of space and time (mere forms of our sensibility), and which, if they are connected and determined in that relation of space and time, according to the laws of the unity of experience, are called objects. The non-sensuous cause of these representations is entirely unknown to us, and we can never perceive it as an object, for such a cause would have to be represented neither in space nor in time, which are conditions of sensuous representations only, and without which we cannot conceive any intuition. We may, however, call that purely intelligible cause of phenomena in general, the transcendental object, in order that we may have something which corresponds to sensibility as a kind of receptivity. We may ascribe to that transcendental object the whole extent and connection of all our possible perceptions, and we may say that it is given by itself antecedently to all experience. Phenomena, however, are given accordingly, not by themselves, but in experience only, because they are mere representations which as perceptions only, signify a real object, provided that the perception is connected with all others, according to the rules of unity in experience. Thus we may say that the real things of time past are given in the transcendental object of experience, but they only are objects to me, and real in time past, on the supposition that I conceive that a regressive series of possible perceptions (whether by the light of history, or by the vestiges of causes and effects), in one word, the course of the world, leads, according to empirical laws, to a past series of time, as a condition of the present time. It is therefore represented as real, not by itself, but in connection with a possible experience, so that all past events from time immemorial and before my own existence mean after all nothing but the possibility of an extension of the chain of experience, beginning with present perception and leading upwards to the conditions which determine it in time. . . . [M. 404-13]

Section VIII.[1] *The Regulative*[2] *Principle of Pure Reason with Regard to the Cosmological Ideas*

As through the cosmological principle of totality no real maximum is *given* of the series of conditions in the world of sense, as a thing by itself, but can only be *required* in the regressus of that series, that principle of pure reason, if thus amended, still retains its validity, not indeed as an *axiom,* requiring us to think the totality in the object as real, but as a *problem* for the understanding, and therefore for the subject, encouraging us to undertake and to continue, according to the completeness in the idea, the regressus in the series of conditions of anything given as conditioned. In our sensibility, that is, in space and time, every condition which we can reach in examining given phenomena is again conditioned, because these phenomena are not objects by themselves, in which something absolutely unconditioned might possibly exist, but empirical representations only, which always must have their condition in intuition, whereby they are determined in space and time. The principle of reason is therefore properly a rule only, which in the series of conditions of given phenomena postulates a regressus which is never allowed to stop at anything absolutely unconditioned. It is therefore no principle of the possibility of experience and of the empirical knowledge of the objects of the senses, and not therefore a principle of the understanding, because every experience is (according to a given intui-

[1] [Cf. M. 413 ff. For Section VII, cf. M. 405-413.]

[2] [A principle is "regulative" when it merely guides our thinking by indicating the goal towards which investigation should be directed and the manner in which thought should operate; it is "constitutive" when it makes definite assertions regarding the existence and nature of the objectively real.]

tion) within its limits; nor is it a *constitutive principle* of reason, enabling us to extend the concept of the world of sense beyond all possible experience, but it is merely a principle of the greatest possible continuation and extension of our experience, allowing no empirical limit to be taken as an absolute limit. It is therefore a principle of reason, which, as a *rule,* postulates what we ought to do in the regressus, but does *not anticipate* what may be given in the *object,* before such regressus. I therefore call it a *regulative* principle of reason, while, on the contrary, the principle of the absolute totality of the series of conditions, as given in the object (the phenomena) by itself, would be a constitutive cosmological principle, the hollowness of which I have tried to indicate by this very distinction, thus preventing what otherwise would have inevitably happened (through a transcendental surreptitious proceeding), namely, an idea, which is to serve as a rule only, being invested with objective reality. . . . [M. 414-19]

SECTION IX.[1] *Of the Empirical Use of the Regulative Principle of Reason with Regard to all Cosmological Ideas*

. . . [M. 419-20]

I. *Solution of the Cosmological Idea of the Totality of the Composition of Phenomena in an Universe*[2]

Here, as well as in the other cosmological problems, the regulative principle of reason is founded on the proposition that, in the empirical regressus, *no experience of an absolute limit,* that is, of any condition as such, which *empirically is absolutely unconditioned,* can

[1] [Cf. M. 419 ff.]
[2] [Cf. M. 420]

exist. The ground of this is that such an experience would contain a limitation of phenomena by nothing or by the void, on which the continued regressus by means of experience must abut; and this is impossible.

This proposition, which says that in an empirical regressus I can only arrive at the condition which itself must be considered empirically conditioned, contains the rule *in terminis,* that however far I may have reached in the ascending series, I must always enquire for a still higher member of that series, whether it be known to me by experience or not.

For the solution, therefore, of the first cosmological problem, nothing more is wanted than to determine whether, in the regressus to the unconditioned extension of the universe (in time and in space), this nowhere limited ascent is to be called a *regressus in infinitum,* or a *regressus in indefinitum.*

The mere general representation of the series of all past states of the world, and of the things which exist together in space, is itself nothing but a possible empirical regressus, which I represent to myself, though as yet as indefinite, and through which alone the concept of such a series of conditions of the perception given to me can arise.[1] Now the universe exists for me as a concept only, and never (as a whole) as an intuition. Hence I cannot from its quantity conclude the quantity of the regressus, and determine the one by the other; but I must first frame to myself a concept of the quantity of the world through the quantity of the empirical regressus. Of this, however, I never know anything

[1] This cosmical series can therefore be neither greater nor smaller than the possible empirical regressus on which alone its concept rests. And as this can give neither a definite infinite, nor a definite finite (absolutely limited), it becomes clear that we cannot accept the quantity of the world, either as finite or as infinite, because the regressus (by which it is represented) admits of neither the one nor the other.

more than that, empirically, I must go on from every given member of the series of conditions to a higher and more distant member. Hence the quantity of the whole of phenomena is not absolutely determined, and we cannot say therefore that it is a *regressus in infinitum*, because this would anticipate the members which the regressus has not yet reached, and represent its number as so large that no empirical synthesis could ever reach it. It would therefore (though negatively only) determine the quantity of the world prior to the regressus, which is impossible, because it is not given to me by any intuition (in its totality), so that its quantity cannot be given prior to the regressus. Hence we cannot say anything of the quantity or extension of the world by itself, not even that there is in it a *regressus in infinitum*; but we must look for the concept of its quantity according to the rule that determines the empirical regressus in it. This rule, however, says no more than that, however far we may have got in the series of empirical conditions, we ought never to assume an absolute limit, but subordinate every phenomenon, as conditioned, to another, as its condition, and that we must proceed further to that condition. This is the *regressus in indefinitum*, which, as it fixes no quantity in the object, can clearly enough be distinguished from the *regressus in infinitum*.

I cannot say therefore that, as to time past or as to space, the world is infinite. For such a concept of quantity, as a given infinity, is empirical, and therefore, with reference to the world as an object of the senses, absolutely impossible. Nor shall I say that the regressus, beginning with a given perception, and going on to everything that limits it in a series, both in space and in time past, goes on *in infinitum*, because this would presuppose an infinite quantity of the world. Nor can

I say again that it is *finite,* for the absolute limit is likewise empirically impossible. Hence it follows that I shall not be able to say anything of the whole object of experience (the world of sense), but only of the rule, according to which experience can take place and be continued in accordance with its object. . . . [M. 423]

From this follows at the same time the affirmative answer, that the regressus in the series of the phenomena of the world, intended as a determination of the quantity of the world, goes on *in indefinitum,* which is the same as if we say that the world of sense has no absolute quantity, but that the empirical regressus (through which alone it can be given on the side of its conditions) has its own rule, namely, to advance from every member of the series, as conditioned, to a more distant member, whether by our own experience, or by the guidance of history, or through the chain of causes and their effects; and never to dispense with the extension of the possible empirical use of the understanding, this being the proper and really only task of reason and its principles. . . . [M. 424-5]

II. *Solution of the Cosmological Idea of the Totality of the Division of a Whole given in Intuition* [1]

If I divide a whole, given in intuition, I proceed from the conditioned to the conditions of its possibility. The division of the parts (*subdivisio* or *decompositio*) is a regressus in the series of those conditions. The absolute totality of *this series* could only be given, if the regressus could reach the *simple* parts. But if all parts in a continuously progressing decomposition are always divisible again, then the division, that is, the regressus from the conditioned to its conditions, goes on *in infini-*

[1] [Cf. M. 425 ff.]

tum; because the conditions (the parts) are contained in the conditioned itself, and as that is given as complete in an intuition enclosed within limits, are all given with it. The regressus must therefore not be called a *regressus in indefinitum,* such as was alone allowed by the former cosmological idea, where from the conditioned we had to proceed to conditions outside it, and therefore not given at the same time through it, but first to be added in the empirical regressus. It is not allowed, however, even in the case of a whole that is divisible *in infinitum,* to say, *that it consists of infinitely many parts.* For although all parts are contained in the intuition of the whole, yet the *whole division* is not contained in it, because it consists in the continuous decomposition, or in the regressus itself, which first makes that series real. As this regressus is infinite, all members (parts) at which it arrives are contained, no doubt, in the given whole as *aggregates*; but not so the *whole series of the division,* which is successively infinite and never complete, and cannot, therefore, represent an infinite number, or any comprehension of it as a whole.

It is easy to apply this remark to space. Every space, perceived within its limits, is such a whole the parts of which, in spite of all decomposition, are always spaces again, and therefore divisible *in infinitum.*

From this follows, quite naturally, the second application to an external phenomenon, enclosed within its limits (body). The divisibility of this is founded on the divisibility of space, which constitutes the possibility of the body, as an extended whole. This is therefore divisible *in infinitum,* without consisting, however, of an infinite number of parts.

It might seem indeed, as a body must be represented as a substance in space, that, with regard to the law of the divisibility of space, it might differ from it, for we might possibly concede, that in the latter case decomposition could never do away with all composition, because in that case all space, which besides has nothing independent of its own, would cease to be (which is impossible), while, even if all composition of matter should be done away with in thought, it would not seem compatible with the concept of a substance that nothing should remain of it, because substance is meant to be the subject of all composition, and ought to remain in its elements, although their connection in space, by which they become a body, should have been removed. But, what applies to a thing by itself, represented by a pure concept of the understanding, does not apply to what is called substance, as a phenomenon. This is not an absolute subject, but only a permanent image of sensibility, nothing in fact but intuition, in which nothing unconditioned can ever be met with. . . . [M. 427-8]

. . . *Preliminary Remark for the Solution of the Transcendental-dynamical Ideas* [1]

. . . [M. 428-9] [Thus far] we have overlooked an essential distinction between the objects, that is, the concepts of the understanding, which reason tries to raise into ideas. Two of them, according to the above table of the categories, imply a *mathematical,* the remaining two a *dynamical* synthesis of phenomena. Hitherto this overlooking was of no great importance, because, in the general representation of all transcendental ideas, we always remained under *phenomenal* conditions, and with regard to the two transcendental-mathematical ideas also, we had to do with no object but the phenomenal only. Now, however, as we have come to consider the *dynamical* concepts of the understanding, so

[1] [Cf. M. 428 ff.]

far as they should be rendered adequate to the idea of reason, that distinction becomes important, and opens to us an entirely new insight into the character of the suit in which reason is implicated. That suit had before been dismissed, as resting on both sides on wrong presuppositions. Now, however, as there seems to be in the dynamical antinomy such a presupposition as may be compatible with the pretensions of reason, and as the judge himself supplies perhaps the deficiency of legal grounds, which had been misunderstood on both sides, the suit may possibly be adjusted, from this point of view, to the satisfaction of both parties, which was impossible in the conflict of the mathematical antinomy.

If we merely look to the extension of the series of conditions, and whether they are adequate to the idea, or whether the idea is too large or too small for them, the series are no doubt all homogeneous. But the concept of the understanding on which these ideas are founded contains either a *synthesis* of the *homogeneous* only (which is presupposed in the composition as well as the decomposition of every quantity), or of the *heterogeneous* also, which must at least be admitted as possible in the dynamical synthesis, both in a causal connection, and in the connection of the necessary with the contingent.

Thus it happens that none but sensuous conditions can enter into the mathematical connection of the series of phenomena, that is, conditions which themselves are part of the series; while the dynamical series of sensuous conditions admits also of a heterogeneous condition, which is not a part of the series, but, as merely intelligible, outside it; so that a certain satisfaction is given to reason by the unconditioned being placed before the phenomena, without disturbing the series of the phenomena, which must always be conditioned, or breaking it off, contrary to the principles of the understanding.

Owing to the dynamical ideas admitting of a condition of the phenomena outside their series, that is, a condition which itself is not a phenomenon, something arises which is totally different from the result of the mathematical antinomy. The result of that antinomy was, that both the contradictory dialectical statements had to be declared false. The throughout conditioned character, however, of the dynamical series, which is inseparable from them as phenomena, if connected with the empirically unconditioned, but at the same time *not sensuous* condition, may give satisfaction to the *understanding* on one, and the *reason* on the other side, [1] because the dialectical arguments which, in some way or other, required unconditioned totality in mere phenomena, vanish; while the propositions of reason, if thus amended, may *both be true*. . . . [M. 431]

III. *Solution of the Cosmological Ideas with Regard to the Totality of the Derivation of Cosmical Events from their Causes* [2]

We can conceive two kinds of causality only with reference to events, causality either of *nature* or of *freedom*. The former is the connection of one state in the world of sense with a preceding state, on which it follows according to a rule. As the *causality* of phenomena depends on conditions of time, and as the preceding state, if it had always existed, could not have produced an effect, which first takes place in time, it follows that the causality of the cause of that which happens or arises must, according to the principle of the understanding, have itself *arisen* and require a cause.

[1] [Note, M. 431]
[2] [Cf. M. 432]

By freedom, on the contrary, in its cosmological meaning, I understand the faculty of beginning a state *spontaneously.* Its causality, therefore, does not depend, according to the law of nature, on another cause, by which it is determined in time. In this sense freedom is a purely transcendental idea, which, first, contains nothing derived from *experience,* and, secondly, the object of which cannot be determined in any *experience*; because it is a general rule, even of the possibility of all *experience,* that everything which happens has a cause, and that therefore the causality also of the cause, which *itself has happened* or arisen, must again have a cause. In this manner the whole field of experience, however far it may extend, has been changed into one great whole of nature. As, however, it is impossible in this way to arrive at an absolute totality of the conditions in causal relations, reason creates for itself the idea of spontaneity, or the power of beginning by itself, without an antecedent cause determining it to action, according to the law of causal connection.

It is extremely remarkable, that the practical concept of freedom is founded on the *transcendental idea of freedom,* which constitutes indeed the real difficulty which at all times has surrounded the question of the possibility of freedom. *Freedom,* in its *practical sense,* is the independence of our (arbitrary) will from the *coercion* through sensuous impulses. Our (arbitrary) will is *sensuous,* so far as it is *affected pathologically* (by sensuous impulses); it is called animal (*arbitrium brutum*), if *necessitated* pathologically. The human will is certainly sensuous, an *arbitrium sensitivum,* but not *brutum,* but *liberum,* because sensuous impulses do not necessitate its action, but there is in man a faculty of determination, independent of the necessitation through sensuous impulses.

It can easily be seen that, if all causality in the world of sense belonged to nature, every event would be determined in time through another, according to necessary laws. As therefore the phenomena, in determining the will, would render every act necessary as their natural effect, the annihilation of transcendental freedom would at the same time destroy all practical freedom. Practical freedom presupposes that, although something has not happened, it *ought* to have happened, and that its cause therefore had not that determining force among phenomena, which could prevent the causality of our will from producing, independently of those natural causes, and even contrary to their force and influence, something determined in the order of time, according to empirical laws, and from originating *entirely by itself* a series of events.

What happens here is what happens generally in the conflict of reason venturing beyond the limits of possible experience, namely, that the problem is not *physiological,* but *transcendental.* Hence the question of the possibility of freedom concerns no doubt psychology; but its solution, as it depends on dialectical arguments of pure reason, belongs entirely to transcendental philosophy. In order to enable that philosophy to give a satisfactory answer, which it cannot decline to do, I must first try to determine more accurately its proper procedure in this task. . . . [M. 434]

All depends here only on the dynamical relation of conditions to the conditioned, so that in the question on nature and freedom we at once meet with the difficulty, whether freedom is indeed possible, and whether, if it is possible, it can exist together with the universality of the natural law of causality. The question in fact arises, whether it is a proper disjunctive proposition to say, that every effect in the world must arise, *either* from nature, *or* from freedom, or whether *both* cannot coexist in the same event in different relations. The correctness of the principle of the unbroken connection of all events in the world of sense, according to unchangeable natural laws, is firmly established by the transcendental Analytic, and admits of no limitation. The question, therefore, can only be whether, in spite of it, freedom also can be found in the same effect which is determined by nature; or whether freedom is entirely excluded by that inviolable rule? Here the common but fallacious supposition of the *absolute reality* of phenomena shows at once its pernicious influence in embarrassing reason. For if phenomena are things by themselves, freedom cannot be saved. Nature in that case is the complete and sufficient cause determining every event, and its condition is always contained in that series of phenomena only which, together with their effect, are necessary under the law of nature. If, on the contrary, phenomena are taken for nothing except what they are in reality, namely, not things by themselves, but representations only, which are connected with each other according to empirical laws, they must themselves have causes, which are not phenomenal. Such an intelligible cause, however, is not determined with reference to its causality by phenomena, although its effects become phenomenal, and can thus be determined by other phenomena. That intelligible cause, therefore, with its causality, is outside the series, though its effects are to be found in the series of empirical conditions. The effect therefore can, with reference to its intelligible cause, be considered as free, and yet at the same time, with reference to phenomena, as resulting from them according to the necessity of nature; a distinction which, if thus represented, in a general and entirely abstract form, may seem extremely subtle and obscure, but will become clear in its practical application. . . . [M. 436]

Whatever in an object of the senses is not itself phenomenal, I call *intelligible*. If, therefore, what in the world of sense must be considered as phenomenal, possesses in itself a faculty which is not the object of sensuous intuition, but through which it can become the cause of phenomena, the *causality* of that being may be considered from *two sides*, as *intelligible* in its *action*, as the causality of a thing by itself, and as *sensible* in the *effects* of the action, as the causality of a phenomenon in the world of sense. Of the faculty of such a being we should have to form both an *empirical* and an *intellectual concept* of its causality, both of which consist together in one and the same effect. This twofold way of conceiving the faculty of an object of the senses does not contradict any of the concepts which we have to form of phenomena and of a possible experience. For as all phenomena, not being things by themselves, must have for their foundation a transcendental object, determining them as mere representations, there is nothing to prevent us from attributing to that transcendental object, besides the quality through which it becomes phenomenal, a *causality* also which is not phenomenal, although its *effect* appears in the phenomenon. Every efficient cause, however, must have a *character*, that is, a rule according to which it manifests its causality, and without which it would not be a cause. According to this we should have in every subject of the world of sense, first, an *empirical character*, through which its acts, as phenomena, stand with other phenomena in an unbroken connection, according to permanent laws of nature, and could be derived from them as their conditions, and in connection with them form the links of one and the same series in the order of nature. Secondly, we should have to allow to it an *intelligible character* also, by which, it is true, it becomes the cause of the same acts as phenomena, but which itself is not subject to any conditions of sensibility, and never phenomenal. We might call the former the character of such a thing as a phenomenon, in the latter the character of the thing by itself.

According to its intelligible character, this active subject would not depend on conditions of time, for time is only the condition of phenomena, and not of things by themselves. In it no *act* would *arise* or *perish,* neither would it be subject therefore to the law of determination in time and of all that is changeable, namely, that everything *which happens* must have its cause in *the phenomena* (of the previous state). In one word its causality, so far as it is intelligible, would not have a place in the series of empirical conditions by which the event is rendered necessary in the world of sense. It is true that that intelligible character could never be known immediately, because we cannot perceive anything, except so far as it appears, but it would nevertheless have to be conceived, according to the empirical character, as we must always admit in thought a transcendental object, as the foundation of phenomena, though we know nothing of what it is by itself. . . . [M. 438-9]

Explanation of the Cosmological Idea of Freedom in Connection with the General Necessity of Nature [1]

. . . [M. 439-41] We require the principle of the causality of phenomena among themselves, in order to be able to look for and to produce natural conditions, that is, phenomenal causes of natural events. If this is admitted and not weakened by any exceptions, the un-

[1] [Cf. M. 439 ff.]

derstanding, which in its empirical employment recognises in all events nothing but nature, and is quite justified in doing so, has really all that it can demand, and the explanations of physical phenomena may proceed without let or hindrance. The understanding would not be wronged in the least, if we assumed, though it be a mere fiction, that some among the natural causes have a faculty which is intelligible only, and whose determination to activity does not rest on empirical conditions, but on mere grounds of the intellect, if only the *phenomenal activity* of that cause is in accordance with all the laws of empirical causality. For in this way the active subject, as *causa phaenomenon,* would be joined with nature through the indissoluble dependence of all its actions, and the noumenon only of that subject (with all its phenomenal causality) would contain certain conditions which, if we want to ascend from the empirical to the transcendental object, would have to be considered as intelligible only. For, if only we follow the rule of nature in that which may be the cause among phenomena, it is indifferent to us what kind of ground of those phenomena, and of their connection, may be conceived to exist in the transcendental subject, which is empirically unknown to us. This intelligible ground does not touch the empirical questions, but concerns only, as it would seem, the thought in the pure understanding; and although the effects of that thought and action of the pure understanding may be discovered in the phenomena, these have nevertheless to be completely explained from their phenomenal cause, according to the laws of nature, by taking their empirical character as the highest ground of explanation, and passing by the intelligible character, which is the transcendental cause of the other, as entirely unknown, except so far as it is indicated by the empirical, as its sensuous sign. Let us apply this to experience. Man is one among the phenomena of the world of sense, and in so far one of the natural causes the causality of which must be subject to empirical laws. As such he must therefore have an empirical character, like all other objects of nature. We perceive it through the forces and faculties which he shows in his actions and effects. In the lifeless or merely animal nature we see no ground for admitting any faculty, except as sensuously conditioned. Man, however, who knows all the rest of nature through his senses only, knows himself through mere apperception also, and this in actions and internal determinations, which he cannot ascribe to the impressions of the senses. Man is thus to himself partly a phenomenon, partly, however, namely with reference to certain faculties, a purely intelligible object, because the actions of these faculties cannot be ascribed to the receptivity of sensibility. We call these faculties understanding and reason. It is the latter, in particular, which is entirely distinguished from all empirically conditioned forces or faculties, because it weighs its objects according to ideas, and determines the understanding accordingly, which then makes an empirical use of its (by themselves, however pure) concepts.

That[1] our reason possesses causality, or that we at least represent to ourselves such a causality in it, is clear from the *imperatives* which, in all practical matters, we impose as rules on our executive powers. The *ought* expresses a kind of necessity and connection with causes, which we do not find elsewhere in the whole of nature. The understanding can know in nature only what is present, past, or future. It is impossible that anything in it *ought to be* different from what it is in

[1] [In the following paragraphs Kant anticipates his own ethical theory, which is fully expounded below. Cf. pp. 268 ff.]

reality, in all these relations of time. Nay, if we only look at the course of nature, the ought has no meaning whatever. We cannot ask, what ought to be in nature, as little as we can ask, what qualities a circle ought to possess. We can only ask what happens in it, and what qualities that which happens has.

This ought expresses a possible action, the ground of which cannot be anything but a mere concept; while in every merely natural action the ground must always be a phenomenon. Now it is quite true that the action to which the ought applies must be possible under natural conditions, but these natural conditions do not affect the determination of the will itself, but only its effects and results among phenomena. There may be ever so many natural grounds which impel me to *will* and ever so many sensuous temptations, but they can never produce the *ought*, but only a willing which is always conditioned, but by no means necessary, and to which the ought, pronounced by reason, opposes measure, ay, prohibition and authority. Whether it be an object of the senses merely (pleasure), or of pure reason (the good), reason does not yield to the impulse that is given empirically, and does not follow the order of things, as they present themselves as phenomena, but frames for itself, with perfect spontaneity, a new order according to ideas to which it adapts the empirical conditions, and according to which it declares actions to be necessary, even though they *have not taken place*, and, maybe, never will take place. Yet it is presupposed that reason may have causality with respect to them, for otherwise no effects in experience could be expected to result from these ideas.

Now let us take our stand here and admit it at least as possible, that reason really possesses causality with reference to phenomena. . . . [M. 444-6] Supposing one could say that reason possesses causality in reference to phenomena, could the action of reason be called free in that case, as it is accurately determined by the empirical character (the disposition) and rendered necessary by it? That character again is determined in the intelligible character (way of thinking). The latter, however, we do not know, but signify only through phenomena, which in reality give us immediately a knowledge of the disposition (empirical character) only.[1] An action, so far as it is to be attributed to the way of thinking as its cause, does nevertheless not result from it according to empirical laws, that is, it is not *preceded* by the conditions of pure reason, but only by its effects in the phenomenal form of the internal sense. Pure reason, as a simple intelligible faculty, is not subject to the form of time, or to the conditions of the succession of time. The causality of reason in its intelligible character does *not arise* or begin at a certain time in order to produce an effect; for in that case it would be subject to the natural law of phenomena, which determines all causal series in time, and its causality would then be nature and not freedom. What, therefore, we can say is, that if reason can possess causality with reference to phenomena, it is a faculty *through which* the sensuous condition of an empirical series of effects first begins. For the condition that lies in reason is not sensuous, and therefore does itself not begin. Thus we get what we missed in all empirical series, namely, that the *condition* of a successive series of events

[1] The true morality of actions (merit or guilt), even that of our own conduct, remains therefore entirely hidden. Our imputations can refer to the empirical character only. How much of that may be the pure effect of freedom, how much should be ascribed to nature only, and to the faults of temperament, for which man is not responsible, or its happy constitution (*merito fortunae*), no one can discover, and no one can judge with perfect justice.

should itself be empirically unconditioned. For here the condition is really *outside* the series of phenomena (in the intelligible), and therefore not subject to any sensuous condition, nor to any temporal determination through preceding causes. . . . [M. 447]

Reason is therefore the constant condition of all free actions by which man takes his place in the phenomenal world. Every one of them is determined beforehand in his empirical character, before it becomes actual. With regard to the intelligible character, however, of which the empirical is only the sensuous schema, there is neither *before* nor *after;* and every action, without regard to the temporal relation which connects it with other phenomena, is the immediate effect of the intelligible character of pure reason. That reason therefore acts freely, without being determined dynamically, in the chain of natural causes, by external or internal conditions, anterior in time. That freedom must then not only be regarded negatively, as independence of empirical conditions (for in that case the faculty of reason would cease to be a cause of phenomena), but should be determined positively also, as the faculty of beginning spontaneously a series of events. Hence nothing begins in reason itself, and being itself the unconditioned condition of every free action, reason admits of no condition antecedent in time above itself, while nevertheless its effect takes its beginning in the series of phenomena, though it can never constitute in that series an *absolutely* first beginning.

In order to illustrate the regulative principle of reason by an example of its empirical application, not in order to confirm it (for such arguments are useless for transcendental propositions), let us take a voluntary action, for example, a malicious lie, by which a man has produced a certain confusion in society, and of which we first try to find out the motives, and afterwards try to determine how far it and its consequences may be imputed to the offender. With regard to the first point, one has first to follow up his empirical character to its very sources, which are to be found in wrong education, bad society, in part also in the viciousness of a natural disposition, and a nature insensible to shame, or ascribed to frivolity and heedlessness, not omitting the occasioning causes at the time. In all this the procedure is exactly the same as in the investigation of a series of determining causes of a given natural effect. But although one believes that the act was thus determined, one nevertheless blames the offender, and not on account of his unhappy natural disposition, not on account of influencing circumstances, not even on account of his former course of life, because one supposes one might leave entirely out of account what that course of life may have been, and consider the past series of conditions as having never existed, and the act itself as totally unconditioned by previous states, as if the offender had begun with it a new series of effects, quite by himself. This blame is founded on a law of reason, reason being considered as a cause which, independent of all the before-mentioned empirical conditions, would and should have determined the behaviour of the man otherwise. Nay, we do not regard the causality of reason as a concurrent agency only, but as complete in itself, even though the sensuous motives did not favour, but even oppose it. The action is imputed to a man's intelligible character. At the moment when he tells the lie, the guilt is entirely his; that is, we regard reason, in spite of all empirical conditions of the act, as completely free, and the act has to be imputed entirely to a fault of reason.

Such an imputation clearly shows that we imagine

that reason is not affected at all by the influences of the senses, and that it does not change (although its manifestations, that is the mode in which it shows itself by its effects, do change): that in it no state precedes as determining a following state, in fact, that reason does not belong to the series of sensuous conditions which render phenomena necessary, according to laws of nature. Reason, it is supposed, is present in all the actions of man, in all circumstances of time, and always the same; but it is itself never in time, never in a new state in which it was not before; it is *determining,* never *determined.* We cannot ask, therefore, why reason has not determined itself differently, but only why it has not differently determined the *phenomena* by its causality. And here no answer is really possible. For a different intelligible character would have given a different empirical character, and if we say that, in spite of the whole of his previous course of life, the offender could have avoided the lie, this only means that it was in the power of reason, and that reason, in its causality, is subject to no phenomenal and temporal conditions, and lastly, that the difference of time, though it makes a great difference in phenomena and their relation to each other, can, as these are neither things nor causes by themselves, produce no difference of action in reference to reason.

We thus see that, in judging of voluntary actions, we can, so far as their causality is concerned, get only so far as the intelligible cause, but not beyond. We can see that that cause is free, that it determines as independent of sensibility, and therefore is capable of being the sensuously unconditioned condition of phenomena. To explain why that intelligible character should, under present circumstances, give these phenomena and this empirical character, and no other, transcends all the powers of our reason, nay, all its rights of questioning, as if we were to ask why the transcendental object of our external sensuous intuition gives us intuition in *space* only and no other. But the problem which we have to solve does not require us to ask or to answer such questions. Our problem was, whether freedom is contradictory to natural necessity in one and the same action: and this we have sufficiently answered by showing that freedom may have relation to a very different kind of conditions from those of nature, so that the law of the latter does not affect the former, and both may exist independent of, and undisturbed by, each other.

* * * * * * * *

It should be clearly understood that, in what we have said, we have had no intention of establishing the *reality* of freedom, as one of the faculties which contain the cause of the phenomenal appearances in our world of sense. For not only would this have been no transcendental consideration at all, which is concerned with concepts only, but it could never have succeeded, because from experience we can never infer anything but what must be represented in thought according to the laws of experience. It was not even our intention to prove the *possibility* of freedom, for in this also we should not have succeeded, because from mere concepts *a priori* we can never know the possibility of any real ground or any causality. We have here treated freedom as a transcendental idea only, which makes reason imagine that it can absolutely begin the series of phenomenal conditions through what is sensuously unconditioned, but by which reason becomes involved in an antinomy with its own laws, which it had prescribed to the empirical use of the understanding. That this antinomy rests on a mere illusion, and that nature does *not contradict* the causality of freedom, that was the only thing which we could prove, and cared to prove.

IV. *Solution of the Cosmological Idea of the Totality of the Dependence of Phenomena, with Regard to their Existence in General* [1]

In the preceding article we considered the changes in the world of sense in their dynamical succession, every one being subordinate to another as its cause. Now, however, the succession of states is to serve only as our guide in order to arrive at an existence that might be the highest condition of all that is subject to change, namely, the *necessary Being.* We are concerned here, not with the unconditioned causality, but with the unconditioned existence of the substance itself. Therefore the succession which we have before us is properly one of concepts and not of intuitions, so far as the one is the condition of the other.

It is easy to see, however, that as everything comprehended under phenomena is changeable, and therefore conditioned in its existence, there cannot be, in the whole series of dependent existence, any unconditioned link the existence of which might be considered as absolutely necessary, and that therefore, if phenomena were things by themselves, and their condition accordingly belonged with the conditioned always to one and the same series of intuitions, a necessary being, as the condition of the existence of the phenomena of the world of sense, could never exist.

The dynamical regressus has this peculiar distinction as compared with the mathematical, that, as the latter is only concerned with the composition of parts in form-

[1] [Cf. M. 452 ff.]

ing a whole or the division of a whole into its parts, the conditions of that series must always be considered as parts of it, and therefore as homogeneous and as phenomena, while in the dynamical regressus, where we are concerned, not with the possibility of an unconditioned whole, consisting of a number of given parts, or of an unconditioned part belonging to a given whole, but with the derivation of a state from its cause, or of the contingent existence of the substance itself from the necessary substance, it is not required that the condition should form one and the same empirical series with the conditioned.

There remains therefore to us another escape from this apparent antinomy: because both conflicting propositions might, under different aspects, be true at the same time. That is, all things of the world of sense might be entirely contingent, and have therefore an empirically conditioned existence only, though there might nevertheless be a non-empirical condition of the whole series, that is, an unconditionally necessary being. For this, as an intelligible condition, would not belong to the series, as a link of it (not even as the highest link), nor would it render any link of that series empirically unconditioned, but would leave the whole world of sense, in all its members, in its empirically conditioned existence. This manner of admitting an unconditional existence as the ground of phenomena would differ from the empirically unconditioned causality (freedom), treated of in the preceding article, because, with respect to freedom, the thing itself, as cause (*substantia phaenomenon*), belonged to the series of conditions, and its causality only was represented as intelligible, while here, on the contrary, the necessary being has to be conceived as lying outside the series of the world of sense (as *ens extramundanum*), and as purely intelligible, by which alone it could be guarded against itself becoming subject to the law of contingency and dependence applying to all phenomena.

The *regulative principle* of reason, with regard to our present problem, is therefore this, that everything in the world of sense has an empirically conditioned existence, and that in it there is never any unconditioned necessity with reference to any quality; that there is no member in the series of conditions of which one ought not to expect, and as far as possible to seek, the empirical condition in some possible experience; and that we are never justified in deriving any existence from a condition outside the empirical series, or in considering it as independent and self-subsistent in the series itself; without however denying in the least that the whole series may depend on some intelligible being, which is free therefore from all empirical conditions, and itself contains rather the ground of the possibility of all those phenomena.

By this we by no means intend to prove the unconditionally necessary existence of such a being, or even to demonstrate the possibility of a purely intelligible condition of the existence of the phenomena of the world of sense. But as on the one side we limit reason, lest it should lose the thread of the empirical condition and lose itself in *transcendent* explanations incapable of being represented *in concreto,* thus, on the other side, we want to limit the law of the purely empirical use of the understanding, lest it should venture to decide on the possibility of things in general, and declare the intelligible to be *impossible,* because it has been shown to be useless for the explanation of phenomena. What is shown by this is simply this, that the complete contingency of all things in nature and of all their (empirical) conditions, may well coexist with the arbitrary presupposition of a necessary, though purely intelligible condition, and that, as there is no real contradiction between these two views, they *may well both be true*. Granted even that such an absolutely necessary being, as postulated by the understanding, is impossible in itself, we still maintain that this cannot be concluded from the general contingency and dependence of all that belongs to the world of sense, nor from the principle that we ought not to stop at any single member so far as it is contingent, and appeal to a cause outside the world. Reason follows its own course in its empirical, and again a peculiar course in its transcendental use. . . . [M. 455-6]

Concluding Remark on the Whole Antinomy of Pure Reason [1]

So long as it is only the totality of the conditions in the world of sense and the interest it can have to reason, that form the object of the concepts of our reason, our ideas are no doubt transcendental, but yet *cosmological*. If, however, we place the unconditioned (with which we are chiefly concerned) in that which is entirely outside the world of sense, therefore beyond all possible experience, our ideas become *transcendent*: for they serve not only for the completion of the empirical use of the understanding (which always remains an idea that must be obeyed, though it can never be fully carried out), but they separate themselves entirely from it, and create to themselves objects the material of which is not taken from experience, and the objective reality of which does not rest on the completion of the empirical series, but

[1] [Cf. M. 457 ff.]

on pure concepts *a priori*. Such transcendent ideas have a merely intelligible object, which may indeed be admitted as a transcendental object, of which, for the rest, we know nothing, but for which, if we wish to conceive it as a thing determined by its internal distinguishing predicates, we have neither grounds of possibility (as independent of all concepts of experience) nor the slightest justification on our side in admitting it as an object, and which, therefore, is a mere creation of our thoughts. Nevertheless that cosmological idea, which owes its origin to the fourth antinomy, urges us on to take that step. For the conditional existence of all phenomena, not being founded in itself, requires us to look out for something different from all phenomena, that is, for an intelligible object in which there should be no more contingency. As, however, if we have once allowed ourselves to admit, outside the field of the whole of sensibility, a reality existing by itself, phenomena can only be considered as contingent modes of representing intelligible objects on the part of beings which themselves are intelligences, nothing remains to us, in order to form some kind of concept of intelligible things, of which in themselves we have not the slightest knowledge, but analogy, applied to the concepts of experience. As we know the contingent by experience only, but have here to deal with things which are not meant to be objects of experience, we shall have to derive our knowledge of them from what is necessary in itself, that is, from pure concepts of things in general. Thus the first step which we take outside the world of sense, obliges us to begin our new knowledge with the investigation of the absolutely necessary Being, and to derive from its concepts the concepts of all things, so far as they are intelligible only; and this we shall attempt to do in the next chapter.

CHAPTER III

THE IDEAL OF PURE REASON

SECTION I. *Of the Ideal in General* [1]

WE have seen that without the conditions of sensibility, it is impossible to represent objects by means of the pure *concepts of the understanding,* because the conditions of their objective reality are absent, and they contain the mere form of thought only. If, however, we apply these concepts to phenomena, they can be represented *in concreto,* because in the phenomena they have the material for forming concepts of experience, which are nothing but concepts of the understanding *in concreto. Ideas,* however, are still further removed from objective reality than the *categories,* because they can meet with no phenomenon in which they could be represented *in concreto.* They contain a certain completeness unattainable by any possible empirical knowledge, and reason aims in them at a systematical unity only, to which the empirically possible unity is to approximate, without ever fully reaching it.

Still further removed from objective reality than the Idea, would seem to be what I call the *Ideal,* by which I mean the idea, not only *in concreto,* but *in individuo,* that is, an individual thing determinable or even determined by the idea alone. . . . [M. 460-2]

In its ideal . . . reason aims at a perfect determination, according to rules *a priori,* and it conceives an object throughout determinable according to principles, though without the sufficient conditions of experience, so that the concept itself is transcendent.

[1] [Cf. M. 459 ff.]

SECTION II. *Of the Transcendental Ideal* [1]

. . . [M. 462-3] The proposition, that *everything which exists is completely determined,* does not signify only that one of every pair of *given* contradictory predicates, but that one of all possible predicates must always belong to a thing, so that by this proposition predicates are not only compared with each other logically, but the thing itself is compared transcendentally with the sum total of all possible predicates. The proposition really means that, in order to know a thing completely, we must know everything that is possible, and thereby determine it either affirmatively or negatively. This complete determination is therefore a concept which *in concreto* can never be represented in its totality, and is founded therefore on an idea which belongs to reason only, reason prescribing to the understanding the rule of its complete application. . . . [M. 464-5]

If, therefore, our reason postulates a transcendental substratum for all determinations, a substratum which contains, as it were, the whole store of material whence all possible predicates of things may be taken, we shall find that such a substratum is nothing but the idea of the sum total of reality (*omnitudo realitatis*). In that case all true negations are nothing but *limitations* which they could not be unless there were the substratum of the unlimited (the All).

By this complete possession of all reality we represent the concept of a *thing by itself* as completely determined, and the concept of an *ens realissimum* is the concept of individual being, because of all possible opposite predicates one, namely, that which absolutely belongs to being, is found in its determination. It is

[1] [Cf. M. 462 ff.]

therefore a transcendental *ideal* which forms the foundations of the complete determination which is necessary for all that exists, and which constitutes at the same time the highest and complete condition of its possibility, to which all thought of objects, with regard to their content, must be traced back. It is at the same time the only true ideal of which human reason is capable, because it is in this case alone that a concept of a thing, which in itself is general, is completely determined by itself, and recognised as the representation of an individual. . . . [M. 466-7]

It is self-evident that . . . in order simply to represent the necessary and complete determination of things, reason does not presuppose the existence of a being that should correspond to the ideal, but its idea only, in order to derive from an unconditioned totality of complete determination the conditioned one, that is the totality of something limited. Reason therefore sees in the ideal the prototypon of all things which, as imperfect copies (*ectypa*), derive the material of their possibility from it, approaching more or less nearly to it, yet remaining always far from reaching it.

Thus all the possibility of things (or of the synthesis of the manifold according to their content) is considered as derivative, and the possibility of that only which includes in itself all reality as original. For all negations (which really are the only predicates by which everything else is distinguished from the truly real being) are limitations only of a greater and, in the last instance, of the highest reality, presupposing it, and, according to their content, derived from it. All the manifoldness of things consist only of so many modes of limiting the concept of the highest reality that forms their common substratum, in the same way as all figures are only different modes of limiting endless space. Hence the object of its ideal which exists in reason only is called the *original Being* (*ens originarium*), and so far as it has nothing above it, the *highest Being* (*ens summum*), and so far as everything as conditioned is subject to it, the Being of all beings (*ens entium*). All this however does not mean the objective relation of any real thing to other things, but of the *idea to concepts,* and leaves us in perfect ignorance as to the existence of a being of such superlative excellence.

Again, as we cannot say that an original being consists of so many derivative beings, because these in reality presuppose the former, and cannot therefore constitute it, it follows that the ideal of the original being must be conceived as simple.

The derivation of all other possibility from that original being cannot therefore, if we speak accurately, be considered as a *limitation* of its highest reality, and, as it were, a *division* of it—for in that case the original being would become to us a mere aggregate of derivative beings, which, according to what we have just explained, is impossible, though we represented it so in our first rough sketch. On the contrary, the highest reality would form the basis of the possibility of all things as a *cause,* and not as a *sum total.* The manifoldness of things would not depend on the limitation of the original being, but on its complete effect, and to this also would belong all our sensibility, together with all reality in phenomenal appearance, which could not, as an ingredient, belong to the idea of a supreme being.

If we follow up this idea of ours and hypostasise it, we shall be able to determine the original being by means of the concept of the highest reality as one, simple, all sufficient, eternal, etc., in one word, determine it in its unconditioned completeness through all predicaments. The concept of such a being is the concept *of God* in its transcendental sense, and thus, as I indicated above, the ideal of pure reason is the object of a transcendental *theology*.[1]

By such an employment of the transcendental idea, however, we should be overstepping the limits of its purpose and admissibility. Reason used it only, as being the *concept* of all reality, for a foundation of the complete determination of things in general, without requiring that all this reality should be given objectively and constitute itself a thing. This is a mere fiction by which we comprehend and realise the manifold of our idea in one ideal, as a particular being. We have no right to do this, not even to assume the possibility of such an hypothesis; nor do all the consequences which flow from such an ideal concern the complete determination of things in general, for the sake of which alone the idea was necessary, or influence it in the least. . . . [M. 469-71]

Section III. *Of the Arguments of Speculative Reason in Proof of the Existence of a Supreme Being*[2]

. . . [M. 471-6] There are only three kinds of proofs of the existence of God from speculative reason.

All the paths that can be followed to this end begin

[1] [The following note appears on M. 471]: This ideal of the most real of all things, although merely a representation, is first *realised,* that is, changed into an object, then *hypostasised,* and lastly, by the natural progress of reason towards unity, as we shall presently show, *personified;* because the regulative unity of experience does not rest on the phenomena themselves (sensibility alone), but on the connection of the manifold, through the *understanding* (in an *apperception*), so that the unity of the highest reality, and the complete determinability (possibility) of all things, seem to reside in a supreme understanding, and therefore in an intelligence.

[2] [Cf. M. 471 ff.]

either from definite experience and the peculiar nature of the world of sense, known to us through experience, and ascend from it, according to the laws of causality, to the highest cause, existing outside the world; or they rest on indefinite experience only, that is, on any existence which is empirically given; or lastly, they leave all experience out of account, and conclude, entirely *a priori* from mere concepts, the existence of a supreme cause. The first proof is the *physico-theological,* the second the *cosmological,* the third the *ontological* proof. There are no more, and there can be no more.

I shall show that neither on the one path, the empirical, nor on the other, the transcendental, can reason achieve anything, and that it stretches its wings in vain, if it tries to soar beyond the world of sense by the mere power of speculation. With regard to the order in which these three arguments should be examined, it will be the opposite of that, followed by reason in its gradual development, in which we placed them also at first ourselves. For we shall be able to show that, although experience gives the first impulse, it is the transcendental concept only which guides reason in its endeavours, and fixes the last goal which reason wishes to retain. I shall therefore begin with the examination of the transcendental proof, and see afterwards how far it may be strengthened by the addition of empirical elements.

SECTION IV. *Of the Impossibility of an Ontological*[1] *Proof of the Existence of God*[2]

. . . [M. 477-8] [1.][3] People have at all times been talking of an *absolutely necessary* Being, but they have tried, not so much to understand whether and how a thing of that kind could even be conceived, as rather to prove its existence. No doubt a verbal definition of that concept is quite easy, if we say that it is something the non-existence of which is impossible. This, however, does not make us much wiser with reference to the conditions that make it necessary to consider the non-existence of a thing as absolutely inconceivable. It is these conditions which we want to know, and whether by that concept we are thinking anything or not. For to use the word *unconditioned,* in order to get rid of all the conditions which the understanding always requires, when wishing to conceive something as necessary, does not render it clear to us in the least whether, after that, we are still thinking anything or perhaps nothing, by the concept of the unconditionally necessary.

[2.] Nay, more than this, people have imagined that by a number of examples they had explained this concept, at first risked at haphazard, and afterwards become quite familiar, and that therefore all further inquiry regarding its intelligibility were unnecessary. It was said that every proposition of geometry, such as,

[1] [Cf. Hume's formulation of this proof: "The idea of infinite perfection implies that of actual existence"; and Descartes': "Existence can no more be separated from the essence of God than the idea of a mountain from that of a valley, or the equality of its three angles from the essence of a rectilinear triangle."]

[2] [Cf. M. 477 ff.]

[3] [The four distinct criticisms which Kant makes of the ontological argument are indicated thus, with Arabic numerals.]

for instance, that a triangle has three angles, is absolutely necessary, and people began to talk of an object entirely outside the sphere of our understanding, as if they understood perfectly well what, by that concept, they wished to predicate of it.

But all these pretended examples are taken without exception from *judgments* only, not from *things,* and their existence. Now the unconditioned necessity of judgments is not the same thing as an absolute necessity of things. The absolute necessity of a judgment is only a conditioned necessity of the thing, or of the predicate in the judgment. The above proposition did not say that three angles were absolutely necessary, but that under the condition of the existence of a triangle, three angles are given (in it) by necessity. Nevertheless, this pure logical necessity has exerted so powerful an illusion, that, after having formed of a thing a concept *a priori* so constituted that it seemed to include existence in its sphere, people thought they could conclude with certainty that, because existence necessarily belongs to the object of that concept, provided always that I accept the thing as given (existing), its existence also must necessarily be accepted (according to the rule of identity), and that the Being therefore must itself be absolutely necessary, because its existence is implied in a concept, which is accepted voluntarily only, and always under the condition that I accept the object of it as given.

If in an identical judgment I reject the predicate and retain the subject, there arises a contradiction, and hence, I say, that the former belongs to the latter necessarily. But if I reject the subject as well as the predicate, there is no contradiction, because there is nothing left that can be contradicted. To accept a triangle and yet to reject its three angles is contradictory, but there is no contradiction at all in admitting the non-existence of the triangle and of its three angles. The same applies to the concept of an absolutely necessary Being. Remove its existence, and you remove the thing itself, with all its predicates, so that a contradiction becomes impossible. There is nothing external to which the contradiction could apply, because the thing is not meant to be externally necessary; nor is there anything internal that could be contradicted, for in removing the thing out of existence, you have removed at the same time all its internal qualities. If you say, God is almighty, that is a necessary judgment, because almightiness cannot be removed, if you accept a deity, that is, an infinite Being, with the concept of which that other concept is identical. But if you say, God is not, then neither his almightiness, nor any other of his predicates is given; they are all, together with the subject, removed out of existence, and therefore there is not the slightest contradiction in that sentence.

[3.] We have seen therefore that, if I remove the predicate of a judgment together with its subject, there can never be an internal contradiction, whatever the predicate may be. The only way of evading this conclusion would be to say that there are subjects which cannot be removed out of existence, but must always remain. But this would be the same as to say that there exist absolutely necessary subjects, an assumption the correctness of which I have called in question, and the possibility of which you had undertaken to prove. For I cannot form to myself the smallest concept of a thing which, if it had been removed together with all its predicates, should leave behind a contradiction; and except contradiction, I have no other test of impossibility by pure concepts *a priori*. Against all these general arguments (which no one can object to) you challenge me with a case, which you represent as a proof by a fact, namely, that there is one, and this one concept only, in which the non-existence or the removal of its object would be self-contradictory, namely, the concept of the most real Being (*ens realissimum*). You say that it possesses all reality, and you are no doubt justified in accepting such a Being as possible. This for the present I may admit, though the absence of self-contradictoriness in a concept is far from proving the possibility of its object.[1] Now reality comprehends existence, and therefore existence is contained in the concept of a thing possible. If that thing is removed, the internal possibility of the thing would be removed, and this is self-contradictory.

I answer:—Even in introducing into the concept of a thing, which you wish to think in its possibility only, the concept of its existence, under whatever disguise it may be, you have been guilty of a contradiction. If you were allowed to do this, you would apparently have carried your point; but in reality you have achieved nothing, but have only committed a tautology. I simply ask you, whether the proposition, that *this or that thing* (which, whatever it may be, I grant you as possible) *exists*, is an analytical or a synthetical proposition? If the former, then by its existence you add nothing to your thought of the thing; but in that case, either the thought within you would be the thing itself, or you have

[1] A concept is always possible, if it is not self-contradictory. This is the logical characteristic of possibility, and by it the object of the concept is distinguished from the *nihil negativum.* But it may nevertheless be an empty concept, unless the objective reality of the synthesis, by which the concept is generated, has been distinctly shown. This, however, as shown above, must always rest on principles of possible experience, and not on the principle of analysis (the principle of contradiction). This is a warning against inferring at once from the possibility of concepts (logical) the possibility of things (real)

presupposed existence, as belonging to possibility, and have according to your own showing deduced existence from internal possibility, which is nothing but a miserable tautology. The mere word *reality,* which in the concept of a thing sounds different from existence in the concept of the predicate, can make no difference. For if you call all accepting or positing (without determining what it is) reality, you have placed a thing, with all its predicates, within the concept of the subject, and accepted it as real, and you do nothing but repeat it in the predicate. If, on the contrary, you admit, as every sensible man must do, that every proposition involving existence is synthetical, how can you say that the predicate of existence does not admit of removal without contradiction, a distinguishing property which is peculiar to analytical propositions only, the very character of which depends on it?

I might have hoped to put an end to this subtle argumentation, without many words, and simply by an accurate definition of the concept of existence, if I had not seen that the illusion, in mistaking a logical predicate for a real one (that is the predicate which determines a thing), resists all correction. Everything can become a *logical predicate,* even the subject itself may be predicated of itself, because logic makes no account of any contents of concepts. *Determination,* however, is a predicate, added to the concept of the subject, and enlarging it, and it must not therefore be contained in it.

[4.] *Being* is evidently not a real predicate, or a concept of something that can be added to the concept of a thing. It is merely the admission of a thing, and of certain determinations in it. Logically, it is merely the copula of a judgment. The proposition, *God is al-*

mighty, contains two concepts, each having its object, namely, God and almightiness. The small word *is,* is not an additional predicate, but only serves to put the predicate *in relation* to the subject. If, then, I take the subject (God) with all its predicates (including that of almightiness), and say, *God is,* or there is a God, I do not put a new predicate to the concept of God, but I only put the subject by itself, with all its predicates, in relation to my concept, as its object. Both must contain exactly the same kind of thing, and nothing can have been added to the concept, which expresses possibility only, by my thinking its object as simply given and saying, it is. And thus the real does not contain more than the possible. A hundred real dollars do not contain a penny more than a hundred possible dollars. For as the latter signify the concept, the former the object and its position by itself, it is clear that, in case the former contained more than the latter, my concept would not express the whole object, and would not therefore be its adequate concept. In my financial position no doubt there exists more by one hundred real dollars, than by their concept only (that is their possibility), because in reality the object is not only contained analytically in my concept, but is added to my concept (which is a determination of my state), synthetically; but the conceived hundred dollars are not in the least increased through the existence which is outside my concept.

By whatever and by however many predicates I may think a thing (even in completely determining it), nothing is really added to it, if I add that the thing exists. Otherwise, it would not be the same that exists, but something more than was contained in the concept, and I could not say that the exact object of my concept existed.

Nay, even if I were to think in a thing all reality, except one, that one missing reality would not be supplied by my saying that so defective a thing exists, but it would exist with the same defect with which I thought it; or what exists would be different from what I thought. If, then, I try to conceive a being, as the highest reality (without any defect), the question still remains, whether it exists or not. For though in my concept there may be wanting nothing of the possible real content of a thing in general, something is wanting in its relation to my whole state of thinking, namely, that the knowledge of that object should be possible *a posteriori* also. And here we perceive the cause of our difficulty. If we were concerned with an object of our senses, I could not mistake the existence of a thing for the mere concept of it; for by the concept the object is thought as only in harmony with the general conditions of a possible empirical knowledge, while by its existence it is thought as contained in the whole content of experience. Through this connection with the content of the whole experience, the concept of an object is not in the least increased; our thought has only received through it one more possible perception. If, however, we are thinking existence through the pure category alone, we need not wonder that we cannot find any characteristic to distinguish it from mere possibility.

Whatever, therefore, our concept of an object may contain, we must always step outside it, in order to attribute to it existence. With objects of the senses, this takes place through their connection with any one of my perceptions, according to empirical laws; with objects of pure thought, however, there is no means of knowing their existence, because it would have to be known entirely *a priori,* while our consciousness of every kind of existence, whether immediately by perception, or by conclusions which connect something with perception, belongs entirely to the unity of experience, and any existence outside that field, though it cannot be declared to be absolutely impossible, is a presupposition that cannot be justified by anything.

[*Conclusion*]

The concept of a Supreme Being is, in many respects, a very useful idea, but being an idea only, it is quite incapable of increasing, by itself alone, our knowledge with regard to what exists. It cannot even do so much as to inform us any further as to its possibility. The analytical characteristic of possibility, which consists in the absence of contradiction in mere positions (realities), cannot be denied to it; but the connection of all real properties in one and the same thing is a synthesis the possibility of which we cannot judge *a priori* because these realities are not given to us as such, and because, even if this were so, no judgment whatever takes place, it being necessary to look for the characteristic of the possibility of synthetical knowledge in experiences only, to which the object of an idea can never belong. Thus we see that the celebrated Leibniz is far from having achieved what he thought he had, namely, to understand *a priori* the possibility of so sublime an ideal Being.

Time and labour therefore are lost on the famous ontological (Cartesian) proof of the existence of a Supreme Being from mere concepts; and a man might as well imagine that he could become richer in knowledge by mere ideas, as a merchant in capital, if, in order to improve his position, he were to add a few noughts to his cash account.

SECTION V. *Of the Impossibility of a Cosmological Proof of the Existence of God*[1]

. . . [M. 486-7.] We shall now proceed to exhibit and to examine this cosmological proof which Leibniz calls also the proof *a contingentia mundi.*

It runs as follows: If there exists anything, there must exist an absolutely necessary Being also. Now I, at least, exist; therefore there exists an absolutely necessary Being. The minor contains an experience, the major the conclusion from experience in general to the existence of the necessary.[2] This proof therefore begins with experience, and is not entirely *a priori,* or ontological; and, as the object of all possible experience is called the world, this proof is called the *cosmological proof.* As it takes no account of any peculiar property of the objects of experience, by which this world of ours may differ from any other possible world, it is distinguished, in its name also, from the physico-theological proof, which employs as arguments, observations of the peculiar property of this our world of sense.

The proof then proceeds as follows: The necessary Being can be determined in one way only, that is, by one only of all possible opposite predicates; it must therefore be determined completely by its own concept. Now, there is only one concept of a thing possible, which *a priori* completely determines it, namely, that of the *ens realissimum.* It follows, therefore, that the concept of the *ens realissimum* is the only one by which a neces-

[1] [Cf. M. 486 ff.]

[2] This conclusion is too well known to require detailed exposition. It rests on the apparently transcendental law of causality in nature, that everything *contingent* has its cause, which, if contingent again, must likewise have a cause, till the series of subordinate causes ends in an absolutely necessary cause, without which it could not be complete.

sary Being can be thought, and therefore it is concluded that a highest Being exists by necessity.

There are so many sophistical propositions in this cosmological argument, that it really seems as if speculative reason had spent all her dialectical skill in order to produce the greatest possible transcendental illusion. Before examining it, we shall draw up a list of them, by which reason has put forward an old argument disguised as a new one, in order to appeal to the agreement of two witnesses, one supplied by pure reason, the other by experience, while in reality there is only one, namely, the first, who changes his dress and voice in order to be taken for a second. In order to have a secure foundation, this proof takes its stand on experience, and pretends to be different from the ontological proof, which places its whole confidence in pure concepts *a priori* only. The cosmological proof, however, uses that experience only in order to make one step, namely, to the existence of a necessary Being in general. What properties that Being may have, can never be learnt from the empirical argument, and for that purpose reason takes leave of it altogether, and tries to find out, from among concepts only, what properties an absolutely necessary Being ought to possess, i.e. which among all possible things contains in itself the requisite conditions (*requisita*) of absolute necessity. This requisite is believed by reason to exist in the concept of an *ens realissimum* only, and reason concludes at once that this must be the absolutely necessary Being. In this conclusion it is simply assumed that the concept of a being of the highest reality is perfectly adequate to the concept of absolute necessity in existence; so that the latter might be concluded from the former. This is the same proposition as that maintained in the ontological argument, and is simply taken over into the cosmological proof, nay, made its foundation, although the intention was to avoid it. For it is clear that absolute necessity is an existence from mere concepts. If, then, I say that the concept of the *ens realissimum* is such a concept, and is the only concept adequate to necessary existence, I am bound to admit that the latter may be deduced from the former. The whole conclusive strength of the so-called cosmological proof rests therefore in reality on the ontological proof from mere concepts, while the appeal to experience is quite superfluous, and, though it may lead us on to the concept of absolute necessity, it cannot demonstrate it with any definite object. For as soon as we intend to do this, we must at once abandon all experience, and try to find out which among the pure concepts may contain the conditions of the possibility of an absolutely necessary Being. But if in this way the possibility of such a Being has been perceived, its existence also has been proved: for what we are really saying is this, that under all possible things there is one which carries with it absolute necessity, or that this Being exists with absolute necessity. . . . [M. 490]

We thus see that the second road taken by speculative reason, in order to prove the existence of the highest Being, is not only as illusory as the first, but commits in addition an *ignoratio elenchi,* promising to lead us by a new path, but after a short circuit bringing us back to the old one, which we had abandoned for its sake.

I said before that a whole nest of dialectical assumptions was hidden in that cosmological proof, and that transcendental criticism might easily detect and destroy it. I shall here enumerate them only, leaving it to the experience of the reader to follow up the fallacies and remove them.

We find, first, the transcendental principle of inferring a cause from the accidental. This principle, that everything contingent must have a cause, is valid in the world of sense only, and has not even a meaning outside it. For the purely intellectual concept of the contingent cannot produce a synthetical proposition like that of causality, and the principle of causality has no meaning and no criterion of its use, except in the world of sense, while here it is meant to help us beyond the world of sense.

Secondly. The inference of a first cause, based on the impossibility of an infinite ascending series of given causes in this world of sense,—an inference which the principles of the use of reason do not allow us to draw even in experience, while here we extend that principle beyond experience, whither that series can never be prolonged.

Thirdly. The false self-satisfaction of reason with regard to the completion of that series, brought about by removing in the end every kind of condition, without which, nevertheless, no concept of necessity is possible, and by then, when any definite concepts have become impossible, accepting this as a completion of our concept. [1]

Fourthly. The mistaking the logical possibility of a concept of all united reality (without any internal contradiction) for the transcendental, which requires a principle for the practicability of such a synthesis, such principle however being applicable to the field of possible experience only, etc. . . . [M. 492-3]

It may be allowable to *admit* the existence of a Being entirely sufficient to serve as the cause of all possible effects, simply in order to assist reason in her search for unity of causes. But to go so far as to say that *such a Being exists necessarily,* is no longer the modest

[1] [Cf. the first criticism of the Ontological Argument, above.]

language of an admissible hypothesis, but the bold assurance of apodictic certainty; for the knowledge of that which is absolutely necessary must itself possess absolute necessity. . . . [M. 493-4]

Discovery and Explanation of the Dialectical Illusion in all Transcendental Proofs of the Existence of a Necessary Being[1]

Both proofs, hitherto attempted, were transcendental, that is, independent of empirical principles. For although the cosmological proof assumes for its foundation an experience in general, it does not rest on any particular quality of it, but on pure principles of reason, with reference to an existence given by the empirical consciousness in general, and abandons even that guidance in order to derive its support from pure concepts only. What then in these transcendental proofs is the cause of the dialectical, but natural, illusion which connects the concepts of necessity and of the highest reality, and realises and hypostasises that which can only be an idea? What is the cause that renders it inevitable to admit something as necessary in itself among existing things, and yet makes us shrink back from the existence of such a Being as from an abyss? What is to be done that reason should understand itself on this point, and, escaping from the wavering state of hesitatingly approving or disapproving, acquire a calm insight into the matter? . . . [M. 495-6]

If, therefore, I am obliged to think something necessary for all existing things, and at the same time am not justified in thinking of anything as in itself necessary, the conclusion is inevitable: that necessity and contingency do not concern things themselves, for otherwise there would be a contradiction, and that therefore

[1] [Cf. M. 495 ff.]

neither of the two principles can be objective; but that they may possibly be subjective principles of reason only, according to which, on one side, we have to find for all that is given as existing, something that is necessary, and thus never to stop except when we have reached an *a priori* complete explanation; while on the other we must never hope for that completion, that is, never admit anything empirical as unconditioned, and thus dispense with its further derivation. In that sense both principles as purely heuristic and *regulative,* and affecting the formal interests of reason only, may well stand side by side. For the one tells us that we ought to philosophise on nature as if there was a necessary first cause for everything that exists, if only in order to introduce systematical unity into our knowledge, by always looking for such an idea as an imagined highest cause. The other warns us against mistaking any single determination concerning the existence of things for such a highest cause, i.e. for something absolutely necessary, and bids us to keep the way always open for further derivation, and to treat it always as conditioned. If, then, everything that is perceived in things has to be considered by us as only conditionally necessary, nothing that is empirically given can ever be considered as absolutely necessary.

It follows from this that the absolutely necessary must be accepted as *outside the world,* because it is only meant to serve as a principle of the greatest possible unity of phenomena, of which it is the highest cause, and that it can never be reached *in the world,* because the second rule bids you always to consider all empirical causes of that unity as derived. . . . [M. 497-8]

The ideal of the Supreme Being is therefore, according to these remarks, nothing but a *regulative principle* of reason, which obliges us to consider all connection in the world as if it arose from an all-sufficient necessary cause, in order to found on it the rule of a systematical unity necessary according to general laws for the explanation of the world; it does not involve the assertion of an existence necessary by itself. It is impossible, however, at the same time, to escape from a transcendental *subreptio,* which leads us to represent that formal principle as constitutive, and to think that unity as hypostasised. It is the same with space. Space, though it is only a principle of sensibility, yet serves originally to make all forms possible, these being only limitations of it. For that very reason, however, it is mistaken for something absolutely necessary and independent, nay, for an object *a priori* existing in itself. It is the same here, and as this systematical unity of nature can in no wise become the principle of the empirical use of our reason, unless we base it on the idea of an *ens realissimum* as the highest cause, it happens quite naturally that we thus represent that idea as a real object, and that object again, as it is the highest condition, as necessary. Thus a *regulative* principle has been changed into a *constitutive* principle, which substitution becomes evident at once because, as soon as I consider that highest Being, which with regard to the world was absolutely (unconditionally) necessary, as a thing by itself, that necessity cannot be conceived, and can therefore have existed in my reason as a formal condition of thought only, and not as a material and substantial condition of existence.

SECTION VI. *Of the Impossibility of the Physico-theological Proof* [1]

. . . [M. 499-500] This present world presents to us so immeasurable a stage of variety, order, fitness, and

[1] [Cf. M. 499 ff.]

beauty, whether we follow it up in the infinity of space or in its unlimited division, that even with the little knowledge which our poor understanding has been able to gather, all language, with regard to so many and inconceivable wonders, loses its vigour, all numbers their power of measuring, and all our thoughts their necessary determination; so that our judgment of the whole is lost in a speechless, but all the more eloquent astonishment. Everywhere we see a chain of causes and effects, of means and ends, of order in birth and death, and as nothing has entered by itself into the state in which we find it, all points to another thing as its cause. As that cause necessitates the same further enquiry, the whole universe would thus be lost in the abyss of nothing, unless we admitted something which, existing by itself, original and independent, outside the chain of infinite contingencies, should support it, and, as the cause of its origin, secure to it at the same time its permanence. Looking at all the things in the world, what greatness shall we attribute to that highest cause? We do not know the whole contents of the world, still less can we measure its magnitude by a comparison with all that is possible. But, as with regard to causality, we cannot do without a last and highest Being, why should we not fix the degree of its perfection *beyond everything else that is possible?* This we can easily do, though only in the faint outline of an abstract concept, if we represent to ourselves all possible perfections united in it as in one substance. Such a concept would agree with the demand of our reason, which requires parsimony in the number of principles; it would have no contradictions in itself, would be favourable to the extension of the employment of reason in the midst of experience, by guiding it towards order and system, and lastly, would never be decidedly opposed to any experience.

This proof will always deserve to be treated with respect. It is the oldest, the clearest, and most in conformity with human reason. It gives life to the study of nature, deriving its own existence from it, and thus constantly acquiring new vigour.

It reveals aims and intention, where our own observation would not by itself have discovered them, and enlarges our knowledge of nature by leading us towards that peculiar unity the principle of which exists outside nature. This knowledge reacts again on its cause, namely, the transcendental idea, and thus increases the belief in a supreme Author to an irresistible conviction.

It would therefore be not only extremely sad, but utterly vain to attempt to diminish the authority of that proof. Reason, constantly strengthened by the powerful arguments that come to hand by themselves, though they are no doubt empirical only, cannot be discouraged by any doubts of subtle and abstract speculation. Roused from every inquisitive indecision, as from a dream, by one glance at the wonders of nature and the majesty of the cosmos, reason soars from height to height till it reaches the highest, from the conditioned to conditions, till it reaches the supreme and unconditioned Author of all.

But although we have nothing to say against the reasonableness and utility of this line of argument, but wish, on the contrary, to commend and encourage it, we cannot approve of the claims which this proof advances to apodictic certainty, and to an approval on its own merits, requiring no favour, and no help from any other quarter. It cannot injure the good cause, if the dogmatical language of the overweening sophist is toned down to the moderate and modest statements of a faith which does not require unconditioned submission, yet is sufficient to give rest and comfort. I therefore maintain that the physico-theological proof can never establish by itself alone the existence of a Supreme Being, but must always leave it to the ontological proof (to which it serves only as an introduction), to supply its deficiency; so that, after all, it is the ontological proof which contains the *only possible argument* (supposing always that any speculative proof is possible), and human reason can never do without it.

The principal points of the physico-theological proof are the following. 1st. There are everywhere in the world clear indications of an intentional arrangement carried out with great wisdom, and forming a whole indescribably varied in its contents and infinite in extent.

2ndly. The fitness of this arrangement is entirely foreign to the things existing in the world, and belongs to them contingently only; that is, the nature of different things could never spontaneously, by the combination of so many means, co-operate towards definite aims, if these means had not been selected and arranged on purpose by a rational disposing principle, according to certain fundamental ideas.

3rdly. There exists, therefore, a sublime and wise cause (or many), which must be the cause of the world, not only as a blind and all-powerful nature, by means of unconscious *fecundity*, but as an intelligence, by *freedom*.

4thly. The unity of that cause may be inferred with certainty from the unity of the reciprocal relation of the parts of the world, as portions of a skilful edifice, so far as our experience reaches, and beyond it, with plausibility, according to the principles of analogy.

Without wishing to argue, for the sake of argument only, with natural reason, as to its conclusion in inferring from the analogy of certain products of nature with the works of human art, in which man does violence to nature, and forces it not to follow its own aims, but to adapt itself to ours (that is, from the similarity of certain products of nature with houses, ships, and watches), in inferring from this, I say, that a similar causality, namely, understanding and will, must be at the bottom of nature, and in deriving the internal possibility of a freely acting nature (which, it may be, renders all human art and even human reason possible) from another though superhuman art—a kind of reasoning, which probably could not stand the severest test of transcendental criticism; we are willing to admit, nevertheless, that if we have to name such a cause, we cannot do better than to follow the analogy of such products of human design, which are the only ones of which we know completely both cause and effect. There would be no excuse, if reason were to surrender a causality which it knows, and have recourse to obscure and indemonstrable principles of explanation, which it does not know.

According to this argument, the fitness and harmony existing in so many works of nature might prove the contingency of the form, but not of the matter, that is, the substance in the world, because, for the latter purpose, it would be necessary to prove in addition, that the things of the world were in themselves incapable of such order and harmony, according to general laws, unless there existed, even in their *substance,* the product of a supreme wisdom. For this purpose, very different arguments would be required from those derived from the analogy of human art. The utmost, therefore, that could be established by such a proof would be an *architect of the world,* always very much hampered by the quality of the material with which he has to work, not a *creator,* to whose idea everything is subject. This would by no means suffice for the purposed aim of proving an all-sufficient original Being. If we wished to prove the contingency of matter itself, we must have recourse to a transcendental argument, and this is the very thing which was to be avoided.

The inference, therefore, really proceeds from the order and design that can everywhere be observed in the world, as an entirely contingent arrangement, to the existence of a cause, *proportionate to it*. The concept of that cause must therefore teach us something quite *definite* about it, and can therefore be no other concept but that of a Being which possesses all might, wisdom, etc., in one word, all perfection of an all-sufficient Being. The predicates of a *very great*, of an astounding, of an immeasurable might and virtue give us no definite concept, and never tell us really what the thing is by itself. They are only relative representations of the magnitude of an object, which the observer (of the world) compares with himself and his own power of comprehension, and which would be equally grand, whether we magnify the object, or reduce the observing subject to smaller proportions in reference to it. Where we are concerned with the magnitude (of the perfection) of a thing in general, there exists no definite concept, except that which comprehends all possible perfection, and only the all (*omnitudo*) of reality is thoroughly determined in the concept.

Now I hope that no one would dare to comprehend the relation of that part of the world which he has observed (in its extent as well as in its contents) to omnipotence, the relation of the order of the world to the highest wisdom, and the relation of the unity of the world to the absolute unity of its author, etc. Physico-theology, therefore, can never give a definite concept of the highest cause of the world, and is insufficient, therefore, as a principle of theology, which is itself to form the basis of religion.

The step leading to absolute totality is entirely impossible on the empirical road. Nevertheless, that step is taken in the physico-theological proof. How then has this broad abyss been bridged over?

The fact is that, after having reached the stage of admiration of the greatness, the wisdom, the power, etc. of the Author of the world, and seeing no further advance possible, one suddenly leaves the argument carried on by empirical proofs, and lays hold of that contingency which, from the very first, was inferred from the order and design of the world. The next step from that contingency leads, by means of transcendental concepts only, to the existence of something absolutely necessary, and another step from the absolute necessity of the first cause to its completely determined or determining concept, namely, that of an all-embracing reality. Thus we see that the physico-theological proof, baffled in its own undertaking, takes suddenly refuge in the cosmological proof, and as this is only the ontological proof in disguise, it really carries out its original intention by means of pure reason only; though it so strongly disclaimed in the beginning all connection with it, and professed to base everything on clear proofs from experience. . . . [M. 506-7]

Thus we have seen that the physico-theological proof rests on the cosmological, and the cosmological on the ontological proof of the existence of one original Being as the Supreme Being; and, as besides these three, there is no other path open to speculative reason, the ontological proof, based exclusively on pure concepts of reason, is the only possible one, always supposing that any proof of a proposition, so far transcending the empirical use of the understanding, is possible at all.

SECTION VII. *Criticism of all Theology based on Speculative Principles of Reason* [1]

. . . [M. 508-13] If people, however, should prefer to call in question all the former proofs of the Analytic, rather than allow themselves to be robbed of their persuasion of the value of the proofs on which they have rested so long, they surely cannot decline my request, when I ask them to justify themselves, at least on this point, in what manner, and by what kind of illumination they trust themselves to soar above all possible experience, on the wings of pure ideas. I must ask to be excused from listening to new proofs, or to the tinkered workmanship of the old. No doubt the choice is not great, for all speculative proofs end in the one, namely, the ontological; nor need I fear to be much troubled by the inventive fertility of the dogmatical defenders of that reason which they have delivered from the bondage of the senses; nor should I even, without considering myself a very formidable antagonist, decline the challenge to detect the fallacy in every one of their attempts, and thus to dispose of their pretensions. But I know too well that the hope of better success will never be surrendered by those who have once accustomed themselves to dogmatical persuasion, and I therefore restrict myself to the one just demand, that my opponents should explain in general, from the nature of the human understanding, or from any other sources of knowledge, what we are to do in order to extend our knowledge entirely *a priori,* and to carry it to a point where no possible experience, and therefore no means whatever, is able to secure to a concept invented by ourselves its objective reality. In whatever way the under-

[1] [Cf. M. 508 ff.]

standing may have reached that concept, it is clearly impossible that the *existence* of its object could be found in it through analysis, because the very knowledge of the existence of the object implies that it exists *outside our thoughts.* We cannot in fact go beyond concepts, nor, unless we follow the empirical connection by which nothing but phenomena can be given, hope to discover new objects and imaginary beings.

Although then reason, in its purely speculative application, is utterly insufficient for this great undertaking, namely, to prove the existence of a Supreme Being, it has nevertheless this great advantage of being able to *correct* our knowledge of it, if it can be acquired from elsewhere,[1] to make it consistent with itself and every intelligible view, and to purify it from everything incompatible with the concept of an original Being, and from all admixture of empirical limitations.

In spite of its insufficiency, therefore, transcendental theology has a very important negative use, as a constant test of our reason, when occupied with pure ideas only, which, as such, admit of a transcendental standard only. For suppose that on practical grounds the *admission* of a highest and all-sufficient Being, as the highest intelligence, were to maintain its validity without contradiction, it would be of the greatest importance that we should be able to determine that concept accurately on its transcendental side, as the concept of a necessary and most real Being, to remove from it what is contradictory to that highest reality and purely phenomenal (anthropomorphic in the widest sense), and at the same time to put an end to all opposite assertions, whether *atheistic, deistic,* or *anthropomorphistic.* Such a critical treatment would not be difficult, because the same

[1] [Cf. Kant's moral proof of God's existence, pp. 360 ff. below.]

arguments by which the insufficiency of human reason in asserting the existence of such a Being has been proved, must be sufficient also to prove the invalidity of opposite assertions. For whence can anybody, through pure speculation of reason, derive his knowledge that there is no Supreme Being, as the cause of all that exists, or that it can claim none of those qualities which we, to judge from their effects, represent to ourselves as compatible with the dynamical realties of a thinking Being, or that, in the latter case, they would be subject to all those limitations which sensibility imposes inevitably on all the intelligences known to us by experience?

For the purely speculative use of reason, therefore, the Supreme Being remains, no doubt, an ideal only, but an ideal *without a flaw,* a concept which finishes and crowns the whole of human knowledge, and the objective reality of which, though it cannot be proved, can neither be disproved in that way. If then there should be an Ethico-theology to supply that deficiency, transcendental theology, which before was problematical only, would prove itself indispensable in determining its concept, and in constantly testing reason, which is so often deceived by sensibility, and not even always in harmony with its own ideas. Necessity, infinity, unity, extramundane existence (not as a world-soul), eternity, free from conditions of time, omnipresence, free from conditions of space, omnipotence, etc., all these are transcendental predicates, and their purified concepts, which are so much required for every theology, can therefore be derived from transcendental theology only.

THEORY OF ETHICS[1]

[I. THE NATURE OF MORALITY]

[1. *Moral Laws are Pure, not Empirical.*]

. . . WE[2] may call all philosophy *empirical,* so far as it is based on grounds of experience: on the other hand, that which delivers its doctrines from *a priori* principles alone we may call *pure* philosophy. When the latter is merely formal, it is *logic;* if it is restricted to definite objects of the understanding, it is *metaphysic.*

In this way there arises the idea of a twofold metaphysic—a *metaphysic of nature* and a *metaphysic of morals.* Physics will thus have an empirical and also a rational part. It is the same with Ethics; but here the empirical part might have the special name of *practical anthropology,* the name *morality* being appropriated to the rational part. . . . [A. 2-3]

As my concern here is with moral philosophy, I limit the question suggested to this: Whether it is not of the utmost necessity to construct a pure moral philosophy, perfectly cleared of everything which is only empirical, and which belongs to anthropology? for that such a philosophy must be possible is evident from the common idea of duty and of the moral laws. Everyone must

[1] [T. K. Abbott's translation of Kant's Ethical writings, under the title *Kant's Theory of Ethics* (Longmans, Green & Co., 6th Ed.) has been used. All page references are to this volume. Most of the translator's notes are omitted, without indication.]

[2] [Cf. A. 2-5, in the *Preface* to the *Fundamental Principles of the Metaphysic of Morals.*]

admit that if a law is to have moral force, i.e. to be the basis of an obligation, it must carry with it absolute necessity; that, for example, the precept, "Thou shalt not lie," is not valid for men alone, as if other rational beings had no need to observe it; and so with all the other moral laws properly so called; that, therefore, the basis of obligation must not be sought in the nature of man, or in the circumstances in the world in which he is placed, but *a priori* simply in the conceptions of pure reason; and although any other precept which is founded on principles of mere experience may be in certain respects universal, yet in as far as it rests even in the least degree on an empirical basis, perhaps only as to a motive, such a precept, while it may be a practical rule, can never be called a moral law.

Thus not only are moral laws with their principles essentially distinguished from every other kind of practical knowledge in which there is anything empirical, but all moral philosophy rests wholly on its pure part. When applied to man, it does not borrow the least thing from the knowledge of man himself (anthropology), but gives laws *a priori* to him as a rational being. No doubt these laws require a judgment sharpened by experience, in order on the one hand to distinguish in what cases they are applicable, and on the other to procure for them access to the will of the man, and effectual influence on conduct; since man is acted on by so many inclinations that, though capable of the idea of a practical pure reason, he is not so easily able to make it effective *in concreto* in his life. . . . [A. 4-5] [But] it is only in a pure philosophy that we can look for the moral law in its purity and genuineness (and, in a practical matter, this is of the utmost consequence): we must, therefore, begin with pure philosophy (metaphysic), and without it there cannot be any moral philosophy at all.

That which mingles these pure principles with the empirical does not deserve the name of philosophy (for what distinguishes philosophy from common rational knowledge is, that it treats in separate sciences what the latter only comprehends confusedly); much less does it deserve that of moral philosophy, since by this confusion it even spoils the purity of morals themselves, and counteracts its own end. . . .

[2. *A Good Will is alone unqualifiedly Good.*]

NOTHING[1] can possibly be conceived in the world, or even out of it, which can be called good without qualification, except a Good Will. Intelligence, wit, judgment, and the other *talents* of the mind, however they may be named, or courage, resolution, perseverance, as qualities of temperament, are undoubtedly good and desirable in many respects; but these gifts of nature may also become extremely bad and mischievous if the will which is to make use of them, and which, therefore, constitutes what is called *character,* is not good. It is the same with the *gifts of fortune.* Power, riches, honour, even health, and the general well-being and contentment with one's condition which is called *happiness, inspire* pride, and often presumption, if there is not a good will to correct the influence of these on the mind, and with this also to rectify the whole principle of acting, and adapt it to its end. The sight of a being who is not adorned with a single feature of a pure and good will, enjoying unbroken prosperity, can never give pleasure to an impartial rational spectator. Thus a good will appears to constitute the indispensable condition even of being worthy of happiness.

There are even some qualities which are of service

[1] [Cf. A. 9-20, in *Section I* of the *Fundamental Principles of the Metaphysic of Morals.*]

to this good will itself, and may facilitate its action, yet which have no intrinsic unconditional value, but always presuppose a good will, and this qualifies the esteem that we justly have for them, and does not permit us to regard them as absolutely good. Moderation in the affections and passions, self-control, and calm deliberation are not only good in many respects, but even seem to constitute part of the intrinsic worth of the person; but they are far from deserving to be called good without qualification, although they have been so unconditionally praised by the ancients. For without the principles of a good will, they may become extremely bad; and the coolness of a villain not only makes him far more dangerous, but also directly makes him more abominable in our eyes than he would have been without it.

A good will is good not because of what it performs or effects, not by its aptness for the attainment of some proposed end, but simply by virtue of the volition, that is, it is good in itself, and considered by itself is to be esteemed much higher than all that can be brought about by it in favour of any inclination, nay, even of the sum total of all inclinations. Even if it should happen that, owing to special disfavour of fortune, or the niggardly provision of a step-motherly nature, this will should wholly lack power to accomplish its purpose, if with its greatest efforts it should yet achieve nothing, and there should remain only the good will (not, to be sure, a mere wish, but the summoning of all means in our power), then, like a jewel, it would still shine by its own light, as a thing which has its whole value in itself. Its usefulness or fruitlessness can neither add to nor take away anything from this value. It would be, as it were, only the setting to enable us to handle it the more conveniently in common commerce, or to attract to it the attention of those who are not yet connoisseurs, but not to recommend it to true connoisseurs, or to determine its value.

There is, however, something so strange in this idea of the absolute value of the mere will, in which no account is taken of its utility, that notwithstanding the thorough assent of even common reason to the idea, yet a suspicion must arise that it may perhaps really be the product of mere high-flown fancy, and that we may have misunderstood the purpose of nature in assigning reason as the governor of our will. Therefore we will examine this idea from this point of view.

In the physical constitution of an organized being, that is, a being adapted suitably to the purposes of life, we assume it as a fundamental principle that no organ for any purpose will be found but what is also the fittest and best adapted for that purpose. Now in a being which has reason and a will, if the proper object of nature were its *conservation,* its *welfare,* in a word, its *happiness,* then nature would have hit upon a very bad arrangement in selecting the reason of the creature to carry out this purpose. For all the actions which the creature has to perform with a view to this purpose, and the whole rule of its conduct, would be far more surely prescribed to it by instinct, and that end would have been attained thereby much more certainly than it ever can be by reason. Should reason have been communicated to this favoured creature over and above, it must only have served it to contemplate the happy constitution of its nature, to admire it, to congratulate itself thereon, and to feel thankful for it to the beneficent cause, but not that it should subject its desires to that weak and delusive guidance, and meddle bunglingly with the purpose of nature. In a word, nature would have taken care that reason should not break forth into *practical exercise,* nor have the presumption, with its weak insight, to think out for itself the plan of happiness, and of the means of attaining it. Nature would not only have taken on herself the choice of the ends, but also of the means, and with wise foresight would have entrusted both to instinct.

And, in fact, we find that the more a cultivated reason applies itself with deliberate purpose to the enjoyment of life and happiness, so much the more does the man fail of true satisfaction. And from this circumstance there arises in many, if they are candid enough to confess it, a certain degree of *misology,* that is, hatred of reason, especially in the case of those who are most experienced in the use of it, because after calculating all the advantages they derive, I do not say from the invention of all the arts of common luxury, but even from the sciences (which seem to them to be after all only a luxury of the understanding), they find that they have, in fact, only brought more trouble on their shoulders, rather than gained in happiness; and they end by envying, rather than despising, the more common stamp of men who keep closer to the guidance of mere instinct, and do not allow their reason much influence on their conduct. And this we must admit, that the judgment of those who would very much lower the lofty eulogies of the advantages which reason gives us in regard to the happiness and satisfaction of life, or who would even reduce them below zero, is by no means morose or ungrateful to the goodness with which the world is governed, but that there lies at the root of these judgments the idea that our existence has a different and far nobler end, for which, and not for happiness, reason is properly intended, and which must, therefore, be regarded as the supreme condition to which the private ends of man must, for the most part, be postponed.

For as reason is not competent to guide the will with

certainty in regard to its objects and the satisfaction of all our wants (which it to some extent even multiplies), this being an end to which an implanted instinct would have led with much greater certainty; and since, nevertheless, reason is imparted to us as a practical faculty, i.e. as one which is to have influence on the *will,* therefore, admitting that nature generally in the distribution of her capacities has adapted the means to the end, its true destination must be to produce a *will,* not merely good as a *means* to something else, but *good in itself,* for which reason was absolutely necessary. This will then, though not indeed the sole and complete good, must be the supreme good and the condition of every other, even of the desire of happiness. Under these circumstances, there is nothing inconsistent with the wisdom of nature in the fact that the cultivation of the reason, which is requisite for the first and unconditional purpose, does in many ways interfere, at least in this life, with the attainment of the second, which is always conditional, namely, happiness. Nay, it may even reduce it to nothing, without nature thereby failing of her purpose. For reason recognizes the establishment of a good will as its highest practical destination, and in attaining this purpose is capable only of a satisfaction of its own proper kind, namely, that from the attainment of an end, which end again is determined by reason only, notwithstanding that this may involve many a disappointment to the ends of inclination.

We have then to develop the notion of a will which deserves to be highly esteemed for itself, and is good without a view to anything further, a notion which exists already in the sound natural understanding, requiring rather to be cleared up than to be taught, and which in estimating the value of our actions always takes the first place, and constitutes the condition of all the rest. In order to do this, we will take the notion of duty, which includes that of a good will, although implying certain subjective restrictions and hindrances. These, however, far from concealing it, or rendering it unrecognizable, rather bring it out by contrast, and make it shine forth so much the brighter.

I omit here all actions which are already recognized as inconsistent with duty, although they may be useful for this or that purpose, for with these the question whether they are done *from duty* cannot arise at all, since they even conflict with it. I also set aside those actions which really conform to duty, but to which men have *no* direct *inclination,* performing them because they are impelled thereto by some other inclination. For in this case we can readily distinguish whether the action which agrees with duty is done *from duty,* or from a selfish view. It is much harder to make this distinction when the action accords with duty, and the subject has besides a *direct* inclination to it. For example, it is always a matter of duty that a dealer should not overcharge an inexperienced purchaser; and wherever there is much commerce the prudent tradesman does not overcharge, but keeps a fixed price for everyone, so that a child buys of him as well as any other. Men are thus *honestly* served; but this is not enough to make us believe that the tradesman has so acted from duty and from principles of honesty: his own advantage required it; it is out of the question in this case to suppose that he might besides have a direct inclination in favour of the buyers, so that, as it were, from love he should give no advantage to one over another. Accordingly the action was done neither from duty nor from direct inclination, but merely with a selfish view.

On the other hand, it is a duty to maintain one's life; and, in addition, everyone has also a direct inclination to do so. But on this account the often anxious care which most men take for it has no intrinsic worth, and their maxim has no moral import. They preserve their life *as duty requires,* no doubt, but not *because duty requires.* On the other hand, if adversity and hopeless sorrow have completely taken away the relish for life; if the unfortunate one, strong in mind, indignant at his fate rather than desponding or dejected, wishes for death, and yet preserves his life without loving it—not from inclination or fear, but from duty—then his maxim has a moral worth.

To be beneficent when we can is a duty; and besides this, there are many minds so sympathetically constituted that, without any other motive of vanity or self-interest, they find a pleasure in spreading joy around them, and can take delight in the satisfaction of others so far as it is their own work. But I maintain that in such a case an action of this kind, however proper, however amiable it may be, has nevertheless no true moral worth, but is on a level with other inclinations, e.g. the inclination to honour, which, if it is happily directed to that which is in fact of public utility and accordant with duty, and consequently honourable, deserves praise and encouragement, but not esteem. For the maxim lacks the moral import, namely, that such actions be done *from duty,* not from inclination. Put the case that the mind of that philanthropist was clouded by sorrow of his own, extinguishing all sympathy with the lot of others, and that while he still has the power to benefit others in distress, he is not touched by their trouble because he is absorbed with his own; and now suppose that he tears himself out of this dead insensibility, and performs the action without any inclination to it, but simply from duty, then first has his action its genuine moral worth. Further still; if nature has put little sympathy in the heart of this or that man; if he, supposed to be an upright man, is by temperament cold and indifferent to the sufferings of others, perhaps because in respect of his own he is provided with the special gift of patience and fortitude, and supposes, or even requires, that others should have the same—and such a man would certainly not be the meanest product of nature—but if nature had not specially framed him for a philanthropist, would he not still find in himself a source from whence to give himself a far higher worth than that of a good-natured temperament could be? Unquestionably. It is just in this that the moral worth of the character is brought out which is incomparably the highest of all, namely, that he is beneficent, not from inclination, but from duty.

To secure one's own happiness is a duty, at least indirectly; for discontent with one's condition, under a pressure of many anxieties and amidst unsatisfied wants, might easily become a great *temptation to transgression of duty*. But here again, without looking to duty, all men have already the strongest and most intimate inclination to happiness, because it is just in this idea that all inclinations are combined in one total. But the precept of happiness is often of such a sort that it greatly interferes with some inclinations, and yet a man cannot form any definite and certain conception of the sum of satisfaction of all of them which is called happiness. It is not then to be wondered at that a single inclination, definite both as to what it promises and as to the time within which it can be gratified, is often able to overcome such a fluctuating idea, and that a gouty patient, for instance, can choose to enjoy what he likes, and to suffer what he may, since, according to his calculation, on this occasion at least, he has [only] not sacrificed the enjoyment of the present moment to a possibly mistaken expectation of a happiness which is supposed to be found in health. But even in this case, if the general desire for happiness did not influence his will, and supposing that in his particular case health was not a necessary element in this calculation, there yet remains in this, as in all other cases, this law, namely, that he should promote his happiness not from inclination but from duty, and by this would his conduct first acquire true moral worth.

It is in this manner, undoubtedly, that we are to understand those passages of Scripture also in which we are commanded to love our neighbour, even our enemy. For love, as an affection, cannot be commanded, but beneficence for duty's sake may; even though we are not impelled to it by any inclination—nay, are even repelled by a natural and unconquerable aversion. This is *practical* love, and not *pathological*—a love which is seated in the will, and not in the propensions of sense—in principles of action and not of tender sympathy; and it is this love alone which can be commanded.

The second [1] proposition is: That an action done from duty derives its moral worth, *not from the purpose* which is to be attained by it, but from the maxim by which it is determined, and therefore does not depend on the realization of the object of the action, but merely on the *principle of volition* by which the action has taken place, without regard to any object of desire. It is clear from what precedes that the purposes which we may have in view in our actions, or their effects regarded as ends and springs of the will, cannot give to actions any unconditional or moral worth. In what, then, can their worth lie, if it is not to consist in the will and in reference to its expected effect? It cannot lie anywhere

[1] [The first proposition was that to have moral worth an action must be done from duty. Tr.'s note.]

but in the *principle of the will* without regard to the ends which can be attained by the action. For the will stands between its *a priori* principle, which is formal, and its *a posteriori* spring, which is material, as between two roads, and as it must be determined by something, it follows that it must be determined by the formal principle of volition when an action is done from duty, in which case every material principle has been withdrawn from it.

The third proposition, which is a consequence of the two preceding, I would express thus: *Duty is the necessity of acting from respect for the law.* I may have *inclination* for an object as the effect of my proposed action, but I cannot have *respect* for it, just for this reason, that it is an effect and not an energy of will. Similarly, I cannot have respect for inclination, whether my own or another's; I can at most, if my own, approve it; if another's, sometimes even love it; i.e. look on it as favourable to my own interest. It is only what is connected with my will as a principle, by no means as an effect—what does not subserve my inclination, but overpowers it, or at least in case of choice excludes it from its calculation—in other words, simply the law of itself, which can be an object of respect, and hence a command. Now an action done from duty must wholly exclude the influence of inclination, and with it every object of the will, so that nothing remains which can determine the will except objectively the *law,* and subjectively *pure respect* for this practical law, and consequently the maxim [1] that I should follow this law even to the thwarting of all my inclinations.

Thus the moral worth of an action does not lie in the

[1] A *maxim* is the subjective principle of volition. The objective principle (i.e. that which would also serve subjectively as a practical principle to all rational beings if reason had full power over the faculty of desire) is the practical *law.*

effect expected from it, nor in any principle of action which requires to borrow its motive from this expected effect. For all these effects—agreeableness of one's condition, and even the promotion of the happiness of others—could have been also brought about by other causes, so that for this there would have been no need of the will of a rational being; whereas it is in this alone that the supreme and unconditional good can be found. The pre-eminent good which we call moral can therefore consist in nothing else than *the conception of law* in itself, *which certainly is only possible in a rational being,* in so far as this conception, and not the expected effect, determines the will. This is a good which is already present in the person who acts accordingly, and we have not to wait for it to appear first in the result.[1]

[1] It might be here objected to me that I take refuge behind the word *respect* in an obscure feeling, instead of giving a distinct solution of the question by a concept of the reason. But although respect is a feeling, it is not a feeling *received* through influence, but is *self-wrought* by a rational concept, and, therefore, is specifically distinct from all feelings of the former kind, which may be referred either to inclination or fear. What I recognize immediately as a law for me, I recognize with respect. This merely signifies the consciousness that my will is *subordinate* to a law, without the intervention of other influences on my sense. The immediate determination of the will by the law, and the consciousness of this, is called *respect,* so that this is regarded as an *effect* of the law on the subject, and not as the *cause* of it. Respect is properly the conception of a worth which thwarts my self-love. Accordingly it is something which is considered neither as an object of inclination nor of fear, although it has something analogous to both. The *object* of respect is the *law* only, and that, the law which we impose on *ourselves,* and yet recognize as necessary in itself. As a law, we are subjected to it without consulting self-love; as imposed by us on ourselves, it is a result of our will. In the former aspect it has an analogy to fear, in the latter to inclination. Respect for a person is properly only respect for the law (of honesty, &c.) of which he gives us an example. Since we also look on the improvement of our talents as a duty, we consider that we see in a

But what sort of law can that be, the conception of which must determine the will, even without paying any regard to the effect expected from it, in order that this will may be called good absolutely and without qualification? As I have deprived the will of every impulse which could arise to it from obedience to any law, there remains nothing but the universal conformity of its actions to law in general, which alone is to serve the will as a principle, i.e. I am never to act otherwise than so *that I could also will that my maxim should become a universal law.* Here, now, it is the simple conformity to law in general, without assuming any particular law applicable to certain actions, that serves the will as its principle, and must so serve it, if duty is not to be a vain delusion and a chimerical notion. The common reason of men in its practical judgments perfectly coincides with this, and always has in view the principle here suggested. Let the question be, for example: May I when in distress make a promise with the intention not to keep it? I readily distinguish here between the two significations which the question may have: Whether it is prudent, or whether it is right, to make a false promise? The former may undoubtedly often be the case. I see clearly indeed that it is not enough to extricate myself from a present difficulty by means of this subterfuge, but it must be well considered whether there may not hereafter spring from this lie much greater inconvenience than that from which I now free myself, and as, with all my supposed *cunning,* the consequences cannot be so easily foreseen but that credit once lost may be much more injurious to me than any mischief which

person of talents, as it were, the *example of a law* (viz. to become like him in this by exercise), and this constitutes our respect. All so-called moral *interest* consists simply in *respect* for the law.

I seek to avoid at present, it should be considered whether it would not be more *prudent* to act herein according to a universal maxim, and to make it a habit to promise nothing except with the intention of keeping it. But it is soon clear to me that such a maxim will still only be based on the fear of consequences. Now it is a wholly different thing to be truthful from duty, and to be so from apprehension of injurious consequences. In the first case, the very notion of the action already implies a law for me; in the second case, I must first look about elsewhere to see what results may be combined with it which would affect myself. For to deviate from the principle of duty is beyond all doubt wicked; but to be unfaithful to my maxim of prudence may often be very advantageous to me, although to abide by it is certainly safer. The shortest way, however, and an unerring one, to discover the answer to this question whether a lying promise is consistent with duty, is to ask myself, Should I be content that my maxim (to extricate myself from difficulty by a false promise) should hold good as a universal law, for myself as well as for others? and should I be able to say to myself, "Every one may make a deceitful promise when he finds himself in a difficulty from which he cannot otherwise extricate himself"? Then I presently become aware that while I can will the lie, I can by no means will that lying should be a universal law. For with such a law there would be no promises at all, since it would be in vain to allege my intention in regard to my future actions to those who would not believe this allegation, or if they over-hastily did so, would pay me back in my own coin. Hence my maxim, as soon as it should be made a universal law, would necessarily destroy itself.

I do not, therefore, need any far-reaching penetration

to discern what I have to do in order that my will may be morally good. Inexperienced in the course of the world, incapable of being prepared for all its contingencies, I only ask myself: Canst thou also will that thy maxim should be a universal law? If not, then it must be rejected, and that not because of a disadvantage accruing from it to myself or even to others, but because it cannot enter as a principle into a possible universal legislation, and reason extorts from me immediate respect for such legislation. I do not indeed as yet *discern* on what this respect is based (this the philosopher may inquire), but at least I understand this, that it is an estimation of the worth which far outweighs all worth of what is recommended by inclination, and that the necessity of acting from *pure* respect for the practical law is what constitutes duty, to which every other motive must give place, because it is the condition of a will being good *in itself*, and the worth of such a will is above everything.

[3. *Knowledge of this Moral Principle is within the Reach of all Men.*]

THUS,[1] then, without quitting the moral knowledge of common human reason, we have arrived at its principle. And although, no doubt, common men do not conceive it in such an abstract and universal form, yet they always have it really before their eyes, and use it as the standard of their decision. Here it would be easy to show how, with this compass in hand, men are well able to distinguish, in every case that occurs, what is good, what bad, conformably to duty or inconsistent with it, if, without in the least teaching them anything new, we only, like Socrates, direct their attention to

[1] [Cf. A. 20-21, in *Section I* of the *Fundamental Principles of the Metaphysic of Morals.*]

the principle they themselves employ; and that, therefore, we do not need science and philosophy to know what we should do to be honest and good, yea, even wise and virtuous. Indeed, we might well have conjectured beforehand that the knowledge of what every man is bound to do, and therefore also to know, would be within the reach of every man, even the commonest. Here we cannot forbear admiration when we see how great an advantage the practical judgment has over the theoretical in the common understanding of men. In the latter, if common reason ventures to depart from the laws of experience and from the perceptions of the senses, it falls into mere inconceivabilities and self-contradictions, at least into a chaos of uncertainty, obscurity, and instability. But in the practical sphere it is just when the common understanding excludes all sensible springs from practical laws that its power of judgment begins to show itself to advantage. It then becomes even subtle, whether it be that it chicanes with its own conscience or with other claims respecting what is to be called right, or whether it desires for its own instruction to determine honestly the worth of actions; and, in the latter case, it may even have as good a hope of hitting the mark as any philosopher whatever can promise himself. Nay, it is almost more sure of doing so, because the philosopher cannot have any other principle, while he may easily perplex his judgment by a multitude of considerations foreign to the matter, and so turn aside from the right way. Would it not therefore be wiser in moral concerns to acquiesce in the judgment of common reason, or at most only to call in philosophy for the purpose of rendering the system of morals more complete and intelligible, and its rules more convenient for use (especially for disputation, but not so as to draw off the common understanding from its happy simplicity, or to bring it by means of philosophy into a new path of inquiry and instruction? [1] . . .

[4. *Refutation of Ethical Empiricism.*]

If [2] we have hitherto drawn our notion of duty from the common use of our practical reason, it is by no means to be inferred that we have treated it as an empirical notion. On the contrary, if we attend to the experience of men's conduct, we meet frequent and, as we ourselves allow, just complaints that one cannot find a single certain example of the disposition to act from pure duty. Although many things are done in *conformity* with what *duty* prescribes, it is nevertheless always doubtful whether they are done strictly *from duty,* so as to have a moral worth. Hence there have at all times been philosophers who have altogether denied that this disposition actually exists at all in human actions, and have ascribed everything to a more or less refined self-

[1] [The following note appears on A 27-8]. I have a letter from the late excellent Sulzer, in which he asks me what can be the reason that moral instruction, although containing much that is convincing for the reason, yet accomplishes so little? My answer was postponed in order that I might make it complete. But it is simply this, that the teachers themselves have not got their own notions clear, and when they endeavour to make up for this by raking up motives of moral goodness from every quarter, trying to make their physic right strong, they spoil it. For the commonest understanding shows that if we imagine, on the one hand, an act of honesty done with steadfast mind, apart from every view to advantage of any kind in this world or another, and even under the greatest temptations of necessity or allurement, and, on the other hand, a similar act which was affected, in however low a degree, by a foreign motive, the former leaves far behind and eclipses the second; it elevates the soul, and inspires the wish to be able to act in like manner oneself. Even moderately young children feel this impression, and one should never represent duties to them in any other light.

[2] [Cf. A. 23-29, in *Section II* of the *Fundamental Principles of Metaphysic of Morals.*]

love. Not that they have on that account questioned the soundness of the conception of morality; on the contrary, they spoke with sincere regret of the frailty and corruption of human nature, which though noble enough to take as its rule an idea so worthy of respect, is yet too weak to follow it, and employs reason, which ought to give it the law only for the purpose of providing for the interest of the inclinations, whether singly or at the best in the greatest possible harmony with one another.

In fact, it is absolutely impossible to make out by experience with complete certainty a single case in which the maxim of an action, however right in itself, rested simply on moral grounds and on the conception of duty. Sometimes it happens that with the sharpest self-examination we can find nothing beside the moral principle of duty which could have been powerful enough to move us to this or that action and to so great a sacrifice; yet we cannot from this infer with certainty that it was not really some secret impulse of self-love, under the false appearance of duty, that was the actual determining cause of the will. We like then to flatter ourselves by falsely taking credit for a more noble motive; whereas in fact we can never, even by the strictest examination, get completely behind the secret springs of action; since, when the question is of moral worth, it is not with the actions which we see that we are concerned, but with those inward principles of them which we do not see. . . . [A. 24-5]

When we add further that, unless we deny that the notion of morality has any truth or reference to any possible object, we must admit that its law must be valid, not merely for men, but for all *rational creatures generally,* not merely under certain contingent conditions or with exceptions, but *with absolute necessity,* then it is clear that no experience could enable us to infer even the possibility of such apodictic laws. For with what right could we bring into unbounded respect as a universal precept for every rational nature that which perhaps holds only under the contingent conditions of humanity? Or how could laws of the determination of *our* will be regarded as laws of the determination of the will of rational beings generally, and for us only as such, if they were merely empirical, and did not take their origin wholly *a priori* from pure but practical reason?

Nor could anything be more fatal to morality than that we should wish to derive it from examples. For every example of it that is set before me must be first itself tested by principles of morality, whether it is worthy to serve as an original example, i.e. as a pattern, but by no means can it authoritatively furnish the conception of morality. Even the Holy One of the Gospels must first be compared with our ideal of moral perfection before we can recognize Him as such; and so He says of Himself, "Why call ye Me (whom you see) good; none is good (the model of good) but God only (whom ye do not see)?" But whence have we the conception of God as the supreme good? Simply from the *idea* of moral perfection, which reason frames *a priori*, and connects inseparably with the notion of a free will. Imitation finds no place at all in morality, and examples serve only for encouragement, i.e. they put beyond doubt the feasibility of what the law commands, they make visible that which the practical rule expresses more generally, but they can never authorize us to set aside the true original which lies in reason, and to guide ourselves by examples. . . . [A. 26-8]

From what has been said, it is clear that all moral conceptions have their seat and origin completely *a priori* in the reason, and that, moreover, in the commonest reason just as truly as in that which is in the highest degree speculative; that they cannot be obtained by abstraction from any empirical, and therefore merely contingent knowledge; that it is just this purity of their origin that makes them worthy to serve as our supreme practical principle, and that just in proportion as we add anything empirical, we detract from their genuine influence, and from the absolute value of actions; that it is not only of the greatest necessity, in a purely speculative point of view, but is also of the greatest practical importance, to derive these notions and laws from pure reason, to present them pure and unmixed, and even to determine the compass of this practical or pure rational knowledge, i.e. to determine the whole faculty of pure practical reason; and, in doing so, we must not make its principles dependent on the particular nature of human reason, though in speculative philosophy this may be permitted, or may even at times be necessary; but since moral laws ought to hold good for every rational creature, we must derive them from the general concept of a rational being. In this way, although for its *application* to man morality has need of anthropology, yet, in the first instance, we must treat it independently as pure philosophy, i.e. as metaphysic, complete in itself (a thing which in such distinct branches of science is easily done); knowing well that unless we are in possession of this, it would not only be vain to determine the moral element of duty in right actions for purposes of speculative criticism, but it would be impossible to base morals on their genuine principles, even for common practical purposes, especially of moral instruction, so as to produce pure moral dispositions, and to engraft them on men's minds to the promotion of the greatest possible good in the world. . . .

[5. *Refutation of Ethical Hedonism.*]

All [1] *material* practical rules place the determining principle of the will in the *lower desires,* and if there were no *purely formal* laws of the will adequate to determine it, then we could not admit *any higher desire* at all.

REMARK I.

It is surprising that men, otherwise acute, can think it possible to distinguish between *higher* and *lower desires,* according as the ideas which are connected with the feeling of pleasure have their origin in the *senses* or in the *understanding;* for when we inquire what are the determining grounds of desire, and place them in some expected pleasantness, it is of no consequence whence the *idea* of this pleasing object is derived, but only how much it *pleases.* Whether an idea has its seat and source in the understanding or not, if it can only determine the choice by presupposing a feeling of pleasure in the subject, it follows that its capability of determining the choice depends altogether on the nature of the inner sense, namely, that this can be agreeably affected by it. However dissimilar ideas of objects may be, though they be ideas of the understanding, or even of the reason in contrast to ideas of sense, yet the feeling of pleasure, by means of which they constitute the determining principle of the will (the expected satisfaction which impels the activity to the production of the object), is of one and the same kind, not only inasmuch as it can only be known empirically, but also inasmuch as it affects one and the same vital force which mani-

[1] [Cf. A. 109-16, in the *Critique of Practical Reason.*]

fests itself in the faculty of desire, and in this respect can only differ in degree from every other ground of determination. Otherwise, how could we compare in respect of *magnitude* two principles of determination, the ideas of which depend upon different faculties, so as to prefer that which affects the faculty of desire in the highest degree. The same man may return unread an instructive book which he cannot again obtain, in order not to miss a hunt; he may depart in the midst of a fine speech, in order not to be late for dinner; he may leave a rational conversation, such as he otherwise values highly, to take his place at the gaming-table; he may even repulse a poor man whom he at other times takes pleasure in benefiting, because he has only just enough money in his pocket to pay for his admission to the theatre. If the determination of his will rests on the feeling of the agreeableness or disagreeableness that he expects from any cause, it is all the same to him by what sort of ideas he will be affected. The only thing that concerns him, in order to decide his choice, is, how great, how long continued, how easily obtained, and how often repeated, this agreeableness is. Just as to the man who wants money to spend, it is all the same whether the gold was dug out of the mountain or washed out of the sand, provided it is everywhere accepted at the same value; so the man who cares only for the enjoyment of life does not ask whether the ideas are of the understanding or the senses, but only *how much* and *how great pleasure* they will give for the longest time. It is only those that would gladly deny to pure reason the power of determining the will, without the presupposition of any feeling, who could deviate so far from their own exposition as to describe as quite heterogeneous what they have themselves previously brought under one and the same principle. Thus, for example, it is observed that we can find pleasure in the mere *exercise of power,* in the consciousness of our strength of mind in overcoming obstacles which are opposed to our designs, in the culture of our mental talents, etc.; and we justly call these more refined pleasures and enjoyments, because they are more in our power than others; they do not wear out, but rather increase the capacity for further enjoyment of them, and while they delight they at the same time cultivate. But to say on this account that they determine the will in a different way, and not through sense, whereas the possibility of the pleasure presupposes a feeling for it implanted in us, which is the first condition of this satisfaction; this is just as when ignorant persons that like to dabble in metaphysics imagine matter so subtle, so super-subtle, that they almost make themselves giddy with it, and then think that in this way they have conceived it as a *spiritual* and yet extended being. If with *Epicurus* we make virtue determine the will only by means of the pleasure it promises, we cannot afterwards blame him for holding that this pleasure is of the same kind as those of the coarsest senses. For we have no reason whatever to charge him with holding that the ideas by which this feeling is excited in us belong merely to the bodily senses. As far as can be conjectured, he sought the source of many of them in the use of the higher cognitive faculty; but this did not prevent him, and could not prevent him, from holding on the principle above stated, that the pleasure itself which those intellectual ideas give us, and by which alone they can determine the will, is just of the same kind. *Consistency* is the highest obligation of a philosopher, and yet the most rarely found. The ancient Greek schools give us more examples of it than we find in our *syncretistic* age, in which a certain shallow and dishonest *system of compromise* of contradictory principles is devised, because it commends itself better to a public which is content to know something of everything and nothing thoroughly, so as to please every party.

The principle of private happiness, however much understanding and reason may be used in it, cannot contain any other determining principles for the will than those which belong to the *lower* desires; and either there are no [higher] desires at all, or *pure* reason must of itself alone be practical: that is, it must be able to determine the will by the mere form of the practical rule without supposing any feeling, and consequently without any idea of the pleasant or unpleasant, which is the matter of the desire, and which is always an empirical condition of the principles. Then only, when reason of itself determines the will (not as the servant of the inclination), it is really a *higher* desire to which that which is pathologically determined is subordinate, and is really, and even specifically, distinct from the latter, so that even the slightest admixture of the motives of the latter impairs its strength and superiority; just as in a mathematical demonstration the least empirical condition would degrade and destroy its force and value. Reason, with its practical law, determines the will immediately, not by means of an intervening feeling of pleasure or pain, not even of pleasure in the law itself, and it is only because it can, as pure reason, be practical, that it is possible for it to be *legislative*.

REMARK II.

To be happy is necessarily the wish of every finite rational being, and this, therefore, is inevitably a determining principle of its faculty of desire. For we are not in possession originally of satisfaction with our whole existence—a bliss which would imply a consciousness of our own independent self-sufficiency—this is a problem imposed upon us by our own finite nature, because we have wants, and these wants regard the matter of our desires, that is, something that is relative to a subjective feeling of pleasure or pain, which determines what we need in order to be satisfied with our condition. But just because this material principle of determination can only be empirically known by the subject, it is impossible to regard this problem as a law; for a law being objective must contain the *very same principle of determination* of the will in all cases and for all rational beings. For, although the notion of happiness is *in every case* the foundation of the practical relation of the *objects* to the desires, yet it is only a general name for the subjective determining principles, and determines nothing specifically; whereas this is what alone we are concerned with in this practical problem, which cannot be solved at all without such specific determination. For it is every man's own special feeling of pleasure and pain that decides in what he is to place his happiness, and even in the same subject this will vary with the difference of his wants according as this feeling changes, and thus a law which is *subjectively necessary* (as a law of nature) is *objectively* a very contingent practical principle, which can and must be very different in different subjects, and therefore can never furnish a law; since, in the desire for happiness it is not the form (of conformity to law) that is decisive, but simply the matter, namely, whether I am to expect pleasure in following the law, and how much. Principles of self-love may, indeed, contain universal precepts of skill (how to find means to accomplish one's purposes), but in that case they are merely theoretical principles;[1] as, for example, how he who would like to eat bread should contrive a mill; but practical precepts founded on them can never be universal, for the determining principle of the desire is based on the feeling of pleasure and pain, which can never be supposed to be universally directed to the same objects.

Even supposing, however, that all finite rational beings were thoroughly agreed as to what were the objects of their feelings of pleasure and pain, and also as to the means which they must employ to attain the one and avoid the other; still, they could *by no means* set up the *principle of self-love* as a *practical law,* for this unanimity itself would be only contingent. The principle of determination would still be only subjectively valid and merely empirical, and would not possess the necessity which is conceived in every law, namely, an objective necessity arising from *a priori* grounds; unless, indeed, we hold this necessity to be not at all practical, but merely physical, viz. that our action is as inevitably determined by our inclination, as yawning when we see others yawn. It would be better to maintain that there are no practical laws at all, but only *counsels* for the service of our desires, than to raise merely subjective principles to the rank of practical laws, which have objective necessity, and not merely subjective, and which must be known by reason *a priori,* not by experi-

[1] Propositions which in mathematics or physics are called *practical* ought properly to be called *technical.* For they have nothing to do with the determination of the will; they only point out how a certain effect is to be produced, and are therefore just as theoretical as any propositions which express the connexion of a cause with an effect. Now whoever chooses the effect must also choose the cause.

ence (however empirically universal this may be). . . . [A. 114-5]

It is, therefore, surprising that intelligent men could have thought of calling the desire of happiness a universal *practical law* on the ground that the desire is universal, and, therefore, also the *maxim* by which everyone makes this desire determine his will. For whereas in other cases a universal law of nature makes everything harmonious; here, on the contrary, if we attribute to the maxim the universality of a law, the extreme opposite of harmony will follow, the greatest opposition, and the complete destruction of the maxim itself, and its purpose. For, in that case, the will of all has not one and the same object, but everyone has his own (his private welfare), which may accidentally accord with the purposes of others which are equally selfish, but it is far from sufficing for a law; because the occasional exceptions which one is permitted to make are endless, and cannot be definitely embraced in one universal rule. In this manner, then, results a harmony like that which a certain satirical poem depicts as existing between a married couple bent on going to ruin, "O, marvellous harmony, what he wishes, she wishes also"; or like what is said of the pledge of Francis I to the Emperor Charles V, "What my brother Charles wishes that I wish also" (viz. Milan). Empirical principles of determination are not fit for any universal external legislation, but just as little for internal; for each man makes his own subject the foundation of his inclination, and in the same subject sometimes one inclination, sometimes another, has the preponderance. To discover a law which would govern them all under this condition, namely, bringing them all into harmony, is quite impossible.

[6. *Formulæ* [1] *of the Categorical Imperative, and the Kingdom of Ends.*]

Everything [2] in nature works according to laws. Rational beings alone have the faculty of acting according *to the conception* of laws, that is according to principles, i.e. have a *will*. Since the deduction of actions from principles requires *reason,* the will is nothing but practical reason. If reason infallibly determines the will, then the actions of such a being which are recognized as objectively necessary are subjectively necessary also, i.e. the will is a faculty to choose *that only* which reason independent on inclination recognizes as practically necessary, i.e. as good. But if reason of itself does not sufficiently determine the will, if the latter is subject also to subjective conditions (particular impulses) which do not always coincide with the objective conditions; in a word, if the will does not *in itself* completely accord with reason (which is actually the case with men), then the actions which objectively are recognized as necessary are subjectively contingent, and the determination of such a will according to objective laws is *obligation,* that is to say, the relation of the objective

[1] [The following note appears on A. 93 as a note to the *Preface* to the *Critique of Practical Reason.*] A reviewer who wanted to find some fault with this work has hit the truth better, perhaps, than he thought, when he says that no new principle of morality is set forth in it, but only a *new formula.* But who would think of introducing a new principle of all morality, and making himself as it were the first discoverer of it, just as if all the world before him were ignorant what duty was or had been in thorough-going error? But whoever knows of what importance to a mathematician a *formula* is, which defines accurately what is to be done to work a problem, will not think that a formula is insignificant and useless which does the same for all duty in general.

[2] [Cf. A. 29-59, in *Section II* of the *Fundamental Principles of the Metaphysic of Morals.*]

laws to a will that is not thoroughly good is conceived as the determination of the will of a rational being by principles of reason, but which the will from its nature does not of necessity follow.

The conception of an objective principle, in so far as it is obligatory for a will, is called a command (of reason), and the formula of the command is called an Imperative.

All imperatives are expressed by the word *ought* [or *shall*], and thereby indicate the relation of an objective law of reason to a will, which from its subjective constitution is not necessarily determined by it (an obligation). They say that something would be good to do or to forbear, but they say it to a will which does not always do a thing because it is conceived to be good to do it. That is practically *good,* however, which determines the will by means of the conceptions of reason, and consequently not from subjective causes, but objectively, that is on principles which are valid for every rational being as such. It is distinguished from the *pleasant,* as that which influences the will only by means of sensation from merely subjective causes, valid only for the sense of this or that one, and not as a principle of reason, which holds for every one.[1]

[1] The dependence of the desires on sensations is called inclination, and this accordingly always indicates a *want.* The dependence of a contingently determinable will on principles of reason is called an *interest.* This, therefore, is found only in the case of a dependent will which does not always of itself conform to reason; in the Divine will we cannot conceive any interest. But the human will can also *take an interest* in a thing without therefore acting *from interest.* The former signifies the *practical* interest in the action, the latter the *pathological* in the object of the action. The former indicates only dependence of the will on principles of reason in themselves; the second, dependence on principles of reason for the sake of inclination, reason supplying only the practical rules how the requirement of the inclination may be satisfied. In the first case the action interests me; in the second the object

A perfectly good will would therefore be equally subject to objective laws (viz. laws of good), but could not be conceived as *obliged* thereby to act lawfully, because of itself from its subjective constitution it can only be determined by the conception of good. Therefore no imperatives hold for the Divine will, or in general for a *holy* will; *ought* is here out of place, because the volition is already of itself necessarily in unison with the law. Therefore imperatives are only formulæ to express the relation of objective laws of all volition to the subjective imperfection of the will of this or that rational being, e.g. the human will.

Now all *imperatives* command either *hypothetically* or *categorically.* The former represent the practical necessity of a possible action as means to something else that is willed (or at least which one might possibly will). The categorical imperative would be that which represented an action as necessary of itself without reference to another end, i.e., as objectively necessary.

Since every practical law represents a possible action as good, and on this account, for a subject who is practically determinable by reason, necessary, all imperatives are formulæ determining an action which is necessary according to the principle of a will good in some respects. If now the action is good only as a means *to something else,* then the imperative is *hypothetical;* if it is conceived as good *in itself* and consequently as being necessarily the principle of a will which of itself conforms to reason, then it is *categorical.*

Thus the imperative declares what action possible by me would be good, and presents the practical rule in

---

of the action (because it is pleasant to me). We have seen in the first section [above pp. 270 ff.] that in an action done from duty we must look not to the interest in the object, but only to that in the action itself, and in its rational principle (viz. the law).

relation to a will which does not forthwith perform an action simply because it is good, whether because the subject does not always know that it is good, or because, even if it know this, yet its maxims might be opposed to the objective principles of practical reason.

Accordingly the hypothetical imperative only says that the action is good for some purpose, *possible* or *actual*. In the first case it is a Problematical, in the second an Assertorial practical principle. The categorical imperative which declares an action to be objectively necessary in itself without reference to any purpose, i.e. without any other end, is valid as an Apodictic (practical) principle.

Whatever is possible only by the power of some rational being may also be conceived as a possible purpose of some will; and therefore the principles of action as regards the means necessary to attain some possible purpose are in fact infinitely numerous. All sciences have a practical part, consisting of problems expressing that some end is possible for us, and of imperatives directing how it may be attained. These may, therefore, be called in general imperatives of Skill. Here there is no question whether the end is rational and good, but only what one must do in order to attain it. The precepts for the physician to make his patient thoroughly healthy, and for a poisoner to ensure certain death, are of equal value in this respect, that each serves to effect its purpose perfectly. Since in early youth it cannot be known what ends are likely to occur to us in the course of life, parents seek to have their children taught a *great many things,* and provide for their *skill* in the use of means for all sorts of arbitrary ends, of none of which can they determine whether it may not perhaps hereafter be an object to their pupil, but which it is at all events *possible* that he might aim at; and this anxiety is so great that they commonly neglect to form and correct their judgment on the value of the things which may be chosen as ends.

There is *one* end, however, which may be assumed to be actually such to all rational beings (so far as imperatives apply to them, viz. as dependent beings), and, therefore, one purpose which they not merely *may* have, but which we may with certainty assume that they all actually *have* by a natural necessity, and this is *happiness*. The hypothetical imperative which expresses the practical necessity of an action as means to the advancement of happiness is Assertorial. We are not to present it as necessary for an uncertain and merely possible purpose, but for a purpose which we may presuppose with certainty and *a priori* in every man, because it belongs to his being. Now skill in the choice of means to his own greatest well-being may be called *prudence*,[1] in the narrowest sense. And thus the imperative which refers to the choice of means to one's own happiness, i.e. the precept of prudence, is still always *hypothetical;* the action is not commanded absolutely, but only as means to another purpose.

Finally, there is an imperative which commands a certain conduct immediately, without having as its condition any other purpose to be attained by it. This imperative is Categorical. It concerns not the matter of the action, or its intended result, but its form and the principle of which it is itself a result; and what is essentially good in it consists in the mental disposition, let the consequence be what it may. This imperative may be called that of Morality.

There is a marked distinction also between the volitions on these three sorts of principles in the *dissimilarity* of the obligation of the will. In order to mark

[1] [Note A 33]

this difference more clearly, I think they would be most suitably named in their order if we said they are either *rules* of skill or *counsels* of prudence, or *commands (laws)* of morality. For it is *law* only that involves the conception of an *unconditional* and objective necessity, which is consequently universally valid; and commands are laws which must be obeyed, that is, must be followed, even in opposition to inclination. *Counsels,* indeed, involve necessity, but one which can only hold under a contingent subjective condition, viz. they depend on whether this or that man reckons this or that as part of his happiness; the categorical imperative, on the contrary, is not limited by any condition, and as being absolutely, although practically, necessary, may be quite properly called a command. We might also call the first kind of imperatives *technical* (belonging to art), the second *pragmatic*[1] (to welfare), the third *moral* (belonging to free conduct generally, that is, to morals). . . . [A. 34-8]

. . . We will first inquire whether the mere conception of a categorical imperative may not perhaps supply us also with the formula of it, containing the proposition which alone can be a categorical imperative . . . [A. 38]

When I conceive a hypothetical imperative, in general I do not know beforehand what it will contain until I am given the condition. But when I conceive a categorical imperative, I know at once what it contains. For as the imperative contains besides the law only the necessity that the maxims[2] shall conform to this law,

[1] [Note A 34.]

[2] A MAXIM is a subjective principle of action, and must be distinguished from the *objective principle,* namely, practical law. The former contains the practical rule set by reason according to the conditions of the subject (often its ignorance or its inclinations), so that it is the principle on which the subject *acts;* but the law is the objective principle valid for

while the law contains no conditions restricting it, there remains nothing but the general statement that the maxim of the action should conform to a universal law, and it is this conformity alone that the imperative properly represents as necessary.

There is therefore but one categorical imperative, namely, this: *Act only on that maxim whereby thou canst at the same time will that it should become a universal law.*

Now if all imperatives of duty can be deduced from this one imperative as from their principle, then, although it should remain undecided whether what is called duty is not merely a vain notion, yet at least we shall be able to show what we understand by it and what this notion means.

Since the universality of the law according to which effects are produced constitutes what is properly called *nature* in the most general sense (as to form), that is the existence of things so far as it is determined by general laws, the imperative of duty may be expressed thus: *Act as if the maxim of thy action were to become by thy will a universal law of nature.*

We will now enumerate a few duties, adopting the usual division of them into duties to ourselves and to others, and into perfect and imperfect duties.[1]

1. A man reduced to despair by a series of misfortunes feels wearied of life, but is still so far in possession of his reason that he can ask himself whether it would not be contrary to his duty to himself to take his own life. Now he inquires whether the maxim of his action could become a universal law of nature. His maxim is: From self-love I adopt it as a principle to

---

every rational being, and is the principle on which it *ought to act* that is an imperative.

[1] [Note A 39].

shorten my life when its longer duration is likely to bring more evil than satisfaction. It is asked then simply whether this principle founded on self-love can become a universal law of nature. Now we see at once that a system of nature of which it should be a law to destroy life by means of the very feeling whose special nature it is to impel to the improvement of life would contradict itself, and therefore could not exist as a system of nature; hence that maxim cannot possibly exist as a universal law of nature, and consequently would be wholly inconsistent with the supreme principle of all duty.

2. Another finds himself forced by necessity to borrow money. He knows that he will not be able to repay it, but sees also that nothing will be lent to him, unless he promises stoutly to repay it in a definite time. He desires to make this promise, but he has still so much conscience as to ask himself: Is it not unlawful and inconsistent with duty to get out of a difficulty in this way? Suppose, however, that he resolves to do so, then the maxim of his action would be expressed thus: When I think myself in want of money, I will borrow money and promise to repay it, although I know that I never can do so. Now this principle of self-love or of one's own advantage may perhaps be consistent with my whole future welfare; but the question now is, Is it right? I change then the suggestion of self-love into a universal law, and state the question thus: How would it be if my maxim were a universal law? Then I see at once that it could never hold as a universal law of nature, but would necessarily contradict itself. For supposing it to be a universal law that everyone when he thinks himself in a difficulty should be able to promise whatever he pleases, with the purpose of not keeping his promise, the promise itself would become impossible, as well as

the end that one might have in view in it, since no one would consider that anything was promised to him, but would ridicule all such statements as vain pretences.

3. A third finds in himself a talent which with the help of some culture might make him a useful man in many respects. But he finds himself in comfortable circumstances, and prefers to indulge in pleasure rather than to take pains in enlarging and improving his happy natural capacities. He asks, however, whether his maxim of neglect of his natural gifts, besides agreeing with his inclination to indulgence, agrees also with what is called duty. He sees then that a system of nature could indeed subsist with such a universal law although men (like the South Sea islanders) should let their talents rest, and resolve to devote their lives merely to idleness, amusement, and propagation of their species—in a word, to enjoyment; but he cannot possibly *will* that this should be a universal law of nature, or be implanted in us as such by a natural instinct. For, as a rational being, he necessarily wills that his faculties be developed, since they serve him, and have been given him, for all sorts of possible purposes.

4. A fourth, who is in prosperity, while he sees that others have to contend with great wretchedness and that he could help them, thinks: What concern is it of mine? Let everyone be as happy as Heaven pleases, or as he can make himself; I will take nothing from him nor even envy him, only I do not wish to contribute anything to his welfare or to his assistance in distress! Now no doubt if such a mode of thinking were a universal law, the human race might very well subsist, and doubtless even better than in a state in which everyone talks of sympathy and good-will, or even takes care occasionally to put it into practice, but, on the other side, also cheats when he can, betrays the rights of men, or

otherwise violates them. But although it is possible that a universal law of nature might exist in accordance with that maxim, it is impossible to *will* that such a principle should have the universal validity of a law of nature. For a will which resolved this would contradict itself, inasmuch as many cases might occur in which one would have need of the love and sympathy of others, and in which, by such a law of nature, sprung from his own will, he would deprive himself of all hope of the aid he desires.

These are a few of the many actual duties, or at least what we regard as such, which obviously fall into two classes on the one principle that we have laid down. We must be *able to will* that a maxim of our action should be a universal law. This is the canon of the moral appreciation of the action generally. Some actions are of such a character that their maxim cannot without contradiction be even *conceived* as a universal law of nature, far from it being possible that we should *will* that it *should* be so. In others this intrinsic impossibility is not found, but still it is impossible to *will* that their maxim should be raised to the universality of a law of nature, since such a will would contradict itself. It is easily seen that the former violate strict or rigorous (inflexible) duty; the latter only laxer (meritorious) duty. Thus it has been completely shown by these examples how all duties depend as regards the nature of the obligation (not the object of the action) on the same principle.

If now we attend to ourselves on occasion of any transgression of duty, we shall find that we in fact do not will that our maxim should be a universal law, for that is impossible for us; on the contrary, we will that the opposite should remain a universal law, only we assume the liberty of making an *exception* in our own favour or (just for this time only) in favour of our inclination. Consequently if we considered all cases from one and the same point of view, namely, that of reason, we should find a contradiction in our own will, namely, that a certain principle should be objectively necessary as a universal law, and yet subjectively should not be universal, but admit of exceptions. As, however, we at one moment regard our action from the point of view of a will wholly conformed to reason, and then again look at the same action from the point of view of a will affected by inclination, there is not really any contradiction, but an antagonism of inclination to the precept of reason, whereby the universality of the principle is changed into a mere generality, so that the practical principle of reason shall meet the maxim half way. Now, although this cannot be justified in our own impartial judgment, yet it proves that we do really recognize the validity of the categorical imperative and (with all respect for it) only allow ourselves a few exceptions, which we think unimportant and forced from us. . . . [A. 42-3]

[It] is of extreme importance to remember that we must not allow ourselves to think of deducing the reality of this principle from the *particular attributes of human nature.* For duty is to be a practical, unconditional necessity of action; it must therefore hold for all rational beings (to whom an imperative can apply at all), and *for this reason only* be also a law for all human wills. On the contrary, whatever is deduced from the particular natural characteristics of humanity, from certain feelings and propensions, nay, even, if possible, from any particular tendency proper to human reason, and which need not necessarily hold for the will of every rational being; this may indeed supply us with a maxim, but not with a law; with a subjective principle on which we may have a propension and inclination to act, but not with an objective principle on which we should be *enjoined* to act, even though all our propensions, inclinations, and natural dispositions were opposed to it. In fact, the sublimity and intrinsic dignity of the command in duty are so much the more evident, the less the subjective impulses favour it and the more they oppose it, without being able in the slightest degree to weaken the obligation of the law or to diminish its validity. . . . [A. 43-4]

The question then is this: Is it a necessary law *for all rational beings* that they should always judge of their actions by maxims of which they can themselves will that they should serve as universal laws? If it is so, then it must be connected (altogether *a priori*) with the very conception of the will of a rational being generally. . . . [A. 44-5]

The will is conceived as a faculty of determining oneself to action *in accordance with the conception of certain laws*. And such a faculty can be found only in rational beings. Now that which serves the will as the objective ground of its self-determination is the *end*, and if this is assigned by reason alone, it must hold for all rational beings. On the other hand, that which merely contains the ground of possibility of the action of which the effect is the end, this is called the *means*. The subjective ground of the desire is the *spring*, the objective ground of the volition is the *motive;* hence the distinction between subjective ends which rest on springs, and objective ends which depend on motives valid for every rational being. Practical principles are *formal* when they abstract from all subjective ends; they are *material* when they assume these, and therefore particular springs of action. The ends which a rational being proposes to himself at pleasure as *effects* of his actions (material ends) are all only relative, for it is only their relation to the particular desires of the subject that gives them their worth, which therefore cannot furnish principles universal and necessary for all rational beings and for every volition, that is to say practical laws. Hence all these relative ends can give rise only to hypothetical imperatives.

Supposing, however, that there were something *whose existence* has *in itself* an absolute worth, something which, being *an end in itself,* could be a source of definite laws, then in this and this alone would lie the source of a possible categorical imperative, i.e. a practical law.

Now I say: man and generally any rational being *exists* as an end in himself, *not merely as a means* to be arbitrarily used by this or that will, but in all his actions, whether they concern himself or other rational beings, must be always regarded at the same time as an end. All objects of the inclinations have only a conditional worth; for if the inclinations and the wants founded on them did not exist, then their object would be without value. But the inclinations themselves being sources of want are so far from having an absolute worth for which they should be desired, that, on the contrary, it must be the universal wish of every rational being to be wholly free from them. Thus the worth of any object which is *to be acquired* by our action is always conditional. Beings whose existence depends not on our will but on nature's, have nevertheless, if they are rational beings, only a relative value as means, and are therefore called *things;* rational beings, on the contrary, are called *persons,* because their very nature points them out as ends in themselves, that is as something which must not be used merely as means, and so far therefore restricts freedom of action (and is an object of respect). These, therefore, are not merely subjective ends whose existence has a worth *for us* as an effect of our action, but *objective ends*, that is things whose existence is an end in itself: an end moreover for which no other can be substituted, which they should subserve *merely* as means, for otherwise nothing whatever would possess *absolute worth;* but if all worth were conditioned and therefore contingent, then there would be no supreme practical principle of reason whatever.

If then there is a supreme practical principle or, in respect of the human will, a categorical imperative, it must be one which, being drawn from the conception of that which is necessarily an end for everyone because it is *an end in itself,* constitutes an *objective* principle of will, and can therefore serve as a universal practical law. The foundation of this principle is: *rational nature exists as an end in itself.* Man necessarily conceives his own existence as being so: so far then this is a *subjective* principle of human actions. But every other rational being regards its existence similarly, just on the same rational principle that holds for me [1]: so that it is at the same time an objective principle, from which as a supreme practical law all laws of the will must be capable of being deduced. Accordingly the practical imperative will be as follows: *So act as to treat humanity, whether in thine own person or in that of any other, in every case as an end withal, never as means only.* We will now inquire whether this can be practically carried out.

To abide by the previous examples:

Firstly, under the head of necessary duty to oneself: He who contemplates suicide should ask himself whether his action can be consistent with the idea of humanity *as an end in itself.* If he destroys himself in order to es-

[1] [Note, A 47]

cape from painful circumstances, he uses a person merely as *a mean* to maintain a tolerant condition up to the end of life. But a man is not a thing, that is to say, something which can be used merely as means, but must in all his actions be always considered as an end in himself. I cannot, therefore, dispose in any way of a man in my own person so as to mutilate him, to damage or kill him. (It belongs to ethics proper to define this principle more precisely, so as to avoid all misunderstanding, e.g. as to the amputation of the limbs in order to preserve myself; as to exposing by life to danger with a view to preserve it, &c. This question is therefore omitted here.)

Secondly, as regards necessary duties, or those of strict obligation, towards others; he who is thinking of making a lying promise to others will see at once that he would be using another man *merely as a mean,* without the latter containing at the same time the end in himself. For he whom I propose by such a promise to use for my own purposes cannot possibly assent to my mode of acting towards him, and therefore cannot himself contain the end of this action. This violation of the principle of humanity in other men is more obvious if we take in examples of attacks on the freedom and property of others. For then it is clear that he who transgresses the rights of men intends to use the person of others merely as means, without considering that as rational beings they ought always to be esteemed also as ends, that is, as beings who must be capable of containing in themselves the end of the very same action.[1]

Thirdly, as regards contingent (meritorious) duties to oneself; it is not enough that the action does not violate humanity in our own person as an end in itself, it must also *harmonize with* it. Now there are in humanity

[1] [Note A 48].

capacities of greater perfection which belong to the end that nature has in view in regard to humanity in ourselves as the subject: to neglect these might perhaps be consistent with the *maintenance* of humanity as an end in itself, but not with the *advancement* of this end.

Fourthly, as regards meritorious duties towards others: the natural end which all men have is their own happiness. Now humanity might indeed subsist, although no one should contribute anything to the happiness of others, provided he did not intentionally withdraw anything from it; but after all, this would only harmonize negatively, not positively, with *humanity, as an end in itself,* if everyone does not also endeavour, as far as in him lies, to forward the ends of others. For the ends of any subject which is an end in himself, ought as far as possible to be *my* ends also, if that conception is to have its *full* effect with me.

This principle, that humanity and generally every rational nature is *an end in itself* (which is the supreme limiting condition of every man's freedom of action), is not borrowed from experience, *firstly,* because it is universal, applying as it does to all rational beings whatever, and experience is not capable of determining anything about them; *secondly,* because it does not present humanity as an end to men (subjectively), that is as an object which men do of themselves actually adopt as an end; but as an objective end, which must as a law constitute the supreme limiting condition of all our subjective ends, let them be what we will; it must therefore spring from pure reason. In fact the objective principle of all practical legislation lies (according to the first principle) in *the rule* and its form of universality which makes it capable of being a law (say, e.g., a law of nature); but the *subjective* principle is in the *end;* now by the second principle the subject of all ends is each rational being inasmuch as it is an end in itself. Hence follows the third practical principle of the will, which is the ultimate condition of its harmony with the universal practical reason, viz.: the idea of *the will of every rational being as a universally legislative will.*

On this principle all maxims are rejected which are inconsistent with the will being itself universal legislator. Thus the will is not subject simply to the law, but so subject that it must be regarded *as itself giving the law,* and on this ground only, subject to the law (of which it can regard itself as the author).

In the previous imperatives, namely, that based on the conception of the conformity of actions to general laws, as in a *physical system of nature,* and that based on the universal *prerogative* of rational beings as *ends* in themselves—these imperatives just because they were conceived as categorical, excluded from any share in their authority all admixture of any interest as a spring of action; they were, however, only *assumed* to be categorical, because such an assumption was necessary to explain the conception of duty. But we could not prove independently that there are practical propositions which command categorically, nor can it be proved in this section; one thing, however, could be done, namely, to indicate in the imperative itself by some determinate expression, that in the case of volition from duty all interest is renounced, which is the specific criterion of categorical as distinguished from hypothetical imperatives. This is done in the present (third) formula of the principle, namely, in the idea of the will of every rational being as a *universally legislating will.*

For although a will *which is subject to laws* may be attached to this law by means of an interest, yet a will which is itself a supreme lawgiver so far as it is such cannot possibly depend on any interest, since a will so dependent would itself still need another law restricting the interest of its self-love by the condition that it should be valid as universal law.

Thus the *principle* that every human will is *a will which in all its maxims gives universal laws,*[1] provided it be otherwise justified, would be very *well adapted* to be the categorical imperative, in this respect, namely, that just because of the idea of universal legislation it is *not based on any interest,* and therefore it alone among all possible imperatives can be *unconditional.* Or still better, converting the proposition, if there is a categorical imperative (i.e., a law for the will of every rational being), it can only command that everything be done from maxims of one's will regarded as a will which could at the same time will that it should itself give universal laws, for in that case only the practical principle and the imperative which it obeys are unconditional, since they cannot be based on any interest.

Looking back now on all previous attempts to discover the principle of morality, we need not wonder why they all failed. It was seen that man was bound to laws by duty, but it was not observed that the laws to which he is subject are *only those of his own giving,* though at the same time they are *universal* and that he is only bound to act in conformity with his own will; a will, however, which is designed by nature to give universal laws. For when one has conceived man only as subject to a law (no matter what), then this law required some interest, either by way of attraction or constraint, since it did not originate as a law from *his own* will, but this will was according to a law obliged by *something else* to act in a certain manner. Now by

[1] I may be excused from adducing examples to elucidate this principle, as those which have already been used to elucidate the categorical imperative and its formula would all serve for the like purpose here.

this necessary consequence all the labour spent in finding a supreme principle of *duty* was irrevocably lost. For men never elicited duty, but only a necessity of acting from a certain interest. Whether this interest was private or otherwise, in any case the imperative must be conditional, and could not by any means be capable of being a moral command. I will therefore call this the principle of *Autonomy* of the will, in contrast with every other which I accordingly reckon as *Heteronomy*.

The conception of every rational being as one which must consider itself as giving in all the maxims of its will universal laws, so as to judge itself and its actions from this point of view—this conception leads to another which depends on it and is very fruitful, namely, that of a *kingdom of ends*.

By a *kingdom* I understand the union of different rational beings in a system by common laws. Now since it is by laws that ends are determined as regards their universal validity, hence, if we abstract from the personal differences of rational beings, and likewise from all the content of their private ends, we shall be able to conceive all ends combined in a systematic whole (including both rational beings as ends in themselves, and also the special ends which each may propose to himself), that is to say, we can conceive a kingdom of ends, which on the preceding principles is possible.

For all rational beings come under the *law* that each of them must treat itself and all others *never merely as means*, but in every case *at the same time as ends in themselves*. Hence results a systematic union of rational beings by common objective laws, i.e., a kingdom which may be called a kingdom of ends, since what these laws have in view is just the relation of these beings to one another as ends and means. It is certainly only an ideal.

A rational being belongs as a *member* to the kingdom of ends when, although giving universal laws in it, he is also himself subject to these laws. He belongs to it *as sovereign* when, while giving laws, he is not subject to the will of any other.

A rational being must always regard himself as giving laws either as member or as sovereign in a kingdom of ends which is rendered possible by the freedom of will. He cannot, however, maintain the latter position merely by the maxims of his will, but only in case he is a completely independent being without wants and with unrestricted power adequate to his will.

Morality consists then in the reference of all action to the legislation which alone can render a kingdom of ends possible. This legislation must be capable of existing in every rational being, and of emanating from his will, so that the principle of this will is, never to act on any maxim which could not without contradiction be also a universal law, and accordingly always so to act *that the will could at the same time regard itself as giving in its maxims universal laws*. If now the maxims of rational beings are not by their own nature coincident with this objective principle, then the necessity of acting on it is called practical necessitation, i.e. *duty*. Duty does not apply to the sovereign in the kingdom of ends, but it does to every member of it and to all in the same degree.

The practical necessity of acting on this principle, i.e. duty, does not rest at all on feelings, impulses, or inclinations, but solely on the relation of rational beings to one another, a relation in which the will of a rational being must always be regarded as *legislative*, since otherwise it could not be conceived as *an end in itself*. Reason then refers every maxim of the will, regarding it as legislating universally, to every other will and also to every action towards oneself; and this not on account of any other practical motive or any future advantage, but from the idea of the *dignity* of a rational being, obeying no law but that which he himself also gives.

In the kingdom of ends everything has either Value or Dignity. Whatever has a value can be replaced by something else which is *equivalent;* whatever, on the other hand, is above all value, and therefore admits of no equivalent, has a dignity.

Whatever has reference to the general inclinations and wants of mankind has a *market value;* whatever, without presupposing a want, corresponds to a certain taste, that is to a satisfaction in the mere purposeless play of our faculties, has a *fancy value;* but that which constitutes the condition under which alone anything can be an end in itself, this has not merely a relative worth, i.e. value, but an intrinsic worth, that is *dignity*.

Now morality is the condition under which alone a rational being can be an end in himself, since by this alone it is possible that he should be a legislating member in the kingdom of ends. Thus morality, and humanity as capable of it, is that which alone has dignity. Skill and diligence in labour have a market value; wit, lively imagination, and humour, have fancy value; on the other hand, fidelity to promises, benevolence from principle (not from instinct), have an intrinsic worth. Neither nature nor art contains anything which in default of these it could put in their place, for their worth consists not in the effects which spring from them, not in the use and advantage which they secure, but in the disposition of mind, that is, the maxims of the will which are ready to manifest themselves in such actions, even though they should not have the desired effect. These actions also need no recommendation from any subjective taste or sentiment, that they may be looked on with immediate favour and satisfaction: they need no immediate propension or feeling for them; they exhibit the will that performs them as an object of an immediate respect, and nothing but reason is required to *impose* them on the will; not to *flatter* it into them, which, in the case of duties, would be a contradiction. This estimation therefore shows that the worth of such a disposition is dignity, and places it infinitely above all value, with which it cannot for a moment be brought into comparison or competition without as it were violating its sanctity.

What then is it which justifies virtue or the morally good disposition, in making such lofty claims? It is nothing less than the privilege it secures to the rational being of participating in the giving of universal laws, by which it qualifies him to be a member of a possible kingdom of ends, a privilege to which he was already destined by his own nature as being an end in himself, and on that account legislating in the kingdom of ends; free as regards all laws of physical nature, and obeying those only which he himself gives, and by which his maxims can belong to a system of universal law, to which at the same time he submits himself. For nothing has any worth except what the law assigns it. Now the legislation itself which assigns the worth of everything must for that very reason possess dignity, that is an unconditional incomparable worth; and the word *respect* alone supplies a becoming expression for the esteem which a rational being must have for it. *Autonomy* then is the basis of the dignity of human and of every rational nature.

The three modes of presenting the principle of morality that have been adduced are at bottom only so many formulæ of the very same law, and each of itself involves the other two. There is, however, a difference in them, but it is rather subjectively than objectively practical, intended namely to bring an idea of the reason nearer to intuition (by means of a certain analogy), and thereby nearer to feeling. All maxims, in fact, have—

1. A *form,* consisting in universality; and in this view the formula of the moral imperative is expressed thus, that the maxims must be so chosen as if they were to serve as universal laws of nature.

2. A *matter,* namely, an end, and here the formula says that the rational being, as it is an end by its own nature and therefore an end in itself, must in every maxim serve as the condition limiting all merely relative and arbitrary ends.

3. A *complete characterisation* of all maxims by means of that formula, namely, that all maxims ought by their own legislation to harmonize with a possible kingdom of ends as with a kingdom of nature.[1] There is a progress here in the order of the categories of *unity* of the form of the will (its universality), *plurality* of the matter (the objects, i.e. the ends), and *totality* of the system of these. In forming our moral *judgment* of actions it is better to proceed always on the strict method, and start from the general formula of the categorical imperative: *Act according to a maxim which can at the same time make itself a universal law.* If, however, we wish to gain an *entrance* for the moral law, it is very

[1] [Note A 55]

useful to bring one and the same action under the three specified conceptions, and thereby as far as possible to bring it nearer to intuition.

We can now end where we started at the beginning, namely, with the conception of a will unconditionally good. *That will* is *absolutely good* which cannot be evil —in other words, whose maxim, if made a universal law, could never contradict itself. This principle, then, is its supreme law: Act always on such a maxim as thou canst at the same time will to be a universal law; this is the sole condition under which a will can never contradict itself; and such an imperative is categorical. Since the validity of the will as a universal law for possible actions is analogous to the universal connexion of the existence of things by general laws, which is the formal notion of nature in general, the categorical imperative can also be expressed thus: *Act on maxims which can at the same time have for their object themselves as universal laws of nature.* Such then is the formula of an absolutely good will.

Rational nature is distinguished from the rest of nature by this, that it sets before itself an end. This end would be the matter of every good will. But since in the idea of a will that is absolutely good without being limited by any condition (of attaining this or that end) we must abstract wholly from every end *to be effected* (since this would make every will only relatively good), it follows that in this case the end must be conceived, not as an end to be effected, but as an *independently* existing end. Consequently it is conceived only negatively, i.e., as that which we must never act against, and which, therefore, must never be regarded merely as means, but must in every volition be esteemed as an end likewise. Now this end can be nothing but the subject of all possible ends, since this is also the subject of a possible absolutely good will; for such a will cannot without contradiction be postponed to any other object. This principle: So act in regard to every rational being (thyself and others), that he may always have place in thy maxim as an end in himself, is accordingly essentially identical with this other: Act upon a maxim which, at the same time, involves its own universal validity for every rational being. For that in using means for every end I should limit my maxim by the condition of its holding good as a law for every subject, this comes to the same thing as that the fundamental principle of all maxims of action must be that the subject of all ends, i.e., the rational being himself, be never employed merely as means, but as the supreme condition restricting the use of all means, that is in every case as an end likewise.

It follows incontestably that, to whatever laws any rational being may be subject, he being an end in himself must be able to regard himself as also legislating universally in respect of these same laws, since it is just this fitness of his maxims for universal legislation that distinguishes him as an end in himself; also it follows that this implies his dignity (prerogative) above all mere physical beings, that he must always take his maxims from the point of view which regards himself, and likewise every other rational being, as lawgiving beings (on which account they are called persons). In this way a world of rational beings (*mundus intelligibilis*) is possible as a kingdom of ends, and this by virtue of the legislation proper to all persons as members. Therefore every rational being must so act as if he were by his maxims in every case a legislating member in the universal kingdom of ends. The formal principle of these maxims is: So act as if thy maxim were to serve likewise as the universal law (of all rational beings). A kingdom of ends is thus only possible on the analogy of a kingdom of nature, the former, however, only by maxims, that is self-imposed rules, the latter only by the laws of efficient causes acting under necessitation from without. Nevertheless, although the system of nature is looked upon as a machine, yet so far as it has reference to rational beings as its ends, it is given on this account the name of a kingdom of nature. Now such a kingdom of ends would be actually realized by means of maxims conforming to the canon which the categorical imperative prescribes to all rational beings, *if they were universally followed.* But although a rational being, even if he punctually follows this maxim himself, cannot reckon upon all others being therefore true to the same, nor expect that the kingdom of nature and its orderly arrangements shall be in harmony with him as a fitting member, so as to form a kingdom of ends to which he himself contributes, that is to say, that it shall favour his expectation of happiness, still that law: Act according to the maxims of a member of a merely possible kingdom of ends legislating in it universally, remains in its full force, inasmuch as it commands categorically. And it is just in this that the paradox lies; that the mere dignity of man as a rational creature, without any other end or advantage to be attained thereby, in other words, respect for a mere idea, should yet serve an as inflexible precept of the will, and that it is precisely in this independence of the maxim on all such springs of action that its sublimity consists; and it is this that makes every rational subject worthy to be a legislative member in the kingdom of ends: for otherwise he would have to be conceived only as subject to the physical law of his wants. And although we should suppose the kingdom of nature and the kingdom of ends to be united under one sovereign, so that the latter kingdom thereby ceased to be a mere idea and acquired true reality, then it would no doubt gain the accession of a strong spring, but by no means any increase of its intrinsic worth. For this sole absolute lawgiver must, notwithstanding this, be always conceived as estimating the worth of rational beings only by their disinterested behaviour, as prescribed to themselves from that idea [the dignity of man] alone. The essence of things is not altered by their external relations, and that which, abstracting from these, alone constitutes the absolute worth of man, is also that by which he must be judged, whoever the judge may be, and even by the Supreme Being. *Morality,* then, is the relation of actions to the autonomy of the will, that is, to the potential universal legislation by its maxims. An action that is consistent with the autonomy of the will is *permitted;* one that does not agree therewith is *forbidden.* A will whose maxims necessarily coincide with the laws of autonomy is a *holy* will, good absolutely. The dependence of a will not absolutely good on the principle of autonomy (moral necessitation) is obligation. This, then, cannot be applied to a holy being. The objective necessity of actions from obligations is called *duty.*

From what has just been said, it is easy to see how it happens that although the conception of duty implies subjection to the law, we yet ascribe a certain *dignity* and sublimity to the person who fulfils all his duties. There is not, indeed, any sublimity in him, so far as he is *subject* to the moral law; but inasmuch as in regard to that very law he is likewise a *legislator,* and on that account alone subject to it, he has sublimity. We have also shown above that neither fear nor inclination, but simply respect for the law, is the spring which can give actions a moral worth. Our own will, so far as we suppose it to act only under the condition that its maxims are potentially universal laws, this ideal will which is possible to us is the proper object of respect; and the dignity of humanity consists just in this capacity of being universally legislative, though with the condition that it is itself subject to this same legislation. . . .

[7. *The Motives of Pure Practical Reason.*]

WHAT [1] is essential in the moral worth of actions is *that the moral law should directly determine the will.* If the determination of the will takes place in conformity indeed to the moral law, but only by means of a feeling, no matter of what kind, which has to be presupposed in order that the law may be sufficient to determine the will, and therefore not *for the sake of the law,* then the action will possess *legality* but not *morality.* Now, if we understand by *motive* [or *spring*] (*elater animi*) the subjective ground of determination of the will of a being whose reason does not necessarily conform to the objective law, by virtue of its own nature, then it will follow, first, that no motives can be attributed to the Divine will, and that the motives of the human will (as well as that of every created rational being) can never be anything else than the moral law, and consequently that the objective principle of determination must always and alone be also the subjectively sufficient determining principle of the action, if this is not merely to fulfil the *letter* of the law, without containing its *spirit.*[2]

Since, then, for the purpose of giving the moral law influence over the will, we must not seek for any other motives that might enable us to dispense with the motive of the law itself, because that would produce mere hypocrisy, without consistency; and it is even *dangerous*

[1] [Cf. 164-82, in the *Critique of Practical Reason.*]
[2] [Note A 164]

to allow other motives (for instance, that of interest) even to co-operate *along with* the moral law; hence nothing is left us but to determine carefully in what way the moral law becomes a motive, and what effect this has upon the faculty of desire. For as to the question how a law can be directly and of itself a determining principle of the will (which is the essence of morality), this is, for human reason, an insoluble problem and identical with the question: how a free will is possible. Therefore what we have to show *a priori* is, not why the moral law in itself supplies a motive, but what effect it, as such, produces (or, more correctly speaking, must produce) on the mind.

The essential point in every determination of the will by the moral law, is that being a free will it is determined simply by the moral law, not only without the co-operation of sensible impulses, but even to the rejection of all such, and to the checking of all inclinations so far as they might be opposed to that law. So far, then, the effect of the moral law as a motive is only negative, and this motive can be known *a priori* to be such. For all inclination and every sensible impulse is founded on feeling, and the negative effect produced on feeling (by the check on the inclinations) is itself feeling; consequently, we can see *a priori* that the moral law, as a determining principle of the will, must by thwarting all our inclinations produce a feeling which may be called pain; and in this we have the first, perhaps the only, instance in which we are able from *a priori* considerations to determine the relation of a cognition (in this case of pure practical reason) to the feeling of pleasure or displeasure. All the inclinations together (which can be reduced to a tolerable system, in which case their satisfaction is called happiness) constitute *self-regard* (*solipsismus*). This is either the *self-love* that consists in an excessive *fondness* for oneself (*philautia*), or satisfaction with oneself (*arrogantia*). The former is called particularly *selfishness;* the latter *self-conceit.* Pure practical reason only *checks* selfishness, looking on it as natural and active in us even prior to the moral law, so far as to limit it to the condition of agreement with this law, and then it is called *rational self-love.* But self-conceit reason *strikes down* altogether, since all claims to self-esteem which precede agreement with the moral law are vain and unjustifiable, for the certainty of a state of mind that coincides with this law is the first condition of personal worth (as we shall presently show more clearly), and prior to this conformity any pretension to worth is false and unlawful. . . . [A. 166-7]

Now whatever checks our self-conceit in our own judgment humiliates; therefore the moral law inevitably humbles every man when he compares with it the physical propensities of his nature. That, the idea of which as a *determining principle of our will* humbles us in our self-consciousness, awakes *respect* for itself, so far as it is itself positive, and a determining principle. Therefore the moral law is even subjectively a cause of respect. Now since everything that enters into self-love belongs to inclination, and all inclination rests on feelings, and consequently whatever checks all the feelings together in self-love has necessarily, by this very circumstance, an influence on feeling; hence we comprehend how it is possible to perceive *a priori* that the moral can produce an effect on feeling, in that it excludes the inclinations and the propensity to make them the supreme practical condition, i.e. self-love, from all participation in the supreme legislation. This effect is on one side merely *negative,* but on the other side, relatively to the restricting principle of pure practical reason, it is *positive.* No special kind of feeling need be assumed for this under the name of a practical or moral feeling as antecedent to the moral law, and serving as its foundation.

The negative effect on feeling (unpleasantness) is *pathological,* like every influence on feeling, and like every feeling generally. But as an effect of the consciousness of the moral law, and consequently in relation to a supersensible cause, namely, the subject of pure practical reason which is the supreme lawgiver, this feeling of a rational being affected by inclinations is called humiliation (intellectual self-depreciation); but with reference to the positive source of this humiliation, the law, it is respect for it. There is indeed no feeling for this law; but inasmuch as it removes the resistance out of the way, this removal of an obstacle is, in the judgment of reason, esteemed equivalent to a positive help to its causality. Therefore this feeling may also be called a feeling of respect for the moral law, and for both reasons together *a moral feeling.* . . . [A. 168-9]

Respect applies always to persons only—not to things. The latter may arouse inclination, and if they are animals (e.g. horses, dogs, &c.), even *love* or *fear,* like the sea, a volcano, a beast of prey; but never *respect.* Something that comes nearer to this feeling is *admiration,* and this, as an affection, astonishment, can apply to things also, e.g. lofty mountains, the magnitude, number, and distance of the heavenly bodies, the strength and swiftness of many animals, &c. But all this is not respect. A man also may be an object to me of love, fear, or admiration, even to astonishment, and yet not be an object of respect. His jocose humour, his courage and strength, his power from the rank he has amongst others, may inspire me with sentiments of this kind, but still inner respect for him is wanting. *Fontenelle* says, "I bow before a great man, but my mind does not bow." I would add, before an humble plain man, in whom I perceive uprightness of character in a higher degree than I am conscious of in myself, *my mind bows* whether I choose it or not, and though I bear my head never so high that he may not forget my superior rank. Why is this? Because his example exhibits to me a law that humbles my self-conceit when I compare it with my conduct: a law, the *practicability* of obedience to which I see proved by fact before my eyes. Now, I may even be conscious of a like degree of uprightness, and yet the respect remains. For since in man all good is defective, the law made visible by an example still humbles my pride, my standard being furnished by a man whose imperfections, whatever they may be, are not known to me as my own are, and who therefore appears to me in a more favourable light. *Respect* is a *tribute* which we cannot refuse to merit, whether we will or not; we may indeed outwardly withhold it, but we cannot help feeling it inwardly. . . . [A. 170-1]

Respect for the moral law is therefore the only and the undoubted moral motive, and this feeling is directed to no object, except on the ground of this law. . . . [A. 171-5] The moral law is in fact for the will of a perfect being a law of *holiness*, but for the will of every finite rational being a law of *duty*, of moral constraint, and of the determination of its actions by *respect* for this law and reverence for its duty. No other subjective principle must be assumed as a motive, else while the action might chance to be such as the law prescribes, yet as it does not proceed from duty, the intention, which is the thing properly in question in this legislation, is not moral.

It is a very beautiful thing to do good to men from love to them and from sympathetic good will, or to be just from love of order; but this is not yet the true moral maxim of our conduct which is suitable to our position amongst rational beings as *men,* when we pretend with fanciful pride to set ourselves above the thought of duty, like volunteers, and, as if we were independent on the command, to want to do of our own good pleasure what we think we need no command to do. We stand under a *discipline* of reason, and in all our maxims must not forget our subjection to it, nor withdraw anything therefrom, or by an egotistic presumption diminish aught of the authority of the law (although our own reason gives it) so as to set the determining principle of our will, even though the law be conformed to, anywhere else but in the law itself and in respect for this law. Duty and obligation are the only names that we must give to our relation to the moral law. We are indeed legislative members of a moral kingdom rendered possible by freedom, and presented to us by reason as an object of respect; but yet we are subjects in it, not the sovereign, and to mistake our inferior position as creatures, and presumptuously to reject the authority of the moral law, is already to revolt from it in spirit, even though the letter of it is fulfilled.

With this agrees very well the possibility of such a command as: *Love God above everything, and thy neighbour as thyself.*[1] For as a command it requires respect for a law which *commands* love and does not leave it to our own arbitrary choice to make this our principle.

[1] This law is in striking contrast with the principle of private happiness which some make the supreme principle of morality. This would be expressed thus: *Love thyself above everything, and God and thy neighbour for thine own sake.*

Love to God, however, considered as an inclination (pathological love), is impossible, for he is not an object of the senses. The same affection towards men is possible no doubt, but cannot be commanded, for it is not in the power of any man to love anyone at command; therefore it is only *practical love* that is meant in that pith of all laws. To love God means, in this sense, to like to do His commandments; to love one's neighbour means to like to practise all duties towards him. But the command that makes this a rule cannot command us to *have* this disposition in actions conformed to duty, but only to *endeavour* after it. For a command to like to do a thing is in itself contradictory, because if we already know of ourselves what we are bound to do, and if further we are conscious of liking to do it, a command would be quite needless; and if we do it not willingly, but only out of respect for the law, a command that makes this respect the motive of our maxim would directly counteract the disposition commanded. That law of all laws, therefore, like all the moral precepts of the Gospel, exhibits the moral disposition in all its perfection, in which, viewed as an Ideal of holiness, it is not attainable by any creature, but yet is the pattern which we should strive to approach, and in an uninterrupted but infinite progress become like to. In fact, if a rational creature could ever reach this point, that he thoroughly *likes* to do all moral laws, this would mean that there does not exist in him even the possibility of a desire that would tempt him to deviate from them; for to overcome such a desire always costs the subject some sacrifice, and therefore requires self-compulsion, that is, inward constraint to something that one does not quite like to do; and no creature can ever reach this stage of moral disposition. For, being a creature, and therefore always dependent with respect to what he requires for complete satisfaction, he can never be quite free from desires and inclinations, and as these rest on physical causes, they can never of themselves coincide with the moral law, the sources of which are quite different; and therefore they make it necessary to found the mental disposition of one's maxims on moral obligation, not on ready inclination, but on respect, which *demands* obedience to the law, even though one may not like it; not on love, which apprehends no inward reluctance of the will towards the law. Nevertheless, this latter, namely, love to the law (which would then cease to be a *command,* and then morality, which would have passed subjectively into holiness, would cease to be *virtue*), must be the constant though unattainable goal of his endeavours. For in the case of what we highly esteem, but yet (on account of the consciousness of our weakness) dread, the increased facility of satisfying it changes the most reverential awe into inclination, and respect into love: at least this would be the perfection of a disposition devoted to the law, if it were possible for a creature to attain it. . . . [A. 178-9]

Duty! Thou sublime and mighty name that dost embrace nothing charming or insinuating, but requirest submission, and yet seekest not to move the will by threatening aught that would arouse natural aversion or terror, but merely holdest forth a law which of itself finds entrance into the mind, and yet gains reluctant reverence (though not always obedience), a law before which all inclinations are dumb, even though they secretly counter-work it; what origin is there worthy of thee, and where is to be found the root of thy noble descent which proudly rejects all kindred with the inclinations; a root to be derived from which is the indispensable condition of the only worth which men can give themselves?

It can be nothing less than a power which elevates man above himself (as a part of the world of sense), a power which connects him with an order of things that only the understanding can conceive, with a world which at the same time commands the whole sensible world, and with it the empirically determinable existence of man in time, as well as the sum-total of all ends (which totality alone suits such unconditional practical laws as the moral). This power is nothing but *personality,* that is, freedom and independence on the mechanism of nature, yet, regarded also as a faculty of a being which is subject to special laws, namely, pure practical laws given by its own reason; so that the person as belonging to the sensible world is subject to his own personality as belonging to the intelligible [supersensible] world. It is, then, not to be wondered at that man, as belonging to both worlds, must regard his own nature in reference to its second and highest characteristic only with reverence, and its laws with the highest respect.

On this origin are founded many expressions which designate the worth of objects according to moral ideas. The moral law is *holy* (inviolable). Man is indeed unholy enough; but he must regard *humanity* in his own person as holy. In all creation everything one chooses, and over which one has any power, may be used *merely as means;* man alone, and with him every rational creature, is an *end in himself.* By virtue of the autonomy of his freedom he is the subject of the moral law, which is holy. Just for this reason every will, even every person's own individual will, in relation to itself, is restricted to the condition of agreement with the *autonomy* of the rational being, that is to say, that it is not to be subject to any purpose which cannot accord with a law which might arise from the will of the passive subject himself; the latter is, therefore, never to be employed merely as means, but as itself also, concurrently, an end. We justly attribute this condition even to the Divine will, with regard to the rational beings in the world, which are His creatures, since it rests on their *personality,* by which alone they are ends in themselves.

This respect-inspiring idea of personality which sets before our eyes the sublimity of our nature (in its higher aspect), while at the same time it shows us the want of accord of our conduct with it, and thereby strikes down self-conceit, is even natural to the commonest reason, and easily observed. Has not every even moderately honourable man sometimes found that, where by an otherwise inoffensive lie he might either have withdrawn himself from an unpleasant business, or even have procured some advantage for a loved and well-deserving friend, he has avoided it solely lest he should despise himself secretly in his own eyes? When an upright man is in the greatest distress, which he might have avoided if he could only have disregarded duty, is he not sustained by the consciousness that he has maintained humanity in its proper dignity in his own person and honoured it, that he has no reason to be ashamed of himself in his own sight, or to dread the inward glance of self-examination? This consolation is not happiness, it is not even the smallest part of it, for no one would wish to have occasion for it, or would perhaps even desire a life in such circumstances. But he lives, and he cannot endure that he should be in his own eyes unworthy of life. This inward peace is therefore merely negative as regards what can make life pleasant; it is, in fact, only the escaping the danger of sinking in personal worth, after everything else that is valuable has been lost. It is the effect of a respect for something quite different from life, something in comparison and contrast with which life with all its enjoyment has no value. He still lives only because it is his duty, not because he finds anything pleasant in life.

Such is the nature of the true motive of pure practical reason; it is no other than the pure moral law itself, inasmuch as it makes us conscious of the sublimity of our own supersensible existence, and subjectively produces respect for their higher nature in men who are also conscious of their sensible existence and of the consequent dependence of their pathologically very susceptible nature. Now with this motive may be combined so many charms and satisfactions of life, that even on this account alone the most prudent choice of a rational *Epicurean* reflecting on the greatest advantage of life would declare itself on the side of moral conduct, and it may even be advisable to join this prospect of a cheerful enjoyment of life with that supreme motive which is already sufficient of itself; but only as a counterpoise to the attractions which vice does not fail to exhibit on the opposite side, and not so as, even in the smallest degree, to place in this the proper moving power when duty is in question. For that would be just the same as to wish to taint the purity of the moral disposition in its source. The majesty of duty has nothing to do with enjoyment of life; it has its special law and its special tribunal, and though the two should be never so well shaken together to be given well mixed, like medicine, to the sick soul, yet they will soon separate of themselves; and if they do not, the former will not act; and although physical life might gain somewhat in force, the moral life would fade away irrecoverably.

[II. THE PROBLEM OF FREEDOM]

[1.] *The Concept of Freedom is the Key that explains the Autonomy of the Will.*

THE [1] *will* is a kind of causality belonging to living beings in so far as they are rational, and *freedom* would be this property of such causality that it can be efficient, independently on foreign causes *determining* it; just as *physical necessity* is the property that the causality of all irrational beings has of being determined to activity by the influence of foreign causes.

The preceding definition of freedom is *negative,* and therefore unfruitful for the discovery of its essence; but it leads to a *positive* conception which is so much the more full and fruitful. Since the conception of causality involves that of laws, according to which, by something that we call cause, something else, namely, the effect, must be produced [laid down]; hence, although freedom is not a property of the will depending on physical laws, yet it is not for that reason lawless; on the contrary, it must be a causality acting according to immutable laws, but of a peculiar kind; otherwise a free will would be an absurdity. Physical necessity is a heteronomy of the efficient causes, for every effect is possible only according to this law, that something else determines the efficient cause to exert its causality. What else then can freedom of the will be but autonomy, that is the property of the will to be a law to itself? But the proposition: The will is in every action a law to itself, only expresses the principle, to act on no other maxim than that which can also have as an object itself as a universal law. Now this is precisely the formula

[1] [Cf. A. 65-6, in *Section III* of the *Fundamental Principles of the Metaphysic of Morals.*]

of the categorical imperative and is the principle of morality, so that a free will and a will subject to moral laws are one and the same. . . .

[2.] *Freedom must be presupposed as a Property of the Will of all Rational Beings.*

It [1] is not enough to predicate freedom of our own will, from whatever reason, if we have not sufficient grounds for predicating the same of all rational beings. For as morality serves as a law for us only because we are *rational beings,* it must also hold for all rational beings; and as it must be deduced simply from the property of freedom, it must be shown that freedom also is a property of all rational beings. It is not enough, then, to prove it from certain supposed experiences of human nature (which indeed is quite impossible, and it can only be shown *a priori*), but we must show that it belongs to the activity of all rational beings endowed with a will. Now I say every being that cannot act except *under the idea of freedom* is just for that reason in a practical point of view really free, that is to say, all laws which are inseparably connected with freedom have the same force for him as if his will had been shown to be free in itself by a proof theoretically conclusive.[2] Now I affirm that we must attribute to every rational being which has a will that it has also the idea of freedom and acts entirely under this idea. For in such a being we conceive a reason that is practical, that is, has causality in reference to its objects. Now we cannot possibly conceive a reason consciously receiving a bias from any other quarter with respect to

[1] [Cf. A. 66-7, in *Section III* of the *Fundamental Principles of the Metaphysic of Morals.*]
[2] [Note A 67.]

its judgments, for then the subject would ascribe the determination of its judgment not to its own reason, but to an impulse. It must regard itself as the author of its principles independent on foreign influences. Consequently as practical reason or as the will of a rational being it must regard itself as free, that is to say, the will of such a being cannot be a will of its own except under the idea of freedom. This idea must therefore in a practical point of view be ascribed to every rational being.

[3.] *How is a Categorical Imperative Possible?*

Every [1] rational being reckons himself *qua* intelligence as belonging to the world of understanding, and it is simply as an efficient cause belonging to that world that he calls his causality a *will.* On the other side he is also conscious of himself as a part of the world of sense in which his actions, which are mere appearances [phenomena] of that causality, are displayed; we cannot, however, discern how they are possible from this causality which we do not know; but instead of that, these actions as belonging to the sensible world must be viewed as determined by other phenomena, namely, desires and inclinations. If therefore I were only a member of the world of understanding, then all my actions would perfectly conform to the principle of autonomy of the pure will; if I were only a part of the world of sense, they would necessarily be assumed to conform wholly to the natural law of desires and inclinations, in other words, to the heteronomy of nature. (The former would rest on morality as the supreme principle, the latter on happiness.) Since, however, *the world of understanding contains the foundation of the world of*

[1] [Cf. A. 73-5, in *Section III* of the *Fundamental Principles of the Metaphysic of Morals.*]

sense, and consequently of its laws also, and accordingly gives the law to my will (which belongs wholly to the world of understanding) directly, and must be conceived as doing so, it follows that, although on the one side I must regard myself as a being belonging to the world of sense, yet on the other side I must recognize myself as subject as an intelligence to the law of the world of understanding, i.e. to reason, which contains this law in the idea of freedom, and therefore as subject to the autonomy of the will: consequently I must regard the laws of the world of understanding as imperatives for me, and the actions which conform to them as duties.

And thus what makes categorical imperatives possible is this, that the idea of freedom makes me a member of an intelligible world, in consequence of which, if I were nothing else, all my actions *would* always conform to the autonomy of the will; but as I at the same time intuit myself as a member of the world of sense, they *ought* so to conform, and this *categorical* "ought" implies a synthetic *a priori* proposition, inasmuch as besides my will as affected by sensible desires there is added further the idea of the same will, but as belonging to the world of the understanding, pure and practical of itself, which contains the supreme condition according to Reason of the former will; precisely as to the intuitions of sense there are added concepts of the understanding which of themselves signify nothing but regular form in general, and in this way synthetic *a priori* propositions become possible, on which all knowledge of physical nature rests.

The practical use of common human reason confirms this reasoning. There is no one, not even the most consummate villain, provided only that he is otherwise accustomed to the use of reason, who, when we set before him examples of honesty of purpose, of steadfastness in following good maxims, of sympathy and general benevolence (even combined with great sacrifices of advantages and comfort), does not wish that he might also possess these qualities. Only on account of his inclinations and impulses he cannot attain this in himself, but at the same time he wishes to be free from such inclinations which are burdensome to himself. He proves by this that he transfers himself in thought with a will free from the impulses of the sensibility into an order of things wholly different from that of his desires in the field of the sensibility; since he cannot expect to obtain by that wish any gratification of his desires, nor any position which would satisfy any of his actual or supposable inclinations (for this would destroy the preeminence of the very idea which wrests that wish from him): he can only expect a greater intrinsic worth of his own person. This better person, however, he imagines himself to be when he transfers himself to the point of view of a member of the world of the understanding, to which he is involuntarily forced by the idea of freedom, i.e., of independence on *determining* causes of the world of sense; and from this point of view he is conscious of a good will, which by his own confession constitutes the law for the bad will that he possesses as a member of the world of sense—a law whose authority he recognizes while transgressing it. What he morally "ought" is then what he necessarily "would" as a member of the world of the understanding, and is conceived by him as an "ought" only inasmuch as he likewise considers himself as a member of the world of sense.

[4.] *The Relation of Freedom to the Moral Law.*

Freedom [1] and an unconditional practical law recip-

[1] [Cf. A. 117-18, in the *Critique of Practical Reason.*]

rocally imply each other. Now I do not ask here whether they are in fact distinct, or whether an unconditional law is not rather merely the consciousness of a pure practical reason, and the latter identical with the positive concept of freedom; I only ask, whence *begins* our *knowledge* of the unconditionally practical, whether it is from freedom or from the practical law? Now it cannot begin from freedom, for of this we cannot be immediately conscious, since the first concept of it is negative; nor can we infer it from experience, for experience gives us the knowledge only of the law of phenomena, and hence of the mechanism of nature, the direct opposite of freedom. It is therefore the moral law, of which we become directly conscious (as soon as we trace for ourselves maxims of the will), that *first* presents itself to us, and leads directly to the concept of freedom, inasmuch as reason presents it as a principle of determination not to be outweighed by any sensible conditions, nay, wholly independent of them. But how is the consciousness of that moral law possible? We can become conscious of pure practical laws just as we are conscious of pure theoretical principles, by attending to the necessity with which reason prescribes them, and to the elimination of all empirical conditions, which it directs. The concept of a pure will arises out of the former, as that of a pure understanding arises out of the latter. That this is the true subordination of our concepts, and that it is morality that first discovers to us the notion of freedom, hence that it is *practical reason* which, with this concept, first proposes to speculative reason the most insoluble problem, thereby placing it in the greatest perplexity, is [thus] evident.[1] . . .

[1] [The following note appears as a note to the *Preface* of the *Critique of Practical Reason,* A. 88]. Lest anyone should imagine that he finds an *inconsistency* here when I call free-

[5.] *The Deduction of the Fundamental Principles of Pure Practical Reason.*

. . . With[1] the *deduction*, that is, the justification of [the] objective and universal validity [of the supreme principle of practical reason], and the discernment of the possibility of such a synthetical proposition *a priori*, we cannot expect to succeed so well as in the case of the principles of pure theoretical reason. For these referred to objects of possible experience, namely, to phenomena; and we could prove that these phenomena could be *known* as objects of experience only by being brought under the categories in accordance with these laws; and consequently that all possible experience must conform to these laws. But I could not proceed in this way with the deduction of the moral law. For this does not concern the knowledge of the properties of objects, which may be given to the reason from some other source; but a knowledge which can itself be the ground of the existence of the objects, and by which reason in a rational being has causality, i.e. pure reason, which can be regarded as a faculty immediately determining the will.

Now all our human insight is at an end as soon as we have arrived at fundamental powers or faculties; for the possibility of these cannot be understood by any

---

dom the condition of the moral law, and hereafter maintain in the treatise itself that the moral law is the condition under which we can first *become conscious* of freedom, I will merely remark that freedom is the *ratio essendi* of the moral law, while the moral law is the *ratio cognoscendi* of freedom. For had not the moral law been previously distinctly thought in our reason, we should never consider ourselves justified in *assuming* such a thing as freedom, although it be not contradictory. But were there no freedom, it would be *impossible* to trace the moral law in ourselves at all.

[1] [Cf. A. 136-40, in the *Critique of Practical Reason.*]

means, and just as little should it be arbitrarily invented and assumed. Therefore, in the theoretic use of reason, it is experience alone that can justify us in assuming them. But this expedient of adducing empirical proofs, instead of a deduction from *a priori* sources of knowledge, is denied us here in respect to the pure practical faculty of reason. For whatever requires to draw the proof of its reality from experience must depend for the grounds of its possibility on principles of experience; and pure, yet practical, reason by its very notion cannot be regarded as such. Further, the moral law is given as a fact of pure reason of which we are *a priori* conscious, and which is apodictically certain, though it be granted that in experience no example of its exact fulfilment can be found. Hence the objective reality of the moral law cannot be proved by any deduction, by any efforts of theoretical reason, whether speculative or empirically supported, and therefore, even if we renounced its apodictic certainty, it could not be proved *a posteriori* by experience, and yet it is firmly established of itself.

But instead of this vainly sought deduction of the moral principle, something else is found which was quite unexpected, namely, that this moral principle serves conversely as the principle of the deduction of an inscrutable faculty which no experience could prove, but of which speculative reason was compelled at least to assume the possibility (in order to find amongst its cosmological ideas the unconditioned in the chain of causality, so as not to contradict itself)—I mean the faculty of freedom. The moral law, which itself does not require a justification, proves not merely the possibility of freedom, but that it really belongs to beings who recognize this law as binding on themselves. The moral law is in fact a law of the causality of free agents, and therefore of the possibility of a supersensible system of nature, just as the metaphysical law of events in the world of sense was a law of causality of the sensible system of nature; and it therefore determines what speculative philosophy was compelled to leave undetermined, namely, the law for a causality, the concept of which in the latter was only negative; and therefore for the first time gives this concept objective reality.

This sort of credential of the moral law, viz. that it is set forth as a principle of the deduction of freedom, which is a causality of pure reason, is a sufficient substitute for all *a priori* justification, since theoretic reason was compelled to assume *at least* the possibility of freedom, in order to satisfy a want of its own. For the moral law proves its reality, so as even to satisfy the critique of the speculative reason, by the fact that it adds a positive definition to a causality previously conceived only negatively, the possibility of which was incomprehensible to speculative reason, which yet was compelled to suppose it. For it adds the notion of a reason that directly determines the will (by imposing on its maxims the condition of a universal legislative form); and thus it is able for the first time to give objective, though only practical, reality to reason, which always became transcendent when it sought to proceed speculatively with its ideas. It thus changes the *transcendent* use of reason into an *immanent* use (so that reason is itself, by means of ideas, an efficient cause in the field of experience).

The determination of the causality of beings in the world of sense, as such, can never be unconditioned; and yet for every series of conditions there must be something unconditioned, and therefore there must be a causality which is determined wholly by itself. Hence, the idea of freedom as a faculty of absolute spontaneity was not found to be a want, but *as far as its possibility is concerned,* an analytic principle of pure speculative reason. But as it is absolutely impossible to find in experience any example in accordance with this idea, because amongst the causes of things as phenomena, it would be impossible to meet with any absolutely unconditioned determination of causality, we were only able to *defend our supposition* that a freely acting cause might be a being in the world of sense, in so far as it is considered in the other point of view as a *noumenon,* showing that there is no contradiction in regarding all its actions as subject to physical conditions so far as they are phenomena, and yet regarding its causality as physically unconditioned, in so far as the acting being belongs to the world of understanding, and in thus making the concept of freedom the regulative principle of reason. By this principle I do not indeed learn what the object is to which that sort of causality is attributed; but I remove the difficulty; for, on the one side, in the explanation of events in the world, and consequently also of the actions of rational beings, I leave to the mechanism of physical necessity the right of ascending from conditioned to condition *ad infinitum,* while on the other side I keep open for speculative reason the place which for it is vacant, namely, the intelligible, in order to transfer the unconditioned thither. But I was not able to *verify* this *supposition;* that is, to change it into the *knowledge* of a being so acting, not even into the knowledge of the possibility of such a being. This vacant place is now filled by pure practical reason with a definite law of causality in an intelligible word (causality with freedom), namely, the moral law. Speculative reason does not hereby gain anything as regards its insight, but only as regards the *certainty* of its problematical notion of freedom, which here obtains *objective reality,* which, though only practical, is nevertheless undoubted. Even the notion of causality—the application, and consequently the signification, of which holds properly only in relation to phenomena, so as to connect them into experience (as is shown by the critique of pure reason)—is not so enlarged as to extend its use beyond these limits. For if reason sought to do this, it would have to show how the logical relation of principle and consequence can be used synthetically in a different sort of intuition from the sensible; that is how a *causa noumenon* is possible. This it can never do; and, as practical reason, it does not even concern itself with it, since it only places the *determining principle* of causality of man as a sensible creature (which is given) in *pure reason* (which is therefore called practical); and therefore it employs the notion of cause, not in order to know objects, but to determine causality in relation to objects in general. It can abstract altogether from the application of this notion to objects with a view to theoretical knowledge (since this concept is always found *a priori* in the understanding, even independently on any intuition). Reason, then, employs it only for a practical purpose, and hence we can transfer the determining principle of the will into the intelligible order of things, admitting, at the same time, that we cannot understand how the notion of cause can determine the knowledge of these things. But reason must cognise causality with respect to the actions of the will in the sensible world in a definite manner; otherwise, practical reason could not really produce any action. But as to the notion which it forms of its own causality as noumenon, it need not determine it theoretically with a view to the cognition of its supersensible existence, so as to give it significance in this way. For it acquires significance apart from this, though only for practical use, namely, through the moral law. Theoretically viewed, it remains always a pure *a priori* concept of the understanding, which can be applied to objects whether they have been given sensibly or not, although in the latter case it has no definite theoretical significance or application, but is only a formal, though essential, conception of the understanding relating to an object in general. The significance which reason gives it through the moral law is merely practical, inasmuch as the idea of the law of causality (of the will) has itself causality, or is its determining principle.

[6.] *Of the Right that Pure Reason in its Practical Use has to an Extension which is not Possible to it in its Speculative Use.*

We [1] have in the moral principle set forth a law of causality, the determining principle of which is set above all the conditions of the sensible world; we have it conceived how the will, as belonging to the intelligible world, is determinable, and therefore we have its subject (man) not merely *conceived* as belonging to a world of pure understanding, and in this respect unknown (which the critique of speculative reason enabled us to do), but also *defined* as regards his causality by means of a law which cannot be reduced to any physical law of the sensible world; and therefore our knowledge is *extended* beyond the limits of that world—a pretension which the critique of the pure reason declared to be futile in all speculation. Now, how is the practical use of pure reason here to be reconciled with the theoretical, as to the determination of the limits of its faculty? . . . [A. 140-3]

[1] [Cf. A. 140-47, in the *Critique of Practical Reason.*]

It resulted . . . from my [previous][1] inquiries, that the objects with which we have to do in experience are by no means things in themselves, but merely phenomena; and that although in the case of things in themselves it is impossible to see how, if A is supposed, it should be contradictory that B, which is quite different from A, should not also be supposed (i.e. to see the necessity of the connexion between A as cause and B as effect); yet it can very well be conceived that, as phenomena, they may be necessarily connected *in one experience* in a certain way (e.g. with regard to time-relations); so that they could not be separated without contradicting that connexion, by means of which this experience is possible in which they are objects, and in which alone they are cognisable by us. And so it was found to be in fact; so that I was able not only to prove the objective reality of the concept of cause in regard to objects of experience, but also to *deduce* it as an *a priori* concept by reason of the necessity of the connexion it implied; that is, to show the possibility of its origin from pure understanding without any empirical sources; and thus, after removing the sources of empiricism, I was also able to overthrow the inevitable consequence of this namely, scepticism, first with regard to physical science, and then with regard to mathematics (in which empiricism has just the same grounds), both being sciences which have reference to objects of possible experience; herewith overthrowing the thorough doubt of whatever theoretic reason professes to discern.

But how is it with the application of this category of causality (and all the others; for without them there can be no knowledge of anything existing) to things

[1] [i.e. in the *Critique of Pure Reason.*]

which are not objects of possible experience, but lie beyond its bounds? For I was able to deduce the objective reality of these concepts only with regard to *objects of possible experience.* But even this very fact, that I have saved them, only in case I have proved that objects may by means of them be thought, though not determined *a priori;* this it is that gives them a place in the pure understanding, by which they are referred to objects in general (sensible or not sensible). If anything is still wanting, it is that which is the condition of the *application* of these categories, and especially that of causality, to objects, namely, intuition; for where this is not given, the application *with a view to theoretic knowledge of the object,* as a noumenon, is impossible; and therefore if anyone ventures on it, is (as in the critique of the pure reason) absolutely forbidden. Still, the objective reality of the concept (of causality) remains, and it can be used even of noumena, but without our being able in the least to define the concept theoretically so as to produce knowledge. For that this concept, even in reference to an object, contains nothing impossible, was shown by this, that even while applied to objects of sense, its seat was certainly fixed in the pure understanding; and although, when referred to things in themselves (which cannot be objects of experience), it is not capable of being determined so as to represent a *definite object* for the purpose of theoretic knowledge; yet for any other purpose (for instance, a practical) it might be capable of being determined so as to have such application. . . . [A. 144]

In order now to discover this condition of the application of the said concept to noumena, we need only recall why we are not content with its application to objects of experience, but desire also to apply it to things in themselves. It will appear, then, that it is not a theoretic but a practical purpose that makes this a necessity. In speculation, even if we were successful in it, we should not really gain anything in the knowledge of nature, or generally with regard to such objects as are given, but we should make a wide step from the sensibly conditioned (in which we have already enough to do to maintain ourselves, and to follow carefully the chain of causes) to the supersensible, in order to complete our knowledge of principles and to fix its limits: whereas there always remains an infinite chasm unfilled between those limits and what we know: and we should have hearkened to a vain curiosity rather than a solid desire of knowledge.

But, besides the relation in which the *understanding* stands to objects (in theoretical knowledge), it has also a relation to the faculty of desire, which is therefore called the will, and the pure will, inasmuch as pure understanding (in this case called reason) is practical through the mere conception of a law. The objective reality of a pure will, or what is the same thing, of a pure practical reason, is given in the moral law *a priori*, as it were, by a fact, for so we may name a determination of the will which is inevitable, although it does not rest on empirical principles. Now, in the notion of a will the notion of causality is already contained, and hence the notion of a pure will contains that of a causality accompanied with freedom, that is, one which is not determinable by physical laws, and consequently is not capable of any empirical intuition in proof of its reality, but, nevertheless, completely justifies its objective reality *a priori* in the pure practical law; not, indeed (as is easily seen) for the purposes of the theoretical, but of the practical use of reason. Now, the notion of a being that has free will is the notion of a *causa nou-*

menon; and that this notion involves no contradiction we are already assured by the fact that, inasmuch as the concept of cause has arisen wholly from pure understanding, and has its objective reality assured by the Deduction, as it is moreover in its origin independent on any sensible conditions, it is, therefore, not restricted to phenomena (unless we wanted to make a definite theoretic use of it), but can be applied equally to things that are objects of the pure understanding. But, since this application cannot rest on any intuition (for intuition can only be sensible), therefore, *causa noumenon,* as regards the theoretic use of reason, although a possible and thinkable, is yet an empty notion. Now I do not desire by means of this to *understand theoretically* the nature of a being, *in so far* as it has a *pure* will; it is enough for me to have thereby designated it as such, and hence to combine the notion of causality with that of freedom (and what is inseparable from it, the moral law, as its determining principle). Now, this right I certainly have by virtue of the pure, not-empirical origin of the notion of cause, since I do not consider myself entitled to make any use of it except in reference to the moral law which determines its reality, that is, only a practical use. . . . [A. 146]

This objective reality of a pure concept of the understanding in the sphere of the supersensible, once brought in, gives an objective reality also to all the other categories, although only so far as they stand in *necessary* connexion with the determining principle of the will (the moral law); a reality only of practical application, which has not the least effect in enlarging our theoretical knowledge of these objects, or the discernment of their nature by pure reason. So we shall find also in the sequel that these categories refer only to beings as *intelligences,* and in them only to the relation of *reason* to the *will;* consequently, always only to the *practical,* and beyond this cannot pretend to any knowledge of these things; and whatever other properties belonging to the theoretical representation of supersensible things may be brought into connexion with these categories, this is not to be reckoned as knowledge, but only as a right (in a practical point of view, however, it is a necessity) to admit and assume such beings, even in the case where we [conceive] supersensible beings (e.g. God) according to analogy, that is, a purely rational relation, of which we make a practical use with reference to what is sensible; and thus the application to the supersensible solely in a practical point of view does not give pure theoretic reason the least encouragement to run riot into the transcendent.

[III. THE SUMMUM BONUM, GOD AND IMMORTALITY]

[1. *The Concept of the Summum Bonum.*]

. . . REASON [1] in its practical use . . . seeks to find the unconditioned for the practically conditioned (which rests on inclinations and natural wants), and this not as the determining principle of the will, but even when this is given (in the moral law) it seeks the unconditioned totality of the *object* of pure practical reason under the name of the *Summum Bonum.* . . . [A. 203-5]

The conception of the *summum* itself contains an ambiguity which might occasion needless disputes if we did not attend to it. The *summum* may mean either the supreme *(supremum)* or the perfect *(consummatum).* The former is that condition which is itself unconditioned, i.e. is not subordinate to any other *(originarium)*; the second is that whole which is not a part of a greater

[1] [Cf. A. 203-9, in the *Critique of Practical Reason.*]

whole of the same kind *(perfectissimum)*. It has been shown in the Analytic that *virtue* (as worthiness to be happy) is the *supreme condition* of all that can appear to us desirable, and consequently of all our pursuit of happiness, and is therefore the *supreme* good. But it does not follow that it is the whole and perfect good as the object of the desires of rational finite beings; for this requires happiness also, and that not merely in the partial eyes of the person who makes himself an end, but even in the judgment of an impartial reason, which regards persons in general as ends in themselves. For to need happiness, to deserve it, and yet at the same time not to participate in it, cannot be consistent with the perfect volition of a rational being possessed at the same time of all power, if, for the sake of experiment, we conceive such a being. Now inasmuch as virtue and happiness together constitute the possession of the *summum bonum* in a person, and the distribution of happiness in exact proportion to morality (which is the worth of the person, and his worthiness to be happy) constitutes the *summum bonum* of a possible world; hence this *summum bonum* expresses the whole, the perfect good, in which, however, virtue as the condition is always the supreme good, since it has no condition above it; whereas happiness, while it is pleasant to the possessor of it, is not of itself absolutely and in all respects good, but always presupposes morally right behaviour as its condition. . . . [A. 207-8]

Now it is clear from the Analytic that the maxims of virtue and those of private happiness are quite heterogeneous as to their supreme practical principle; and although they belong to one *summum bonum* which together they make possible, yet they are so far from coinciding that they restrict and check one another very much in the same subject. Thus the question, *How is the summum bonum practically possible?* still remains an unsolved problem, notwithstanding all the *attempts at coalition* that have hitherto been made. The Analytic has, however, shown what it is that makes the problem difficult to solve; namely, that happiness and morality are two specifically *distinct elements of the summum bonum,* and therefore their combination *cannot* be *analytically* cognized (as if the man that seeks his own happiness should find by mere analysis of his conception that in so acting he is virtuous, or as if the man that follows virtue should in the consciousness of such conduct find that he is already happy *ipso facto*) but must be a *synthesis* of concepts. Now since this combination is recognized as *a priori,* and therefore as practically necessary, and consequently not as derived from experience, so that the possibility of the *summum bonum* does not rest on any empirical principle, it follows that the *deduction* [legitimation] of this concept must be *transcendental.* It is *a priori* (morally) necessary to *produce the summum bonum by freedom of will:* therefore the condition of its possibility must rest solely on *a priori* principles of cognition.

[2.] *The Antinomy of Practical Reason [and its Critical Solution].*

In [1] the *summum bonum* which is practical for us, i.e. to be realized by our will, virtue and happiness are thought as necessarily combined, so that the one cannot be assumed by pure practical reason without the other also being attached to it. Now this combination (like every other) is either *analytical* or *synthetical.* It has been shown that it cannot be analytical; it must then be synthetical, and, more particularly, must be conceived

[1] [Cf. A. 209-16, in the *Critique of Practical Reason.*]

as the connexion of cause and effect, since it concerns a practical good, i.e. one that is possible by means of action; consequently either the desire of happiness must be the motive to maxims of virtue, or the maxim of virtue must be the efficient cause of happiness. The first is *absolutely* impossible, because (as was proved in the Analytic) maxims which place the determining principle of the will in the desire of personal happiness are not moral at all, and no virtue can be founded on them. But the second is *also impossible,* because the practical connexion of causes and effects in the world, as the result of the determination of the will, does not depend upon the moral dispositions of the will, but on the knowledge of the laws of nature and the physical power to use them for one's purposes; consequently we cannot expect in the world by the most punctilious observance of the moral laws any necessary connexion of happiness with virtue adequate to the *summum bonum.* Now as the promotion of this *summum bonum,* the conception of which contains this connexion, is *a priori* a necessary object of our will, and inseparably attached to the moral law, the impossibility of the former must prove the falsity of the latter. If then the supreme good is not possible by practical rules, then the moral law also which commands us to promote it is directed to vain imaginary ends, and must consequently be false.

The antinomy of pure speculative reason exhibits a similar conflict between freedom and physical necessity in the causality of events in the world. It was solved by showing that there is no real contradiction when the events and even the world in which they occur are regarded (as they ought to be) merely as appearances; since one and the same acting being, *as an appearance* (even to his own inner sense), has a causality in the world of sense that always conforms to the mechanism of nature, but with respect to the same events, so far as the acting person regards himself at the same time as a noumenon (as pure intelligence in an existence not dependent on the condition of time), he can contain a principle by which that causality acting according to laws of nature is determined, but which is itself free from all laws of nature.

It is just the same with the foregoing antinomy of pure practical reason. The first of the two propositions —That the endeavour after happiness produces a virtuous mind, is *absolutely false;* but the second, That a virtuous mind necessarily produces happiness, is *not absolutely false,* but only in so far as virtue is considered as a form of causality in the sensible world, and consequently only if I suppose existence in it to be the only sort of existence of a rational being; it is then only *conditionally* false. But as I am not only justified in thinking that I exist also as a noumenon in a world of the understanding, but even have in the moral law a purely intellectual determining principle of my causality (in the sensible world), it is not impossible that morality of mind should have a connexion as cause with happiness (as an effect in the sensible world) if not immediate yet mediate (viz.: through an intelligent author of nature), and moreover necessary; while in a system of nature which is merely an object of the senses this combination could never occur except contingently, and therefore could not suffice for the *summum bonum.*

Thus, notwithstanding this seeming conflict of practical reason with itself, the *summum bonum,* which is the necessary supreme end of a will morally determined, is a true object thereof; for it is practically possible, and the maxims of the will which as regards their matter refer to it have objective reality, which at first was threatened by the antinomy that appeared in the connexion of morality with happiness by a general law; but this was merely from a misconception, because the relation between appearances was taken for a relation of the things in themselves to these appearances. . . . [A. 211-15]

From this solution of the antinomy of pure practical reason it follows that in practical principles we may at least conceive as possible a natural and necessary connexion between the consciousness of morality and the expectation of a proportionate happiness as its result, though it does not follow that we can know or perceive this connexion; that, on the other hand, principles of the pursuit of happiness cannot possibly produce morality; that, therefore, morality is the *supreme* good (as the first condition of the *summum bonum*), while happiness constitutes its second element, but only in such a way that it is the morally conditioned, but necessary consequence of the former. Only with this subordination is the *summum bonum* the whole object of pure practical reason, which must necessarily conceive it as possible, since it commands us to contribute to the utmost of our power to its realization. But since the possibility of such connexion of the conditioned with its condition belongs wholly to the supersensual relation of things, and cannot be given according to the laws of the world of sense, although the practical consequences of the idea belong to the world of sense, namely, the actions that aim at realizing the *summum bonum*; we will therefore endeavour to set forth the grounds of that possibility, first, in respect of what is immediately in our power, and then, secondly, in that which is not in our power, but which reason presents to us as the supplement of our impotence, for the realization of the *summum bonum* (which by practical principles is necessary).

[3.] *Of the Primacy of Pure Practical Reason in its Union with the Speculative Reason.*

. . . If [1] practical reason could not assume or think as given anything further than what speculative reason of itself could offer it from its own insight, the latter would have the primacy. But supposing that it had of itself original *a priori* principles with which certain theoretical positions were inseparably connected, while these were withdrawn from any possible insight of speculative reason (which, however, they must not contradict); then the question is, which interest is the superior (not which must give way, for they are not necessarily conflicting), whether speculative reason, which knows nothing of all that the practical offers for its acceptance, should take up these propositions, and (although they transcend it) try to unite them with its own concepts as a foreign possession handed over to it, or whether it is justified in obstinately following its own separate interest, and . . . rejecting as vain subtlety everything that cannot accredit its objective reality by manifest examples to be shown in experience, even though it should be never so much interwoven with the interest of the practical (pure) use of reason, and in itself not contradictory to the theoretical, merely because it infringes on the interest of the speculative reason to this extent, that it removes the bounds which this latter had set to itself, and gives it up to every nonsense or delusion of imagination?

In fact, so far as practical reason is taken as dependent on pathological conditions, that is, as merely regulating the inclinations under the sensible principle of happiness, we could not require speculative reason

[2] [Cf. A. 220-29, in the *Critique of Practical Reason.*]

to take its principles from such a source. *Mohammed's* paradise, or the absorption into the Deity of the *theosophists* and *mystics,* would press their monstrosities on the reason according to the taste of each, and one might as well have no reason as surrender it in such fashion to all sorts of dreams. But if pure reason of itself can be practical and is actually so, as the consciousness of the moral law proves, then it is still only one and the same reason which, whether in a theoretical or a practical point of view, judges according to *a priori* principles; and then it is clear that although it is in the first point of view incompetent to establish certain propositions positively, which, however, do not contradict it, then as soon as these propositions are *inseparably* attached *to the practical interest* of pure reason, then it must accept them, though it be as something offered to it from a foreign source, something that has not grown on its own ground, but yet is sufficiently authenticated; and it must try to compare and connect them with everything that it has in its power as speculative reason. It must remember, however, that these are not additions to its insight, but yet are extensions of its employment in another, namely, a practical aspect; and this is not in the least opposed to its interest, which consists in the restriction of wild speculation.

Thus, when pure speculative and pure practical reason are combined in one cognition, the latter has the *primacy,* provided, namely, that this combination is not *contingent* and arbitrary, but founded *a priori* on reason itself and therefore *necessary.* For without this subordination there would arise a conflict of reason with itself; since if they were merely co-ordinate, the former would close its boundaries strictly and admit nothing from the latter into its domain, while the latter would extend its bounds over everything, and when its needs required would seek to embrace the former within them. Nor could we reverse the order, and require pure practical reason to be subordinate to the speculative, since all interest is ultimately practical, and even that of speculative reason is conditional, and it is only in the practical employment of reason that it is complete.

[4.] *The Immortality of the Soul as a Postulate of Pure Practical Reason.*

The [1] realization of the *summum bonum* in the world is the necessary object of a will determinable by the moral. But in this will the *perfect accordance* of the mind with the moral law is the supreme condition of the *summum bonum.* This then must be possible, as well as its object, since it is contained in the command to promote the latter. Now, the perfect accordance of the will with the moral law is *holiness,* a perfection of which no rational being of the sensible world is capable at any moment of his existence. Since, nevertheless, it is required as practically necessary, it can only be found in a *progress in infinitum* towards that perfect accordance, and on the principles of pure practical reason it is necessary to assume such a practical progress as the real object of our will.

Now, this endless progress is only possible on the supposition of an *endless* duration of the *existence* and personality of the same rational being (which is called the immortality of the soul). The *summum bonum,* then, practically is only possible on the supposition of the immortality of the soul; consequently this immortality, being inseparably connected with the moral law, is a postulate of pure practical reason (by which I mean a *theoretical* proposition, not demonstrable as such,

[1] [Cf. A. 218-20, in the *Critique of Practical Reason.*]

but which is an inseparable result of an unconditional *a priori practical* law).

This principle of the moral destination of our nature, namely, that it is only in an endless progress that we can attain perfect accordance with the moral law, is of the greatest use, not merely for the present purpose of supplementing the impotence of speculative reason, but also with respect to religion. In default of it, either the moral law is quite degraded from its *holiness,* being made out to be *indulgent,* and conformable to our convenience, or else men strain their notions of their vocation and their expectation to an unattainable goal, hoping to acquire complete holiness of will, and so they lose themselves in fantastical *theosophic* dreams, which wholly contradict self-knowledge. In both cases the unceasing *effort* to obey punctually and thoroughly a strict and inflexible command of reason, which yet is not ideal but real, is only hindered. For a rational but finite being, the only thing possible is an endless progress from the lower to higher degrees of moral perfection. The *Infinite* Being, to whom the condition of time is nothing, sees in this to us endless succession a whole of accordance with the moral law; and the holiness which His command inexorably requires, in order to be true to His justice in the share which He assigns to each in the *summum bonum,* is to be found in a single intellectual intuition of the whole existence of rational beings. All that can be expected of the creature in respect of the hope of this participation would be the consciousness of his tried character, by which, from the progress he has hitherto made from the worse to the morally better, and the immutability of purpose which has thus become known to him, he may hope for a further unbroken continuance of the same, however long his existence may last, even beyond this life,[1] and thus he may hope, not indeed here, nor in any imaginable point of his future existence, but only in the endlessness of his duration (which God alone can survey) to be perfectly adequate to his will (without indulgence or excuse, which do not harmonize with justice).

[5.] *The Existence of God as a Postulate of Pure Practical Reason.*

In[2] the foregoing analysis the moral law led to a practical problem which is prescribed by pure reason alone, without the aid of any sensible motives, namely, that of the necessary completeness of the first and principal element of the *summum bonum,* viz. Morality; and as this can be perfectly solved only in eternity, to the postulate of *immortality.* The same law must also lead us to affirm the possibility of the second element of the

[1] It seems, nevertheless, impossible for a creature to have the *conviction* of his unwavering firmness of mind in the progress towards goodness. On this account the Christian religion makes it come only from the same Spirit that works sanctification, that is, this firm purpose, and with it the consciousness of steadfastness in the moral progress. But naturally one who is conscious that he has persevered through a long portion of his life up to the end in the progress to the better, and this from genuine moral motives, may well have the comforting hope, though not the certainty, that even in an existence prolonged beyond this life he will continue steadfast in these principles; and although he is never justified here in his own eyes, nor can ever hope to be so in the increased perfection of his nature, to which he looks forward, together with an increase of duties, nevertheless in this progress which, though it is directed to a goal infinitely remote, yet is in God's sight regarded as equivalent to possession, he may have a prospect of a *blessed* future; for this is the word that reason employs to designate perfect *well-being* independent on all contingent causes of the world, and which, like *holiness,* is an idea that can be contained only in an endless progress and its totality, and consequently is never fully attained by a creature.

[2] [Cf. A. 220-29, in the *Critique of Practical Reason.*]

summum bonum, viz. Happiness proportioned to that morality, and this on grounds as disinterested as before, and solely from impartial reason; that is, it must lead to the supposition of the existence of a cause adequate to this effect; in other words, it must postulate the *existence of God,* as the necessary condition of the possibility of the *summum bonum* (an object of the will which is necessarily connected with the moral legislation of pure reason). We proceed to exhibit this connexion in a convincing manner.

Happiness is the condition of a rational being in the world with whom *everything goes according to his wish and will;* it rests, therefore, on the harmony of physical nature with his whole end, and likewise with the essential determining principle of his will. Now the moral law as a law of freedom commands by determining principles, which ought to be quite independent on nature and on its harmony with our faculty of desire (as springs). But the acting rational being in the world is not the cause of the world and of nature itself. There is not the least ground, therefore, in the moral law for a necessary connexion between morality and proportionate happiness in a being that belongs to the world as part of it, and therefore dependent on it, and which for that reason cannot by his will be a cause of this nature, nor by his own power make it thoroughly harmonize, as far as his happiness is concerned, with his practical principles. Nevertheless, in the practical problem of pure reason, i.e. the necessary pursuit of the *summum bonum,* such a connexion is postulated as necessary: we ought to endeavour to promote the *summum bonum,* which, therefore, must be possible. Accordingly, the existence of a cause of all nature, distinct from nature itself, and containing the principle of this connexion, namely, of the exact harmony of happiness with morality, is also *postulated.* Now, this supreme cause must contain the principle of the harmony of nature, not merely with a law of the will of rational beings, but with the conception of this *law,* in so far as they make it the *supreme determining principle of the will,* and consequently not merely with the form of morals, but with their morality as their motive, that is, with their moral character. Therefore, the *summum bonum* is possible in the world only on the supposition of a Supreme Being having a causality corresponding to moral character. Now a being that is capable of acting on the conception of laws is an *intelligence* (a rational being), and the causality of such a being according to this conception of laws is his *will;* therefore the supreme cause of nature, which must be presupposed as a condition of the *summum bonum* is a being which is the cause of nature by *intelligence* and *will,* consequently its author, that is God. It follows that the postulate of the possibility of the *highest derived good* (the best world) is likewise the postulate of the reality of a *highest original good,* that is to say, of the existence of God. Now it was seen to be a duty for us to promote the *summum bonum;* consequently it is not merely allowable, but it is a necessity connected with duty as a requisite, that we should presuppose the possibility of this *summum bonum;* and as this is possible only on condition of the existence of God, it inseparably connects the supposition of this with duty; that is, it is morally necessary to assume the existence of God.

It must be remarked here that this moral necessity is *subjective,* that is, it is a want, and not *objective,* that is, itself a duty, for there cannot be a duty to suppose the existence of anything (since this concerns only the theoretical employment of reason). Moreover, it is not meant by this that it is necessary to suppose the existence of God *as a basis of all obligation in general* (for this rests, as has been sufficiently proved, simply on the autonomy of reason itself). What belongs to duty here is only the endeavour to realize and promote the *summum bonum* in the world, the possibility of which can therefore be postulated; and as our reason finds it not conceivable except on the supposition of a supreme intelligence, the admission of this existence is therefore connected with the consciousness of our duty, although the admission itself belongs to the domain of speculative reason. Considered in respect of this alone, as a principle of explanation, it may be called a *hypothesis,* but in reference to the intelligibility of an object given us by the moral law (the *summum bonum*), and consequently of a requirement for practical purposes, it may be called *faith,* that is to say a pure *rational faith,* since pure reason (both in its theoretical and its practical use) is the sole source from which it springs. . . . [A. 223-4]

The doctrine of Christianity,[1] even if we do not yet consider it as a religious doctrine, gives, touching this point, a conception of the *summum bonum* (the kingdom of God), which alone satisfies the strictest demand of practical reason. The moral law is holy (unyielding) and demands holiness of morals, although all the moral perfection to which man can attain is still only virtue, that is, a rightful disposition arising from *respect* for the law, implying consciousness of a constant propensity to transgression, or at least a want of purity, that is, a mixture of many spurious (not moral) motives of obedience to the law, consequently a self-esteem combined with humility. In respect, then, of the holiness which the Christian law requires, this leaves the creature nothing but a progress *in infinitum,* but for that very reason

[1] [Note A. 224-5]

it justifies him in hoping for an endless duration of his existence. The *worth* of a character *perfectly* accordant with the moral law is infinite, since the only restriction on all possible happiness in the judgment of a wise and all-powerful distributor of it is the absence of conformity of rational beings to their duty. But the moral law of itself does not *promise* any happiness, for according to our conceptions of an order of nature in general, this is not necessarily connected with obedience to the law. Now Christian morality supplies this defect (of the second indispensable element of the *summum bonum*) by representing the world, in which rational beings devote themselves with all their soul to the moral law, as a *kingdom of God,* in which nature and morality are brought into a harmony foreign to each of itself, by a holy Author who makes the derived *summum bonum* possible. *Holiness* of life is prescribed to them as a rule even in this life, while the welfare proportioned to it, namely, *bliss,* is represented, as attainable only in an eternity; because the *former* must always be the pattern of their conduct in every state, and progress towards it is already possible and necessary in this life; while the *latter,* under the name of happiness, cannot be attained at all in this world (so far as our own power is concerned), and therefore is made simply an object of hope. Nevertheless, the Christian principle of *morality* itself is not theological (so as to be heteronomy), but is autonomy of pure practical reason, since it does not make the knowledge of God and His will the foundation of these laws, but only of the attainment of the *summum bonum,* on condition of following these laws, and it does not even place the proper *spring* of this obedience in the desired results, but solely in the conception of duty, as that of which the faithful observance alone constitutes the worthiness to obtain those happy consequences.

In this manner the moral laws lead through the conception of the *summum bonum* as the object and final end of pure practical reason to *religion,* that is, to the *recognition of all duties as divine commands, not as sanctions, that is to say, arbitrary ordinances of a foreign will and contingent in themselves,* but as essential *laws* of every free will in itself, which, nevertheless, must be regarded as commands of the Supreme Being, because it is only from a morally perfect (holy and good) and at the same time all-powerful will, and consequently only through harmony with this will, that we can hope to attain the *summum bonum* which the moral law makes it our duty to take as the object of our endeavours. Here again, then, all remains disinterested and founded merely on duty; neither fear nor hope being made the fundamental springs, which if taken as principles would destroy the whole moral worth of actions. The moral law commands me to make the highest possible good in a world the ultimate object of all my conduct. But I cannot hope to effect this otherwise than by the harmony of my will with that of a holy and good Author of the world; and although the conception of the *summum bonum* as a whole, in which the greatest happiness is conceived as combined in the most exact proportion with the highest degree of moral perfection (possible in creatures), includes *my own happiness,* yet it is not this that is the determining principle of the will which is enjoined to promote the *summum bonum,* but the moral law, which, on the contrary, limits by strict conditions my unbounded desire of happiness.

Hence also morality is not properly the doctrine how we should *make* ourselves happy, but how we should become *worthy* of happiness. It is only when religion is added that there also comes in the hope of participating some day in happiness in proportion as we have endeavoured to be not unworthy of it.

A man is *worthy* to possess a thing or a state when his possession of it is in harmony with the *summum bonum*. We can now easily see that all worthiness depends on moral conduct, since in the conception of the *summum bonum* this constitutes the condition of the rest (which belongs to one's state), namely, the participation of happiness. Now it follows from this that *morality* should never be treated as a *doctrine of happiness*, that is, an instruction how to become happy; for it has to do simply with the rational condition *(conditio sine qua non)* of happiness, not with the means of attaining it. But when morality has been completely expounded (which merely imposes duties instead of providing rules for selfish desires), then first, after the moral desire to promote the *summum bonum* (to bring the kingdom of God to us) has been awakened, a desire founded on a law, and which could not previously arise in any selfish mind, and when for the behoof of this desire the step to religion has been taken, then this ethical doctrine may be also called a doctrine of happiness because the *hope* of happiness first begins with religion only.

We can also see from this that, when we ask what is *God's ultimate end* in creating the world, we must not name the *happiness* of the rational beings in it, but the *summum bonum*, which adds a further condition to that wish of such beings, namely, the condition of being worthy of happiness, that is, the *morality* of these same rational beings, a condition which alone contains the rule by which only they can hope to share in the former at the hand of a *wise* Author. For as *wisdom* theoretically considered signifies *the knowledge of the summum bonum,* and practically *the accordance of the will with the summum bonum,* we cannot attribute to a supreme independent wisdom an end based merely on *goodness.* For we cannot conceive the action of this goodness (in respect of the happiness of rational beings) as suitable to the highest original good, except under the restrictive conditions of harmony with the holiness [1] of His will. Therefore those who placed the end of creation in the glory of God (provided that this is not conceived anthropomorphically as a desire to be praised) have perhaps hit upon the best expression. For nothing glorifies God more than that which is the most estimable thing in the world, respect for His command, the observance of the holy duty that His law imposes on us, when there is added thereto His glorious plan of crowning such a beautiful order of things with corresponding happiness. If the latter (to speak humanly) makes Him worthy of love, by the *former* He is an object of adoration. Even men can never acquire respect by benevolence alone, though they may gain love, so that the greatest beneficence only procures them honour when it is regulated by worthiness.

That in the order of ends, man (and with him every

[1] In order to make these characteristics of these conceptions clear, I add the remark that whilst we ascribe to God various attributes, the quality of which we also find applicable to creatures, only that in Him they are raised to the highest degree, e.g. power, knowledge, presence, goodness, &c., under the designations of omnipotence, omniscience, omnipresence, &c., there are three that are ascribed to God exclusively, and yet without the addition of greatness, and which are all moral. He is the *only holy,* the *only blessed,* the *only wise,* because these conceptions already imply the absence of limitation. In the order of these attributes He is also the *holy lawgiver* (and creator), the *good governor* (and preserver), and the *just judge,* three attributes which include everything by which God is the object of religion, and in conformity with which the metaphysical perfections are added of themselves in the reason.

rational being) is *an end in himself*, that is, that he can never be used merely as a means by any (not even by God) without being at the same time an end also himself, that therefore *humanity* in our person must be *holy* to ourselves, this follows now of itself because he is the *subject of the moral law*, in other words, of that which is holy in itself, and on account of which and in agreement with which alone can anything be termed holy. For this moral law is founded on the autonomy of his will, as a free will which by its universal laws must necessarily be able to agree with that to which it is to submit itself.

[6.] *The Postulates of Pure Practical Reason in General.*

They[1] all proceed from the principle of morality, which is not a postulate but a law, by which reason determines the will directly, which will, because it is so determined as a pure will, requires these necessary conditions of obedience to its precept. These postulates are not theoretical dogmas, but suppositions practically necessary; while then they do [not] extend our speculative knowledge, they give objective reality to the ideas of speculative reason in general (by means of their reference to what is practical), and give it a right to concepts, the possibility even of which it could not otherwise venture to affirm.

These postulates are those of *immortality, freedom* positively considered (as the causality of a being so far as he belongs to the intelligible world), and the *existence of God*. The *first* results from the practically necessary condition of a duration adequate to the complete fulfilment of the moral law; the *second* from the

[1] [Cf. A. 229-31, in the *Critique of Practical Reason.*]

necessary supposition of independence on the sensible world, and of the faculty of determining one's will according to the law of an intelligible world, that is, of freedom; the *third* from the necessary condition of the existence of the *summum bonum* in such an intelligible world, by the supposition of the supreme independent good, that is, the existence of God.

Thus the fact that respect for the moral law necessarily makes the *summum bonum* an object of our endeavours, and the supposition thence resulting of its objective reality, lead through the postulates of practical reason to conceptions which speculative reason might indeed present as problems, but could never solve. Thus it leads—1. To that one in the solution of which the latter could do nothing but commit *paralogisms* (namely, that of immortality), because it could not lay hold of the character of permanence, by which to complete the psychological conception of an ultimate subject necessarily ascribed to the soul in self-consciousness, so as to make it the real conception of a substance, a character which practical reason furnishes by the postulates of a duration required for accordance with the moral law in the *summum bonum,* which is the whole end of practical reason. 2. It leads to that of which speculative reason contained nothing but *antinomy,* the solution of which it could only found on a notion problematically conceivable indeed, but whose objective reality it could not prove or determine, namely, the *cosmological* idea of an intelligible world and the consciousness of our existence in it, by means of the postulate of freedom (the reality of which it lays down by virtue of the moral law), and with it likewise the law of an intelligible world, to which speculative reason could only point, but could not define its conception. 3. What speculative reason was able to think, but was obliged to leave undetermined as a mere transcendental *ideal,* viz. the *theological* conception of the First Being, to this it gives significance (in a practical view, that is, as a condition of the possibility of the object of a will determined by that law), namely, as the supreme principle of the *summum bonum* in an intelligible world, by means of moral legislation in it invested with sovereign power.

Is our knowledge, however, actually extended in this way by pure practical reason, and is that *immanent* in practical reason which for the speculative was only *transcendent?* Certainly, but *only in a practical point of view.* For we do not thereby take knowledge of the nature of our souls, nor of the intelligible world, nor of the Supreme Being, with respect to what they are in themselves, but we have merely combined the conceptions of them in the *practical* concept of the *summum bonum* as the object of our will, and this altogether *a priori,* but only by means of the moral law, and merely in reference to it, in respect of the object which it commands. But how freedom is possible, and how we are to conceive this kind of causality theoretically and positively, is not thereby discovered; but only that there is such a causality is postulated by the moral law and in its behoof. It is the same with the remaining ideas, the possibility of which no human intelligence will ever fathom, but the truth of which, on the other hand, no sophistry will ever wrest from the conviction even of the commonest man.[1]

[7.] *Modification of the Moral Proof of God's Existence in Kant's Opus Postumum*

[In 1920 Erich Adickes published, under the title

[1] [For a further exposition of morality and religion cf. below, pp. 513 ff.]

Kants Opus Postumum, dargestellt und beurteilt, an exhaustive digest of Kant's private notes which were found in manuscript at his death. It appears from these notes that, in the last years of his life, Kant thought less highly of the proof of God's existence which he had developed in the *Critique of Practical Reason,* than he did at the time of the publication of that work. Professor Kemp Smith has summarized the general trend of Kant's thought during these last years, as indicated in Adickes' volume, with such clarity and brevity, that a portion of his summary is here appended. Cf. N. Kemp Smith, *A Commentary to Kant's Critique of Pure Reason,* Second Edition, pp. 638-41. Professor Kemp Smith's footnotes have been omitted.

"We have to bear in mind," says Professor Kemp Smith, "that the manuscripts were not intended for immediate publication, but are Kant's private notes, in which, with frequent failure and at best with only comparative success, constantly restating and modifying, with words and sentences crossed out, and with notes added on the margins, as suggestions occurred to him, he endeavored to arrive at a satisfactory formulation of certain new positions to which he was tentatively feeling his way." [1] Ed.]

". . . Kant now rejects as being untenable, and as being illegitimately theoretical, the proof of God's existence upon which he has relied in the *Critique of Practical Reason,* namely, by reference to the *Summum Bonum.* Though Kant nowhere, in explicit terms, avows this change of standpoint, or at least does not do so in any passage quoted by Adickes, the whole tenor of his argument is towards substituting a proof of a more strictly moral character, all the emphasis being laid upon the direct relation in which the Idea of God stands

[1] N. Kemp Smith, *Commentary,* p. 608.

to the moral imperative. This new proof Kant tentatively formulates in at least three distinguishable forms.

(1) In one set of passages Kant maintains that the religious interpretation of all duties as divine commands is not a supplementary, later interpretation, but is, for every moral being, immediately and necessarily given together with the apprehension of the duties, i.e. the categorical imperative leads directly to God, and affords surety of His reality. 'In the morally-practical Reason lies the categorical imperative, to regard all human duties as divine commands.' 'The realism of the Idea of God can be proved only through the duty-imperative.' 'Beings must be thought which, although they exist only in the thoughts of the philosopher, yet in these have morally practical reality. These are God, the world-all, and man as subjected in the world to the duty-concept according to the categorical imperative, which as categorical is also a principle of freedom.' 'A being which is capable of holding sway over all rational beings in accordance with laws of duty (the categorical imperative), and is justified in so doing, is God. But the existence of such a being can be *postulated* only in a practical reference, namely [in view of] the necessity of so acting as if in the knowledge of all my duties as divine commands *(tanquam non ceu)* I stood under this awful but also at the same time salutary guidance and surety. Accordingly the *existence* of such a being is not postulated in this formula; such postulating would be self-contradictory.'

The concluding sentence is far from clear; comparison of it with other passages shows that Kant intends to signify that the certainty obtained of God's existence is a certainty of practical belief, not of theoretical demonstration.

(2) In a second set of passages, Kant makes no ref-

erence to the existence of God but only to the Idea of God. But in these passages also, duties are alleged to be not apprehensible only as divine commands. 'The categorical imperative of the command of duty is grounded in the Idea of an *imperantis,* who is all-powerful and holds universal sway (formal). This is the Idea of God.' 'What constrains us to the Idea of God? No empirical concept; no metaphysic. What presents this *a priori* concept is Transcendental Philosophy, the concept of duty.' 'The imperative of duty proves to men their freedom, and at the same time conducts them to the Idea of God.'

(3) In yet another set of passages Kant suggests that God Himself, and not merely the Idea of God as a trans-subjective Being, is immanent in the human spirit. 'God is not a being outside me, but merely a thought in me. God is the morally practical self-legislative Reason. Therefore only a God in me, about me, and over me.' 'The proposition: There is a God says nothing more than: There is in the human morally self-determining Reason a highest principle which determines itself, and finds itself compelled unremittingly to act in accordance with such a principle.' 'God can be sought only in us.' 'There is a God, namely, in the Idea of the morally practical Reason which [determines] itself to a continuous oversight as well as guidance of the actions according to *one* principle. . . .'

Many of the passages are directed against the view of God as a substance. 'Cosmotheology. It is an object of the morally practical Reason, which contains the principle of all human duties as being divine commands, and yet does not require us to assume a special substance existing outside man.' 'There is a Being *(Wesen)* in me, which though distinct from me stands to me in relations of causal efficacy, and which, itself free, i.e. not dependent upon the law of nature in space and time, inwardly directs me (justifies or condemns), and I, as man, am myself this Being. It is not a substance outside me; and what is strangest of all, the causality is a determination to action in freedom, and not as a necessity of nature.' 'God must be represented not as substance outside me, but as [the] highest moral principle in me. But indirectly as a power in me (gods do not exist) [it] is the Ideal of power and wisdom in *one* concept; if it is [represented as the Ideal?] outside me, it is the determining ground of my [? its] omnipresence.' 'The Idea (not concept) of God is not the concept of a substance. The personality which we ascribe to it, which is also bound up with the singleness of its object (not a plurality of gods) [passage ends abruptly]. 'The Idea of that which human reason itself makes out of the World-All is the active representation of God. Not as a special personality, *substance outside me* but as a thought in me.'

Clearly Kant's views have undergone considerable change since the writing of the *Critique of Practical Reason*. God is no longer viewed as a Being who must be postulated in order to make possible the coincidence of virtue with happiness. God speaks with the voice of the categorical imperative, and thereby reveals Himself in a direct manner. But as the passages above quoted also show, this new point of view is suggested merely; it is nowhere developed in a systematic manner; and even as thus suggested, it is formulated in at least three diverse ways."

CRITIQUE OF THE AESTHETICAL JUDGEMENT [1]

as contained in

Part I of the *Critique of Judgement*

I. ANALYTIC OF THE AESTHETIC JUDGEMENT

[I.] Analytic of the Beautiful

FIRST MOMENT OF THE JUDGEMENT OF TASTE [2] ACCORDING TO QUALITY

§ 1. *The judgement of Taste is aesthetical*

In order to decide whether anything is beautiful or not, we refer the representation, not by the Understanding to the Object for cognition but, by the Imagination (perhaps in conjunction with the Understanding) to the subject, and its feeling of pleasure or pain. The judgement of taste is therefore not a judgement of cognition,

[1] [J. H. Bernard's translation of the *Critique of Judgement* (Macmillan, 2d Edition, revised) has been used. All page references are to this volume. As the original numbering of the sections in the *Critique of Judgement* has not been changed, the reader will find it easy to discover what sections have been omitted, and to find these sections in Bernard's complete translation. Bernard's indications of changes in the Second Edition have been omitted but the Second Edition reading has invariably been selected. Unfortunately most of Bernard's explanatory notes have had to be omitted.]

[2] [Note B. 45.]

and is consequently not logical but aesthetical, by which we understand that whose determining ground can be *no other than subjective.* Every reference of representations, even that of sensations, may be objective (and then it signifies the real in an empirical representation); save only the reference to the feeling of pleasure and pain, by which nothing in the Object is signified, but through which there is a feeling in the subject, as it is affected by the representation.

To apprehend a regular, purposive building by means of one's cognitive faculty (whether in a clear or a confused way of representation) is something quite different from being conscious of this representation as connected with the sensation of satisfaction. Here the representation is altogether referred to the subject and to its feeling of life, under the name of the feeling of pleasure or pain. This establishes a quite separate faculty of distinction and of judgement, adding nothing to cognition, but only comparing the given representation in the subject with the whole faculty of representations, of which the mind is conscious in the feeling of its state. . . . [B. 46]

§ 2. *The satisfaction which determines the judgement of Taste is disinterested*

The satisfaction which we combine with the representation of the existence of an object is called interest. Such satisfaction always has reference to the faculty of desire, either as its determining ground or as necessarily connected with its determining ground. Now when the question is if a thing is beautiful, we do not want to know whether anything depends or can depend on the existence of the thing either for myself or for any one else, but how we judge it by mere observation (intuition or reflection). If any one asks me if I find that palace beautiful which I see before me, I may answer: I do not like things of that kind which are made merely to be stared at. Or I can answer like that Iroquois *sachem* who was pleased in Paris by nothing more than by the cook-shops. Or again after the manner of *Rousseau* I may rebuke the vanity of the great who waste the sweat of the people on such superfluous things. In fine I could easily convince myself that if I found myself on an uninhabited island without the hope of ever again coming among men, and could conjure up just such a splendid building by my mere wish, I should not even give myself the trouble if I had a sufficiently comfortable hut. This may all be admitted and approved; but we are not now talking of this. We wish only to know if this mere representation of the object is accompanied in me with satisfaction, however indifferent I may be as regards the existence of the object of this representation. We easily see that in saying it is *beautiful* and in showing that I have taste, I am concerned, not with that in which I depend on the existence of the object, but with that which I make out of this representation in myself. Every one must admit that a judgement about beauty, in which the least interest mingles, is very partial and is not a pure judgement of taste. We must not be in the least prejudiced in favour of the existence of the things, but be quite indifferent in this respect, in order to play the judge in things of taste.[1] . . . [B. 48-53]

[1] . . . A judgement upon an object of satisfaction may be quite *disinterested,* but yet very *interesting,* i.e. not based upon an interest, but bringing an interest with it; of this kind are all pure moral judgements. Judgements of taste, however, do not in themselves establish any interest. Only in society is it *interesting* to have taste: the reason of this will be shown in the sequel. [Cf. below § 41, pp. 380 ff.]

§ 5. *Comparison of the three specifically different kinds of satisfaction*

The pleasant and the good have both a reference to the faculty of desire; and they bring with them—the former a satisfaction pathologically conditioned (by impulses, *stimuli*)—the latter a pure practical satisfaction, which is determined not merely by the representation of the object, but also by the represented connexion of the subject with the existence of the object. It is not merely the object that pleases, but also its existence. On the other hand, the judgement of taste is merely *contemplative;* i.e. it is a judgement which, indifferent as regards the being of an object, compares its character with the feeling of pleasure and pain. But this contemplation itself is not directed to concepts; for the judgement of taste is not a cognitive judgement (either theoretical or practical), and thus is not *based* on concepts, nor has it concepts as its *purpose.*

The Pleasant, the Beautiful, and the Good, designate then, three different relations of representations to the feeling of pleasure and pain, in reference to which we distinguish from each other objects or methods of representing them. And the expressions corresponding to each, by which we mark our complacency in them, are not the same. That which GRATIFIES a man is called *pleasant;* that which merely PLEASES him is *beautiful;* that which is ESTEEMED OR APPROVED by him, i.e. that to which he accords an objective worth, is *good.* Pleasantness concerns irrational animals also; but Beauty only concerns men, i.e. animal, but still rational, beings—not merely *quâ* rational (e.g. spirits), but *quâ* animal also; and the Good concerns every rational being in general. This is a proposition which can only be completely established and explained in the sequel. We may say that of all these three kinds of satisfaction, that of taste in the Beautiful is alone a disinterested and *free* satisfaction; for no interest, either of Sense or of Reason, here forces our assent. Hence we may say of satisfaction that it is related in the three aforesaid cases to *inclination*, to *favour*, or to *respect*. Now *favour* is the only free satisfaction. An object of inclination, and one that is proposed to our desire by a law of Reason, leave us no freedom in forming for ourselves anywhere an object of pleasure. All interest presupposes or generates a want; and, as the determining ground of assent, it leaves the judgement about the object no longer free.

As regards the interest of inclination in the case of the Pleasant, every one says that hunger is the best sauce, and everything that is eatable is relished by people with a healthy appetite; and thus a satisfaction of this sort does not indicate choice directed by taste. It is only when the want is appeased that we can distinguish which of many men has or has not taste. In the same way there may be manners (conduct) without virtue, politeness without good-will, decorum without modesty, etc. For where the moral law speaks there is no longer, objectively, a free choice as regards what is to be done; and to display taste in its fulfilment (or in judging of another's fulfilment of it) is something quite different from manifesting the moral attitude of thought. For this involves a command and generates a want, whilst moral taste only plays with the objects of satisfaction, without attaching itself to one of them.

§ 41. *Of the empirical interest in the Beautiful*

That the judgement of taste by which something is declared beautiful must have no interest *as its determining ground* has been sufficiently established above. But it does not follow that after it has been given as a pure aesthetical judgement, no interest can be combined with it. This combination, however, can only be indirect, i.e. taste must first of all be represented as combined with something else, in order that we may unite with the satisfaction of mere reflection upon an object a *pleasure in its existence* (as that wherein all interest consists). For here also in aesthetical judgements what we say in cognitive judgements (of things in general) is valid; *a posse ad esse non valet consequentia.* This something else may be empirical, viz. an inclination proper to human nature, or intellectual, as the property of the Will of being capable of *a priori* determination by Reason. Both these involve a satisfaction in the presence of an Object, and so can lay the foundation for an interest in what has by itself pleased without reference to any interest whatever.

Empirically the Beautiful interests only in *society.* If we admit the impulse to society as natural to man, and his fitness for it, and his propension towards it, i.e. *sociability,* as a requisite for man as a being destined for society, and so as a property belonging to *humanity,* we cannot escape from regarding taste as a faculty for judging everything in respect of which we can communicate our *feeling* to all other men, and so as a means of furthering that which every one's natural inclination desires.

A man abandoned by himself on a desert island would adorn neither his hut nor his person; nor would he seek for flowers, still less would he plant them, in order to adorn himself therewith. It is only in society that it occurs to him to be not merely a man, but a refined man after his kind (the beginning of civilisation). For such do we judge him to be who is both inclined and apt to communicate his pleasure to others, and who is not contented with an Object if he cannot feel satisfaction in it in common with others. Again, every one expects and requires from every one else this reference to universal communication [of pleasure], as it were from an original compact dictated by humanity itself. Thus, doubtless, in the beginning only those things which attracted the senses, e.g. colours for painting oneself (roucou among the Carabs and cinnabar among the Iroquois), flowers, mussel shells, beautiful feathers, etc.,—but in time beautiful forms also e.g. in their canoes, and clothes, etc., which bring with them no gratification, or satisfaction of enjoyment—were important in society, and were combined with great interest. Until at last civilisation, having reached its highest point, makes out of this almost the main business of refined inclination; and sensations are only regarded as of worth in so far as they can be universally communicated. Here, although the pleasure which every one has in such an object is inconsiderable and in itself without any marked interest, yet the Idea of its universal communicability increases its worth in an almost infinite degree.

But this interest that indirectly attaches to the Beautiful through our inclination to society, and consequently is empirical, is of no importance for us here; because we have only to look to what may have a reference, although only indirectly, to the judgement of taste *a priori*. For if even in this form an interest bound up therewith should discover itself, taste would discover a transition of our judging faculty from sense-enjoyment to moral feeling; and so not only would we be the better guided in employing taste purposively, but there would be thus presented a link in the chain of the human faculties *a priori,* on which all legislation must depend. We can only say thus much about the empirical interest in objects of taste and in taste itself. Since it is subservient to inclination, however refined the latter may be, it may easily be confounded with all the inclinations and passions, which attain their greatest variety and highest degree in society; and the interest in the Beautiful, if it is grounded thereon, can only furnish a very ambiguous transition from the Pleasant to the Good. But whether this can or cannot be furthered by taste, taken in its purity, is what we now have to investigate.

EXPLANATION OF THE BEAUTIFUL RESULTING FROM THE FIRST MOMENT

Taste is the faculty of judging of an object or a method of representing it by an *entirely disinterested* satisfaction or dissatisfaction. The object of such satisfaction is called *beautiful.*

SECOND MOMENT OF THE JUDGEMENT OF TASTE, ACCORDING TO QUANTITY

§ 6. *The Beautiful is that which apart from concepts is represented as the object of a universal satisfaction*

This explanation of the beautiful can be derived from the preceding explanation of it as the object of an entirely disinterested satisfaction. For the fact of which every one is conscious, that the satisfaction is for him quite disinterested, implies in his judgement a ground of satisfaction for every one. For since it does not rest on any inclination of the subject (nor upon any other premeditated interest), but since he who judges feels himself quite *free* as regards the satisfaction which he attaches to the object, he cannot find the ground of this satisfaction in any private conditions connected with his own subject; and hence it must be regarded as grounded on what he can presuppose in every other man. Consequently he must believe that he has reason for attributing a similar satisfaction to every one. He will therefore speak of the beautiful, as if beauty were a characteristic of the object and the judgement logical (constituting a cognition of the Object by means of concepts of it); although it is only aesthetical and involves merely a reference of the representation of the object to the subject. . . . [B. 56] That is, there must be bound up with it a title to subjective universality.

§ 7. *Comparison of the Beautiful with the Pleasant and the Good by means of the above characteristic*

As regards the Pleasant every one is content that his judgement, which he bases upon private feeling, and by which he says of an object that it pleases him, should be limited merely to his own person. Thus he is quite contented that if he says "Canary wine is pleasant," another man may correct his expression and remind him that he ought to say "It is pleasant *to me*." And this is the case not only as regards the taste of the tongue, the palate, and the throat, but for whatever is pleasant to any one's eyes and ears. To one violet colour is soft and lovely, to another it is faded and dead. One man likes the tone of wind instruments, another that of strings. To strive here with the design of reproving as incorrect another man's judgement which is different from our own, as if the judgements were logically opposed, would be folly. As regards the pleasant therefore the fundamental proposition is valid, *every one has his own taste* (the taste of Sense).

The case is quite different with the Beautiful. It would (on the contrary) be laughable if a man who imagined anything to his own taste, thought to justify himself by saying: "This object (the house we see, the coat that person wears, the concert we hear, the poem submitted to our judgement) is beautiful *for me.*" For he must not call it *beautiful* if it merely pleases himself. Many things may have for him charm and pleasantness; no one troubles himself at that; but if he gives out anything as beautiful, he supposes in others the same satisfaction—he judges not merely for himself, but for every one, and speaks of beauty as if it were a property of things. Hence he says "The *thing* is beautiful"; and he does not count on the agreement of others with this his judgement of satisfaction, because he has found this agreement several times before, but he *demands* it of them. He blames them if they judge otherwise and he denies them taste, which he nevertheless requires from them. Here then we cannot say that each man has his own particular taste. For this would be as much as to say that there is no taste whatever; i.e. no aesthetical judgement, which can make a rightful claim upon every one's assent.

At the same time we find as regards the Pleasant that there is an agreement among men in their judgements upon it, in regard to which we deny Taste to some and attribute it to others; by this not meaning one of our organic senses, but a faculty of judging in respect of the pleasant generally. Thus we say of a man who knows how to entertain his guests with pleasures (of enjoyment for all the senses), so that they are all pleased, "He has taste." But here the universality is only taken comparatively; and there emerge rules which are only *general* (like all empirical ones), and not *universal;* which latter the judgement of Taste upon the beautiful undertakes or lays claim to. It is a judgement in reference to sociability, so far as this rests on empirical rules. In respect of the Good it is true that judgements make rightful claim to validity for every one; but the Good is represented only *by means of a concept* as the Object of a universal satisfaction, which is the case neither with the Pleasant nor with the Beautiful.

§ 8. *The universality of the satisfaction is represented in a judgement of Taste only as subjective*

. . . [B. 59-60] Here we must, in the first place, remark that a universality which does not rest on concepts of Objects (not even on empirical ones) is not logical but aesthetical, i.e. it involves no objective quantity of the judgement but only that which is subjective. For this I use the expression *general validity* which signifies the validity of the reference of a representation, not to the cognitive faculty, but to the feeling of pleasure and pain for every subject. (We can avail ourselves also of the same expression for the logical quantity of the judgement, if only we prefix *objective* to "universal validity," to distinguish it from that which is merely subjective and aesthetical.)

A judgement with *objective universal validity* is also always valid subjectively; i.e. if the judgement holds for everything contained under a given concept, it holds also for every one who represents an object by means of this concept. But from a *subjective universal validity,* i.e. aesthetical and resting on no concept, we cannot infer that which is logical; because that kind of judgement does not extend to the Object. Hence the aesthetical universality which is ascribed to a judgement must be of a particular kind, because it does not unite the predicate of beauty with the concept of the *Object,* considered in its whole logical sphere, and yet extends it to the whole sphere of judging persons. . . . [B. 61-2]

If we judge Objects merely according to concepts, then all representation of beauty is lost. Thus there can be no rule according to which any one is to be forced to recognise anything as beautiful. We cannot press [upon others] by the aid of any reasons or fundamental propositions our judgement that a coat, a house, or a flower is beautiful. We wish to submit the Object to our own eyes, as if the satisfaction in it depended on sensation; and yet if we then call the object beautiful, we believe that we speak with a universal voice, and we claim the assent of every one, although on the contrary all private sensation can only decide for the observer himself and his satisfaction.[1]

[1] [The following passage, which comes later in the text (§33, B. 157-9), is inserted here as bearing on the present discussion.] The judgement of taste is not determinable by grounds of proof, just as if it were merely *subjective.*

If a man, *in the first place,* does not find a building, a prospect, or a poem beautiful, a hundred voices all highly praising it will not force his inmost agreement. He may indeed feign that it pleases him in order that he may not be regarded as devoid of taste; he may even begin to doubt whether he has formed his taste on a knowledge of a sufficient number of objects of a certain kind (just as one, who believes that he recognises in the distance as a forest, something which all others regard as a town, doubts the judgement of his own sight). But he clearly sees that the agreement of others gives no valid proof of the judgement about beauty. Others might perhaps see and observe for him; and what many have seen in one way, although he believes that he has seen it differently, might serve him as an adequate ground of proof of a theoretical and consequently logical judgement. But that a thing has pleased others could never serve as the basis of an aestheti-

We may see now that in the judgement of taste nothing is postulated but such a *universal voice,* in respect of the satisfaction without the intervention of concepts;

---

cal judgement. A judgement of others which is unfavourable to ours may indeed rightly make us scrutinise our own with care, but it can never convince us of its incorrectness. There is therefore no empirical *ground of proof* which would force a judgement of taste upon any one.

Still less, *in the second place,* can an *a priori* proof determine according to definite rules a judgement about beauty. If a man reads me a poem of his or brings me to a play, which does not after all suit my taste, he may bring forward in proof of the beauty of his poem *Batteux* or *Lessing* or still more ancient and famous critics of taste, and all the rules laid down by them; certain passages which displease me may agree very well with rules of beauty (as they have been put forth by these writers and are universally recognised): but I stop my ears, I will listen to no arguments and no reasoning; and I will rather assume that these rules of the critics are false, or at least that they do not apply to the case in question, than admit that my judgement should be determined by grounds of proof *a priori.* For it is to be a judgement of Taste and not of Understanding or Reason.

It seems that this is one of the chief reasons why this aesthetical faculty of judgement has been given the name of Taste. For though a man enumerate to me all the ingredients of a dish, and remark that each is separately pleasant to me and further extol with justice the wholesomeness of this particular food—yet am I deaf to all these reasons; I try the dish with *my* tongue and *my* palate, and thereafter (and not according to universal principles) do I pass my judgement.

In fact the judgement of Taste always takes the form of a singular judgement about an Object. The Understanding can form a universal judgement by comparing the Object in point of the satisfaction it affords with the judgement of others upon it: e.g. "All tulips are beautiful." But then this is not a judgement of taste but a logical judgement, which takes the relation of an Object to taste as the predicate of things of a certain species. That judgement, however, in which I find an individual tulip beautiful, i.e. in which I find my satisfaction in it to be universally valid, is alone a judgement of taste. Its peculiarity consists in the fact that, although it has merely subjective validity, it claims the assent of *all* subjects, exactly as it would do if it were an objective judgement resting on grounds of knowledge, that could be established by a proof.

and thus the *possibility* of an aesthetical judgement that can, at the same time, be regarded as valid for every one. The judgement of taste itself does not *postulate* the agreement of every one (for that can only be done by a logically universal judgement because it can adduce reasons); it only *imputes* this agreement to every one, as a case of the rule in respect of which it expects, not confirmation by concepts, but assent from others. The universal voice is, therefore, only an Idea (we do not yet inquire upon what it rests). It may be uncertain whether or not the man, who believes that he is laying down a judgement of taste, is, as a matter of fact, judging in conformity with that Idea; but that he refers his judgement thereto, and, consequently, that it is intended to be a judgement of taste, he announces by the expression "beauty." He can be quite certain of this for himself by the mere consciousness of the separation of everything belonging to the Pleasant and the Good from the satisfaction which is left; and this is all for which he promises himself the agreement of every one—a claim which would be justifiable under these conditions, provided only he did not often make mistakes, and thus lay down an erroneous judgement of taste.

§ 9. *Investigation of the question whether in the judgement of Taste the feeling of pleasure precedes or follows the judging of the object*

The solution of this question is the key to the Critique of Taste, and so is worthy of all attention.

If the pleasure in the given object precedes, and it is only its universal communicability that is to be acknowledged in the judgment of taste about the representation of the object, there would be a contradiction. For such pleasure would be nothing different from the mere pleasantness in the sensation, and so in accordance with its nature could have only private validity, because it is immediately dependent on the representation through which the object *is given.*

Hence, it is the universal capability of communication of the mental state in the given representation which, as the subjective condition of the judgement of taste, must be fundamental, and must have the pleasure in the object as its consequent. But nothing can be universally communicated except cognition and representation, so far as it belongs to cognition. For it is only thus that this latter can be objective; and only through this has it a universal point of reference, with which the representative power of every one is compelled to harmonise. If the determining ground of our judgement as to this universal communicability of the representation is to be merely subjective, i.e. is conceived independently of any concept of the object, it can be nothing else than the state of mind, which is to be met with in the relation of our representative powers to each other, so far as they refer a given representation to *cognition in general.*

The cognitive powers, which are involved by this representation, are here in free play, because no definite concept limits them to a particular rule of cognition. Hence, the state of mind in this representation must be a feeling of the free play of the representative powers in a given representation with reference to a cognition in general. Now a representation by which an object is given, that is to become a cognition in general, requires *Imagination,* for the gathering together the manifold of intuition, and *Understanding,* for the unity of the concept uniting the representations. This state of *free play* of the cognitive faculties in a representation by which an object is given, must be universally communicable; because cognition, as the determination of the Object with which given representations (in whatever subject) are to agree, is the only kind of representation which is valid for every one.

The subjective universal communicability of the mode of representation in a judgement of taste, since it is to be possible without presupposing a definite concept, can refer to nothing else than the state of mind in the free play of the Imagination and the Understanding (so far as they agree with each other, as is requisite for *cognition in general*). We are conscious that this subjective relation, suitable for cognition in general, must be valid for every one, and thus must be universally communicable, just as if it were a definite cognition, resting always on that relation as its subjective condition.

This merely subjective (aesthetical) judging of the object, or of the representation by which it is given, precedes the pleasure in it, and is the ground of this pleasure in the harmony of the cognitive faculties; but on the universality of the subjective conditions for judging of objects is alone based the universal subjective validity of the satisfaction bound up by us with the representation of the object that we call beautiful.

The power of communicating one's state of mind, even though only in respect of the cognitive faculties, carries a pleasure with it, as we can easily show from the natural propension of man towards sociability (empirical and psychological). But this is not enough for our design. The pleasure that we feel is, in a judgement of taste, necessarily imputed by us to every one else; as if, when we call a thing beautiful, it is to be regarded as a characteristic of the object which is determined in it according to concepts; though beauty, without a reference to the feeling of the subject, is nothing by itself. But we must reserve the examination of this question until we have answered another, viz. "If and how aesthetical judgements are possible *a priori?*"

We now occupy ourselves with the easier question, in what way we are conscious of a mutual subjective harmony of the cognitive powers with one another in the judgement of taste; is it aesthetically by mere internal sense and sensation? or is it intellectually by the consciousness of our designed activity, by which we bring them into play?

If the given representation, which occasions the judgement of taste, were a concept uniting Understanding and Imagination in the judging of the object, into a cognition of the Object, the consciousness of this relation would be intellectual. . . . [B. 66] But then the judgement would not be laid down in reference to pleasure and pain, and consequently would not be a judgement of taste. But the judgement of taste, independently of concepts, determines the Object in respect of satisfaction and of the predicate of beauty. Therefore that subjective unity of relation can only make itself known by means of sensation. The excitement of both faculties (Imagination and Understanding) to indeterminate, but yet, through the stimulus of the given sensation, harmonious activity, viz. that which belongs to cognition in general, is the sensation whose universal communicability is postulated by the judgement of taste. An objective relation can only be thought, but yet, so far as it is subjective according to its conditions, can be felt in its effect on the mind; and, of a relation based on no concept (like the relation of the representative powers to a cognitive faculty in general), no other consciousness is possible than that through the sensation of the effect, which consists in the more lively play of both mental powers (the Imagination and the Understanding) when animated by mutual agreement. A representation which, as singular and apart from comparison with others, yet has an agreement with the conditions of universality which it is the business of the Understanding to supply, brings the cognitive faculties into that proportionate accord which we require for all cognition, and so regard as holding for every one who is determined to judge by means of Understanding and Sense in combination (i.e. for every man).

EXPLANATION OF THE BEAUTIFUL RESULTING FROM THE SECOND MOMENT

The *beautiful* is that which pleases universally, without a concept.

THIRD MOMENT OF JUDGEMENTS OF TASTE, ACCORDING TO THE RELATION OF THE PURPOSES WHICH ARE BROUGHT INTO CONSIDERATION THEREIN.

§ 10. *Of purposiveness in general*

. . . [B. 67] Where . . . not merely the cognition of an object, but the object itself (its form and existence) is thought as an effect only possible by means of the concept of this latter, there we think a purpose. The representation of the effect is here the determining ground of its cause and precedes it. . . . [B. 68]

The faculty of desire, so far as it is determinable only through concepts, i.e. to act in conformity with the representation of a purpose, would be the Will. But an Object, or a state of mind, or even an action, is called purposive, although its possibility does not necessarily presuppose the representation of a purpose, merely because its possibility can be explained and conceived by us only so far as we assume for its ground a causality according to purposes, i.e. a will which would have so disposed it according to the representation of a certain rule. There can be, then, purposiveness without purpose, so far as we do not place the causes of this form in a will, but yet can only make the explanation of its possibility intelligible to ourselves by deriving it from a will. Again, we are not always forced to regard what we observe (in respect of its possibility) from the point of view of Reason. Thus we can at least observe a purposiveness according to form, without basing it on a purpose (as the material of the *nexus finalis*), and we can notice it in objects, although only by reflection.

§§ 11 [and 12] *The judgement of taste has nothing at its basis but the* form of the purposiveness *of an object (or of its mode of representation)*

Every purpose, if it be regarded as a ground of satisfaction, always carries with it an interest—as the determining ground of the judgement—about the object of pleasure. Therefore no subjective purpose can lie at the basis of the judgement of taste. But neither can the judgement of taste be determined by any representation of an objective purpose, i.e. of the possibility of the object itself in accordance with principles of purposive combination, and consequently it can be determined by no concept of the good; because it is an aesthetical and not a cognitive judgement. It therefore has to do with no *concept* of the character and internal or external possibility of the object by means of this or that cause. But merely with the relation of the representative powers [1] to one another, so far as they are determined by a representation. . . . [B. 69]

Thus it is the mere form of purposiveness in the representation by which an object is *given* to us, so far as we are conscious of it, which constitutes the satisfaction that we without a concept judge to be universally communicable; and, consequently, this is the determining ground of the judgement of taste. . . . [B. 70-1]

The consciousness of the mere formal purposiveness in the play of the subject's cognitive powers, in a representation through which an object is given, is the pleasure itself; because it contains a determining ground of the activity of the subject in respect of the excitement of its cognitive powers, and therefore an inner causality (which is purposive) in respect of cognition in general without however being limited to any definite cognition; and consequently contains a mere form of the subjective purposiveness of a representation in an aesthetical judgement. This pleasure is in no way practical, neither like that arising from the pathological ground of pleasantness, nor that from the intellectual ground of the represented good. But yet it involves causality, viz. of *maintaining* the state of the representation itself, and the exercise of the cognitive powers without further design. We *linger* over the contemplation of the beautiful, because this contemplation strengthens and reproduces itself, which is analogous to (though not of the same kind as) that lingering which takes place when a [physical] charm in the representation of the object repeatedly arouses the attention, the mind being passive.

[1] [i.e., Imagination and Understanding.]

§§ 13 [and 14] *The pure judgement of Taste is independent of charm and emotion*

Every interests spoils the judgement of taste and takes from its impartiality, especially if the purposiveness is not, as with the interest of Reason, placed before the feeling of pleasure but grounded on it. This last always happens in an aesthetical judgement upon anything so far as it gratifies or grieves us. Hence judgements so affected can lay no claim at all to a universally valid satisfaction, or at least so much the less claim, in proportion as there are sensations of this sort among the determining grounds of taste. That taste is still barbaric which needs a mixture of *charms* and *emotions* in order that there may be satisfaction, and still more so if it make these the measure of its assent. . . . [B. 72-3]

Now here many objections present themselves, which fallaciously put forward charm not merely as a necessary ingredient of beauty, but as alone sufficient [to justify] a thing's being called beautiful. A mere colour, e.g. the green of a grass plot, a mere tone (as distinguished from sound and noise) like that of a violin, are by most people described as beautiful in themselves; although both seem to have at their basis merely the matter of representations, viz. simply sensation, and therefore only deserve to be called pleasant. . . . [B. 73-4]

But as regards the beauty attributed to the object on account of its form, to suppose it to be capable of augmentation through the charm of the object is a common error, and one very prejudicial to genuine, uncorrupted, well-founded taste. We can doubtless add these charms to beauty, in order to interest the mind by the representation of the object, apart from the bare satisfaction [received]; and thus they may serve as a recommendation of taste and its cultivation, especially when it is yet crude and unexercised. But they actually do injury to the judgement of taste if they draw attention to themselves as the grounds for judging of beauty. So far are they from adding to beauty that they must only be admitted by indulgences as aliens; and provided always that they do not disturb the beautiful form, in cases when taste is yet weak and untrained.

In painting, sculpture, and in all the formative arts—in architecture, and horticulture, so far as they are beautiful arts—the *delineation* is the essential thing; and here it is not what gratifies in sensation but what pleases by means of its form that is fundamental for taste. The colours which light up the sketch belong to the charm; they may indeed enliven the object for sensation, but they cannot make it worthy of contemplation and beautiful. In most cases they are rather limited by the requirements of the beautiful form; and even where charm is permissible it is ennobled solely by this.

Every form of the objects of sense (both of external sense and also mediately of internal) is either *figure* or *play*. In the latter case it is either play of figures (in space, viz. pantomime and dancing), or the mere play of sensations (in time). The *charm* of colours or of the pleasant tones of an instrument may be added; but the *delineation* in the first case and the composition in the second constitute the proper object of the pure judgement of taste. To say that the purity of colours and of tones, or their variety and contrast, seems to add to beauty, does not mean that they supply a homogeneous addition to our satisfaction in the form because they are pleasant in themselves; but they do so, because they make the form more exactly, definitely, and completely, intuitible, and besides by their charm excite the representation, whilst they awaken and fix our attention on the object itself.

Even what we call *ornaments* [parerga], i.e. those things which do not belong to the complete representation of the object internally as elements but only externally as complements, and which augment the satisfaction of taste, do so only by their form; as for example the frames of pictures, or the draperies of statues or the colonnades of palaces. But if the ornament does not itself consist in beautiful form, and if it is used as a golden frame is used, merely to recommend the painting by its *charm,* it is then called *finery* and injures genuine beauty.

Emotion, i.e. a sensation in which pleasantness is produced by means of a momentary checking and a consequent more powerful outflow of the vital force, does not belong at all to beauty. But sublimity with which the feeling of emotion is bound up requires a different standard of judgement from that which is at the foundation of taste; and thus a pure judgement of taste has for its determining ground neither charm nor emotion, in a word, no sensation as the material of the aesthetical judgement.

§ 15. *The judgement of Taste is quite independent of the concept of perfection*

Objective purposiveness can only be cognised by means of the reference of the manifold to a definite purpose, and therefore only through a concept. From this alone it is plain that the Beautiful, the judging of which has at its basis a merely formal purposiveness, i.e. a purposiveness without purpose, is quite independent of the concept of the Good; because the latter presupposes an objective purposiveness, i.e. the reference of the object to a definite purpose.

Objective purposiveness is either external, i.e. the *utility*, or internal, i.e. the *perfection* of the object. That the satisfaction in an object, on account of which we call it beautiful, cannot rest on the representation of its utility, is sufficiently obvious from the two preceding sections; because in that case it would not be an immediate satisfaction in the object, which is the essential condition of a judgement about beauty. But objective internal purposiveness, i.e. perfection, comes nearer to the predicate of beauty; and it has been regarded by celebrated philosophers as the same as beauty, with the proviso, *if it is thought in a confused way*. It is of the greatest importance in a Critique of Taste to decide whether beauty can thus actually be resolved into the concept of perfection. . . . [B. 78-9]

Now the judgement of taste is an aesthetical judgement, i.e. such as rests on subjective grounds, the determining ground of which cannot be a concept, and consequently cannot be the concept of a definite purpose. Therefore in beauty, regarded as a formal subjective purposiveness, there is in no way thought a perfection of the object, as a would-be formal purposiveness, which yet is objective. And thus to distinguish between the concepts of the Beautiful and the Good, as if they were only different in logical form, the first being a confused, the second a clear concept of perfection, but identical in content and origin, is quite fallacious. For then there would be no *specific* difference between them, but a judgement of taste would be as much a cognitive judgement as the judgement by which a thing is described as good; just as when the ordinary man says that fraud is unjust he bases his judgement on confused grounds, whilst the philosopher bases it on clear grounds, but both on identical principles of Reason. I have already, however, said that an aesthetical judgement is unique of its kind, and gives absolutely no cognition (not even a confused cognition) of the Object; this is only supplied by a logical judgement. On the contrary, it simply refers the representation, by which an Object is given, to the subject; and brings to our notice no characteristic of the object, but only the purposive form in the determination of the representative powers which are occupying themselves therewith. The judgement is called aesthetical just because its determining ground is not a concept, but the feeling (of internal sense) of that harmony in the play of the mental powers, so far as it can be felt in sensation. . . . [B. 80]

§ 16. *The judgement of Taste, by which an object is declared to be beautiful under the condition of a definite concept, is not pure*

There are two kinds of beauty; free beauty *(pulchritudo vaga)* or merely dependent beauty *(pulchritudo adhaerens)*. The first presupposes no concept of what the object ought to be; the second does presuppose such a concept and the perfection of the object in accordance therewith. The first is called the (self-subsistent) beauty of this or that thing; the second, as dependent upon a concept (conditioned beauty), is ascribed to Objects which come under the concept of a particular purpose.

Flowers are free natural beauties. Hardly any one but a botanist knows what sort of a thing a flower ought to be; and even he, though recognising in the flower the reproductive organ of the plant, pays no regard to this natural purpose if he is passing judgement on the flower by Taste. There is then at the basis of this judgement no perfection of any kind, no internal purposiveness, to which the collection of the manifold is referred. Many birds (such as the parrot, the humming bird, the bird of paradise), and many sea shells are beauties in themselves, which do not belong to any object determined in respect of its purpose by concepts, but please freely and in themselves. So also delineations *à la grecque,* foliage for borders or wall-papers, mean nothing in themselves; they represent nothing—no Object under a definite concept,—and are free beauties. We can refer to the same class what are called in music phantasies (i.e. pieces without any theme), and in fact all music without words.

In the judging of a free beauty (according to the mere form) the judgement of taste is pure. There is presupposed no concept of any purpose, for which the manifold should serve the given Object, and which therefore is to be represented therein. By such a concept the freedom of the Imagination which disports itself in the contemplation of the figure would be only limited.

But human beauty (i.e. of a man, a woman, or a child), the beauty of a horse, or a building (be it church, palace, arsenal, or summer-house) presupposes a concept of the purpose which determines what the thing is to be, and consequently a concept of its perfection; it is therefore adherent beauty. Now as the combination of the Pleasant (in sensation) with Beauty, which properly is only concerned with form, is a hindrance to the purity of the judgement of taste; so also is its purity injured by the combination with Beauty of the Good (viz. that manifold which is good for the thing itself in accordance with its purpose).

We could add much to a building which would immediately please the eye, if only it were not to be a church. We could adorn a figure with all kinds of spirals and light but regular lines, as the New Zealanders do with their tattooing, if only it were not the figure of a human being. And again this could have much finer features and a more pleasing and gentle cast of countenance provided it were not intended to represent a man, much less a warrior. . . . [B. 82-3]

It is true that taste gains by this combination of aesthetical with intellectual satisfaction, inasmuch as it becomes fixed; and though it is not universal, yet in respect to certain purposively determined Objects it becomes possible to prescribe rules for it. These, however, are not rules of taste, but merely rules for the unification of Taste with Reason, i.e. of the Beautiful with the Good, by which the former becomes available as an instrument of design in respect of the latter. Thus the tone of mind which is self-maintaining and of subjective universal validity is subordinated to the way of thinking which can be maintained only by painful resolve, but is of objective universal validity. Properly speaking, however, perfection gains nothing by beauty or beauty by perfection; but, when we compare the representation by which an object is given to us with the Object (as regards what it ought to be) by means of a concept, we cannot avoid considering along with it the sensation in the subject. And thus when both states of mind are in harmony our *whole faculty* of representative power gains.

A judgement of taste, then, in respect of an object with a definite internal purpose, can only be pure, if either the person judging has no concept of this purpose, or else abstracts from it in his judgement. Such a person, although forming an accurate judgement of taste in judging of the object as free beauty, would yet by another who considers the beauty in it only as a dependent attribute (who looks to the purpose of the object) be blamed, and accused of false taste; although both are right in their own way, the one in reference to what he has before his eyes, the other in reference to what he has in his thought. By means of this distinction we can settle many disputes about beauty between judges of taste; by showing that the one is speaking of free, the other of dependent, beauty,—that the first is making a pure, the second an applied, judgement of taste.

§ 17. *Of the Ideal of beauty*

There can be no objective rule of taste which shall determine by means of concepts what is beautiful. For every judgement from this source is aesthetical; i.e. the feeling of the subject, and not a concept of the Object, is its determining ground. To seek for a principle of taste which shall furnish, by means of definite concepts, a universal criterion of the beautiful, is fruitless trouble; because what is sought is impossible and self-contradictory. The universal communicability of sensation (satisfaction or dissatisfaction) without the aid of a concept—the agreement, as far as is possible, of all times and peoples as regards this feeling in the representation of certain objects—this is the empirical criterion, although weak and hardly sufficing for probability, of the derivation of a taste, thus confirmed by examples, from the deep-lying grounds of agreement common to all men, in judging of the forms under which objects are given to them.

Hence, we consider some products of taste as *exemplary*. Not that taste can be acquired by imitating others; for it must be an original faculty. He who imitates a model shows, no doubt, in so far as he attains to it, skill; but only shows taste in so far as he can judge of this model itself.[1] It follows from hence that the highest model, the archetype of taste, is a mere Idea, which every one must produce in himself; and according to which he must judge every Object of taste, every example of judgement by taste, and even the taste of every one. *Idea* properly means a rational concept, and *Ideal* the representation of an individual being, regarded as adequate to an Idea. Hence that archetype of taste, which certainly rests on the indeterminate Idea that Reason has of a maximum, but which cannot be represented by concepts, but only in an individual presentation, is better called the Ideal of the beautiful. Although we are not in possession of this, we yet strive to produce it in ourselves. But it can only be an Ideal of the Imagination, because it rests on a presentation and not on concepts, and the Imagination is the faculty of presentation.— How do we arrive at such an Ideal of beauty? *A priori,* or empirically? Moreover, what species of the beautiful is susceptible of an Ideal?

First, it is well to remark that the beauty for which an Ideal is to be sought cannot be *vague* beauty, but is *fixed* by a concept of objective purposiveness; and thus it cannot appertain to the Object of a quite pure judgement of taste, but to that of a judgement of taste which is in part intellectual. That is, in whatever grounds of judgement an Ideal is to be found, an Idea of Reason in accordance with definite concepts must lie at its basis; which determines *a priori* the purpose on which the internal possibility of the object rests. An Ideal of beautiful flowers, of a beautiful piece of furniture, of a beautiful view, is inconceivable. But neither can an Ideal be represented of a beauty dependent on definite purposes, e.g. of a beautiful dwelling-house, a beautiful tree, a beautiful garden, etc.; presumably because their

[1] [Note B. 85.]

purpose is not sufficiently determined and fixed by the concept, and thus the purposiveness is nearly as free as in the case of *vague* beauty. The only being which has the purpose of its existence in itself is *man,* who can determine his purposes by Reason; or, where he must receive them from external perception, yet can compare them with essential and universal purposes, and can judge this their accordance aesthetically. This *man* is, then, alone of all objects in the world, susceptible of an Ideal of *beauty;* as it is only *humanity* in his person, as an intelligence, that is susceptible of the Ideal of *perfection.*

But there are here two elements. *First,* there is the aesthetical *normal Idea,* which is an individual intuition (of the Imagination), representing the standard of our judgement [upon man] as a thing belonging to a particular animal species. *Secondly,* there is the *rational Idea* which makes the purposes of humanity, so far as they cannot be sensibly represented, the principle for judging of a figure through which, as their phenomenal effect, those purposes are revealed. The normal Idea of the figure of an animal of a particular race must take its elements from experience. But the greatest purposiveness in the construction of the figure, that would be available for the universal standard of aesthetical judgement upon each individual of this species—the image which is as it were designedly at the basis of nature's Technic, to which only the whole race and not any isolated individual is adequate—this lies merely in the Idea of the judging [subject]. And this, with its proportions, as an aesthetical Idea, can be completely presented *in concreto* in a model. In order to make intelligible in some measure (for who can extract her whole secret from nature?) how this comes to pass, we shall attempt a psychological explanation.

We must remark that, in a way quite incomprehensible by us, the Imagination can not only recall, on occasion, the signs for concepts long past, but can also reproduce the image of the figure of the object out of an unspeakable number of objects of different kinds or even of the same kind. Further, if the mind is concerned with comparisons, the Imagination can, in all probability, actually though unconsciously let one image glide into another, and thus by the concurrence of several of the same kind come by an average, which serves as the common measure of all. Every one has seen a thousand full-grown men. Now if you wish to judge of their normal size, estimating it by means of comparison, the Imagination (as I think) allows a great number of images (perhaps the whole thousand) to fall on one another. If I am allowed to apply here the analogy of optical presentation, it is in the space where most of them are combined and inside the contour, where the place is illuminated with the most vivid colours, that the *average size* is cognisable; which, both in height and breadth, is equally far removed from the extreme bounds of the greatest and smallest stature. And this is the stature of a beautiful man. (We could arrive at the same thing mechanically, by adding together all thousand magnitudes, heights, breadths, and thicknesses, and dividing the sum by a thousand. But the Imagination does this by means of a dynamical effect, which arises from the various impressions of such figures on the organ of internal sense.) If now in a similar way for this average man we seek the average head, for this head the average nose, etc., such figure is at the basis of the normal Idea in the country where the comparison is instituted. Thus necessarily under these empirical conditions a negro must have a different normal Idea of the beauty of the [human figure] from a white man, a Chinaman a different normal Idea from a European, etc. And the same is the case with the model of a beautiful horse or dog (of a certain breed).— This *normal Idea* is not derived from proportions got from experience [and regarded] *as definite rules;* but in accordance with it rules for judging become in the first instance possible. It is the image for the whole race, which floats among all the variously different intuitions of individuals, which nature takes as archetype in her productions of the same species, but which seems not to be fully reached in any individual case. It is by no means the whole *archetype of beauty* in the race, but only the form constituting the indispensable condition of all beauty, and thus merely *correctness* in the [mental] presentation of the race. It is, like the celebrated *Doryphorus of Polycletus,*[1] the *rule* (*Myron's* Cow might also be used thus for its kind). It can therefore contain nothing specifically characteristic, for otherwise it would not be the *normal Idea* for the race. Its presentation pleases, not by its beauty, but merely because it contradicts no condition, under which alone a thing of this kind can be beautiful. The presentation is merely correct.[2]

[1] [Polycletus of Argos flourished about 430 B. C. His statue of the *spearbearer* (*Doryphorus*), afterwards became known as the *Canon;* because in it the artist was supposed to have embodied a perfect representation of the ideal of the human figure. Tr.'s note.]

[2] It will be found that a perfectly regular countenance, such as a painter might wish to have for a model, ordinarily tells us nothing; because it contains nothing characteristic, and therefore rather expresses the Idea of the race than the specific [traits] of a person. The exaggeration of a characteristic of this kind, i.e. such as does violence to the normal Idea (the purposiveness of the race) is called *caricature.* Experience also shows that these quite regular countenances commonly indicate internally only a mediocre man; presumably (if it may be assumed that external nature expresses the proportions of internal) because, if no mental disposition exceeds that

We must yet distinguish the *normal Idea* of the beautiful from the *Ideal,* which latter, on grounds already alleged, we can only expect in the *human* figure. In this the Ideal consists in the expression of the *moral,* without which the object would not please universally and thus positively (not merely negatively in a correct presentation). The visible expression of moral Ideas that rule men inwardly, can indeed only be got from experience; but to make its connexion with all which our Reason unites with the morally good in the Idea of the highest purposiveness,—goodness of heart, purity, strength, peace, etc.,—visible as it were in bodily manifestation (as the effect of that which is internal), requires a union of pure Ideas of Reason with great imaginative power, even in him who wishes to judge of it, still more in him who wishes to present it. The correctness of such an Ideal of beauty is shown by its permitting no sensible charm to mingle with the satisfaction in the Object and yet allowing us to take a great interest therein. This shows that a judgement in accordance with such a standard can never be purely aesthetical, and that a judgement in accordance with an Ideal of beauty is not a mere judgement of taste.

EXPLANATION OF THE BEAUTIFUL DERIVED FROM THIS THIRD MOMENT

Beauty is the form of the *purposiveness* of an object, so far as this is perceived in it *without any representation of a purpose.*[1]

---

proportion which is requisite in order to constitute a man free from faults, nothing can be expected of what is called *genius,* in which nature seems to depart from the ordinary relations of the mental powers on behalf of some special one.

[1] It might be objected to this explanation that there are things, in which we see a purposive form without cognising

FOURTH MOMENT OF THE JUDGEMENT OF TASTE, ACCORDING TO THE MODALITY OF THE SATISFACTION IN THE OBJECT

§ 18. *What the modality in a judgement of Taste is*

I can say of every representation that it is at least *possible* that (as a cognition) it should be bound up with a pleasure. Of a representation that I call *pleasant* I say that it *actually* excites pleasure in me. But the *beautiful* we think as having a *necessary* reference to satisfaction. Now this necessity is of a peculiar kind. It is not a theoretical objective necessity; in which case it would be cognised *a priori* that every one *will feel* this satisfaction in the object called beautiful by me. It is not a practical necessity; in which case, by concepts of a pure rational will serving as a rule for freely acting beings, the satisfaction is the necessary result of an objective law and only indicates that we absolutely (without any further design) ought to act in a certain way. But the necessity which is thought in an aesthetical judgement can only be called *exemplary;* i.e. a necessity of the assent of *all* to a judgement which is regarded as the example of a universal rule that we cannot state. Since an aesthetical judgement is not an objective cog-

---

any [definite] purpose in them, like the stone implements often got from old sepulchral tumuli with a hole in them as if for a handle. These, although they plainly indicate by their shape a purposiveness of which we do not know the purpose, are nevertheless not described as beautiful. But if we regard a thing as a work of art, that is enough to make us admit that its shape has reference to some design and definite purpose. And hence there is no immediate satisfaction in the contemplation of it. On the other hand a flower, e.g., a tulip, is regarded as beautiful; because in perceiving it we find a certain purposiveness which, in our judgement, is referred to no purpose at all.

nitive judgement, this necessity cannot be derived from definite concepts, and is therefore not apodictic. Still less can it be inferred from the universality of experience (of a complete agreement of judgements as to the beauty of a certain object). For not only would experience hardly furnish sufficiently numerous vouchers for this; but also, on empirical judgements we can base no concept of the necessity of these judgements.

§ 19. *The subjective necessity, which we ascribe to the judgement of Taste, is conditioned*

The judgement of taste requires the agreement of every one; and he who describes anything as beautiful claims that every one *ought* to give his approval to the object in question and also describe it as beautiful. The *ought* in the aesthetical judgement is therefore pronounced in accordance with all the data which are required for judging and yet is only conditioned. We ask for the agreement of every one else, because we have for it a ground that is common to all; and we could count on this agreement, provided we were always sure that the case was correctly subsumed under that ground as rule of assent.

§ 20. *The condition of necessity which a judgement of Taste asserts is the Idea of a common sense*

If judgements of taste (like cognitive judgements) had a definite objective principle, then the person who lays them down in accordance with this latter would claim an unconditioned necessity for his judgement. If they were devoid of all principle, like those of the mere taste of sense, we would not allow them in thought any necessity whatever. Hence they must have a subjective principle which determines what pleases or displeases only by feeling and not by concepts, but yet with universal validity. But such a principle could only be regarded as a *common sense,* which is essentially different from common Understanding which people sometimes call common Sense *(sensus communis);* for the latter does not judge by feeling but always by concepts, although ordinarily only as by obscurely represented principles.

Hence it is only under the presupposition that there is a common sense (by which we do not understand an external sense, but the effect resulting from the free play of our cognitive powers)—it is only under this presupposition, I say, that the judgement of taste can be laid down.

§ 21. *Have we ground for presupposing a common sense?*

Cognitions and judgements must, along with the conviction that accompanies them, admit of universal communicability; for otherwise there would be no harmony between them and the Object, and they would be collectively a mere subjective play of the representative powers, exactly as scepticism would have it. But if cognitions are to admit of communicability, so must also the state of mind,—i.e. the accordance of the cognitive powers with a cognition generally, and that proportion of them which is suitable for a representation (by which an object is given to us), in order that a cognition may be made out of it—admit of universal communicability. For without this as the subjective condition of cognition, knowledge as an effect could not arise. This actually always takes place when a given object by means of Sense excites the Imagination to collect the manifold, and the Imagination in its turn excites the Understanding to bring about a unity of this collective process in concepts. But this accordance of the cognitive powers has a different proportion according to the variety of the Objects which are given. However, it must be such that this internal relation, by which one mental faculty is excited by another, shall be generally the most beneficial for both faculties in respect of cognition (of given objects); and this accordance can only be determined by feeling (not according to concepts). Since now this accordance itself must admit of universal communicability, and consequently also our feeling of it (in a given representation), and since the universal communicability of a feeling presupposes a common sense, we have grounds for assuming this latter. And this common sense is assumed without relying on psychological observations, but simply as the necessary condition of the universal communicability of our knowledge, which is presupposed in every Logic and in every principle of knowledge that is not sceptical. . . . [B. 94-5]

EXPLANATION OF THE BEAUTIFUL RESULTING FROM THE FOURTH MOMENT

The *beautiful* is that which without any concept is cognised as the object of a *necessary* satisfaction. . . . [B. 96-152]

[II.] DEDUCTION OF PURE AESTHETICAL JUDGEMENTS

§ 31. *Of the method of deduction of judgements of Taste*

A Deduction, i.e. the guarantee of the legitimacy of a class of judgements, is only obligatory if the judgement lays claim to necessity. This it does, if it demands even subjective universality or the agreement of every one, although it is not a judgement of cognition but only one of pleasure or pain in a given object; i.e. it assumes a subjective purposiveness thoroughly valid for every one, which must not be based on any concept of the thing, because the judgement is one of taste. . . . [B. 152-3]

[Hence we must] explain how it is possible that a thing can please in the mere act of judging it (without sensation or concept), and how the satisfaction of one man can be proclaimed as a rule for every other; just as the act of judging of an object for the sake of a *cognition* in general has universal rules.

If now this universal validity is not to be based on any collecting of the suffrages of others, or on any questioning of them as to the kind of sensations they have, but is to rest, as it were, on an autonomy of the judging subject in respect of the feeling of pleasure (in the given representation), i.e. on his own taste, and yet is not to be derived from concepts; then a judgement like this—such as the judgement of taste is, in fact—has a twofold logical peculiarity. *First,* there is its *a priori* universal validity, which is not a logical universality in accordance with concepts, but the universality of a singular judgement. *Secondly,* it has a necessity (which must always rest on *a priori* grounds), which however does not depend on any *a priori* grounds of proof, through the representation of which the assent that every one concedes to the judgement of taste could be exacted.

The solution of these logical peculiarities, wherein a judgement of taste is different from all cognitive judgements—if we at the outset abstract from all content, viz. from the feeling of pleasure, and merely compare the aesthetical form with the form of objective judgements as logic prescribes it—is sufficient by itself for the deduction of this singular faculty. . . . [B. 153-163] [1]

This problem then may be thus represented: how is a judgement possible, in which merely from *our own* feeling of pleasure in an object, independently of its concept, we judge that this pleasure attaches to the representation of the same Object *in every other subject*, and that *a priori* without waiting for the accordance of others? . . . [B. 164-5]

§ 38. *Deduction of judgements of Taste*

If [2] pleasure is bound up with the mere apprehension (*apprehensio*) of the form of an object of intuition, without reference to a concept for a definite cognition, then the representation is thereby not referred to the Object, but simply to the subject; and the pleasure can express nothing else than its harmony with the cognitive faculties which come into play in the reflective Judgement, and so far as they are in play; and hence can only express a subjective formal purposiveness of the Object. For that apprehension of forms in the Imagination can never take place without the reflective Judgement, though undesignedly, at least comparing them with its faculty of referring intuitions to concepts. If now in this comparison the Imagination (as the faculty of *a priori* intuitions) is placed by means of a given representation undesignedly in agreement with the Understanding, as the faculty of concepts, and thus a feeling of pleasure is aroused, the object must then be regarded as purposive for the reflective Judgement.

[1] [B. 157-9 will be found above, pp. 386-7, as a note.]

[2] [This paragraph is part of Sec. VII of the *Introduction* to the *Critique of Judgement,* B. 31-3.]

Such a judgement is an aesthetical judgement upon the purposiveness of the Object, which does not base itself upon any present concept of the object, nor does it furnish any such. In the case of an object whose form (not the matter of its representation, as sensation), in the mere reflection upon it (without reference to any concept to be obtained of it), is judged as the ground of a pleasure in the representation of such an Object, this pleasure is judged as bound up with the representation necessarily; and, consequently, not only for the subject which apprehends this form, but for every judging being in general. The object is then called beautiful; and the faculty of judging by means of such a pleasure (and, consequently, with universal validity) is called Taste. For since the ground of the pleasure is placed merely in the form of the object for reflection in general—and, consequently, in no sensation of the object, and also without reference to any concept which anywhere involves design—it is only the conformity to law in the empirical use of the Judgement in general (unity of the Imagination with the Understanding) in the subject, with which the representation of the Object in reflection, whose conditions are universally valid *a priori,* harmonises. And since this harmony of the object with the faculties of the subject is contingent, it brings about the representation of its purposiveness in respect of the cognitive faculties of the subject.

If [1] it be admitted that in a pure judgement of taste the satisfaction in the object is combined with the mere act of judging its form, it is nothing else than its subjective purposiveness for the Judgement which we feel to be mentally combined with the representation of the object. The Judgement, as regards the formal rules of its action, apart from all matter (whether sensation

[1] [Cf. B. 165 ff.]

or concept), can only be directed to the subjective conditions of its employment in general (it is applied neither to a particular mode of sense nor to a particular concept of the Understanding); and consequently to that subjective [element] which we can presuppose in all men (as requisite for possible cognition in general). Thus the agreement of a representation with these conditions of the Judgement must be capable of being assumed as valid *a priori* for every one. I.e. we may rightly impute to every one the pleasure or the subjective purposiveness of the representation for the relation between the cognitive faculties in the act of judging a sensible object in general.[1]

Remark

This Deduction is thus easy, because it has no need to justify the objective reality of any concept, for Beauty is not a concept of the Object and the judgement of taste is not cognitive. It only maintains that we are justified in presupposing universally in every man those subjective conditions of the Judgement which we find in ourselves; and further, that we have rightly subsumed the given Object under these conditions. The

[1] In order to be justified in claiming universal assent for an aesthetical judgement that rests merely on subjective grounds, it is sufficient to assume, (1) that the subjective conditions of the Judgement, as regards the relation of the cognitive powers thus put into activity to a cognition in general, are the same in all men. This must be true, because otherwise men would not be able to communicate their representations or even their knowledge. (2) The judgement must merely have reference to this relation (consequently to the *formal condition* of the Judgement) and be pure, i.e. not mingled either with concepts of the Object or with sensations, as determining grounds. If there has been any mistake as regards this latter condition, then there is only an inaccurate application of the privilege, which a law gives us, to a particular case; but that does not destroy the privilege itself in general.

latter has indeed unavoidable difficulties which do not beset the logical Judgement. There we subsume under concepts, but in the aesthetical Judgement under a merely sensible relation between the Imagination and Understanding mutually harmonising in the representation of the form of the Object,—in which case the subsumption may easily be fallacious. Yet the legitimacy of the claim of the Judgement in counting upon universal assent is not thus annulled; it reduces itself merely to the correctness of the principle of judging validly for every one from subjective grounds. For as to the difficulty or doubt concerning the correctness of the subsumption under that principle, it makes the legitimacy of the claim of an aesthetical judgement in general to such validity and the principle of the same, as little doubtful, as the like faulty (though neither so commonly nor readily faulty) subsumption of the logical Judgement under its principle can make the latter, an objective principle, doubtful. . . . [B. 167-187][1]

[III. The Nature of Art and Genius]

§ 45. *Beautiful Art is an art, in so far as it seems like nature*

In a product of beautiful art we must become conscious that it is Art and not Nature; but yet the purposiveness in its form must seem to be as free from all constraint of arbitrary rules as if it were a product of mere nature. On this feeling of freedom in the play of our cognitive faculties, which must at the same time be purposive, rests that pleasure which alone is universally communicable, without being based on concepts. Nature

[1] [§ 41 (B. 173-6) has been inserted above pp. 380 ff., and part of § 42 (B. 176-180) on pp. 439 ff. below.]

is beautiful because it looks like Art; and Art can only be called beautiful if we are conscious of it as Art while yet it looks like Nature.

For whether we are dealing with natural or with artificial beauty we can say generally: *That is beautiful which pleases in the mere act of judging it* (not in the sensation of it, or by means of a concept). Now art has always a definite design of producing something. But if this something were bare sensation (something merely subjective), which is to be accompanied with pleasure, the product would please in the act of judgement only by meditation of sensible feeling. And again, if the design were directed towards the production of a definite Object, then, if this were attained by art, the Object would only please by means of concepts. But in both cases the art would not please *in the mere act of judging;* i.e. it would not please as beautiful, but as mechanical.

Hence the purposiveness in the product of beautiful art, although it is designed, must not seem to be designed; i.e. beautiful art must *look* like nature, although we are conscious of it as art. But a product of art appears like nature when, although its agreement with the rules, according to which alone the product can become what it ought to be, is *punctiliously* observed, yet this is not *painfully* apparent; the form of the schools does not obtrude itself—it shows no trace of the rule having been before the eyes of the artist and having fettered his mental powers.

§ 46. *Beautiful Art is the art of genius*

Genius is the talent (or natural gift) which gives the rule to Art. Since talent, as the innate productive faculty of the artist, belongs itself to Nature, we may express the matter thus: *Genius* is the innate mental disposition (*ingenium*) *through which* Nature gives the rule to Art.

Whatever may be thought of this definition, whether it is merely arbitrary or whether it is adequate to the concept that we are accustomed to combine with the word *genius* (which is to be examined in the following paragraphs), we can prove already beforehand that according to the signification of the word here adopted, beautiful arts must necessarily be considered as arts of *genius*.

For every art presupposes rules by means of which in the first instance a product, if it is to be called artistic, is represented as possible. But the concept of beautiful art does not permit the judgement upon the beauty of a product to be derived from any rule, which has a *concept* as its determining ground, and therefore has as its basis a concept of the way in which the product is possible. Therefore, beautiful art cannot itself devise the rule according to which it can bring about its product. But since at the same time a product can never be called Art without some precedent rule, Nature in the subject must (by the harmony of its faculties) give the rule to Art; i.e. beautiful Art is only possible as a product of Genius.

We thus see (1) that genius is a *talent* for producing that for which no definite rule can be given; it is not a mere aptitude for what can be learnt by a rule. Hence *originality* must be its first property. (2) But since it also can produce original nonsense, its products must be models, i.e. *exemplary;* and they consequently ought not to spring from imitation, but must serve as a standard or rule of judgement for others. (3) It cannot describe or indicate scientifically how it brings about its products, but it gives the rule just as nature does. Hence the author of a product for which he is indebted to his genius does not himself know how he has come by his Ideas; and he has not the power to devise the like at pleasure or in accordance with a plan, and to communicate it to others in precepts that will enable them to produce similar products. (Hence it is probable that the word genius is derived from *genius,* that peculiar guiding and guardian spirit given to a man at his birth, from whose suggestion these original Ideas proceed.) (4) Nature by the medium of genius does not prescribe rules to Science, but to Art; and to it only in so far as it is to be beautiful Art.

§ 47. *Elucidation and confirmation of the above explanation of Genius*

Every one is agreed that genius is entirely opposed to the *spirit of imitation.* Now since learning is nothing but imitation, it follows that the greatest ability and teachableness (capacity) regarded *qua* teachableness, cannot avail for genius. Even if a man thinks or invents for himself, and does not merely take in what others have taught, even if he discovers many things in art and science, this is not the right ground for calling such a (perhaps great) *head,* a genius (as opposed to him who because he can only learn and imitate is called a *shallow-pate*). For even these things could be learned, they lie in the natural path of him who investigates and reflects according to rules; and they do not differ specifically from what can be acquired by industry through imitation. Thus we can readily learn all that *Newton* has set forth in his immortal work on the Principles of Natural Philosophy, however great a head was required to discover it; but we cannot learn to write spirited poetry, however express may be the precepts of the art and however excellent its models. The reason is that *Newton* could make all his steps, from the first elements of geometry to his own great and profound discoveries, intuitively plain and definite as regards consequence, not only to himself but to every one else. But a *Homer* or a *Wieland* cannot show how his Ideas, so rich in fancy and yet so full of thought, come together in his head, simply because he does not know and therefore cannot teach others. In Science then the greatest discoverer only differs in degree from his laborious imitator and pupil; but he differs specifically from him whom Nature has gifted for beautiful Art. And in this there is no depreciation of those great men to whom the human race owes so much gratitude, as compared with nature's favourites in respect of the talent for beautiful art. For in the fact that the former talent is directed to the ever-advancing greater perfection of knowledge and every advantage depending on it, and at the same time to the imparting this same knowledge to others—in this it has a great superiority over [the talent of] those who deserve the honour of being called geniuses. For art stands still at a certain point; a boundary is set to it beyond which it cannot go, which presumably has been reached long ago and cannot be extended further. Again, artistic skill cannot be communicated; it is imparted to every artist immediately by the hand of nature; and so it dies with him, until nature endows another in the same way, so that he only needs an example in order to put in operation in a similar fashion the talent of which he is conscious.

If now it is a natural gift which must prescribe its rule to art (as beautiful art), of what kind is this rule? It cannot be reduced to a formula and serve as a precept, for then the judgement upon the beautiful would be determinable according to concepts; but the rule must be abstracted from the fact, i.e. from the product, on which others may try their own talent by using it as a model, not to be *copied* but to be *imitated*. How this is possible is hard to explain. The Ideas of the artist excite like Ideas in his pupils if nature has endowed them with a like proportion of their mental powers. Hence models of beautiful art are the only means of handing down these Ideas to posterity. This cannot be done by mere descriptions, especially not in the case of the arts of speech, and in this latter classical models are only to be had in the old dead languages, now preserved only as "the learned languages."

Although mechanical and beautiful art are very different, the first being a mere art of industry and learning and the second of genius, yet there is no beautiful art in which there is not a mechanical element that can be comprehended by rules and followed accordingly, and in which therefore there must be something *scholastic* as an essential condition. For [in every art] some purpose must be conceived; otherwise we could not ascribe the product to art at all, and it would be a mere product of chance. But in order to accomplish a purpose, definite rules from which we cannot dispense ourselves are requisite. Now since the originality of the talent constitutes an essential (though not the only) element in the character of genius, shallow heads believe that they cannot better show themselves to be full-blown geniuses than by throwing off the constraint of all rules; they believe, in effect, that one could make a braver show on the back of a wild horse than on the back of a trained animal. Genius can only furnish rich *material* for products of beautiful art; its execution and its *form* require talent cultivated in the schools, in order to make such a use of this material as will stand examination by the Judgement. But it is quite ridiculous for a man to speak and decide like a genius in things which require the most careful investigation by Reason. One does not know whether to laugh more at the impostor who spreads such a mist round him that we cannot clearly use our Judgement and so use our Imagination the more, or at the public which naïvely imagines that his inability to cognise clearly and to comprehend the masterpiece before him arises from new truths crowding in on him in such abundance that details (duly weighed definitions and accurate examination of fundamental propositions) seem but clumsy work.

§ 48. *Of the relation of Genius to Taste*

For *judging* of beautiful objects as such, taste is requisite; but for beautiful art, i.e. for the *production* of such objects, *genius* is requisite.

If we consider genius as the talent for beautiful art (which the special meaning of the word implies) and in this point of view analyse it into the faculties which must concur to constitute such a talent, it is necessary in the first instance to determine exactly the difference between natural beauty, the judging of which requires only Taste, and artificial beauty, whose possibility (to which reference must be made in judging such an object) requires Genius.

A natural beauty is a *beautiful thing;* artificial beauty is a *beautiful representation* of a thing.

In order to judge of a natural beauty as such I need not have beforehand a concept of what sort of thing the object is to be; i.e. I need not know its material purposiveness (the purpose), but its mere form pleases by itself in the act of judging it without any knowledge of the purpose. But if the object is given as a product of art, and as such is to be declared beautiful, then, because art always supposes a purpose in the cause (and its causality), there must be at bottom in the first instance a concept of what the thing is to be. And as the agreement of the manifold in a thing with its inner destination, its purpose, constitutes the perfection of the thing, it follows that in judging of artificial beauty the perfection of the thing must be taken into account; but in judging of natural beauty (as *such*) there is no question at all about this.— It is true that in judging of objects of nature, especially objects endowed with life, e.g. a man or a horse, their objective purposiveness also is commonly taken into consideration in judging of their beauty; but then the judgement is no longer purely aesthetical, i.e. a mere judgement of taste. Nature is no longer judged inasmuch as it appears like art, but in so far as it *is* actual (although superhuman) art; and the teleological judgement serves as the basis and condition of the aesthetical, as a condition to which the latter must have respect. In such a case, e.g. if it is said, "That is a beautiful woman," we think nothing else than this: nature represents in her figure the purposes in view in the shape of a woman's figure. For we must look beyond the mere form to a concept, if the object is to be thought in such a way by means of a logically conditioned aesthetical judgement.

Beautiful art shows its superiority in this, that it describes as beautiful things which may be in nature ugly or displeasing. The Furies, diseases, the devastations of war, etc., may, even regarded as calamitous, be described as very beautiful, and even represented in a picture. There is only one kind of ugliness which cannot be represented in accordance with nature, without destroying all aesthetical satisfaction and consequently artificial beauty; viz. that which excites *disgust.* For in this peculiar sensation, which rests on mere imagination, the object is represented as it were obtruding itself for our enjoyment while we strive against it with all our might. And the artistic representation of the object is no longer distinguished from the nature of the object itself in our sensation, and thus it is impossible that it can be regarded as beautiful. The art of sculpture again, because in its products art is almost interchangeable with nature, excludes from its creations the immediate representation of ugly objects; e.g. it represents death by a beautiful genius, the warlike spirit by Mars, and permits [all such things] to be represented only by an allegory or attribute that has a pleasing effect, and thus only indirectly by the aid of the interpretation of Reason, and not for the mere aesthetical Judgement.

So much for the beautiful representation of an object, which is properly only the form of the presentation of a concept, and the means by which the latter is communicated universally.— But to give this form to the product of beautiful art, mere taste is requisite. By taste, after he has exercised and corrected it by manifold examples from art or nature, the artist checks his work; and after many, often toilsome, attempts to content taste he finds the form which satisfies him. Hence this form is not, as it were, a thing of inspiration or the result of a free swing of the mental powers, but of a slow and even painful process of improvement, by which he seeks to render it adequate to his thought, without detriment to the freedom of the play of his powers.

But taste is merely a judging and not a productive faculty; and what is appropriate to it is not therefore a work of beautiful art. It may be only a product belonging to useful and mechanical art or even to science, produced according to definite rules that can be learned and must be exactly followed. But the pleasing form that is given to it is only the vehicle of communication, and a mode, as it were, of presenting it, in respect of which we remain free to a certain extent, although it is combined with a definite purpose. Thus we desire that table appointments, a moral treatise, even a sermon, should have in themselves this form of beautiful art, without it seeming to be *sought*: but we do not therefore call these things works of beautiful art. Under the latter class are reckoned a poem, a piece of music, a picture gallery, etc.; and in some would-be works of beautiful art we find genius without taste, while in others we find taste without genius.

§ 49. *Of the faculties of the mind that constitute Genius*

We say of certain products of which we expect that they should at least in part appear as beautiful art, they are without *spirit* [1]; although we find nothing to blame in them on the score of taste. A poem may be very neat and elegant, but without spirit. A history may be exact and well arranged, but without spirit. A festal discourse may be solid and at the same time elaborate, but without spirit. Conversation is often not devoid of entertainment, but yet without spirit: even of a woman we say that she is pretty, an agreeable talker, and courteous, but without spirit. What then do we mean by spirit?

Spirit, in an aesthetical sense, is the name given to the animating principle of the mind. But that whereby this principle animates the soul, the material which it applies to that [purpose], is that which puts the mental

[1] [In English we would rather say "without *soul*"; but I prefer to translate *Geist* consistently by *spirit,* to avoid the confusion of it with *Seele*. Tr.'s note.]

powers purposively into swing, i.e. into such a play as maintains itself and strengthens the [mental] powers in their exercise.

Now I maintain that this principle is no other than the faculty of presenting *aesthetical Ideas.* And by an aesthetical Idea I understand that representation of the Imagination which occasions much thought without, however, any definite thought, i.e. any *concept,* being capable of being adequate to it; it consequently cannot be completely compassed and made intelligible bv language.— We easily see that it is the counterpart (pendant) of a *rational Idea,* which conversely is a concept to which no *intuition* (or representation of the Imagination) can be adequate.

The Imagination (as a productive faculty of cognition) is very powerful in creating another nature, as it were, out of the material that actual nature gives it. We entertain ourselves with it when experience proves too commonplace, and by it we remould experience, always indeed in accordance with analogical laws, but yet also in accordance with principles which occupy a higher place in Reason (laws too which are just as natural to us as those by which Understanding comprehends empirical nature). Thus we feel our freedom from the law of association (which attaches to the empirical employment of Imagination), so that the material which we borrow from nature in accordance with this law can be worked up into something different which surpasses nature.

Such representations of the Imagination we may call *Ideas,* partly because they at least strive after something which lies beyond the bounds of experience, and so seek to approximate to a presentation of concepts of Reason (intellectual Ideas), thus giving to the latter the appearance of objective reality,—but especially because no concept can be fully adequate to them as internal intuitions. The poet ventures to realise to sense, rational Ideas of invisible beings, the kingdom of the blessed, hell, eternity, creation, etc.; or even if he deals with things of which there are examples in experience, —e.g. death, envy and all vices, also love, fame, and the like,—he tries, by means of Imagination, which emulates the play of Reason in its quest after a maximum, to go beyond the limits of experience and to present them to Sense with a completeness of which there is no example in nature. It is, properly speaking, in the art of the poet, that the faculty of aesthetical Ideas can manifest itself in its full measure. But this faculty, considered in itself, is properly only a talent (of the Imagination).

If now we place under a concept a representation of the Imagination belonging to its presentation, but which occasions solely by itself more thought than can ever be comprehended in a definite concept, and which therefore enlarges aesthetically the concept itself in an unbounded fashion,—the Imagination is here creative, and it brings the faculty of intellectual Ideas (the Reason) into movement; i.e. a movement, occasioned by a representation, towards more thought (though belonging, no doubt, to the concept of the object) than can be grasped in the representation or made clear.

Those forms which do not constitute the presentation of a given concept itself but only, as approximate representations of the Imagination, express the consequences bound up with it and its relationship to other concepts, are called (aesthetical) *attributes* of an object, whose concept as a rational Idea cannot be adequately presented. Thus Jupiter's eagle with the lightning in its claws is an attribute of the mighty king of heaven, as the peacock is of its magnificent queen. They do not, like *logical attributes,* represent what lies in our concepts of the sublimity and majesty of creation, but something different, which gives occasion to the Imagination to spread itself over a number of kindred representations, that arouse more thought than can be expressed in a concept determined by words. They furnish an *aesthetical Idea,* which for that rational Idea takes the place of logical presentation; and thus as their proper office they enliven the mind by opening out to it the prospect into an illimitable field of kindred representations. But beautiful art does this not only in the case of painting or sculpture (in which the term "attribute" is commonly employed): poetry and rhetoric also get the spirit that animates their works simply from the aesthetical attributes of the object, which accompany the logical and stimulate the Imagination, so that it thinks more by their aid, although in an undeveloped way, than could be comprehended in a concept and therefore in a definite form of words. . . . [B. 200-1]

Thus, for example, a certain poet says, in his description of a beautiful morning:

"The sun arose
As calm from virtue springs."

The consciousness of virtue, even if one only places oneself in thought in the position of a virtuous man, diffuses in the mind a multitude of sublime and restful feelings and a boundless prospect of a joyful future, to which no expression measured by a definite concept completely attains.[1]

In a word the aesthetical Idea is a representation of the Imagination associated with a given concept, which

[1] Perhaps nothing more sublime was ever said and no sublimer thought ever expressed than the famous inscription on the Temple of *Isis* (Mother *Nature*): "I am all that is and that was and that shall be, and no mortal hath lifted my veil." . . . [B. 201, N]

is bound up with such a multiplicity of partial representations in its free employment, that for it no expression marking a definite concept can be found; and such a representation, therefore, adds to a concept much ineffable thought, the feeling of which quickens the cognitive faculties, and with language, which is the mere letter, binds up spirit also.

The mental powers, therefore, whose union (in a certain relation) constitutes *genius* are Imagination and Understanding. In the employment of the Imagination for cognition it submits to the constraint of the Understanding and is subject to the limitation of being conformable to the concept of the latter. On the other hand, in an aesthetical point of view it is free to furnish unsought, over and above that agreement with a concept, abundance of undeveloped material for the Understanding; to which the Understanding paid no regard in its concept, but which it applies, though not objectively for cognition, yet subjectively to quicken the cognitive powers and therefore also indirectly to cognitions. Thus genius properly consists in the happy relation [between these faculties], which no science can teach and no industry can learn, by which Ideas are found for a given concept; and on the other hand, we thus find for these Ideas the *expression,* by means of which the subjective state of mind brought about by them, as an accompaniment of the concept, can be communicated to others. The latter talent is properly speaking what is called spirit; for to express the ineffable element in the state of mind implied by a certain representation and to make it universally communicable—whether the expression be in speech or painting or statuary—this requires a faculty of seizing the quickly passing play of Imagination and of unifying it in a concept (which is even on that account original and discloses a new rule that could not have been inferred from any preceding principles or examples), that can be communicated without any constraint of rules.

If after this analysis we look back to the explanation given above of what is called *genius,* we find: *first,* that it is a talent for Art, not for Science, in which clearly known rules must go beforehand and determine the procedure. *Secondly,* as an artistic talent it presupposes a definite concept of the product, as the purpose, and therefore Understanding; but it also presupposes a representation (although an indeterminate one) of the material, i.e. of the intuition, for the presentment of this concept; and, therefore, a relation between the Imagination and the Understanding. *Thirdly,* it shows itself not so much in the accomplishment of the proposed purpose in a presentment of a definite *concept,* as in the enunciation or expression of *aesthetical Ideas,* which contain abundant material for that very design; and consequently it represents the Imagination as free from all guidance of rules and yet as purposive in reference to the presentment of the given concept. Finally, in the *fourth* place, the unsought undesigned subjective purposiveness in the free accordance of the Imagination with the legality of the Understanding presupposes such a proportion and disposition of these faculties as no following of rules, whether of science or of mechanical imitation, can bring about, but which only the nature of the subject can produce.

In accordance with these suppositions genius is the exemplary originality of the natural gifts of a subject in the *free* employment of his cognitive faculties. In this way the product of a genius (as regards what is to be ascribed to genius and not to possible learning or schooling) is an example, not to be imitated (for then that which in it is genius and constitutes the spirit of the work would be lost), but to be followed, by another genius; whom it awakens to a feeling of his own originality and whom it stirs so to exercise his art in freedom from the constraint of rules, that thereby a new rule is gained for art, and thus his talent shows itself to be exemplary. But because a genius is a favourite of nature and must be regarded by us as a rare phenomenon, his example produces for other good heads a school, i.e. a methodical system of teaching according to rules, so far as these can be derived from the peculiarities of the products of his spirit. For such persons beautiful art is so far imitation, to which nature through the medium of a genius supplied the rule.

But this imitation becomes a mere *aping,* if the scholar *copies* everything down to the deformities, which the genius must have let pass only because he could not well remove them without weakening his Idea. This mental characteristic is meritorious only in the case of a genius. A certain *audacity* in expression—and in general many a departure from common rules—becomes him well, but it is in no way worthy of imitation; it always remains a fault in itself which we must seek to remove, though the genius is as it were privileged to commit it, because the inimitable rush of his spirit would suffer from over-anxious carefulness. *Mannerism* is another kind of aping, viz. of mere *peculiarity* (originality) in general; by which a man separates himself as far as possible from imitators, without however possessing the talent to be at the same time *exemplary.*— There are indeed in general two ways (*modi*) in which such a man may put together his notions of expressing himself; the one is called a *manner* (*modus aestheticus*), the other a *method* (*modus logicus*). They differ in this, that the former has no other standard than the *feeling* of unity in the presentment, but the latter follows definite *principles;* hence the former alone avails for beautiful art. But an artistic product is said to show *mannerism* only when the exposition of the artist's Idea is *founded* on its very singularity, and is not made appropriate to the Idea itself. The ostentatious (*précieux*), contorted, and affected [manner, adopted] to differentiate oneself from ordinary persons (though devoid of spirit) is like the behaviour of a man of whom we say, that he hears himself talk, or who stands and moves about as if he were on a stage in order to be stared at; this always betrays a bungler.

§ 50. *Of the combination of Taste with Genius in the products of beautiful Art*

To ask whether it is more important for the things of beautiful art that Genius or Taste should be displayed, is the same as to ask whether in it more depends on Imagination or on Judgement. Now, since in respect of the first an art is rather said to be *full of spirit,* but only deserves to be called a *beautiful* art on account of the second; this latter is at least, as its indispensable condition (*conditio sine qua non*), the most important thing to which one has to look in the judging of art as beautiful art. Abundance and originality of Ideas are less necessary to beauty than the accordance of the Imagination in its freedom with the conformity to law of the Understanding. For all the abundance of the former produces in lawless freedom nothing but nonsense; on the other hand, the Judgement is the faculty by which it is adjusted to the Understanding.

Taste, like the Judgement in general, is the discipline (or training) of Genius; it clips its wings closely, and makes it cultured and polished; but, at the same time, it gives guidance as to where and how far it may extend itself, if it is to remain purposive. And while it brings clearness and order into the multitude of the thoughts, it makes the Ideas susceptible of being permanently and, at the same time, universally assented to, and capable of being followed by others, and of an ever-progressive culture. If, then, in the conflict of these two properties in a product something must be sacrificed, it should be rather on the side of genius; and the Judgement, which in the things of beautiful art gives its decision from its own proper principles, will rather sacrifice the freedom and wealth of the Imagination than permit anything prejudicial to the Understanding.

For beautiful art, therefore, *Imagination, Understanding, Spirit,* and *Taste are requisite.*[1] . . . [B. 206-228]

II. DIALECTIC OF THE AESTHETICAL JUDGEMENT . . . [B. 229-30]

[I. The Antinomy of Taste and Its Solution.]

§ 56. *Representation of the antinomy of Taste*

The first commonplace of taste is contained in the proposition, with which every tasteless person proposes to avoid blame: *every one has his own taste.* That is as much as to say that the determining ground of this judgement is merely subjective (gratification or grief), and that the judgement has no right to the necessary assent of others.

The second commonplace invoked even by those who admit for judgements of taste the right to speak with

[1] [N. 206.]

validity for every one is: *there is no disputing about taste.* That is as much as to say that the determining ground of a judgement of taste may indeed be objective, but that it cannot be reduced to definite concepts, and that consequently about the judgement itself nothing can be *decided* by proofs, although much may rightly be *contested.* For *contesting* [quarrelling] and *disputing* [controversy] are doubtless the same in this, that by means of the mutual opposition of judgements they seek to produce their accordance; but different in that the latter hopes to bring this about according to definite concepts as determining grounds, and consequently assumes *objective concepts* as grounds of the judgement. But where this is regarded as impracticable, controversy is regarded as alike impracticable.

We easily see that between these two commonplaces there is a proposition wanting, which, though it has not passed into a proverb, is yet familiar to every one, viz. *there may be a quarrel about taste* (although there can be no controversy). But this proposition involves the contradictory of the former one. For wherever quarrelling is permissible, there must be a hope of mutual reconciliation; and consequently we can count on grounds of our judgement that have not merely private validity, and therefore are not merely subjective. And to this the proposition, *every one has his own taste,* is directly opposed.

There emerges therefore in respect of the principle of taste the following Antinomy:—

(1) *Thesis.* The judgement of taste is not based upon concepts; for otherwise it would admit of controversy (would be determinable by proofs).

(2) *Antithesis.* The judgement of taste is based on concepts; for otherwise, despite its diversity, we could

not quarrel about it (we could not claim for our judgement the necessary assent of others).

§ 57. *Solution of the antinomy of Taste*

There is no possibility of removing the conflict between these principles that underlie every judgement of taste (which are nothing else than the two peculiarities of the judgement of taste exhibited above in the Analytic), except by showing that the concept to which we refer the Object in this kind of judgement is not taken in the same sense in both maxims of the aesthetical Judgement. This twofold sense or twofold point of view is necessary to our transcendental Judgement; but also the illusion which arises from the confusion of one with the other is natural and unavoidable.

The judgement of taste must refer to some concept; otherwise it could make absolutely no claim to be necessarily valid for every one. But it is not therefore capable of being proved *from* a concept; because a concept may be either determinable or in itself undetermined and undeterminable. The concepts of the Understanding are of the former kind; they are determinable through predicates of sensible intuition which can correspond to them. But the transcendental rational concept of the supersensible, which lies at the basis of all sensible intuition, is of the latter kind, and therefore cannot be theoretically determined further.

Now the judgement of taste is applied to objects of Sense, but not with a view of determining a *concept* of them for the Understanding; for it is not a cognitive judgement. It is thus only a private judgement, in which a singular representation intuitively perceived is referred to the feeling of pleasure; and so far would be limited as regards its validity to the individual judging. The object is *for me* an object of satisfaction; by others it may be regarded quite differently—every one has his own taste.

Nevertheless there is undoubtedly contained in the judgement of taste a wider reference of the representation of the Object (as well as of the subject), whereon we base an extension of judgements of this kind as necessary for every one. At the basis of this there must necessarily be a concept somewhere; though a concept which cannot be determined through intuition. But through a concept of this sort we know nothing, and consequently it can *supply no proof* for the judgement of taste. Such a concept is the mere pure rational concept of the supersensible which underlies the object (and also the subject judging it), regarded as an Object of sense and thus as phenomenon. For if we do not admit such a reference, the claim of the judgement of taste to universal validity would not hold good. If the concept on which it is based were only a mere confused concept of the Understanding, like that of perfection, with which we could bring the sensible intuition of the Beautiful into correspondence, it would be at least possible in itself to base the judgement of taste on proofs; which contradicts the thesis.

But all contradiction disappears if I say: the judgement of taste is based on a concept (viz. the concept of the general ground of the subjective purposiveness of nature for the Judgement); from which, however, nothing can be known and proved in respect of the Object, because it is in itself undeterminable and useless for knowledge. Yet at the same time and on that very account the judgement has validity for every one (though of course for each only as a singular judgement immediately accompanying his intuition); because its determining ground lies perhaps in the concept of that which may be regarded as the supersensible substrate of humanity.

The solution of an antinomy only depends on the possibility of showing that two apparently contradictory propositions do not contradict one another in fact, but that they may be consistent; although the explanation of the possibility of their concept may transcend our cognitive faculties. That this illusion is natural and unavoidable by human Reason, and also why it is so, and remains so, although it ceases to deceive after the analysis of the apparent contradiction, may be thus explained.

In the two contradictory judgements we take the concept, on which the universal validity of a judgement must be based, in the same sense; and yet we apply to it two opposite predicates. In the Thesis we mean that the judgement of taste is not based upon *determinate* concepts; and in the Antithesis that the judgement of taste is based upon a concept, but an *indeterminate* one (viz. of the supersensible substrate of phenomena). Between these two there is no contradiction.

We can do nothing more than remove this conflict between the claims and counter-claims of taste. It is absolutely impossible to give a definite objective principle of taste, in accordance with which its judgements could be derived, examined, and established; for then the judgement would not be one of taste at all. The subjective principle, viz. the indefinite Idea of the supersensible in us, can only be put forward as the sole key to the puzzle of this faculty whose sources are hidden from us: it can be made no further intelligible.

The proper concept of taste, that is of a merely reflective aesthetical Judgement, lies at the basis of the antinomy here exhibited and adjusted. Thus the two apparently contradictory principles are reconciled—*both can be true;* which is sufficient. . . . [B. 234-5]

Hence we see that the removal of the antinomy of the aesthetical Judgement takes a course similar to that pursued by the Critique in the solution of the antinomies of pure theoretical Reason. And thus here, as also in the Critique of practical Reason, the antinomies force us against our will to look beyond the sensible and to seek in the supersensible the point of union for all our *a priori* faculties; because no other expedient is left to make our Reason harmonious with itself.

Remark [*on Genius.*]

. . . [B. 235-8] We can consequently explain *genius* as the faculty of *aesthetical Ideas;* by which at the same time is shown the reason why in the products of genius it is the nature (of the subject) and not a premeditated purpose that gives the rule to the art (of the production of the beautiful). For since the beautiful must not be judged by concepts, but by the purposive attuning of the Imagination to agreement with the faculty of concepts in general, it cannot be rule and precept which can serve as the subjective standard of that aesthetical but unconditioned purposiveness in beautiful art, that can rightly claim to please every one. It can only be that in the subject which is nature and cannot be brought under rules or concepts, i.e. the supersensible substrate of all his faculties (to which no concept of the Understanding extends), and consequently that with respect to which it is the final purpose given by the intelligible [part] of our nature to harmonise all our cognitive faculties. Thus alone is it possible that there should be *a priori* at the basis of this purposiveness, for which we can prescribe no objective principle, a principle subjective and yet of universal validity. . . . [B. 239-48]

[II. Relation of Beauty to Goodness.]

§ 42. *Of the intellectual interest in the Beautiful*

With the best intentions those persons who refer all activities, to which their inner natural dispositions impel men, to the final purpose of humanity, viz. the morally good, have regarded the taking an interest in the Beautiful in general as a mark of good moral character. But it is not without reason that they have been contradicted by others who rely on experience; for this shows that connoisseurs in taste, not only often but generally, are given up to idle, capricious, and mischievous passions, and that they could perhaps make less claim than others to any pre-eminent attachment to moral principles. Thus it would seem that the feeling for the Beautiful is not only (as actually is the case) specifically different from the Moral feeling; but that the interest which can be bound up with it is hardly compatible with moral interest, and certainly has no inner affinity therewith.

Now I admit at once that the interest in the *Beautiful of Art* (under which I include the artificial use of natural beauties for adornment and so for vanity) furnishes no proof whatever of a disposition attached to the morally good or even inclined thereto. But on the other hand, I maintain that to take an *immediate interest* in the Beauty of Nature (not merely to have taste in judging it) is always a mark of a good soul; and that when this interest is habitual it at least indicates a frame of mind favourable to the moral feeling, if it is voluntarily bound up with the *contemplation of nature.* It is to be remembered, however, that I here speak strictly of the beautiful *forms* of Nature, and I set aside the *charms*, that she is wont to combine so abundantly with them; because, though the interest in the latter is indeed immediate, it is only empirical.

He who by himself (and without any design of communicating his observations to others) regards the beautiful figure of a wild flower, a bird, an insect, etc., with admiration and love—who would not willingly miss it in Nature, although it may bring him some hurt, who still less wants any advantage from it—*he* takes an immediate and also an intellectual interest in the beauty of Nature: i.e. it is not merely the form of the product of nature which pleases him, but its very presence pleases him, the charms of sense having no share in this pleasure and no purpose whatever being combined with it.

But it is noteworthy that if we secretly deceived this lover of the beautiful by planting in the ground artificial flowers (which can be manufactured exactly like natural ones), or by placing artificially carved birds on the boughs of trees, and he discovered the deceit, the immediate interest that he previously took in them would disappear at once; though, perhaps, a different interest, viz. the interest of vanity in adorning his chamber with them for the eyes of others, would take its place. This thought then must accompany our intuition and reflection on beauty, viz. that nature has produced it; and on this alone is based the immediate interest that we take in it. Otherwise, there remains a mere judgement of taste, either devoid of all interest, or bound up with a mediate interest, viz. in that it has reference to society; which latter [interest] furnishes no certain indications of a morally good disposition.

This superiority of natural to artificial beauty in that it alone arouses an immediate interest, although as regards form the first may be surpassed by the second, harmonises with the refined and well-grounded habit of thought of all men who have cultivated their moral feeling. If a man who has taste enough to judge of the products of beautiful Art with the greatest accuracy and refinement willingly leaves a chamber where are to be found those beauties that minister to vanity or to any social joys, and turns to the beautiful in Nature in order to find, as it were, delight for his spirit in a train of thought that he can never completely evolve, we will regard this choice of his with veneration, and attribute to him a beautiful soul, to which no connoisseur or lover [of Art] can lay claim on account of the interest he takes in his [artistic] objects.—What now is the difference in our estimation of these two different kinds of Objects, which in the judgement of mere taste it is hard to compare in point of superiority?

We have a faculty of mere aesthetical Judgement by which we judge forms without the aid of concepts, and find a satisfaction in this mere act of judgement; this we make into a rule for every one, without this judgement either being based on or producing any interest.—On the other hand, we have also a faculty of intellectual Judgement which determines an *a priori* satisfaction for the mere forms of practical maxims (so far as they are in themselves qualified for universal legislation); this we make into a law for every one, without our judgement being based on any interest whatever, *though in this case it produces such an interest.* The pleasure or pain in the former judgement is called that of taste, in the latter, that of moral feeling.

But it also interests Reason that the Ideas (for which in moral feeling it arouses an immediate interest) should have objective reality; i.e. that nature should at least show a trace or give an indication that it contains in itself some ground for assuming a regular agreement of its products with our entirely disinterested satisfaction (which we recognise *a priori* as a law for every one, without being able to base it upon proofs). Hence Reason must take an interest in every expression on the part of nature of an agreement of this kind. Consequently, the mind cannot ponder upon the beauty of *Nature* without finding itself at the same time interested therein. But this interest is akin to moral, and he who takes such an interest in the beauties of nature can do so only in so far as he previously has firmly established his interest in the morally good. If, therefore, the beauty of Nature interests a man immediately we have reason for attributing to him, at least, a basis for a good moral disposition. . . . [B. 180-2]

§ 59. *Of Beauty as the symbol of Morality*

. . . [B. 248-9] All intuitions, which we supply to concepts *a priori*, are . . . either *schemata* or *symbols*, of which the former contain direct, the latter indirect, presentations of the concept. The former do this demonstratively; the latter by means of an analogy (for which we avail ourselves even of empirical intuitions) in which the Judgement exercises a double function; first applying the concept to the object of a sensible intuition, and then applying the mere rule of the reflection made upon that intuition to a quite different object of which the first is only the symbol. Thus a monarchical state is represented by a living body, if it is governed by national laws, and by a mere machine (like a hand-mill) if governed by an individual absolute will; but in both cases only *symbolically*. For between a despotic state and a hand-mill there is, to be sure, no similarity; but there is a similarity in the rules according to which we reflect upon these two things and their causality. . . . [B. 250]

Now I say the Beautiful is the symbol of the morally Good, and that it is only in this respect (a reference which is natural to every man and which every man postulates in others as a duty) that it gives pleasure with a claim for the agreement of every one else. By this the mind is made conscious of a certain ennoblement and elevation above the mere sensibility to pleasure received through sense, and the worth of others is estimated in accordance with a like maxim of their Judgement. That is the *intelligible,* to which . . . Taste looks; with which our higher cognitive faculties are in accord; and without which a downright contradiction would arise between their nature and the claims made by taste. In this faculty the Judgement does not see itself, as in empirical judging, subjected to a heteronomy of empirical laws; it gives the law to itself in respect of the objects of so pure a satisfaction, just as the Reason does in respect of the faculty of desire. Hence, both on account of this inner possibility in the subject and of the external possibility of a nature that agrees with it, it finds itself to be referred to something within the subject as well as without him, something which is neither nature nor freedom, but which yet is connected with the supersensible ground of the latter. In this supersensible ground, therefore, the theoretical faculty is bound together in unity with the practical, in a way which though common is yet unknown. We shall indicate some points of this analogy, while at the same time we shall note the differences.

(1) The beautiful pleases *immediately* (but only in reflective intuition, not, like morality, in its concept). (2) It pleases *apart from any interest* (the morally good is indeed necessarily bound up with an interest,

though not with one which precedes the judgement upon the satisfaction, but with one which is first of all produced by it). (3) The *freedom* of the Imagination (and therefore of the sensibility of our faculty) is represented in judging the beautiful as harmonious with the conformity to law of the Understanding (in the moral judgement the freedom of the will is thought as the harmony of the latter with itself according to universal laws of Reason). (4) The subjective principle in judging the beautiful is represented as *universal,* i.e. as valid for every man, though not cognisable through any universal concept. (The objective principle of morality is also expounded as universal, i.e. for every subject and for every action of the same subject, and thus as cognisable by means of a universal concept). Hence the moral judgement is not only susceptible of definite constitutive principles, but is possible *only* by grounding its maxims on these in their universality. . . . [B. 252]

§ 60. *Of the method of Taste*

. . . [B. 253-4] The propaedeutic to all beautiful art, regarded in the highest degree of its perfection, seems to lie, not in precepts, but in the culture of the mental powers by means of those elements of knowledge called *humaniora,* probably because *humanity* on the one side indicates the universal *feeling of sympathy,* and on the other the faculty of being able to *communicate* universally our inmost [feelings]. For these properties taken together constitute the characteristic social spirit of humanity by which it is distinguished from the limitations of animal life. The age and peoples, in which the impulse towards a *law-abiding* social life, by which a people becomes a permanent community, contended with the great difficulties presented by the difficult problem of uniting freedom (and therefore equality also) with compulsion (rather of respect and submission from a sense of duty than of fear)—such an age and such a people naturally first found out the art of reciprocal communication of Ideas between the cultivated and uncultivated classes and thus discovered how to harmonise the large-mindedness and refinement of the former with the natural simplicity and originality of the latter. In this way they first found that mean between the higher culture and simple nature which furnishes that true standard for taste as a sense common to all men which no universal rules can supply.

With difficulty will a later age dispense with those models, because it will be always farther from nature; and in fine, without having permanent examples before it, a concept will hardly be possible, in one and the same people, of the happy union of the law-abiding constraint of the highest culture with the force and truth of free nature which feels its own proper worth.

Now taste is at bottom a faculty for judging of the sensible illustration of moral Ideas (by means of a certain analogy involved in our reflection upon both these); and it is from this faculty also and from the greater susceptibility grounded thereon for the feeling arising from the latter (called moral feeling), that the pleasure is derived which taste regards as valid for mankind in general and not merely for the private feeling of each. Hence it appears plain that the true propaedeutic for the foundation of taste is the development of moral Ideas and the culture of the moral feeling; because it is only when sensibility is brought into agreement with this that genuine taste can assume a definite invariable form.

CRITIQUE OF THE TELEOLOGICAL JUDGEMENT

as contained in

Part II of the *Critique of Judgement*

I. INTRODUCTION [1]

IX. *Of the Connexion of the Legislation of Understanding with that of Reason by means of the Judgement* [2]

The Understanding legislates *a priori* for nature as an Object of sense—for a theoretical knowledge of it in a possible experience. Reason legislates *a priori* for freedom and its peculiar causality; as the supersensible in the subject, for an unconditioned practical knowledge. The realm of the natural concept under the one legislation and that of the concept of freedom under the other are entirely removed from all mutual influence which they might have on one another (each according to its fundamental laws) by the great gulf that separates the supersensible from phenomena. The concept of freedom determines nothing in respect of the theoretical cognition of nature; and the natural concept determines nothing in respect of the practical laws of freedom. So far then it is not possible to throw a bridge from the one realm to the other. But although

[1] [Sections I, III and VIII have been omitted. Part of Sec. VII appears above pp. 413-4]

[2] [B. 39 ff.]

the determining grounds of causality according to the concept of freedom (and the practical rules which it contains) are not resident in nature, and the sensible cannot determine the supersensible in the subject, yet this is possible conversely (not, to be sure, in respect of the cognition of nature, but as regards the effects of the supersensible upon the sensible). This in fact is involved in the concept of a causality through freedom, the *effect* of which is to take place in the world according to its formal laws. The word *cause,* of course, when used of the supersensible only signifies the *ground* which determines the causality of natural things to an effect in accordance with their proper natural laws, although harmoniously with the formal principle of the laws of Reason. Although the possibility of this cannot be comprehended, yet the objection of a contradiction alleged to be found in it can be sufficiently answered.[1]— The effect in accordance with the concept of freedom is the final purpose which (or its phenomenon in the world of sense) ought to exist; and the condition of the possibility of this is presupposed in nature (in the nature of the subject as a sensible being, that is, as man). The

[1] One of the various pretended contradictions in this whole distinction of the causality of nature from that of freedom is this. It is objected that if I speak of *obstacles* which nature opposes to causality according to (moral) laws of freedom or of the *assistance* it affords, I am admitting an *influence* of the former upon the latter. But if we try to understand what has been said, this misinterpretation is very easy to avoid. The opposition or assistance is not between nature and freedom, but between the former as phenomenon and the *effects* of the latter as phenomena in the world of sense. The causality of freedom itself (of pure and practical Reason) is the causality of a natural cause subordinated to freedom i.e. of the subject considered as man and therefore as phenomenon). The intelligible, which is thought under freedom, contains the ground of the *determination* of this [natural cause] in a way not explicable any further (just as that intelligible does which constitutes the supersensible substrate of nature).

Judgement presupposes this *a priori* and without reference to the practical; and thus furnishes the mediating concept between the concepts of nature and that of freedom. It makes possible the transition from the conformity to law in accordance with the former to the final purpose in accordance with the latter, and this by the concept of a *purposiveness* of nature. For thus is cognised the possibility of the final purpose which alone can be actualised in nature in harmony with its laws.

The Understanding by the possibility of its *a priori* laws for nature, gives a proof that nature is only cognised by us as phenomenon; and implies at the same time that it has a supersensible substrate, though it leaves this quite *undetermined.* The Judgement by its *a priori* principle for the judging of nature according to its possible particular laws, makes the supersensible substrate (both in us and without us) *determinable by means of the intellectual faculty.* But the Reason by its practical *a priori* law *determines* it; and thus the Judgement makes possible the transition from the realm of the concept of nature to that of the concept of freedom.

As regards the faculties of the soul in general, in their higher aspect, as containing an antonomy; the Understanding is that which contains the *constitutive* principles *a priori* for the *cognitive faculty* (the theoretical cognition of nature). For the *feeling of pleasure and pain* there is the Judgement, independently of concepts and sensations which relate to the determination of the faculty of desire and can thus be immediately practical. For the *faculty of desire* there is the Reason which is practical without the mediation of any pleasure whatever. It determines for the faculty of desire, as a superior faculty, the final purpose which carries with it the pure intellectual satisfaction in the Object. . . .

[B. 41-2] The following table may facilitate the review of all the higher faculties according to their systematic unity.[1]

	All the faculties of the mind	
Cognitive faculties.	Feeling of pleasure and pain.	Faculties of desire.
	Cognitive faculties	
Understanding.	Judgement.	Reason.
	A priori principles	
Conformity to law.	Purposiveness.	Final purpose.
	Application to	
Nature.	Art.	Freedom.

IV. *Of Judgement as a Faculty legislating a priori.*[2]

Judgement in general is the faculty of thinking the particular as contained under the Universal. If the universal (the rule, the principle, the law) be given, the Judgement which subsumes the particular under it (even if, as transcendental Judgement, it furnishes *a priori* the conditions in conformity with which subsumption under that universal is alone possible) is *determinant*. But if only the particular be given for which the universal has to be found, the Judgement is merely *reflective*.

The determinant Judgement only subsumes under universal transcendental laws given by the Understanding; the law is marked out for it, *a priori*, and it has therefore no need to seek a law for itself in order to be able to subordinate the particular in nature to the universal.— But the forms of nature are so manifold, and

[1] [Note, B. 42.]
[2] [B. 17 ff.]

there are so many modifications of the universal transcendental natural concepts left undetermined by the laws given, *a priori,* by the pure Understanding,—because these only concern the possibility of a nature in general (as an object of sense),—that there must be laws for these [forms] also. These, as empirical, may be contingent from the point of view of *our* Understanding, and yet, if they are to be called laws (as the concept of a nature requires), they must be regarded as necessary in virtue of a principle of the unity of the manifold, though it be unknown to us.— The reflective Judgement, which is obliged to ascend from the particular in nature to the universal, requires on that account a principle that it cannot borrow from experience, because its function is to establish the unity of all empirical principles under higher ones, and hence to establish the possibility of their systematic subordination. Such a transcendental principle, then, the reflective Judgement can only give as a law from and to itself. It cannot derive it from outside (because then it would be the determinant Judgement); nor can it prescribe it to nature, because reflection upon the laws of nature adjusts itself by nature, and not nature by the conditions according to which we attempt to arrive at a concept of it which is quite contingent in respect of these.

This principle can be no other than the following: As universal laws of nature have their ground in our Understanding, which prescribes them to nature (although only according to the universal concept of it as nature); so particular empirical laws, in respect of what is in them left undetermined by these universal laws, must be considered in accordance with such a unity as they would have if an Understanding (although not our Understanding) had furnished them to our cognitive faculties, so as to make possible a system of experience, according to particular laws of nature. Not as if, in this way, such an Understanding must be assumed as actual (for it is only our reflective Judgement to which this Idea serves as a principle—for reflecting, not for determining); but this faculty thus gives a law only to itself and not to nature.

Now the concept of an Object, so far as it contains the ground of the actuality of this Object, is the *purpose*; and the agreement of a thing with that constitution of things, which is only possible according to purposes, is called the *purposiveness* of its form. Thus the principle of Judgement, in respect of the form of things of nature under empirical laws generally, is the *purposiveness of nature* in its manifoldness. That is, nature is represented by means of this concept, as if an Understanding contained the ground of the unity of the manifold of its empirical laws.

The purposiveness of nature is therefore a particular concept, *a priori*, which has its origin solely in the reflective Judgement. For we cannot ascribe to natural products anything like a reference of nature in them to purposes; we can only use this concept to reflect upon such products in respect of the connexion of phenomena which is given in nature according to empirical laws. This concept is also quite different from practical purposiveness (in human art or in morals), though it is certainly thought according to the analogy of these last.

V. *The Principle of the formal Purposiveness of Nature is a Transcendental Principle of Judgement.*[1]

. . . [B. 20-1] That the concept of a purposiveness of nature belongs to transcendental principles can be

[1] [B. 20 ff.]

sufficiently seen from the maxims of the Judgement, which lie at the basis of the investigation of nature *a priori,* and yet do not go further than the possibility of experience, and consequently of the cognition of nature—not indeed nature in general, but nature as determined through a variety of particular laws. These maxims present themselves in the course of this science often enough, though in a scattered way, as sentences of metaphysical wisdom, whose necessity we cannot demonstrate from concepts. "Nature takes the shortest way *(lex parsimoniae);* at the same time it makes no leaps, either in the course of its changes or in the juxtaposition of specifically different forms *(lex continui in natura);* its great variety in empirical laws is yet unity under a few principles *(principia praeter necessitatem non sunt multiplicanda),*" etc.

If we propose to set forth the origin of these fundamental propositions and try to do so by the psychological method, we violate their sense. For they do not tell us what happens, i.e. by what rule our cognitive powers actually operate, and how we judge, but how we ought to judge; and this logical objective necessity does not emerge if the principles are merely empirical. Hence that purposiveness of nature for our cognitive faculties and their use, which is plainly apparent from them, is a transcendental principle of judgements, and needs therefore also a Transcendental Deduction, by means of which the ground for so judging must be sought in the sources of cognition *a priori.*

We find in the grounds of the possibility of an experience in the very first place something necessary, viz. the universal laws without which nature in general (as an object of sense) cannot be thought; and these rest upon the Categories, applied to the formal conditions of all intuition possible for us, so far as it is also given *a priori*. Now under these laws the Judgement is determinant, for it has nothing to do but to subsume under given laws. For example, the Understanding says that every change has its cause (universal law of nature); the transcendental Judgement has nothing further to do than to supply *a priori* the condition of subsumption under the concept of the Understanding placed before it, i.e. the succession [in time] of the determinations of one and the same thing. For nature in general (as an object of possible experience) that law is cognised as absolutely necessary.— But now the objects of empirical cognition are determined in many other ways than by that formal time-condition, or, at least as far as we can judge *a priori*, are determinable. . . . [B. 23]

We must therefore think in nature, in respect of its merely empirical laws, a possibility of infinitely various empirical laws, which are, as far as our insight goes, contingent (cannot be cognised *a priori*), and in respect of which we judge nature, according to empirical laws and the possibility of the unity of experience (as a system according to empirical laws), to be contingent. But such a unity must be necessarily presupposed and assumed, for otherwise there would be no thoroughgoing connexion of empirical cognitions in a whole of experience. The universal laws of nature no doubt furnish such a connexion of things according to their kind as things of nature in general, but not specifically, as such particular beings of nature. Hence the Judgement must assume for its special use this principle *a priori*, that what in the particular (empirical) laws of nature is from the human point of view contingent, yet contains a unity of law in the combination of its manifold into an experience possible in itself—a unity not indeed to be fathomed by us, but yet thinkable. Consequently as the unity of law in a combination, which we cognise as contingent in itself, although in conformity with a necessary design (a need) of Understanding, is represented as the purposiveness of Objects (here of nature); so must the Judgement, which in respect of things under possible (not yet discovered) empirical laws is merely reflection, think of nature in respect of the latter according to a *principle of purposiveness* for our cognitive faculty, which then is expressed in the above maxims of the Judgement. This transcendental concept of a purposiveness of nature is neither a natural concept nor a concept of freedom, because it ascribes nothing to the Object (of nature), but only represents the peculiar way in which we must proceed in reflection upon the objects of nature in reference to a thoroughly connected experience, and is consequently a subjective principle (maxim) of the Judgement. Hence, as if it were a lucky chance favouring our design, we are rejoiced (properly speaking, relieved of a want), if we meet with such systematic unity under merely empirical laws; although we must necessarily assume that there is such a unity without our comprehending it or being able to prove it.

In order to convince ourselves of the correctness of this Deduction of the concept before us, and the necessity of assuming it as a transcendental principle of cognition, just consider the magnitude of the problem. The problem, which lies *a priori* in our Understanding, is to make a connected experience out of given perceptions of a nature containing at all events an infinite variety of empirical laws. The Understanding is, no doubt, in possession *a priori* of universal laws of nature, without which nature could not be an object of experience; but it needs in addition a certain order of nature in its particular rules, which can only be empirically known and which are, as regards the Understanding, contingent. These rules, without which we could not proceed from the universal analogy of a possible experience in general to the particular, must be thought by it as laws (i.e. as necessary), for otherwise they would not constitute an order of nature although their necessity can never be cognised or comprehended by it. Although, therefore, the Understanding can determine nothing *a priori* in respect of Objects, it must, in order to trace out these empirical so-called laws, place at the basis of all reflection upon Objects an *a priori* principle, viz. that a cognisable order of nature is possible in accordance with these laws. . . . [B. 25-6]

The Judgement has therefore also in itself a principle *a priori* of the possibility of nature, but only in a subjective aspect; by which it prescribes, not to nature (autonomy), but to itself (heautonomy) a law for its reflection upon nature. This we might call the *law of the specification of nature* in respect of its empirical laws. The Judgement does not cognise this *a priori* in nature, but assumes it on behalf of a natural order cognisable by our Understanding in the division which it makes of the universal laws of nature when it wishes to subordinate to these the variety of particular laws. If then we say that nature specifies its universal laws according to the principles of purposiveness for our cognitive faculty, i.e. in accordance with the necessary business of the human Understanding of finding the universal for the particular which perception offers it, and again of finding connexion for the diverse (which however is a universal for each species) in the unity of a principle,—we thus neither prescribe to nature a law, nor do we learn one from it by observation (although such a principle may be confirmed by this means). For it is not a principle of the determinant but merely of the reflective Judgement. We only require that, be nature disposed as it may as regards its universal laws, investigation into its empirical laws may be carried on in accordance with that principle and the maxims founded thereon, because it is only so far as that holds that we can make any progress with the use of our Understanding in experience, or gain knowledge.

VI. *Of the Combination of the Feeling of Pleasure with the Concept of the Purposiveness of Nature.*[1]

. . . [B. 27-8] So far as we can see, it is contingent that the order of nature according to its particular laws, in all its variety and heterogeneity possibly at least transcending our comprehension, should be actually conformable to these [laws]. The discovery of this [order] is the business of the Understanding which is designedly borne towards a necessary purpose, viz. the bringing of unity of principles into nature, which purpose then the Judgement must ascribe to nature, because the Understanding cannot here prescribe any law to it.

The attainment of that design is bound up with the feeling of pleasure, and since the condition of this attainment is a representation *a priori,*—as here a principle for the reflective Judgement in general,—therefore the feeling of pleasure is determined by a ground *a priori* and valid for every man, and that merely by the reference of the Object to the cognitive faculty, the concept of purposiveness here not having the least reference to the faculty of desire. It is thus quite distinguished from all practical purposiveness of nature.

In fact, although from the agreement of perceptions with laws in accordance with universal natural concepts

[1] [B. 27 ff.]

(the categories), we do not and cannot find in ourselves the slightest effect upon the feeling of pleasure, because the Understanding necessarily proceeds according to its nature without any design; yet, on the other hand, the discovery that two or more empirical heterogeneous laws of nature may be combined under one principle comprehending them both, is the ground of a very marked pleasure, often even of an admiration, which does not cease, though we may be already quite familiar with the objects of it. We no longer find, it is true, any marked pleasure in the comprehensibility of nature and in the unity of its divisions into genera and species, whereby are possible all empirical concepts, through which we cognise it according to its particular laws. But this pleasure has certainly been present at one time, and it is only because the commonest experience would be impossible without it that it is gradually confounded with mere cognition and no longer arrests particular attention. There is then something in our judgements upon nature which makes us attentive to its purposiveness for our Understanding—an endeavour to bring, where possible, its dissimilar laws under higher ones, though still always empirical—and thus, if successful, makes us feel pleasure in that harmony of these with our cognitive faculty, which harmony we regard as merely contingent. On the other hand, a representation of nature would altogether displease, by which it should be foretold to us that in the smallest investigation beyond the commonest experience we should meet with a heterogeneity of its laws, which would make the union of its particular laws under universal empirical laws impossible for our Understanding. For this would contradict the principle of the subjectively-purposive specification of nature in its genera, and also of our reflective Judgement in respect of such principle.

This presupposition of the Judgement is, however, at the same time so indeterminate as to how far that ideal purposiveness of nature for our cognitive faculty should be extended, that if we were told that a deeper or wider knowledge of nature derived from observation must lead at last to a variety of laws, which no human Understanding could reduce to a principle, we should at once acquiesce. But still we more gladly listen to one who offers hope that the more we know nature internally, and can compare it with external members now unknown to us, the more simple shall we find it in its principles, and that the further our experience reaches the more uniform shall we find it amid the apparent heterogeneity of its empirical laws. For it is a mandate of our Judgement to proceed according to the principle of the harmony of nature with our cognitive faculty so far as that reaches, without deciding (because it is not the determinant Judgement which gives us this rule) whether or not it is bounded anywhere. For although in respect of the rational use of our cognitive faculty we can determine such bounds, this is not possible in the empirical field.

II. ANALYTIC OF THE TELEOLOGICAL JUDGEMENT

§ 61. *Of the objective purposiveness of Nature* [1]

. . . [B. 259] That the things of nature serve one another as means to purposes, and that their possibility is only completely intelligible through this kind of causality—for this we have absolutely no ground in the universal Idea of nature, as the complex of the objects of sense. In the above-mentioned case, the represen-

[1] [Cf. B. 259 ff.]

tation of things, because it is something in ourselves, can be quite well thought *a priori* as suitable and useful for the internally purposive determination of our cognitive faculties; but that purposes, which neither are our own nor belong to nature (for we do not regard nature as an intelligent being), could or should constitute a particular kind of causality, at least a quite special conformity to law—this we have absolutely no *a priori* reason for presuming. Yet more, experience itself cannot prove to us the actuality of this; there must then have preceded a rationalising subtlety which only sportively introduces the concept of purpose into the nature of things, but which does not derive it from Objects or from their empirical cognition. To this latter it is of more service to make nature comprehensible according to analogy with the subjective ground of the connexion of our representations, than to cognise it from objective grounds.

Further, objective purposiveness, as a principle of the possibility of things of nature, is so far removed from *necessary* connexion with the concept of nature, that it is much oftener precisely that upon which one relies to prove the contingency of nature and of its form. When, e.g. we adduce the structure of a bird, the hollowness of its bones, the disposition of its wings for motion and of its tail for steering, etc., we say that all this is contingent in the highest degree according to the mere *nexus effectivus* of nature, without calling in the aid of a particular kind of causality, namely that of purpose (*nexus finalis*). In other words, nature, considered as mere mechanism, could have produced its forms in a thousand other ways without stumbling upon the unity which is in accordance with such a principle. It is not in the concept of nature but quite apart from it that we can hope to find the least ground *a priori* for this.

Nevertheless the teleological act of judgement is rightly brought to bear, at least problematically, upon the investigation of nature; but only in order to bring it under principles of observation and inquiry according to the *analogy* with the causality of purpose, without any pretence to *explain* it thereby. It belongs therefore to the reflective and not to the determinant judgement. The concept of combinations and forms of nature in accordance with purposes is then at least *one principle more* for bringing its phenomena under rules where the laws of simply mechanical causality do not suffice. For we bring in a teleological ground, where we attribute causality in respect of an Object to the concept of an Object, as if it were to be found in nature (not in ourselves); or rather when we represent to ourselves the possibility of the Object after the analogy of that causality which we experience in ourselves, and consequently think nature technically as through a special faculty. If we did not ascribe to it such a method of action, its causality would have to be represented as blind mechanism. If, on the contrary, we supply to nature causes acting *designedly,* and consequently place at its basis teleology, not merely as a *regulative* principle for the mere *judging* of phenomena, to which nature can be thought as subject in its particular laws, but as a *constitutive* principle of the *derivation* of its products from their causes; then would the concept of a natural purpose no longer belong to the reflective but to the determinant Judgement. Then, in fact, it would not belong specially to the Judgement (like the concept of beauty regarded as formal subjective purposiveness), but as a rational concept it would introduce into natural science a new causality, which we only borrow from ourselves and ascribe to other beings, without meaning to assume them to be of the same kind with ourselves. . . . [B. 262-8]

§ 63. *Of the relative, as distinguished from the inner, purposiveness of Nature*

Experience leads our Judgement to the concept of an objective and material purposiveness, i.e. to the concept of a purpose of nature, only when [1] we have to judge of a relation of cause to effect which we find ourselves able to apprehend as legitimate only by presupposing the Idea of the effect of the causality of the cause as the fundamental condition, in the cause, of the possibility of the effect. This can take place in two ways. We may regard the effect directly as an art product, or only as material for the art of other possible natural beings; in other words, either as a purpose or as a means towards the purposive employment of other causes. This latter purposiveness is called utility (for man) or mere advantage (for other creatures), and is merely relative; while the former is an inner purposiveness of the natural being. . . . [B. 268-9]

To give an example of the advantageousness of certain natural things as means for other creatures (if we suppose them to be means), no soil is more suitable to pine trees than a sandy soil. Now the deep sea, before it withdrew from the land, left behind large tracts of sand in our northern regions, so that on this soil, so unfavourable for all cultivation, widely extended pine forests were enabled to grow, for the unreasoning destruction of which we frequently blame our ancestors. We may ask if this original deposit of tracts of sand was a purpose of nature for the benefit of the possible pine forests? So much is clear, that if we regard this

[1] [Note, B. 268.]

as a purpose of nature, we must also regard the sand as a relative purpose, in reference to which the ocean strand and its withdrawal were means: for in the series of the mutually subordinated members of a purposive combination, every member must be regarded as a purpose (though not as a final purpose), to which its proximate cause is the means. So too if cattle, sheep, horses, etc., are to exist, there must be grass on the earth, but there must also be saline plants in the desert if camels are to thrive; and again these and other herbivorous animals must be met with in numbers if there are to be wolves, tigers, and lions. Consequently the objective purposiveness, which is based upon advantage, is not an objective purposiveness of things in themselves; as if the sand could not be conceived for itself as an effect of a cause, viz. the sea, without attributing to the latter a purpose, and regarding the effect, namely, the sand, as a work of art. It is a merely relative purposiveness contingent upon the thing to which it is ascribed; and although in the examples we have cited, the different kinds of grass are to be judged as in themselves organised products of nature, and consequently as artificial, yet are they to be regarded, in reference to the beasts which feed upon them, as mere raw material.

But above all, though man, through the freedom of his causality, finds certain natural things of advantage for his designs—designs often foolish, such as using the variegated plumage of birds to adorn his clothes, or coloured earths and the juices of plants for painting his face; often again reasonable as when the horse is used for riding, the ox or (as in Minorca) the ass or pig for ploughing—yet we cannot even here assume a relative natural purpose. For his Reason knows how to give things a conformity with his own arbitrary fancies for which he was not at all predestined by nature. Only, *if* we assume that men are to live upon the earth, then the means must be there without which they could not exist as animals, and even as rational animals (in however low a degree of rationality); and thereupon those natural things, which are indispensable in this regard, must be considered as natural purposes.

We can hence easily see that external purposiveness (advantage of one thing in respect of others) can be regarded as an external natural purpose only under the condition, that the existence of that [being], to which it is immediately or distantly advantageous, is in itself a purpose of nature. Since that can never be completely determined by mere contemplation of nature, it follows that relative purposiveness, although it hypothetically gives indications of natural purposes, yet justifies no absolute teleological judgement.

Snow in cold countries protects the crops from the frost; it makes human intercourse easier (by means of sleighs). The Laplander finds in his country animals by whose aid this intercourse is brought about, i.e. reindeer, who find sufficient sustenance in a dry moss which they have to scratch out for themselves from under the snow, and who are easily tamed and readily permit themselves to be deprived of that freedom in which they could have remained if they chose. For other people in the same frozen regions marine animals afford rich stores; in addition to the food and clothing which are thus supplied, and the wood which is floated in by the sea to their dwellings, these marine animals provide material for fuel by which their huts are warmed. Here is a wonderful concurrence of many references of nature to one purpose; and all this applies to the cases of the Greenlander, the Lapp, the Samoyede, the inhabitant of Yakutsk, etc. But then we do not see why, generally, men must live there at all. Therefore to say that vapour falls out of the atmosphere in the form of snow, that the sea has its currents which float down wood that has grown in warmer lands, and that there are in it great sea monsters filled with oil, *because* the idea of advantage for certain poor creatures is fundamental for the cause which collects all these natural products, would be a very venturesome and arbitrary judgement. . . . [B. 272]

§ 64. *Of the peculiar character of things as natural purposes*

In order to see that a thing is only possible as a purpose, that is, to be forced to seek the causality of its origin not in the mechanism of nature but in a cause whose faculty of action is determined through concepts, it is requisite that its form be not possible according to mere natural laws, i.e. laws which can be cognised by us through the Understanding alone when applied to objects of Sense; but that even the empirical knowledge of it as regards its cause and effect presupposes concepts of Reason. This *contingency* of its form in all empirical natural laws in reference to Reason affords a ground for regarding its causality as possible only through Reason. For Reason, which must cognise the necessity of every form of a natural product in order to comprehend even the conditions of its genesis, cannot assume such [natural] necessity in that particular given form. The causality of its origin is then referred to the faculty of acting in accordance with purposes (a will); and the Object which can only thus be represented as possible is represented as a purpose.

If in a seemingly uninhabited country a man perceived a geometrical figure, say a regular hexagon, inscribed on the sand, his reflection busied with such a concept would attribute, although obscurely, the unity in the principle of its genesis to Reason, and consequently would not regard as a ground of the possibility of such a shape the sand, or the neighbouring sea, or the winds, or beasts with familiar footprints, or any other irrational cause. For the chance against meeting with such a concept, which is only possible through Reason, would seem so infinitely great, that it would be just as if there were no natural law, no cause in the mere mechanical working of nature capable of producing it; but as if only the concept of such an Object, as a concept which Reason alone can supply and with which it can compare the thing, could contain the causality for such an effect. This then would be regarded as a purpose, but as a product of *art,* not as a natural purpose *(vestigium hominis video).*

But in order to regard a thing cognised as a natural product as a purpose also—consequently as a *natural purpose,* if this is not a contradiction—something more is required. I would say provisionally: a thing exists as a natural purpose, if it is, although in a double sense, both *cause and effect of itself.* For herein lies a causality the like of which cannot be combined with the mere concept of a nature without attributing to it a purpose; it can certainly be thought without contradiction, but cannot be comprehended. We shall elucidate the determination of this Idea of a natural purpose by an example, before we analyse it completely.

In the *first* place, a tree generates another tree according to a known natural law. But the tree produced is of the same genus; and so it produces itself *generically.* On the one hand, as effect it is continually self-produced; on the other hand, as cause it continually produces itself, and so perpetuates itself generically.

Secondly, a tree produces itself as an *individual.* This kind of effect no doubt we call growth; but it is quite different from any increase according to mechanical laws, and is to be reckoned as generation, though under another name. The matter that the tree incorporates it previously works up into a specifically peculiar quality, which natural mechanism external to it cannot supply; and thus it develops itself by aid of a material which, as compounded, is its own product. No doubt, as regards the constituents got from nature without, it must only be regarded as an educt; but yet in the separation and recombination of this raw material we see such an originality in the separating and formative faculty of this kind of natural being, as is infinitely beyond the reach of art, if the attempt is made to reconstruct such vegetable products out of elements obtained by their dissection or material supplied by nature for their sustenance.

Thirdly, each part of a tree generates itself in such a way that the maintenance of any one part depends reciprocally on the maintenance of the rest. A bud of one tree engrafted on the twig of another produces in the alien stock a plant of its own kind, and so also a scion engrafted on a foreign stem. Hence we may regard each twig or leaf of the same tree as merely engrafted or inoculated into it, and so as an independent tree attached to another and parasitically nourished by it. At the same time, while the leaves are products of the tree they also in turn give support to it; for the repeated defoliation of a tree kills it, and its growth thus depends on the action of the leaves upon the stem. The self-help of nature in case of injury in the vegetable creation, when the want of a part that is necessary for the maintenance of its neighbours is supplied by the remaining parts; and the abortions or malformations in growth, in which certain parts, on account of casual defects or hindrances, form themselves in a new way to maintain what exists, and so produce an anomalous creature, I shall only mention in passing, though they are among the most wonderful properties of organised creatures.

§ 65. *Things regarded as natural purposes are organised beings*

According to the character alleged in the preceding section, a thing, which, though a natural product, is to be cognised as only possible as a natural purpose, must bear itself alternately as cause and as effect. This, however, is a somewhat inexact and indeterminate expression which needs derivation from a determinate concept. . . . [B. 276]

For a thing to be a natural purpose in the *first* place it is requisite that its parts (as regards their being and their form) are only possible through their reference to the whole. For the thing itself is a purpose and so is comprehended under a concept or an Idea which must determine *a priori* all that is to be contained in it. But so far as a thing is only thought as possible in this way, it is a mere work of art; i.e. a product of one rational cause distinct from the matter (of the parts), whose causality (in the collection and combination of the parts) is determined through its Idea of a whole possible by their means (and consequently not through external nature).

But if a thing as a natural product is to involve in itself and in its internal possibility a reference to purposes,—i.e. to be possible only as a natural purpose, and without the causality of the concepts of rational beings external to itself,—then it is requisite *secondly* that its parts should so combine in the unity of a whole that they are reciprocally cause and effect of each other's form. Only in this way can the Idea of the whole conversely (reciprocally) determine the form and combination of all the parts; not indeed as cause—for then it would be an artificial product—but as the ground of cognition, for him who is judging it, of the systematic unity and combination of all the manifold contained in the given material.

For a body then which is to be judged in itself and its internal possibility as a natural purpose, it is requisite that its parts mutually depend upon each other both as to their form and their combination, and so produce a whole by their own causality; while conversely the concept of the whole may be regarded as its cause according to a principle (in a being possessing a causality according to concepts adequate to such a product). In this case then the connexion of *effective causes* may be judged as an *effect through final causes.*

In such a product of nature every part not only exists *by means of* the other parts, but is thought as existing *for the sake of* the others and the whole, that is as an (organic) instrument. Thus, however, it might be an artificial instrument, and so might be represented only as a purpose that is possible in general; but also its parts are all organs reciprocally *producing* each other. This can never be the case with artificial instruments, but only with nature which supplies all the material for the instruments (even for those of art). Only a product of such a kind can be called a *natural purpose,* and this because it is an *organised* and *self-organising being.*

In a watch one part is the instrument for moving the other parts, but the wheel is not the effective cause of the production of the others; no doubt one part is for the sake of the others, but it does not exist by their means. In this case the producing cause of the parts and of their form is not contained in the nature (of the material), but is external to it in a being which can produce effects according to Ideas of a whole possible by means of its causality. Hence a watch wheel does not produce other wheels, still less does one watch produce other watches, utilising (organising) foreign material for that purpose; hence it does not replace of itself parts of which it has been deprived, nor does it make good what is lacking in a first formation by the addition of the missing parts, nor if it has gone out of order does it repair itself—all of which, on the contrary, we may expect from organised nature.— An organised being is then not a mere machine, for that has merely *moving* power, but it possesses in itself *formative* power of a self-propagating kind which it communicates to its materials though they have it not of themselves; it organises them, in fact, and this cannot be explained by the mere mechanical faculty of motion.

We say of nature and its faculty in organised products far too little if we describe it as an *analogon of art;* for this suggests an artificer (a rational being) external to it. Much rather does it organise itself and its organised products in every species, no doubt after one general pattern but yet with suitable deviations, which self-preservation demands according to circumstances. . . . [B. 279] To speak strictly . . . the organisation of nature has in it nothing analogous to any causality we know.[1] Beauty in nature can be rightly described as an analogon of art, because it is ascribed to objects only in reference to reflection upon their *external* aspect, and consequently only on account of the form of their external surface. But *internal natural perfection,* as it belongs to those things which are only possible as *natural purposes,* and are therefore called organised beings,

[1] [Note, B. 279.]

is not analogous to any physical, i.e. natural, faculty known to us; nay even, regarding ourselves as, in the widest sense, belonging to nature, it is not even thinkable or explicable by means of any exactly fitting analogy to human art. . . . [B. 280]

Organised beings are then the only beings in nature which, considered in themselves and apart from any relation to other things, can be thought as possible only as purposes of nature. Hence they first afford objective reality to the concept of a *purpose of nature,* as distinguished from a practical purpose; and so they give to the science of nature the basis for a teleology, i.e. a mode of judgement about natural Objects according to a special principle which otherwise we should in no way be justified in introducing (because we cannot see *a priori* the possibility of this kind of causality).

§ 66. *Of the principle of judging of internal purposiveness in organised beings*

This principle, which is at the same time a definition, is as follows: *An organised product of nature is one in which every part is reciprocally purpose* [*end*] *and means.* In it nothing is vain, without purpose, or to be ascribed to a blind mechanism of nature.

This principle, as regards its occasion, is doubtless derived from experience, viz. from that methodised experience called observation; but on account of the universality and necessity which it ascribes to such purposiveness it cannot rest solely on empirical grounds, but must have at its basis an *a priori* principle, although it be merely regulative and these purposes lie only in the idea of the judging [subject] and not in an effective cause. We may therefore describe the aforesaid principle as a *maxim* for judging of the internal purposiveness of organised beings.

It is an acknowledged fact that the dissectors of plants and animals, in order to investigate their structure and to find out the reasons, why and for what end such parts, such a disposition and combination of parts, and just such an internal form have been given them, assume as indisputably necessary the maxim that nothing in such a creature is *vain;* just as they lay down as the fundamental proposition of the universal science of nature, that *nothing* happens *by chance.* In fact, they can as little free themselves from this teleological proposition as from the universal physical proposition; for as without the latter we should have no experience at all, so without the former we should have no guiding thread for the observation of a species of natural things which we have thought teleologically under the concept of natural purposes.

Now this concept brings the Reason into a quite different order of things from that of a mere mechanism of nature, which is no longer satisfying here. An Idea is to be the ground of the possibility of the natural product. But because this is an absolute unity of representation, instead of the material being a plurality of things that can supply by itself no definite unity of composition,—if that unity of the Idea is to serve at all as the *a priori* ground of determination of a natural law of the causality of such a form of composition,—the purpose of nature must be extended to *everything* included in its product. For if we once refer action of this sort *on the whole* to any supersensible ground of determination beyond the blind mechanism of nature, we must judge of it altogether according to this principle; and we have then no reason to regard the form of such a thing as partly dependent on mechanism—for by such mixing up of disparate principles no certain rule of judging would be left.

For example, it may be that in an animal body many parts can be conceived as concretions according to mere mechanical laws (as the hide, the bones, the hair). And yet the cause which brings together the required matter, modifies it, forms it, and puts it in its appropriate place, must always be judged of teleologically; so that here everything must be considered as organised, and everything again in a certain relation to the thing itself is an organ.

§ 67. *Of the principle of the teleological judging of nature in general as a system of purposes*

. . . [B. 282-4] It is only so far as matter is organised that it necessarily carries with it the concept of a natural purpose, because this its specific form is at the same time a product of nature. But this concept leads necessarily to the Idea of collective nature as a system in accordance with the rule of purposes, to which Idea all the mechanism of nature must be subordinated according to principles of Reason (at least in order to investigate natural phenomena therein). The principle of Reason belongs to it only as a subjective principle or a maxim: viz. everything in the world is some way good for something; nothing is vain in it. By the example that nature gives us in its organic products we are justified, nay called upon, to expect of it and of its laws nothing that is not purposive on the whole. . . . [B. 285-7]

If [then] we have once discovered in nature a faculty of bringing forth products that can only be thought by us in accordance with the concept of final causes, we go further still. We venture to judge that things belong to a system of purposes, which yet do not (either in themselves or in their purposive relations) necessitate our seeking for any principle of their possibility beyond the mechanism of causes working blindly. For the first Idea, as concerns its ground, already brings us beyond the world of sense; since the unity of the supersensible principle must be regarded as valid in this way not merely for certain species of natural beings, but for the whole of nature as a system. . . . [B. 287-91]

III. DIALECTIC OF THE TELEOLOGICAL JUDGEMENT

. . . [B. 292-3]

§ 70. *Representation of* [*the*] *Antinomy* [*of Judgement and its preliminary solution.*]

So far as Reason has to do with nature, as the complex of objects of external sense, it can base itself partly upon laws which the Understanding itself prescribes *a priori* to nature, partly upon laws which it can extend indefinitely by means of the empirical determinations occurring in experience. To apply the former kind of laws, i.e. the *universal* laws of material nature in general, the Judgement needs no special principle of reflection, since it is there determinant because an objective principle is given to it through Understanding. But as regards the particular laws that can only be made known to us through experience, there can be under them such great manifoldness and diversity, that the Judgement must serve as its own principle in order to investigate and search into the phenomena of nature in accordance with a law. Such a guiding thread is needed, if we are only to hope for a connected empirical cognition according to a thoroughgoing conformity of nature to law, even its unity according to empirical laws. In this contingent unity of particular laws it may very well happen that the Judgement in its reflection proceeds from two maxims. One of these is suggested to it *a priori* by the mere Understanding; but the other is prompted by particular experiences, which bring the Reason into play in order to form a judgement upon corporeal nature and its laws in accordance with a particular principle. Hence it comes about that these two kinds of maxims seem to be incapable of existing together, and consequently a Dialectic arises which leads the Judgement into error in the principle of its reflection.

The *first maxim* of Judgement is the *proposition:* All production of material things and their forms must be judged to be possible according to merely mechanical laws.

The *second maxim* is the *counter-proposition*: Some products of material nature cannot be judged to be possible according to merely mechanical laws. (To judge them requires quite a different law of causality, namely, that of final causes.)

If these regulative principles of investigation be converted into constitutive principles of the possibility of Objects, they will run thus:

Proposition: All production of material things is possible according to merely mechanical laws.

Counter-proposition: Some production of material things is not possible according to merely mechanical laws.

In this latter aspect, as objective principles for the determinant Judgement, they would contradict each other; and consequently one of the two propositions must necessarily be false. We shall then, it is true, have an antinomy, but not of Judgement; there will be a conflict in the legislation of Reason. Reason, however, can prove neither the one nor the other of these fundamental propositions, because we can have *a priori* no determinant principle of the possibility of things according to mere empirical laws of nature.

On the other hand, as regards the first-mentioned maxims of a reflective Judgement, they involve no contradiction in fact. For if I say, I must *judge,* according to merely mechanical laws, of the possibility of all events in material nature, and consequently of all forms regarded as its products, I do not therefore say: *They are possible in this way alone* (apart from any other kind of causality). All that is implied is: I *must* always *reflect* upon them *according to the principle* of the mere mechanism of nature, and consequently investigate this as far as I can; because unless this lies at the basis of investigation, there can be no proper knowledge of nature at all. But this does not prevent us, if occasion offers, from following out the second maxim in the case of certain natural forms (and even by occasion of these in the whole of nature), in order to reflect upon them according to the principle of final causes, which is quite a different thing from explaining them according to the mechanism of nature. Reflection in accordance with the first maxim is thus not abrogated; on the contrary, we are told to follow it as far as we can. Nor is it said that these forms would not be possible in accordance with the mechanism of nature. It is only asserted that *human Reason* in following up this maxim and in this way could never find the least ground for that which constitutes the specific [character] of a natural purpose, although it would increase its knowledge of natural laws. Thus it is left undecided whether or not in the unknown inner ground of nature, physico-mechanical and purposive combination may be united in the same things in one principle. We only say that our Reason is not in a position so to unite them; and that therefore the Judgement (as *reflective*—from subjective grounds, not as determinant, in consequence of an objective principle of the possibility of things in themselves) is compelled to think a different principle from that of natural mechanism as the ground of the possibility of certain forms in nature. . . . [B. 296-8]

§ 72. *Of the different systems which deal with the purposiveness of nature*

. . . [B. 298-300] If we . . . speak of systems explanatory of nature in regard of final causes, it must be remarked that they all controvert each other dogmatically, i.e. as to objective principles of the possibility of things, whether there are causes which act designedly or whether they are quite without design. They do not dispute as to the subjective maxims, by which we merely judge of the causes of such purposive products. In this latter case *disparate* principles could very well be unified; but in the former, contradictorily opposed laws annul each other and cannot subsist together.

There are two sorts of systems as to the Technic of nature, i.e. its productive power in accordance with the rule of purposes; viz. *Idealism* or *Realism* of natural purposes. The first maintains that all purposiveness of nature is *undesigned;* the second that some (in organised beings) is *designed.* From this latter the hypothetical consequence can be deduced that the Technic of Nature, as concerns all its other products in reference to the whole of nature, is also designed, i.e. is a purpose.

(1) The *Idealism* of purposiveness (I always understand here by this, objective purposiveness) is either that of the *causality* or the *fatality* of the determination

of nature in the purposive form of its products. The former principle treats of the reference of matter to the physical basis of its form, viz. the laws of motion; the second, its reference to the *hyperphysical* basis of itself and of the whole of nature. The system of *causality* that is ascribed to *Epicurus* or *Democritus* is, taken literally, so plainly absurd that it need not detain us. Opposed to this is the system of fatality, of which *Spinoza* is taken as the author, although it is much older according to all appearance. This, as it appeals to something supersensible to which our insight does not extend, is not so easy to controvert; but that is because its concept of the original Being is not possible to understand. But so much is clear, that on this theory the purposive combination in the world must be taken as undesigned; for although derived from an original Being, it is not derived from its Understanding or from any design on its part, but rather from the necessity of its nature and of the world-unity which emanates therefrom. Consequently the Fatalism of purposiveness is at the same time an Idealism.

(2) The *Realism* of the purposiveness of nature is also either physical or hyperphysical. The *former* bases the purposes in nature, by the analogy of a faculty acting with design, on the *life of matter* (either its own or the life of an inner principle in it, a world-soul) and is called *Hylozoism*. The *latter* derives them from the original ground of the universe, as from an intelligent Being (originally living), who produces them with design, and is *Theism*.[1]

[1] We thus see that in most speculative things of pure Reason, as regards dogmatic assertions, the philosophical schools have commonly tried all possible solutions of a given question. To explain the purposiveness of nature men have tried either *lifeless matter* or a *lifeless God*, or again, *living matter* or a *living God*. It only remains for us, if the need should arise, to abandon all these objective *assertions* and to examine

§ 73. *None of the above systems give what they pretend*

What do all these systems desire? They desire to explain our teleological judgements about nature, and they go so to work therewith that some deny their truth and, consequently, explain them as an Idealism of Nature (represented as Art); others recognise them as true, and promise to establish the possibility of a nature in accordance with the Idea of final causes.

(1) The systems which defend the Idealism of final causes in nature grant, it is true, on the one hand to their principle a causality in accordance with the laws of motion (through which [causality] natural things exist purposively); but they deny to it *intentionality*, i.e. that it designedly determines itself to this its purposive production; in other words, they deny that the cause is a purpose. This is *Epicurus's* method of explanation, according to which the distinction between a Technic of nature and mere mechanism is altogether denied. Blind chance is taken as the explanatory ground not only of the agreement of the developed products with our concepts of the purpose, and consequently of [nature's] Technic; but also of the determination of the causes of this production in accordance with the laws of motion, and consequently of their mechanism. Thus nothing is explained, not even the illusion in our teleological judgements, and consequently, the would-be Idealism of these in no way established.

On the other hand, *Spinoza* wishes to dispense with all inquiries into the ground of the possibility of pur-

---

critically our judgement merely in reference to our cognitive faculties, in order to supply to their principle a validity which, if not dogmatic, shall at least be that of a maxim sufficient for the sure employment of Reason.

poses of nature, and to take away all reality from this Idea. He allows their validity in general not as products but as accidents inhering in an original Being; and to this Being, as substrate of those natural things, he ascribes not causality in regard to them but mere subsistence. On account of its unconditioned necessity, and also that of all natural things as accidents inhering in it, he secures, it is true, to the forms of nature that unity of ground which is requisite for all purposiveness; but at the same time he tears away their contingence, without which no *unity of purpose* can be thought, and with it all *design,* inasmuch as he takes away all intelligence from the original ground of natural things.

But Spinozism does not furnish what it desires. It desires to afford an explanatory ground of the purposive connexion (which it does not deny) of the things of nature, and it merely speaks of the unity of the subject in which they all inhere. But even if we concede to it that the beings of the world exist in this way, such ontological unity is not therefore a *unity of purpose,* and does not make this in any way comprehensible. For this latter is a quite particular kind of unity which does not follow from the connexion of things (the beings of the world) in a subject (the original Being), but implies in itself reference to a *cause* which has Understanding; and even if we unite all these things in a simple subject, this never exhibits a purposive reference. For we do not think of them, first, as the inner *effects* of the substance, as if it were a *cause;* nor, secondly, of this cause as a cause producing effects *by means of its Understanding.* Without these formal conditions all unity is mere natural necessity; and, if it is ascribed as well to things which we represent as external to one another, blind necessity. But if we wish to give the name of purposiveness of nature to that which the schoolmen call the transcendental perfection of things (in reference to their proper being), according to which everything has in itself that which is requisite to make it one thing and not another, then we are only like children playing with words instead of concepts. For if all things must be thought as purposes, then to be a thing is the same as to be a purpose, and there is at bottom nothing which specially deserves to be represented as a purpose.

We hence see at once that Spinoza by his reducing our concepts of the purposive in nature to our own consciousness of existing in an all-embracing (though simple) Being, and by his seeking that form merely in the unity of this Being, must have intended to maintain not the realism, but the idealism of its purposiveness. Even this he was not able to accomplish, because the mere representation of the unity of the substrate cannot bring about the Idea of a purposiveness, even that which is only undesigned.

(2) Those who not only maintain the *Realism* of natural purposes, but also set about explaining it, believe that they can comprehend, at least as regards its possibility, a practical kind of causality, viz. that of causes working designedly; otherwise they could not undertake to supply this explanation. For to authorise even the most daring of hypotheses, at least the *possibility* of what we assume as basis must be *certain,* and we must be able to assure objective reality to its concept.

But the possibility of living matter cannot even be thought; its concept involves a contradiction because lifelessness, *inertia,* constitutes the essential character of matter. The possibility of matter endowed with life, and of collective nature regarded as an animal, can only be used in an adequate way (in the interests of the hypothesis of purposiveness in the whole of nature), so far as it is manifested by experience in the organisation of nature on a small scale; but in no way can we have insight into its possibility *a priori*. There must then be a circle in the explanation, if we wish to derive the purposiveness of nature in organised beings from the life of matter, and yet only know this life in organised beings, and can form no concept of its possibility without experience of this kind. Hylozoism, therefore, does not furnish what it promises.

Finally, *Theism* can just as little establish dogmatically the possibility of natural purposes as a key to Teleology; although it certainly is superior to all other grounds of explanation in that, through the Understanding which it ascribes to the original Being, it rescues in the best way the purposiveness of nature from Idealism, and introduces a causality acting with design for its production.

But we must first prove satisfactorily to the determinant Judgement the impossibility of the unity of purpose in matter resulting from its mere mechanism, before we are justified in placing the ground of this beyond nature in a determinate way. We can, however, advance no further than this. In accordance with the constitution and limits of our cognitive faculties (whilst we do not comprehend even the first inner ground of this mechanism) we must in no wise seek in matter a principle of determinate purposive references; but no other way of judging of the origination of its products as natural purposes remains to us than that by means of a supreme Understanding as cause of the world. But this is only a ground for the reflective, not for the determinant Judgement, and can justify absolutely no objective assertion. . . . [B. 306-9]

§ 75. [*Critical Solution of the Antinomy of Judgement.*] *The concept of an objective purposiveness of nature is a critical principle of Reason for the reflective Judgement*

It is then one thing to say, "The production of certain things of nature or that of collective nature is only possible through a cause which determines itself to action according to design"; and quite another to say, "I can *according to the peculiar constitution of my cognitive faculties* judge concerning the possibility of these things and their production, in no other fashion than by conceiving for this a cause working according to design, i.e. a Being which is productive in a way analogous to the causality of an intelligence." In the former case I wish to establish something concerning the Object, and am bound to establish the objective reality of an assumed concept; in the latter, Reason only determines the use of my cognitive faculties, conformably to their peculiarities and to the essential conditions of their range and their limits. Thus the former principle is an objective proposition for the determinant Judgement, the latter merely a subjective proposition for the reflective Judgement, i.e. a maxim which Reason prescribes to it.

We are in fact indispensably obliged to ascribe the concept of design to nature if we wish to investigate it, though only in its organised products, by continuous observation; and this concept is therefore an absolutely necessary maxim for the empirical use of our Reason. It is plain that once such a guiding thread for the study of nature is admitted and verified, we must at least try the said maxim of Judgement in nature as a whole; because thereby many of nature's laws might discover themselves, which otherwise, on account of the limitation of our insight into its inner mechanism, would remain hidden. But though in regard to this latter employment that maxim of Judgement is certainly useful, it is not indispensable, for nature as a whole is not given as organised (in the narrow sense of the word above indicated). On the other hand, in regard to those natural products, which must be judged of as designed and not formed otherwise (if we are to have empirical knowledge of their inner constitution), this maxim of the reflective Judgement is essentially necessary; because the very thought of them as organised beings is impossible without combining therewith the thought of their designed production.

Now the concept of a thing whose existence or form we represent to ourselves as possible under the condition of a purpose is inseparably bound up with the concept of its contingency (according to natural laws). Hence the natural things that we find possible only as purposes supply the best proof of the contingency of the world-whole; to the common Understanding and to the philosopher alike they are the only valid ground of proof for its dependence on and origin from a Being existing outside the world—a Being who must also be intelligent on account of that purposive form. Teleology then finds the consummation of its investigations only in Theology.

But what now in the end does the most complete Teleology prove? Does it prove that there is such an intelligent Being? No. It only proves that according to the constitution of our cognitive faculties and in the consequent combination of experience with the highest principles of Reason, we can form absolutely no concept of the possibility of such a world [as this] save by thinking a *designedly-working* supreme cause thereof.

Objectively we cannot therefore lay down the proposition, there is an intelligent original Being; but only subjectively, for the use of our Judgement in its reflection upon the purposes in nature, which can be thought according to no other principle than that of a designing causality of a highest cause. . . . [B. 311-12]

Now if this proposition, based on an inevitably necessary maxim of our Judgement, is completely satisfactory from every *human* point of view for both the speculative and practical use of our Reason, I should like to know what we lose by not being able to prove it as also valid for higher beings, from objective grounds (which unfortunately are beyond our faculties). It is indeed quite certain that we cannot adequately cognise, much less explain, organised beings and their internal possibility, according to mere mechanical principles of nature; and we can say boldly it is alike certain that it is absurd for men to make any such attempt or to hope that another *Newton* will arise in the future, who shall make comprehensible by us the production of a blade of grass according to natural laws which no design has ordered. We must absolutely deny this insight to men. But then how do we know that in nature, if we could penetrate to the principle by which it specifies the universal laws known to us, there *cannot* lie hidden (in its mere mechanism) a sufficient ground of the possibility of organised beings without supposing any design in their production? would it not be judged by us presumptuous to say this? Probabilities here are of no account when we have to do with judgements of pure Reason.— We cannot therefore judge objectively, either affirmatively or negatively, concerning the proposition: "Does a Being acting according to design lie at the basis of what we rightly call natural purposes, as the cause of the world (and consequently as its author)?" So much only is sure, that if we are to judge according to what is permitted us to see by our own proper nature (the conditions and limitations of our Reason), we can place at the basis of the possibility of these natural purposes nothing else than an intelligent Being. This alone is in conformity with the maxim of our reflective Judgement and therefore with a ground which, though subjective, is inseparably attached to the human race. . . . [B. 313-33]

METHODOLOGY OF THE TELEOLOGICAL JUDGEMENT

[I. THE FINAL PURPOSE OF THE ORDER AND EXISTENCE OF NATURE]

. . . [B. 334-6]

§ 80. *Of the necessary subordination of the mechanical to the teleological principle in the explanation of a thing as a natural purpose.*

The *privilege of aiming at* a merely mechanical method of explanation of all natural products is in itself quite unlimited; but the *faculty of attaining* thereto is by the constitution of our Understanding, so far as it has to do with things as natural purposes, not only very much limited but also clearly bounded. For, according to a principle of the Judgement, by this process alone nothing can be accomplished towards an explanation of these things; and consequently the judgement upon such products must always be at the same time subordinated by us to a teleological principle.

It is therefore rational, even meritorious, to pursue natural mechanism, in respect of the explanation of natural products, so far as can be done with probability; and if we give up the attempt it is not because it is impossible *in itself* to meet in this path with the purposiveness of nature, but only because it is impossible *for us* as men. For there would be required for that an intuition other than sensuous, and a determinate knowledge of the intelligible substrate of nature from which a ground could be assigned for the mechanism of phenomena according to particular laws, which quite surpasses our faculties.

Hence if the naturalist would not waste his labour he must, in judging of things, the concept of any of which is indubitably established as a natural purpose (organised beings), always lay down as basis an original organisation, which uses that very mechanism in order to produce fresh organised forms or to develop the existing ones into new shapes (which, however, always result from that purpose and conformably to it).

It is praiseworthy by the aid of comparative anatomy to go through the great creation of organised natures, in order to see whether there may not be in it something similar to a system and also in accordance with the principle of production. For otherwise we should have to be content with the mere principle of judgement (which gives no insight into their production) and, discouraged, to give up all claim to *natural insight* in this field. The agreement of so many genera of animals in a certain common schema, which appears to be fundamental not only in the structure of their bones but also in the disposition of their remaining parts,—so that with an admirable simplicity of original outline, a great variety of species has been produced by the shortening of one member and the lengthening of another, the involution of this part and the evolution of that,—allows a ray of hope, however faint, to penetrate into our minds, that here something may be accomplished by the aid of the principle of the mechanism of nature (without which there can be no natural science in general). This analogy of forms, which with all their differences seem to have been produced according to a common original type, strengthens our suspicions of an actual relationship between them in their production from a common parent, through the gradual approximation of one animal-genus to another—from those in which the principle of purposes seems to be best authenticated, i.e. from man, down to the polype, and again from this down to mosses and lichens, and finally to the lowest stage of nature noticeable by us, viz. to crude matter. And so the whole Technic of nature, which is so incomprehensible to us in organised beings that we believe ourselves compelled to think a different principle for it, seems to be derived from matter and its powers according to mechanical laws (like those by which it works in the formation of crystals).

Here it is permissible for the *archaeologist* of nature to derive from the surviving traces of its oldest revolutions, according to all its mechanism known or supposed by him, that great family of creatures (for so we must represent them if the said thoroughgoing relationship is to have any ground). He can suppose the bosom of mother earth, as she passed out of her chaotic state (like a great animal), to have given birth in the beginning to creatures of less purposive form, that these again gave birth to others which formed themselves with greater adaptation to their place of birth and their relations to each other; until this womb becoming torpid and ossified, limited its births to definite species not further modifiable, and the manifoldness remained as it was at the end of the operation of that fruitful formative power.— Only he must still in the end ascribe to this universal mother an organisation purposive in respect of all these creatures; otherwise it would not be possible to think the possibility of the purposive form of the products of the animal and vegetable kingdoms.[1] He has then only pushed further back the ground of explanation and cannot pretend to have made the development of those two kingdoms independent of the condition of final causes.

Even as concerns the variation to which certain individuals of organised genera are accidentally subjected, if we find that the character so changed is hereditary and is taken up into the generative power, then we cannot pertinently judge the variation to be anything else than an occasional development of purposive capacities originally present in the species with a view to the preservation of the race. For in the complete inner purposiveness of an organised being, the generation of its like is closely bound up with the condition of taking nothing up into the generative power which does not belong, in such a system of purposes, to one of its undeveloped original capacities. Indeed, if we depart from this principle, we cannot know with certainty whether several parts of the form which is now apparent in a species have not a contingent and unpurposive origin; and the principle of Teleology, to judge nothing in an organised being as unpurposive which maintains

[1] We may call a hypothesis of this kind a daring venture of reason, and there may be few even of the most acute naturalists through whose head it has not sometimes passed. For it is not absurd, like that *generatio aequivoca* by which is understood the production of an organised being through the mechanics of crude unorganised matter. It would always remain *generatio univoca* in the most universal sense of the word, for it only considers one organic being as derived from another organic being, although from one which is specifically different; e.g. certain water-animals transform themselves gradually into marsh-animals and from these, after some generations, into land-animals. . . . [B. 339]

it in its propagation, would be very unreliable in its application and would be valid solely for the original stock (of which we have no further knowledge). . . . [B. 340-2]

§ 81. *Of the association of mechanism with the teleological principle in the explanation of a natural purpose as a natural product.*

According to the preceding paragraphs the mechanism of nature alone does not enable us to think the possibility of an organised being; but (at least according to the constitution of our cognitive faculty) it must be originally subordinated to a cause working designedly. But, just as little is the mere teleological ground of such a being sufficient for considering it and judging it as a product of nature, if the mechanism of the latter be not associated with the former, like the instrument of a cause working designedly, to whose purposes nature is subordinated in its mechanical laws. The possibility of such a unification of two quite different kinds of causality,—of nature in its universal conformity to law with an Idea which limits it to a particular form, for which it contains no ground in itself—is not comprehended by our Reason. It lies in the supersensible substrate of nature, of which we can determine nothing positively, except that it is the being in itself of which we merely know the phenomenon. But the principle, "all that we assume as belonging to this nature (*phenomenon*) and as its product, must be thought as connected therewith according to mechanical laws," has none the less force, because without this kind of causality organised beings (as purposes of nature) would not be natural products. . . . [B. 342-6]

§ 82. *Of the teleological system in the external relations of organised beings.*

By external purposiveness I mean that by which one thing of nature serves another as means to a purpose. . . . [B. 346-8]

But if we go through the whole of nature we find in it, as nature, no being which could make claim to the eminence of being the final purpose of creation; and we can even prove *a priori* that what might be for nature an *ultimate purpose,* according to all the thinkable determinations and properties wherewith one could endow it, could yet as a natural thing never be a *final purpose.*

If we consider the vegetable kingdom we might at first sight, on account of the immeasurable fertility with which it spreads itself almost on every soil, be led to take it for a mere product of that mechanism which nature displays in the formations of the mineral kingdom. But a more intimate knowledge of its indescribably wise organisation does not permit us to hold to this thought, but prompts the question: What are these things created for? If it is answered: For the animal kingdom, which is thereby nourished and has thus been able to spread over the earth in genera so various, then the further question comes: What are these plant-devouring animals for? The answer would be something like this: For beasts of prey, which can only be nourished by that which has life. Finally we have the question: What are these last, as well as the first-mentioned natural kingdoms, good for? For man, in reference to the manifold use which his Understanding teaches him to make of all these creatures. He is the ultimate purpose of creation here on earth, because he is the only being upon it who can form a concept of purposes, and who can by his Reason make out of an aggregate of purposively formed things a system of purposes.

We might also with the chevalier *Linnaeus* go the apparently opposite way and say: The herbivorous animals are there to moderate the luxurious growth of the vegetable kingdom, by which many of its species are choked. The carnivora are to set bounds to the voracity of the herbivora. Finally man, by his pursuit of these and his diminution of their numbers, preserves a certain equilibrium between the producing and the destructive powers of nature. And so man, although in a certain reference he might be esteemed a purpose, yet in another has only the rank of a means.

If an objective purposiveness in the variety of the genera of creatures and their external relations to one another, as purposively constructed beings, be made a principle, then it is conformable to Reason to conceive in these relations a certain organisation and a system of all natural kingdoms according to final causes. Only here experience seems flatly to contradict the maxims of Reason, especially as concerns an ultimate purpose of nature, which is indispensable for the possibility of such a system and which we can put nowhere else but in man. For regarding him as one of the many animal genera, nature has not in the least excepted him from its destructive or its productive powers, but has subjected everything to a mechanism thereof without any purpose.

The first thing that must be designedly prepared in an arrangement for a purposive complex of natural beings on the earth would be their place of habitation, the soil and the element on and in which they are to thrive. But a more exact knowledge of the constitution of this basis of all organic production indicates no other causes than those working quite undesignedly, causes which rather destroy than favour production, order, and purposes. Land and sea not only contain in themselves memorials of ancient mighty desolations which have confounded them and all creatures that are in them; but their whole structure, the strata of the one and the boundaries of the other, have quite the appearance of being the product of the wild and violent forces of a nature working in a state of chaos. Although the figure, the structure, and the slope of the land might seem to be purposively ordered for the reception of water from the air, for the welling up of streams between strata of different kinds (for many kinds of products), and for the course of rivers—yet a closer investigation shows that they are merely the effects of volcanic eruptions or of inundations of the ocean, as regards not only the first production of this figure, but, above all, its subsequent transformation, as well as the disappearance of its first organic productions.[1] Now if the place of habitation of all these creatures, the soil (of the land) or the bosom (of the sea), indicates nothing but a quite undesigned mechanism of its production, how and with what right can we demand and maintain a different origin for these latter products? The closest examination, indeed (in *Camper's* judgement), of the remains of the aforesaid devastations of nature seems to show that man was not comprehended in these revolutions; but yet he is so dependent on the remaining creatures that, if a universally directing mechanism of nature be admitted in the case of the others, he must also be regarded as comprehended under it; even though his Understanding (for the most part at least) has been able to deliver him from these devastations.

But this argument seems to prove more than was

[1] [Note, B. 350.]

intended by it. It seems to prove not merely that man cannot be the ultimate purpose of nature, and that on the same grounds the aggregate of the organised things of nature on the earth cannot be a system of purposes; but also that the natural products formerly held to be natural purposes have no other origin than the mechanism of nature.

But in the solution given above of the Antinomy of the principles of the mechanical and teleological methods of production of organic beings of nature, we have seen that they are merely principles of the reflective Judgement in respect of Nature as it produces forms in accordance with particular laws (for the systematic connexion of which we have no key). They do not determine the origin of these beings in themselves; but only say that we, by the constitution of our Understanding and our Reason, cannot conceive it in this kind of being except according to final causes. The greatest possible effort, even audacity, in the attempt to explain them mechanically is not only permitted, but we are invited to it by Reason; notwithstanding that we know from the subjective grounds of the particular species and limitations of our Understanding (not e.g. because the mechanism of production would contradict in itself an origin according to purposes) that we can never attain thereto. Finally, the compatibility of both ways of representing the possibility of nature may lie in the supersensible principle of nature (external to us, as well as in us); whilst the method of representation according to final causes may be only a subjective condition of the use of our Reason, when it not merely wishes to form a judgement upon objects as phenomena, but desires to refer these phenomena together with their principles to their supersensible substrate, in order to find certain laws of their unity possible, which it cannot represent to itself except through purposes (of which the Reason also has such as are supersensible).

§ 83. *Of the ultimate purpose of nature as a teleological system*

We have shown in the preceding that, though not for the determinant but for the reflective Judgement, we have sufficient cause for judging man to be, not merely like all organised beings a *natural purpose,* but also the *ultimate purpose* of nature here on earth; in reference to whom all other natural things constitute a system of purposes according to fundamental propositions of Reason. If now that must be found in man himself, which is to be furthered as a purpose by means of his connexion with nature, this purpose must either be of a kind that can be satisfied by nature in its beneficence; or it is the aptitude and skill for all kinds of purposes for which nature (external and internal) can be used by him. The first purpose of nature would be man's *happiness,* the second his *culture.*

The concept of happiness is not one that man derives by abstraction from his instincts and so deduces from his animal nature; but it is a mere *Idea* of a state, that he wishes to make adequate to the Idea under merely empirical conditions (which is impossible). This Idea he projects in such different ways on account of the complication of his Understanding with Imagination and Sense, and changes so often, that nature, even if it were entirely subjected to his elective will, could receive absolutely no determinate, universal and fixed law, so as to harmonise with this vacillating concept and thus with the purpose which each man arbitrarily sets before himself. And even if we reduce this to the true natural wants as to which our race is thoroughly agreed, or on the other hand, raise ever so high man's skill to accomplish his imagined purposes; yet, even thus, what man understands by happiness, and what is in fact his proper, ultimate, natural purpose (not purpose of freedom), would never be attained by him. For it is not his nature to rest and be contented with the possession and enjoyment of anything whatever. On the other side, too, there is something wanting. Nature has not taken him for her special darling and favoured him with benefit above all animals. Rather, in her destructive operations,—plague, hunger, perils of waters, frost, assaults of other animals great and small, etc.,—in these things has she spared him as little as any other animal. Further, the inconsistency of his own *natural dispositions* drives him into self-devised torments, and also reduces others of his own race to misery, by the oppression of lordship, the barbarism of war, and so forth; he, himself, as far as in him lies, works for the destruction of his own race; so that even with the most beneficent external nature, its purpose, if it were directed to the happiness of our species, would not be attained in an earthly system, because our nature is not susceptible of it. Man is then always only a link in the chain of natural purposes; a principle certainly in respect of many purposes, for which nature seems to have destined him in her disposition, and towards which he sets himself, but also a means for the maintenance of purposiveness in the mechanism of the remaining links. As the only being on earth which has an Understanding and, consequently, a faculty of setting arbitrary purposes before itself, he is certainly entitled to be the lord of nature; and if it be regarded as a teleological system he is, by his destination, the ultimate purpose of nature. But this is subject to the condition of his having an Understanding and the Will to give to it and to himself such a reference to purposes, as can be self-sufficient independently of nature, and, consequently, can be a final purpose; which, however, must not be sought in nature itself.

But in order to find out where in man we have to place that *ultimate purpose* of nature, we must seek out what nature can supply to prepare him for what he must do himself in order to be a final purpose, and we must separate it from all those purposes whose possibility depends upon things that one can expect only from nature. Of the latter kind is earthly happiness, by which is understood the complex of all man's purposes possible through nature, whether external nature or man's nature; i.e. the matter of all his earthly purposes, which, if he makes it his whole purpose, renders him incapable of positing his own existence as a final purpose, and being in harmony therewith. There remains therefore of all his purposes in nature only the formal subjective condition; viz. the aptitude of setting purposes in general before himself, and (independent of nature in his purposive determination) of using nature, conformably to the maxims of his free purposes in general, as a means. This nature can do in regard to the final purpose that lies outside it, and it therefore may be regarded as its ultimate purpose. The production of the aptitude of a rational being for arbitrary purposes in general (consequently in his freedom) is *culture*. Therefore, culture alone can be the ultimate purpose which we have cause for ascribing to nature in respect to the human race (not man's earthly happiness or the fact that he is the chief instrument of instituting order and harmony in irrational nature external to himself).

But all culture is not adequate to this ultimate purpose of nature. The culture of *skill* is indeed the chief subjective condition of aptitude for furthering one's purposes in general; but it is not adequate to furthering the *will* in the determination and choice of purposes, which yet essentially belongs to the whole extent of an aptitude for purposes. The latter condition of aptitude, which we might call the culture of training (discipline), is negative, and consists in the freeing of the will from the despotism of desires. By these, tied as we are to certain natural things, we are rendered incapable even of choosing, while we allow those impulses to serve as fetters, which Nature has given us as guiding threads that we should not neglect or violate the destination of our animal nature—we being all the time free enough to strain or relax, to extend or diminish them, according as the purposes of Reason require.

Skill cannot be developed in the human race except by means of inequality among them; for the great majority provide the necessities of life, as it were, mechanically, without requiring any art in particular, for the convenience and leisure of others who work at the less necessary elements of culture, science and art. In an oppressed condition they have hard work and little enjoyment, although much of the culture of the higher classes gradually spreads to them. Yet with the progress of this culture (the height of which is called luxury, reached when the propensity to what can be done without begins to be injurious to what is indispensable), their calamities increase equally in two directions, on the one hand through violence from without, on the other hand through internal discontent; but still this splendid misery is bound up with the development of the natural capacities of the human race, and the purpose of nature itself, although not our purpose, is thus attained. The formal condition under which nature can alone attain this its final design, is that arrangement of men's relations to one another, by which lawful authority in a whole, which we call a *civil community,* is opposed to the abuse of their conflicting freedoms; only in this can the greatest development of natural capacities take place. For this also there would be requisite,—if men were clever enough to find it out and wise enough to submit themselves voluntarily to its constraint,—a *cosmopolitan* whole, i.e. a system of all states that are in danger of acting injuriously upon each other. Failing this, and with the obstacles which ambition, lust of dominion, and avarice, especially in those who have the authority in their hands, oppose even to the possibility of such a scheme, there is, inevitably, *war* (by which sometimes states subdivide and resolve themselves into smaller states, sometimes a state annexes other smaller states and strives to form a greater whole). Though war is an undesigned enterprise of men (stirred up by their unbridled passions), yet is it perhaps a deep-hidden and designed enterprise of supreme wisdom for preparing, if not for establishing, conformity to law amid the freedom of states, and with this a unity of a morally grounded system of those states. In spite of the dreadful afflictions with which it visits the human race, and the perhaps greater afflictions with which the constant preparation for it in time of peace oppresses them, yet is it (although the hope for a restful state of popular happiness is ever further off) a motive for developing all talents serviceable for culture, to the highest possible pitch.

As concerns the discipline of the inclinations,—for which our natural capacity in regard of our destination as an animal race is quite purposive, but which render the development of humanity very difficult,—there is manifest in respect of this second requirement for culture a purposive striving of nature to a cultivation which makes us receptive of higher purposes than nature itself can supply. We cannot strive against the preponderance of evil, which is poured out upon us by the refinement of taste pushed to idealisation, and even by the luxury of science as affording food for pride, through the insatiable number of inclinations thus aroused. But yet we cannot mistake the purpose of nature—ever aiming to win us away from the rudeness and violence of those inclinations (inclinations to enjoyment) which belong rather to our animality, and for the most part are opposed to the cultivation of our higher destiny, and to make way for the development of our humanity. The beautiful arts and the sciences which, by their universally-communicable pleasure, and by the polish and refinement of society, make man more civilised, if not morally better, win us in large measure from the tyranny of sense-propensions, and thus prepare men for a lordship, in which Reason alone shall have authority; whilst the evils with which we are visited, partly by nature, partly by the intolerant selfishness of men, summon, strengthen, and harden the powers of the soul not to submit to them, and so make us feel an aptitude for higher purposes, which lies hidden in us. [1]

[1] The value of life for us, if it is estimated by that *which we enjoy* (by the natural purpose of the sum of all inclinations, i.e. happiness), is easy to decide. It sinks below zero; for who would be willing to enter upon life anew under the same conditions? who would do so even according to a new, self-chosen plan (yet in conformity with the course of nature), if it were merely directed to enjoyment? We have shown above what value life has in virtue of what it contains in itself, when lived in accordance with the purpose that nature has along with us, and which consists in what we do (not merely what we enjoy), in which, however, we are always but means towards an undetermined final purpose. There remains then nothing but the value which we ourselves give our life, through what we can not only do, but do purposively in such independence of nature that the existence of nature itself can only be a purpose under this condition.

§ 84. *Of the final purpose of the existence of a world, i.e. of creation itself*

A *final purpose* is that purpose which needs no other as condition of its possibility.

If the mere mechanism of nature be assumed as the ground of explanation of its purposiveness, we cannot ask: What are things in the world there for? For according to such an idealistic system it is only the physical possibility of things (to think which as purposes would be mere subtlety without any Object) that is under discussion; whether we refer this form of things to chance or to blind necessity, in either case the question would be vain. If, however, we assume the purposive combination in the world to be real and to be [brought about] by a particular kind of causality, viz. that of a *designedly-working* cause, we cannot stop at the question: Why have things of the world (organised beings) this or that form? Why are they placed by nature in this or that relation to one another? But once an Understanding is thought that must be regarded as the cause of the possibility of such forms as are actually found in things, it must be also asked on objective grounds: Who could have determined this productive Understanding to an operation of this kind? This being is then the final purpose in reference to which such things are there.

I have said above that the final purpose is not a purpose which nature would be competent to bring about and to produce in conformity with its Idea, because it is unconditioned. For there is nothing in nature (regarded as a sensible being) for which the determining ground present in itself would not be always conditioned; and this holds not merely of external (material) nature, but also of internal (thinking) nature—it being of course understood that I only am considering that in myself which is nature. But a thing that is to exist necessarily, on account of its objective constitution, as the final purpose of an intelligent cause, must be of the kind that in the order of purposes it is dependent on no further condition than merely its Idea.

Now we have in the world only one kind of beings whose causality is teleological, i.e. is directed to purposes and is at the same time so constituted that the law according to which they have to determine purposes for themselves is represented as unconditioned and independent of natural conditions, and yet as in itself necessary. The being of this kind is man, but man considered as noumenon; the only natural being in which we can recognise, on the side of its peculiar constitution, a supersensible faculty (*freedom*) and also the law of causality, together with its Object, which this faculty may propose to itself as highest purpose (the highest good in the world).

Now of man (and so of every rational creature in the world) as a moral being it can no longer be asked, why (*quem in finem*) he exists? His existence involves the highest purpose to which, as far as is in his power, he can subject the whole of nature; contrary to which at least he cannot regard himself as subject to any influence of nature.— If now things of the world, as beings dependent in their existence, need a supreme cause acting according to purposes, man is the final purpose of creation; since without him the chain of mutually subordinated purposes would not be complete as regards its ground. Only in man, and only in him as subject of morality, do we meet with unconditioned legislation in respect of purposes, which therefore alone renders him capable of being a final purpose, to which the whole of nature is teleologically subordinated. [1]

[II. Teleological and Moral Proofs of God's Existence]

§ 85. *Of Physico-theology*

Physico-theology is the endeavour of Reason to infer the Supreme Cause of nature and its properties from the *purposes* of nature (which can only be empirically known). *Moral theology* (ethico-theology) would be the endeavour to infer that Cause and its properties from the moral purpose of rational beings in nature (which can be known *a priori*). . . . [B. 362]

Now I say that Physico-theology, however far it may be pursued, can disclose to us nothing of a *final purpose* of creation; for it does not even extend to the question as to this. It can, it is true, justify the concept of an intelligent World Cause, as a subjective concept (only available for the constitution of our cognitive faculty) of the possibility of things that we can make intelligible to ourselves according to purposes; but it cannot determine this concept further, either in a theoretical or a practical point of view. Its endeavour does not come up to its design of being the basis of a Theology, but it always remains only a physical Teleology; because the purposive reference therein is and must be always considered only as conditioned in nature, and it consequently cannot inquire into the purpose for which nature itself exists (for which the ground must be sought outside nature),—notwithstanding that it is upon the determinate Idea of this that the determinate concept of

[1] [Note, B. 361.]

that Supreme Intelligent World Cause, and the consequent possibility of a Theology, depend.

What the things in the world are mutually useful for; what good the manifold in a thing does for the thing; how we have ground to assume that nothing in the world is in vain, but that everything *in nature* is good for something,—the condition being granted that certain things are to exist (as purposes), whence our Reason has in its power for the Judgement no other principle of the possibility of the Object, which it inevitably judges teleologically, than that of subordinating the mechanism of nature to the Architectonic of an intelligent Author of the world—all this the teleological consideration of the world supplies us with excellently and to our extreme admiration. But because the data, and so the principles, for *determining* that concept of an intelligent World Cause (as highest artist) are merely empirical, they do not enable us to infer any of its properties beyond those which experience reveals in its effects. Now experience, since it can never embrace collective nature as a system, must often (apparently) happen upon this concept (and by mutually conflicting grounds of proof); but it can never, even if we had the power of surveying empirically the whole system as far as it concerns mere nature, raise us above nature to the purpose of its existence, and so to the determinate concept of that supreme Intelligence.

If we lessen the problem with the solution of which Physico-theology has to do, its solution appears easy. If we reduce the concept of a *Deity* to that of an intelligent being sought by us, of which there may be one or more, which possesses many and very great properties, but not all the properties which are requisite for the foundation of a nature in harmony with the greatest possible purpose; or if we do not scruple in a theory to supply by arbitrary additions what is deficient in the grounds of proof, and so, where we have only ground for assuming *much* perfection (and what is "much" for us?), consider ourselves entitled to presuppose *all possible* perfection; thus indeed physical Teleology may make weighty claims to the distinction of being the basis of a Theology. But if we are desired to point out what impels and moreover authorises us to add these supplements, then we shall seek in vain for a ground of justification in the principles of the theoretical use of Reason, which is ever desirous in the explanation of an Object of experience to ascribe to it no more properties than those for which empirical data of possibility are to be found. On closer examination we should see that properly speaking an Idea of a Supreme Being, which rests on a quite different use of Reason (the practical use), lies in us fundamentally *a priori*, impelling us to supplement, by the concept of a Deity, the defective representation, supplied by a physical Teleology, of the original ground of the purposes in nature; and we should not falsely imagine that we had worked out this Idea, and with it a Theology by means of the theoretical use of Reason in the physical cognition of the world—much less that we had proved its reality.

One cannot blame the ancients much, if they thought of their gods as differing much from each other both as regards their faculties and as regards their designs and volitions, but yet thought of all of them, the Supreme One not excepted, as always limited after human fashion. For if they considered the arrangement and the course of things in nature, they certainly found ground enough for assuming something more than mechanism as its cause, and for conjecturing behind the machinery of this world designs of certain higher causes, which they could not think otherwise than superhuman. But because they met with good and evil, the purposive and the unpurposive, mingled together (at least as far as our insight goes), and could not permit themselves to assume nevertheless that wise and benevolent purposes of which they saw no proof lay hidden at bottom, on behalf of the arbitrary Idea of a supremely perfect original Author, their judgement upon the supreme World Cause could hardly have been other than it was, so long as they proceeded consistently according to maxims of the mere theoretical use of Reason. . . . [B. 366-7]

Physical Teleology impels us, it is true, to seek a Theology; but it cannot produce one, however far we may investigate nature by means of experience and, in reference to the purposive combination apparent in it, call in Ideas of Reason (which must be theoretical for physical problems). What is the use, one might well complain, of placing at the basis of all these arrangements a great Understanding incommensurable by us, and supposing it to govern the world according to design, if nature does not and cannot tell us anything of the final design? For without this we cannot refer all these natural purposes to any common point, nor can we form any teleological principle, sufficient either for cognising the purposes collected in a system, or for forming a concept of the Supreme Understanding, as Cause of such a nature, that could serve as a standard for our Judgement reflecting teleologically thereon. I should thus have an *artistic Understanding* for scattered purposes, but no *Wisdom* for a final purpose, in which final purpose nevertheless must be contained the determining ground of the said Understanding. But in the absence of a final purpose which pure Reason alone can supply (because all purposes in the world are empirically conditioned, and can contain nothing absolutely good but only what is good for this or that regarded as a contingent design), and which alone would teach me what properties, what degree, and what relation of the Supreme Cause to nature I have to think in order to judge of nature as a teleological system; how and with what right do I dare to extend at pleasure my very limited concept of that original Understanding (which I can base on my limited knowledge of the world), of the Might of that original Being in actualising its Ideas, and of its Will to do so, and complete this into the Idea of an All-wise, Infinite Being? If this is to be done theoretically, it would presuppose omniscience in me, in order to see into the purposes of nature in their whole connexion, and in addition the power of conceiving all possible plans, in comparison with which the present plan would be judged on [sufficient] grounds as the best. For without this complete knowledge of the effect I can arrive at no determinate concept of the Supreme Cause, which can only be found in the concept of an Intelligence infinite in every respect, i.e. the concept of a Deity, and so I can supply no foundation for Theology. . . . [B. 369]

Hence Physico-theology is a misunderstood physical Teleology, only serviceable as a preparation (propaedeutic) for Theology; and it is only adequate to this design by the aid of a foreign principle on which it can rely, and not in itself, as its name would intimate.

§ 86. *Of Ethico-theology*

The commonest Understanding, if it thinks over the presence of things in the world, and the existence of the world itself, cannot forbear from the judgement that all the various creatures, no matter how great the art displayed in their arrangement, and how various their purposive mutual connexion,—even the complex of their numerous systems (which we incorrectly call worlds), —would be for nothing, if there were not also men (rational beings in general). Without men the whole creation would be a mere waste, in vain, and without final purpose. But it is not in reference to man's cognitive faculty (theoretical Reason) that the being of everything else in the world gets its worth; he is not there merely that there may be some one to *contemplate* the world. For if the contemplation of the world only afforded a representation of things without any final purpose, no worth could accrue to its being from the mere fact that it is known; we must presuppose for it a final purpose, in reference to which its contemplation itself has worth. Again it is not in reference to the feeling of pleasure, or to the sum of pleasures, that we think a final purpose of creation as given; i.e. we do not estimate that absolute worth by well-being or by enjoyment (whether bodily or mental), or in a word, by happiness. For the fact that man, if he exists, takes this for his final design, gives us no concept as to why in general he should exist, and as to what worth he has in himself to make his existence pleasant. He must, therefore, be supposed to be the final purpose of creation, in order to have a rational ground for holding that nature must harmonise with his happiness, if it is considered as an absolute whole according to principles of purposes.— Hence there remains only the faculty of desire; not, however, that which makes man dependent (through sensuous impulses) upon nature, nor that in respect of which the worth of his being depends upon what he receives and enjoys. But the worth which he alone can give to himself, and which consists in what he does, how and according to what principles he acts, and that not as a link in nature's chain but in the *free-*

dom of his faculty of desire—i.e. a good will—is that whereby alone his being can have an absolute worth, and in reference to which the being of the world can have a *final purpose*.

The commonest judgement of healthy human Reason completely accords with this, that it is only as a moral being that man can be a final purpose of creation; if we but direct men's attention to the question and incite them to investigate it. What does it avail, one will say, that this man has so much talent, that he is so active therewith, and that he exerts thereby a useful influence over the community, thus having a great worth both in relation to his own happy condition and to the benefit of others, if he does not possess a good will? He is a contemptible Object considered in respect of his inner self; and if the creation is not to be without any final purpose at all, he, who as man belongs to it, must, in a world under moral laws, inasmuch as he is a bad man, forfeit his subjective purpose (happiness). This is the only condition under which his existence can accord with the final purpose.

If now we meet with purposive arrangements in the world and, as Reason inevitably requires, subordinate the purposes that are only conditioned to an unconditioned, supreme, i.e. final, purpose; then we easily see in the first place that we are thus concerned not with a purpose of nature (internal to itself), so far as it exists, but with the purpose of its existence along with all its ordinances, and, consequently, with the ultimate *purpose of creation,* and specially with the supreme condition under which can be posited a final purpose (i.e. the ground which determines a supreme Understanding to produce the beings of the world).

Since now it is only as a moral being that we recognise man as the purpose of creation, we have in the first place a ground (at least, the chief condition) for regarding the world as a whole connected according to purposes, and as a *system* of final causes. And, more especially, as regards the reference (necessary for us by the constitution of our Reason) of natural purposes to an intelligent World Cause, we have *one principle* enabling us to think the nature and properties of this First Cause as supreme ground in the kingdom of purposes, and to determine its concept. This physical Teleology could not do; it could only lead to indeterminate concepts thereof, unserviceable alike in theoretical and in practical use.

From the principle, thus determined, of the causality of the Original Being we must not think Him merely as Intelligence and as legislative for nature, but also as legislating supremely in a moral kingdom of purposes. In reference to the *highest good,* alone possible under His sovereignty, viz. the existence of rational beings under moral laws, we shall think this Original Being as *all-knowing*: thus our inmost dispositions (which constitute the proper moral worth of the actions of rational beings of the world) will not be hid from Him. We shall think Him as *all-mighty*: thus He will be able to make the whole of nature accord with this highest purpose. We shall think Him as *all-good,* and at the same time as *just*: because these two properties (which when united constitute *Wisdom*) are the conditions of the causality of a supreme Cause of the world, as highest good, under moral laws. So also all the other transcendental properties, such as *Eternity, Omnipresence,* etc. (for goodness and justice are moral properties), which are presupposed in reference to such a final purpose, must be thought in Him.— In this way *moral Teleology* supplies the deficiency in *physical Teleology,* and first establishes a *Theology;* because the latter, if it did not borrow from the former without being observed, but were to proceed consistently, could only found a *Demonology,* which is incapable of any definite concept.

But the principle of the reference of the world to a supreme Cause, as Deity, on account of the moral purposive destination of certain beings in it, does not accomplish this by completing the physico-teleological ground of proof and so taking this necessarily as its basis. It is sufficient *in itself* and directs attention to the purposes of nature and the investigation of that incomprehensible great art lying hidden behind its forms, in order to confirm incidentally by means of natural purposes the Ideas that pure practical Reason furnishes. For the concept of beings of the world under moral laws is a principle (*a priori*) according to which man must of necessity judge himself. Further, if there is in general a World Cause acting designedly and directed towards a purpose, this moral relation must be just as necessarily the condition of the possibility of a creation, as that in accordance with physical laws (if, that is, this intelligent Cause has also a final purpose). This is regarded *a priori* by Reason as a necessary fundamental proposition for it in its teleological judging of the existence of things. It now only comes to this, whether we have sufficient ground for Reason (either speculative or practical) to ascribe to the supreme Cause, acting in accordance with purposes, a *final purpose.* For it may *a priori* be taken by us as certain that this, by the subjective constitution of our Reason and even of the Reason of other beings as far as we can think it, can be nothing else than *man under moral laws*: since otherwise the purposes of nature in the physical order could not be known *a priori,* especially as it can in no way be seen that nature could not exist without such purposes.

Remark

Suppose the case of a man at the moment when his mind is disposed to a moral sensation. If surrounded by the beauties of nature, he is in a state of restful, serene enjoyment of his being, he feels a want, viz. to be grateful for this to some being or other. Or if another time he finds himself in the same state of mind when pressed by duties that he can and will only adequately discharge by a voluntary sacrifice, he again feels in himself a want, viz. to have thus executed a command and obeyed a Supreme Lord. Or, again; if he has in some heedless way transgressed his duty, but without becoming answerable to men, his severe self-reproach will speak to him with the voice of a judge to whom he has to give account. In a word, he needs a moral Intelligence, in order to have a Being for the purpose of his existence, which may be, conformably to this purpose, the cause of himself and of the world. It is vain to assign motives behind these feelings, for they are immediately connected with the purest moral sentiment, because *gratitude, obedience,* and *humiliation* (submission to deserved chastisement) are mental dispositions that make for duty; and the mind which is inclined towards a widening of its moral sentiment here only voluntarily conceives an object that is not in the world in order where possible to render its duty before such an one. It is therefore at least possible and grounded too in our moral disposition to represent a pure moral need of the existence of a Being, by which our morality gains strength or even (at least according to our representation) more scope, viz. a new object for its exercise.

That is, [there is a need] to assume a morally-legislating Being outside the world, without any reference to theoretical proofs, still less to self-interest, from pure moral grounds free from all foreign influence (and consequently only subjective), on the mere recommendation of a pure practical Reason legislating by itself alone. And although such a mental disposition might seldom occur or might not last long, but be transient and without permanent effect, or might even pass away without any meditation on the object represented in such shadowy outline, or without care to bring it under clear concepts —there is yet here unmistakably the ground why our moral capacity, as a subjective principle, should not be contented in its contemplation of the world with its purposiveness by means of natural causes, but should ascribe to it a supreme Cause governing nature according to moral principles.— In addition, we feel ourselves constrained by the moral law to strive for a universal highest purpose which yet we, in common with the rest of nature, are incapable of attaining; and it is only so far as we strive for it that we can judge ourselves to be in harmony with the final purpose of an intelligent World Cause (if such there be). Thus is found a pure moral ground of practical Reason for assuming this Cause (since it can be done without contradiction), in order that we may no more regard that effort of Reason as quite idle, and so run the risk of abandoning it from weariness.

With all this, so much only is to be said, that though *fear* first produces *gods* (demons), it is *Reason* by means of its moral principles that can first produce the concept of *God* (even when, as commonly is the case, one is unskilled in the Teleology of nature, or is very doubtful on account of the difficulty of adjusting by a sufficiently established principle its mutually contradictory phenomena). Also, the inner *moral* purposive destination of man's being supplies that in which natural knowledge is deficient, by directing us to think, for the final purpose of the being of all things (for which no other principle than an *ethical* one is satisfactory to Reason), the supreme Cause [as endowed] with properties, whereby it is able to subject the whole of nature to that single design (for which nature is merely the instrument),—i.e. to think it as a *Deity*.

§ 87. *Of the moral proof of the Being of God*

. . . [B. 377-80] The moral law as the formal rational condition of the use of our freedom obliges us by itself alone, without depending on any purpose as material condition; but it nevertheless determines for us, and indeed *a priori,* a final purpose towards which it obliges us to strive; and this purpose is the *highest good in the world* possible through freedom.

The subjective condition under which man (and, according to all our concepts, every rational finite being) can set a final purpose before himself under the above law is happiness. Consequently, the highest physical good possible in the world, to be furthered as a final purpose as far as in us lies, is *happiness,* under the objective condition of the harmony of man with the law of *morality* as worthiness to be happy.

But it is impossible for us in accordance with all our rational faculties to represent these two requirements of the final purpose proposed to us by the moral law, as *connected* by merely natural causes, and yet as conformable to the Idea of that final purpose. Hence the concept of the *practical* necessity of such a purpose through the application of our powers does not harmonise with the theoretical concept of the *physical possi-*

bility of working it out, if we connect with our freedom no other causality (as a means) than that of nature.

Consequently, we must assume a moral World-Cause (an Author of the world), in order to set before ourselves a final purpose consistently with the moral law; and in so far as the latter is necessary, so far (i.e. in the same degree and on the same ground) the former also must be necessarily assumed; i.e. we must admit that there is a God.[1]

This proof, to which we can easily give the form of logical precision, does not say: it is as necessary to assume the Being of God as to recognise the validity of the moral law; and consequently he who cannot convince himself of the first, can judge himself free from the obligations of the second. No! there must in such case only be given up the *aiming at* the final purpose in the world, to be brought about by the pursuit of the second (viz. a happiness of rational beings in harmony with the pursuit of moral laws, regarded as the highest good). Every rational being would yet have to cognise himself as straitly bound by the precepts of morality, for its laws are formal and command unconditionally without respect to purposes (as the matter of volition). But the one requisite of the final purpose, as practical Reason prescribes it to beings of the world, is an irresistible purpose imposed on them by their nature (as finite beings), which Reason wishes to know

[1] This moral argument does not supply any *objectively-valid* proof of the Being of God; it does not prove to the sceptic that there is a God, but proves that if he wishes to think in a way consonant with morality, he must admit the *assumption* of this proposition under the maxims of his practical Reason.— We should therefore not say: it is necessary *for morals* [Sittlichkeit], to assume the happiness of all rational beings of the world in proportion to their morality [Moralität]; but rather, this is necessitated *by* morality. Accordingly, this is a *subjective* argument sufficient for moral beings.

as subject only to the moral law as inviolable *condition*, or even as universally set up in accordance with it. Thus Reason takes for final purpose the furthering of happiness in harmony with morality. To further this so far as is in our power (i.e. in respect of happiness) is commanded us by the moral law; be the issue of this endeavour what it may. The fulfilling of duty consists in the form of the earnest will, not in the intermediate causes of success.

Suppose then that partly through the weakness of all the speculative arguments so highly extolled, and partly through many irregularities in nature and the world of sense which comes before him, a man is persuaded of the proposition, There is no God; he would nevertheless be contemptible in his own eyes if on that account he were to imagine the laws of duty as empty, invalid and inobligatory, and wished to resolve to transgress them boldly. Such an one, even if he could be convinced in the sequel of that which he had doubted at the first, would always be contemptible while having such a disposition, although he should fulfil his duty as regards its [external] effect as punctiliously as could be desired, for [he would be acting] from fear or from the aim at recompense, without the sentiment of reverence for duty. If, conversely, as a believer [in God] he performs his duty according to his conscience, uprightly and disinterestedly, and nevertheless believes that he is free from all moral obligation so soon as he is convinced that there is no God, this could accord but badly with an inner moral disposition.

We may then suppose the case of a righteous man e.g. *Spinoza,* who holds himself firmly persuaded that there is no God, and also (because in respect of the Object of morality a similar consequence results) no future life; how is he to judge of his own inner purposive destination, by means of the moral law, which he reveres in practice? He desires no advantage to himself from following it, either in this or another world; he wishes, rather, disinterestedly to establish the good to which that holy law directs all his powers. But his effort is bounded; and from nature, although he may expect here and there a contingent accordance, he can never expect a regular harmony agreeing according to constant rules (such as his maxims are and must be, internally), with the purpose that he yet feels himself obliged and impelled to accomplish. Deceit, violence, and envy will always surround him, although he himself be honest, peaceable, and kindly; and the righteous men with whom he meets will, notwithstanding all their worthiness of happiness, be yet subjected by nature which regards not this, to all the evils of want, disease, and untimely death, just like the beasts of the earth. So it will be until one wide grave engulfs them together (honest or not, it makes no difference), and throws them back—who were able to believe themselves the final purpose of creation—into the abyss of the purposeless chaos of matter from which they were drawn.—The purpose, then, which this well-intentioned person had and ought to have before him in his pursuit of moral laws, he must certainly give up as impossible. Or else, if he wishes to remain dependent upon the call of his moral internal destination, and not to weaken the respect with which the moral law immediately inspires him, by assuming the nothingness of the single, ideal, final purpose adequate to its high demand (which cannot be brought about without a violation of moral sentiment), he must, as he well can—since there is at least no contradiction from a practical point of view in forming a concept of the possibility of a morally prescribed final purpose—assume the being of a *moral* author of the world, that is, a God. . . . [B. 384-91]

Remark [on man's rational nature as the basis of the moral proof]

This moral proof is not one newly discovered, although perhaps its basis is newly set forth; since it has lain in man's rational faculty from its earliest germ, and is only continually developed with its advancing cultivation. So soon as men begin to reflect upon right and wrong—at a time when, quite indifferent as to the purposiveness of nature, they avail themselves of it without thinking anything more of it than that it is the accustomed course of nature—this judgement is inevitable, viz. that the issue cannot be the same, whether a man has behaved candidly or falsely, fairly or violently, even though up to his life's end, as far as can be seen, he has met with no happiness for his virtues, no punishment for his vices. It is as if they perceived a voice within [saying] that the issue must be different. And so there must lie hidden in them a representation, however obscure, of something after which they feel themselves bound to strive; with which such a result would not agree,—with which, if they looked upon the course of the world as the only order of things, they could not harmonise that inner purposive determination of their minds. Now they might represent in various rude fashions the way in which such an irregularity could be adjusted (an irregularity which must be far more revolting to the human mind than the blind chance that we are sometimes willing to use as a principle for judging of nature). But they could never think any other principle of the possibility of the unification of nature with its inner ethical laws, than a supreme Cause governing the world according to moral laws; because a final purpose in them proposed as duty, and a nature without any final purpose beyond them in which that purpose might be actualised, would involve a contradiction. As to the inner constitution of that World-Cause they could contrive much nonsense. But that moral relation in the government of the world would remain always the same, which by the uncultivated Reason, considered as practical, is universally comprehensible, but with which the speculative Reason can make far from the like advance. . . . [B. 392]

[III. Religion and Faith.]

§ 89. *Of the use of the moral argument*

The limitation of Reason in respect of all our Ideas of the supersensible to the conditions of its practical employment has, as far as the Idea of God is concerned, undeniable uses. For it prevents *Theology* from rising into Theosophy (into transcendent concepts which confound Reason), or from sinking into Demonology (an anthropomorphic way of representing the highest Being). And it also prevents *Religion* from turning into *Theurgy* (a fanatical belief that we can have a feeling of other supersensible beings and can reciprocally influence them), or into *Idolatry* (a superstitious belief that we can please the Supreme Being by other means than by a moral sentiment.)[1]

[1] In a practical sense that religion is always idolatry which conceives the Supreme Being with properties, according to which something else besides morality can be a fit condition for that which man can do being in accordance with His Will. For however pure and free from sensible images the concept that we have formed may be in a theoretical point of view, yet it will be in a practical point of view still represented as

For if we permit the vanity or the presumption of sophistry to determine the least thing theoretically (in a way that extends our knowledge) in respect of what lies beyond the world of sense, or if we allow any pretence to be made of insight into the being and constitution of the nature of God, of His Understanding and Will, of the laws of both and of His properties which thus affect the world, I should like to know where and at what point we will bound these assumptions of Reason. For wherever such insight can be derived, there may yet more be expected (if we only strain our reflection, as we have a mind to do). Bounds must then be put to such claims according to a certain principle, and not merely because we find that all attempts of the sort have hitherto failed, for that proves nothing against the possibility of a better result. But here no principle is possible, except either to assume that in respect of the supersensible absolutely nothing can be theoretically determined (except mere negations); or else that our Reason contains in itself a yet unused mine of cognitions, reaching no one knows how far, stored up for ourselves and our posterity.— But as concerns Religion, i.e. morals in reference to God as legislator, if the theoretical cognition of Him is to come first, morals must be adjusted in accordance with Theology; and not only is an external arbitrary legislation of a Supreme Being introduced in place of an internal necessary legislation of Reason, but also whatever is defective in our insight into the nature of this Being must extend to ethical precepts, and thus make Religion immoral and perverted. . . . [B. 394-423][1]

[Thus Ethico-] Theology leads immediately to *Re-*

an *idol,* i.e. in regard to the character of His Will, anthropomorphically.

[1] [For B. 407-8 and 409-11, on moral faith, see below pp. 524 ff.]

ligion, i.e. *the recognition of our duties as divine commands;* because it is only the recognition of our duty and of the final purpose enjoined upon us by Reason which brings out with definiteness the concept of God. This concept, therefore, is inseparable in its origin from obligation to that Being. On the other hand, even if the concept of the original Being could be also found determinately by the merely theoretical path (viz. the concept of it as mere Cause of nature), it would afterwards be very difficult—perhaps impossible without arbitrary interpolation [of elements]—to ascribe to this Being by well-grounded proofs a causality in accordance with moral laws; and yet without this that quasi-theological concept could furnish no foundation for religion. Even if a religion could be established by this theoretical path, it would actually, as regards sentiment (wherein its essence lies) be different from that in which the concept of God and the (practical) conviction of His Being originate from the fundamental Ideas of morality. For if we must suppose the Omnipotence, Omniscience, etc., of an Author of the world as concepts given to us from another quarter, in order afterwards only to apply our concepts of duties to our relation to Him, then these latter concepts must bear very markedly the appearance of compulsion and forced submission. If, instead of this, the respect for the moral law, quite freely, in virtue of the precept of our own Reason, represents to us the final purpose of our destination, we admit among our moral views a Cause harmonising with this and with its accomplishment, with the sincerest reverence, which is quite distinct from pathological fear; and we willingly submit ourselves thereto.[1] . . . [B. 424-5]

[1] The admiration for beauty, and also the emotion aroused by the manifold purposes of nature, which a reflective mind

General Remark
[*on the Application of the Categories to God*]

The [1] alleged contradiction between the possibility of a Theology asserted here and that which the Critique of speculative Reason said of the Categories—viz. that they can only produce knowledge when applied to objects of sense, but in no way when applied to the supersensible—vanish, if we see that they are here used for a cognition of God not in a theoretical point of view (in accordance with what His own nature, inscrutable to us, may be) but simply in a practical.— In order then at this opportunity to make an end of the misinterpretation of that very necessary doctrine of the Critique, which, to the chagrin of the blind dogmatist, refers Reason to its bounds, I add here the following elucidation.

If I ascribe to a body *motive force* and thus think it by means of the category of *causality,* then I at the same time *cognise* it by that [category]; i.e. I determine the concept of it, as of an Object in general, by means of what belongs to it by itself (as the condition of the possibility of that relation) as an object of sense. If the motive force ascribed to it is repulsive, then there belongs to it (although I do not place near it any other body upon which it may exert force) a

---

is able to feel even prior to a clear representation of a rational Author of the world, have something in themselves like *religious* feeling. They seem in the first place by a method of judging analogous to moral to produce an effect upon the moral feeling (gratitude to, and veneration for, the unknown cause); and thus by exciting moral Ideas to produce an effect upon the mind, when they inspire that admiration which is bound up with far more interest than mere theoretical observation can bring about.

[1] [Cf. B. 425-8]

place in space, and moreover extension, i.e. space in itself, besides the filling up of this by means of the repulsive forces of its parts. In addition there is the law of this filling up (that the ground of the repulsion of the parts must decrease in the same proportion as the extension of the body increases, and as the space, which it fills with the same parts by means of this force, is augmented).— On the contrary, if I think a supersensible Being as the first *mover,* and thus by the category of causality as regards its determination of the world (motion of matter), I must not think it as existing in any place in space nor as extended; I must not even think it as existing in time or simultaneously with other beings. Hence I have no determinations whatever, which could make intelligible to me the condition of the possibility of motion by means of this Being as its ground. Consequently, I do not in the very least cognise it by means of the predicate of Cause (as first mover), for itself; but I have only the representation of a something containing the ground of the motions in the world; and the relation of the latter to it as their cause, since it does not besides furnish me with anything belonging to the constitution of the thing which is cause, leaves its concept quite empty. The reason of this is, that by predicates which only find their Object in the world of sense I can indeed proceed to the being of something which must contain their ground, but not to the determination of its concept as a supersensible being, which excludes all these predicates. By the category of causality then, if I determine it by the concept of a *first mover,* I do not in the very least cognise what God is. Perhaps, however, I shall have better success if I start from the order of the world, not merely to *think* its causality as that of a supreme *Understanding,* but to *cognise* it by means of this determination of the said concept; because here the troublesome condition of space and of extension disappears.— At all events the great purposiveness in the world compels us to *think* a supreme cause of it, and to *think* its causality as that of an Understanding; but we are not therefore entitled to *ascribe* this to it. (E.g. we think of the eternity of God as presence in all time, because we can form no other concept of mere being as a quantum, i.e. as duration; or we think of the divine Omnipresence as presence in all places in order to make comprehensible to ourselves His immediate presence in things which are external to one another; without daring to ascribe to God any of these determinations, as something cognised in Him.) If I determine the causality of a man, in respect of certain products which are only explicable by designed purposiveness, by thinking it as that of Understanding, I need not stop here, but I can ascribe to him this predicate as a well-known property and cognise him accordingly. For I know that intuitions are given to the senses of men and are brought by the Understanding under a concept and thus under a rule; that this concept only contains the common characteristic (with omission of the particular ones) and is thus discursive; and that the rules for bringing given representations under a consciousness in general are given by Understanding before those intuitions, etc. I therefore ascribe this property to man as a property by means of which I *cognise* him. However, if I wish to *think* a supersensible Being (God) as an intelligence, this is not only permissible in a certain aspect of my employment of Reason—it is unavoidable; but to ascribe to Him Understanding and to flatter ourselves that we can *cognise* Him by means of it as a property of His, is in no way permissible. For I must omit all those conditions under which alone I know an Understanding, and thus the predicate which only serves for determining man cannot be applied at all to a supersensible Object; and therefore by a causality thus determined, I cannot cognise what God is. And so it is with all Categories, which can have no significance for cognition in a theoretical aspect, if they are not applied to objects of possible experience.— However, according to the analogy of an Understanding I can in a certain other aspect think a supersensible being, without at the same time meaning thereby to cognise it theoretically; viz. if this determination of its causality concerns an effect in the world, which contains a design morally necessary but unattainable by a sensible being. For then a cognition of God and of His Being (Theology) is possible by means of properties and determinations of His causality merely thought in Him according to analogy, which has all requisite reality in a practical reference though *only in respect of this* (as moral). . . . [B. 428-9]

§ 91. *Of the kind of belief produced by a practical faith*

. . . [B. 403-7] Belief in things of faith is a belief in a pure practical point of view, i.e. a moral faith, which proves nothing for theoretical pure rational cognition, but only for that which is practical and directed to the fulfilment of its duties; it in no way extends speculation or the practical rules of prudence in accordance with the principle of self-love. If the supreme principle of all moral laws is a postulate, so is also the possibility of its highest Object; and consequently, too, the condition under which we can think this possibility is postulated along with it and by it. Thus the cognition of the latter is neither knowledge nor opinion of the being and character of these conditions, regarded as theoretical cognition; but is a mere assumption in a reference which is practical and commanded for the moral use of our Reason. . . . [B. 408-9]

Faith (as *habitus,* not as *actus*) is the moral attitude of Reason as to belief in that which is unattainable by theoretical cognition. It is therefore the constant principle of the mind, to assume as true, on account of the obligation in reference to it, that which it is necessary to presuppose as condition of the possibility of the highest moral final purpose; [1] although its possibility or impossibility be alike impossible for us to see into. Faith (absolutely so called) is trust in the attainment of a design, the promotion of which is a duty, but the possibility of the fulfilment of which (and consequently also that of the only conditions of it thinkable by us) is not to be *comprehended* by us. Faith, then, that refers to particular objects, which are not objects of possible knowledge or opinion (in which latter case it ought to be called, especially in historical matters, credulity and not faith), is quite moral. It is a free belief, not in that for which dogmatical proofs for the theoretically determinant Judgement are to be found, or in that to

[1] It is a trust in the promise of the moral law; not however such as is contained in it, but such as I put into it and that on morally adequate grounds. For a final purpose cannot be commanded by any law of Reason without this latter at the same time promising, however uncertainly, its attainableness; and thus justifying our belief in the special conditions under which alone our Reason can think it as attainable. The word *fides* expresses this; and it can only appear doubtful, how this expression and this particular Idea came into moral philosophy, since it first was introduced with Christianity, and the adoption of it perhaps might seem to be only a flattering imitation of Christian terminology. But this is not the only case in which this wonderful religion with its great simplicity of statement has enriched philosophy with far more definite and purer concepts of morality, than it had been able to furnish before; but which, once they are there, are *freely* assented to by Reason and are assumed as concepts to which it could well have come of itself and which it could and should have introduced.

which we hold ourselves bound, but in that which we assume on behalf of a design in accordance with laws of freedom. This, however, is not like opinion, without any adequate ground; but, is grounded as in Reason (although only in respect of its practical employment), and *adequately for its design.* For without this, the moral attitude of thought in its repudiation of the claim of the theoretical Reason for proofs (of the possibility of the Objects of morality) has no permanence; but wavers between practical commands and theoretical doubts. To be *incredulous* means to cling to maxims, and not to believe testimony in general; but he is *unbelieving,* who denies all validity to rational Ideas, because there is wanting a *theoretical* ground of their reality. He judges therefore dogmatically. A dogmatical *unbelief* cannot subsist together with a moral maxim dominant in the mental attitude (for Reason cannot command one to follow a purpose, which is cognised as nothing more than a chimera); but a *doubtful faith* can. To this the absence of conviction by grounds of speculative Reason is only a hindrance, the influence of which upon conduct a critical insight into the limits of this faculty can remove, while it substitutes by way of compensation a paramount practical belief.